FOREWORD BY WILL

President Emeritus, United State

Chairman and CEO, El Pomai ruundation

Understanding Nonprofit Law and Finance

48 Key Principles for Philanthropic Leaders

Erik Estrada

University of Colorado School of Public Affairs

ROWMAN & LITTLEFIELD

Lanham • Boulder • New York • London

Dedicated to Sara, Carolyn, and Camden.

Carolyn and Camden, our wish for you is to always dare greatly.

It is not the critic who counts; not the man who points out how the strong man stumbles, or where the doer of deeds could have done them better. The credit belongs to the man who is actually in the arena, whose face is marred by dust and sweat and blood; who strives valiantly; who errs, who comes short again and again, because there is no effort without error and shortcoming; but who does actually strive to do the deeds; who knows great enthusiasms, the great devotions; who spends himself in a worthy cause; who at the best knows in the end the triumph of high achievement, and who at the worst, if he fails, at least fails while daring greatly. —Theodore Roosevelt

Executive Editor: Traci Crowell
Assistant Editor: Deni Remsberg
Senior Marketing Manager: Karin Cholak

Credits and acknowledgments for material borrowed from other sources, and reproduced with permission, appear on the appropriate page within the text.

Published by Rowman & Littlefield
An imprint of The Rowman & Littlefield Publishing Group, Inc.
4501 Forbes Boulevard, Suite 200, Lanham, Maryland 20706
www.rowman.com

6 Tinworth Street, London SE11 5AL, United Kingdom

Copyright © 2020 by The Rowman & Littlefield Publishing Group, Inc.

All rights reserved. No part of this book may be reproduced in any form or by any electronic or mechanical means, including information storage and retrieval systems, without written permission from the publisher, except by a reviewer who may quote passages in a review.

British Library Cataloguing in Publication Information Available

Library of Congress Cataloging-in-Publication Data

Names: Estrada, Erik, 1979– author.
Title: Understanding nonprofit law and finance: forty-eight key principles for philanthropic leaders / Erik Estrada, University of Colorado School of Public Affairs; foreword by William J. Hybl, President Emeritus, United States Olympic Committee, and Chairman and CEO, El Pomar Foundation.
Description: Lanham: Rowman & Littlefield, 2019. | Includes bibliographical references and index.
Identifiers: LCCN 2019008419 (print) | LCCN 2019009651 (ebook) | ISBN 9781538126936 (electronic) | ISBN 9781538126912 (cloth: alk. paper) | ISBN 9781538126929 (pbk.: alk. paper)
Subjects: LCSH: Nonprofit organizations—Law and legislation—United States—Miscellanea. | Nonprofit organizations—Finance—United States—Miscellanea.
Classification: LCC KF1388 (ebook) | LCC KF1388.E88 2019 (print) | DDC 346.73/064—dc23
LC record available at https://lccn.loc.gov/2019008419

♾™ The paper used in this publication meets the minimum requirements of American National Standard for Information Sciences—Permanence of Paper for Printed Library Materials, ANSI/NISO Z39.48–1992.

Contents

■ ■ ■

Foreword

■ ■ ■

On the night of August 31, 1772, a hurricane hit the Caribbean island of St. Croix.[1] At the time, Alexander Hamilton was a resident of the island.[2] He was only a teenager when the hurricane hit, but after witnessing its devastating effects, he wrote about it in a letter to his father.[3] The local newspaper, the *Royal Danish American Gazette*, serendipitously published Hamilton's letter about the hurricane: "The following letter was written the week after the late hurricane, by a youth of this island, to his father; the copy of it fell by accident into the hands of a gentleman, who, being pleased with it himself, showed it to others whom it gave equal satisfaction, and who all agreed that it might not prove unentertaining to the public."[4] His detailed letter moved so many people on the island, including wealthy traders, that they decided to start a fund to raise monies to send him to North America to receive a formal education.[5] Even as a teenager, Hamilton had a gift for writing and that gift prompted others to act.

Because of the generosity of the people of St. Croix, Hamilton enrolled in King's College in New York City, now Columbia University, shortly after the hurricane.[6] Later in life, Hamilton reflected on the generosity bestowed upon him by writing, "The changes in the human condition are uncertain and frequent. Many, on whom fortune has bestowed her favours, may trace their family to a more unprosperous station; and many who are now in obscurity, may look back upon the affluence and exalted rank of their ancestors."[7] Hamilton grew up in impoverished circumstances on St. Croix, but his eloquent writings unintentionally inspired a sense of charity amongst his fellow citizens. In turn, that philanthropy allowed Hamilton to pursue an outstanding education and meet other leaders of the American Revolution, including George Washington. Hamilton became a key leader of the founding of the United States, and without philanthropy, his indelible legacy may have never occurred.

Like Hamilton, Erik Estrada has experienced first-hand the power of philanthropy in his life. His experiences range from his upbringing, to his scholarly pursuits and passions, to his work at various philanthropic organizations including the Boettcher Foundation, Tony Grampsas Fund, Level 3 Foundation, and El Pomar Foundation, which is where I first met Erik. I have served as the Chairman and C.E.O. of El Pomar Foundation for more than four decades. Established by Julie and Spencer Penrose in 1937, El Pomar Foundation is one of the oldest and largest private foundations in the nation, and they founded it to "enhance, encourage, and promote the current and future well-being of the people of Colorado." One of the foundation's key initiatives is its Fellowship Program, which brings together exceptional recent college graduates who share a passion for leadership and making a difference in their communities. To date, the Fellowship Program has produced more than 250 leaders in the public, private, and nonprofit sectors throughout the country.

Shortly after Erik completed the Fellowship Program, the other Trustees and I asked him to serve on the foundation's board of directors. During his year of service on the El Pomar Foundation Board of Trustees, I was able to gain a deeper understanding of his passions, visions, and intellectual curiosity, which is evidenced by his completion of four degrees, including a Doctor of Jurisprudence and two master's degrees. Thus, when Erik first notified me of this book he was writing, I was not surprised that he desired to share his knowledge of nonprofit law and finance, which he's accumulated from his experiences over the past two decades as a scholar, practitioner, and professor. This book is a manifestation of Erik's dedication to philanthropy, teaching, and scholarship, all with the goal of intentionally empowering and serving others who desire to make a difference in their communities.

This book will give you an effective framework for understanding the fundamental principles related to both nonprofit law and finance. Erik has conveyed these rules in an easy-to-understand format with numerous stories and case studies from the philanthropic sector, thereby giving you context for how to use these principles in the nonprofit arena. In each chapter of this book, Erik applies these principles to real-world scenarios. Application leads to understanding, and that understanding will help you achieve the goals you have for your involvement, or soon-to-be involvement, with the nonprofit sector. We can never be certain how a life impacted by philanthropy, just like Hamilton's life, may one day pay it forward. Through this book, Erik is paying it forward so that other beneficiaries of the nonprofit sector may one day do the same.

William J. Hybl
Chairman & C.E.O., El Pomar Foundation, and
President Emeritus, United States Olympic Committee

About the Author

■　■　■

ERIK ESTRADA, JD, MPA, LLM, has taught graduate and law school classes at the University of Colorado School of Public Affairs, the University of Denver College of Law, and the University of Denver's Organizational Leadership Program for nearly a decade. Erik is a graduate of the Boston University School of Law, the University of Denver College of Law, the University of Colorado School of Public Affairs, and the University of Colorado at Boulder. He also served as a Graduate Fellow at Texas A&M University's School of Government and Public Service.

Erik served as the General Counsel for the Level 3 Foundation, a 501(c)(3) nonprofit corporation. Before graduating from law school, he served as a Grants Program Officer for the Boettcher Foundation and as a Trustee, Program Director, and Senior Fellow for El Pomar Foundation, where he directed the nation's second largest youth grant-making program. Erik presently serves or has served on the Board of Directors for El Pomar Foundation, Colorado Center on Law & Policy, Foothills United Way, Community Resource Center, Tony Grampsas Fund (appointed by then Governor Bill Ritter), Colorado State Housing Board (appointed by then Governor John Hickenlooper), and the University of Colorado at Boulder Alumni Association.

In 2002, Erik bicycled from San Francisco, California, to Washington, DC, to raise funds and awareness for people with disabilities through his participation in the *Journey of Hope*. In 2015, Erik received both the "40 Under 40" award from the *Denver Business Journal* and the Outstanding Lecturer in Public Administration award from the University of Colorado School of Public Affairs. In 2016, Erik was inducted into the inaugural class of the Colorado Governors' Fellowship Program, which is based on the best-selling book *Leadocracy*.

How to Use This Book

■ ■ ■

Chapter Summaries and Recap of Key Principles

This book covers a lot of material. Accordingly, we offer an expanded outline to help you remember the key stories, principles, and case studies addressed in the forty-eight chapters. This twelve-page "How to Use This Book" guide may be accessed at https://textbooks.rowman.com/supplements/estrada.

You should use this book often as a reference guide. Think of it as your survival guide for maneuvering through the key issues related to both nonprofit law and nonprofit finance. There are 144 key principles set forth, as well as approximately seventy-five case studies from the nonprofit sector applying these principles to real-world scenarios.

Introduction

■ ■ ■

Simon Sinek, author of *The New York Times* best-selling book *Start with Why*, notes that "People don't buy what you do, they buy *why* you do it."[1] His TEDx talk on the same topic, entitled "How Great Leaders Inspire Action," has been viewed approximately 10 million times on YouTube.[2] One of Sinek's key examples is Apple's *why*, which is simply "Think Different."[3] He asserts that when we buy Apple products, such as an iPhone, an iPod, or a Mac, it's because our desire to challenge the status quo aligns with Apple's *why* of also challenging the status quo.[4] We're proud of the fact that we own the latest iPhone because it actually reflects who we are as individuals: we too like to "Think Different."[5] Similarly, if you've picked up this book, then I presume that we share a *why*, or will soon share a *why*, for the nonprofit sector. As noted by Sinek, your interest in this book is a reflection of who you are and what you value.

After we understand an organization's or a person's *why*, we should then, and only then, focus on the *how* and *what*.[6] This leadership strategy is what Simon Sinek calls "The Golden Circle": *why* followed by *how* followed by *what*.[7] Along with Apple, however, how many organizations or individuals first share their *why*? Despite this simple yet powerful framework, most organizations and individuals focus solely on the *how* and *what*, and ignore the importance of *why*. For example, *how* and *what* I do is both serve as an attorney—providing legal services to clients—and as a professor—teaching graduate students about nonprofits, law, finance, leadership, and management. Likewise, most book introductions focus solely on the *how* and *what*. As a voracious reader of nonfiction books, I've read numerous introductions that only address *how* the book is structured and *what* the author hopes you'll learn from it. Before I address those fundamental issues, however, I'd like to follow Sinek's advice of first telling you about my *why*.

In 2017, I delivered a commencement speech to graduates of the University of Colorado addressing my *why* for the nonprofit sector. Earlier that spring, Dean Paul Teske had asked me to give the speech. In that speech, I addressed why I care deeply about helping nonprofits, their leaders, and their future leaders become agents of social change. This passion was unknowingly instilled in me at a young age because I was the recipient of nonprofits' good works and philanthropy. Before I had the good fortune of being able to help fund nonprofits through my work at three different foundations, I was the recipient of other people's generosity. I'm not aware of all of the nonprofits, including their leadership, staff, and volunteers, that assisted my family during my youth, but I do know they helped change my life for the better. I know that my experience is also shared by countless other individuals, each of whom have benefitted from other people's generosity. Thus, while the nonprofit sector only represents approximately 10 percent of the US economy, I firmly believe that it represents the greatest 10 percent of our economy.

Philanthropic organizations in America, including 501(c)(3)-public charities, educate millions of students every year, help advance important scientific research, address the health care needs of millions of patients, and help America's communities become vibrant social centers through the promotion of arts and culture, to give a few examples. Without the nonprofit sector, many of the museums, universities, hospitals, and countless other institutions that Americans revere and rely upon would not exist. What makes the American experiment unique is not only a "Government of the people, by the people, and for the people," but also our longing to associate with others who share our passions.[8] In 1835, French political scientist and diplomat, Alexis de Tocqueville, in his book, *Democracy in America*, commented on this spirit:

> Americans of all ages, all conditions, and all minds are constantly joining together in groups . . . . If, finally, they wish to publicize a truth or foster a sentiment with the help of a great example, they associate . . . . In America I came across types of associations which I confess I had no idea existed, and I frequently admired the boundless skill of Americans in setting large numbers of people toward a common goal and inducing them to strive toward that goal voluntarily.[9]

After delivering the commencement speech, and at the urging of one of my good friends, I was inspired to write this book. With this book, my goal is to further empower nonprofit leaders who help make our communities, and our world, better places in which to live. Indeed, Alexis de Tocqueville's observations are true today, just as they were nearly 200 years ago. This book is a manifestation of my desire to help nonprofit leaders understand two complicated yet essential subjects: nonprofit law and nonprofit finance. Accordingly, this book addresses forty-eight fundamental principles that the leaders of any nonprofit should know. I've been teaching graduate students, including students of nonprofits, law, finance, leadership, and management, for nearly a decade. In this time, I've been able to distill the forty-eight key questions addressed in this book's table of contents: twenty-four related to nonprofit law and twenty-four related to nonprofit finance.

By addressing these forty-eight questions through numerous stories and case studies from the nonprofit sector, I provide an effective framework for understanding the fundamentals of nonprofit law and nonprofit finance. Not only does each chapter address these key principles, but the chapters also apply these fundamental rules of law and finance to real-world nonprofits to help you better comprehend the material presented in each chapter. My goal for this book is to empower and to serve; and I hope that the rules of law and finance contained within these pages, along with numerous case studies bringing these rules to life, empower you as you pursue your visions and reaffirm your commitment to serve others. Your involvement in the nonprofit sector will surely help make our world a better place, and in turn, will likely change your life for the better. Gandhi once observed, "The best way to find yourself is to lose yourself in the service of others."

As I noted in my commencement speech, various nonprofit leaders altered my trajectory in life and changed it for the better. Whether you're an executive director, board member, staff member, volunteer, donor, fundraiser, educator, student, or any other leader or stakeholder of a nonprofit, your *why* for nonprofits is critically important. What cause or causes are you passionate about? What brings you joy? And why are you committed to a particular nonprofit, or perhaps to the nonprofit sector as a whole? With a firm understanding of your *why* for nonprofits, which is your fuel for making a difference, we can turn to the key legal and financial principles contained within this book. To run an effective nonprofit, every philanthropic leader should learn these principles. The great American experiment is in all of our hands, and I hope that this book helps you fulfill your *why* for nonprofits by providing a firm understanding of the essential principles of both nonprofit law and nonprofit finance.

1

What's the Difference between a Nonprofit Corporation and a Tax-Exempt Entity?

■ ■ ■

How wonderful it is that nobody need wait a single moment before starting to improve the world.

—Anne Frank

TIAA

TIAA, previously known as TIAA-CREF (Teachers Insurance and Annuity Association-College Retirement Equities Fund), is one of the nation's largest financial services firms.[1] Currently, it's listed on the Fortune 100 list and has more than "$1 trillion in assets under management."[2] Approximately 5 million individuals, including "college professors, nurses, administrators, researchers, and government employees," entrust their retirement savings to TIAA.[3] TIAA was established in 1918 by the Carnegie Foundation for the Advancement of Teaching to provide "guaranteed retirement income and life insurance to educators."[4] When the Carnegie Foundation established TIAA, its overarching goal was to create a "sustainable retirement system for teachers."[5] Today, a century after its initial establishment as a financial services firm for educators, TIAA is known for being an industry leader in "serving the financial needs of people in academic, government, medical, cultural, and other nonprofit fields."[6]

At its inception, TIAA was formed as a nonprofit corporation under the laws of the state of New York.[7] Andrew Carnegie established TIAA because he was "concerned about the poverty that seemed the common fate of retired teachers, [thus] he gave the then colossal sum of $10 million to fund the pensions of teachers at thirty universities."[8] TIAA subsequently obtained tax-exempt status from the Internal Revenue Service (IRS) under Section 501(c)(3) of the Internal Revenue Code (hereinafter, the "Code") as a public charity.[9] However, since 1998, TIAA has been subject to federal income taxes because Congress revoked

TIAA's tax-exempt status under Section 501(c)(3) of the Code with the passage of the Taxpayer Relief Act of 1997.[10] Since losing its tax-exempt status, TIAA is no longer a "not-for-profit company" but is now owned by another nonprofit corporation.[11] TIAA's history and existing corporate structure, including the fact that it's no longer a tax-exempt entity, highlights that there's a difference between a "nonprofit corporation" and a "tax-exempt entity."

The difference between a "nonprofit corporation" and a "tax-exempt entity" is often confused, even amongst professionals working in the nonprofit sector. People often use these two terms interchangeably because they think they mean the same thing. Thus, nonprofit leaders should understand the difference between these two terms. As the case study of TIAA demonstrates, an entity can be both or it can be one without being the other.

NONPROFIT CORPORATIONS VS. TAX-EXEMPT ENTITIES

To understand the difference between an entity being a "nonprofit corporation" and a "tax-exempt organization," it's helpful to understand the difference between state law and federal law. First, state law creates nonprofit corporations. That is, a nonprofit corporation is a "creature of [a state] statute," and most states have adopted the Model Nonprofit Corporation Act for this purpose.[12] For example, the state of Colorado has the Colorado Revised Nonprofit Corporation Act. Each state statute applicable to nonprofits addresses the steps that must be followed to create a nonprofit corporation under that state's sovereignty.

Typically, to create a nonprofit corporation under applicable state law, articles of incorporation must be filed in that state. As Lisa Runquist notes in her book, *The ABCs of Nonprofits*, "To form a corporation, a person (the incorporator) files articles of incorporation (sometimes called a corporate charter) with the state."[13] In Colorado, for instance, articles of incorporation must be filed with the Colorado Secretary of State. Similarly, in Oregon, articles of incorporation must be filed with the Oregon Secretary of State.[14] This first step, which requires nonprofit leaders to affirmatively take action to create a nonprofit by filing a document with the appropriate state agency, kick-starts the establishment of a "nonprofit corporation."

After a nonprofit corporation has been created under state law, the leaders of that nonprofit corporation may then seek tax-exemption under federal law. Nonprofit leaders accomplish this objective by filing either (1) the Form 1023, if that nonprofit corporation is seeking tax-exempt status as either a "public charity" or a "private foundation" under Section 501(c)(3) of the Code; (2) the Form 1024, if that nonprofit corporation is seeking tax-exempt status under numerous other provisions of Section 501(c) of the Code, including 501(c)(2), 501(c)(6), or 501(c)(7); or (3) the Form 1024-A, if that nonprofit corporation is seeking tax-exempt status as a "social welfare organization" under Section 501(c)(4) of the Code. All of these exemptions from federal income tax are either granted or recognized by the IRS under applicable federal law.

If tax-exempt status is granted or recognized by the IRS upon a review of those forms, the IRS will issue a "determination letter." After the Form 1023, the Form 1024, or the Form 1024-A is filed by a nonprofit applicant, it typically takes the IRS at least a month before issuing a determination with respect to that application. Regarding the Form 1023, there's a shorter version, called the Form 1023-EZ, that the IRS may review in a shorter period of time if certain qualifications are met by the applicant.[15] A determination letter is simply a one- to two-page "written statement issued by the Exempt Organizations (EO) Rulings and Agreements or an Appeals Office in response to an application for recognition of exemption."[16] This process outlines the difference between a nonprofit corporation, which is created under state law, and a tax-exempt entity, which is recognized under federal law.

CASE STUDY: CORPORATE GIVING BY A DENTIST

One of my acquaintances, Jennifer, desired to start a corporate foundation related to her prominent dental practice. She's a dentist in the Denver metro area and is passionate about giving back to her community. Over the past few years, she's provided free dental services and screenings to underprivileged individuals throughout the area. As a small business owner, she wanted to formalize her philanthropic initiatives by creating a corporate foundation that engages in both educational and charitable activities. Like many business owners desiring to formalize their philanthropic initiatives, she knew that she wanted to create a corporate foundation; however, she didn't know the steps she had to follow to accomplish this goal.

Thus, Jennifer and I met for coffee one day, and I explained to her the difference between a nonprofit corporation and a tax-exempt entity. I informed Jennifer that she must first file articles of incorporation to create a nonprofit corporation. In this case, Jennifer filed articles of incorporation for a Colorado nonprofit corporation with the Colorado Secretary of State. Next, Jennifer obtained an employer identification number (EIN) for this legal entity. Obtaining an EIN is required before either the Form 1023, Form 1024, or Form 1024-A may be filed with the IRS, as these forms ask for the entity's EIN.[17] Having obtained an EIN, Jennifer then filed the Form 1023-EZ and paid the requisite IRS filing fee. The Form 1023-EZ is a variation of the full Form 1023 for organizations having annual gross receipts and total assets below $50,000 and $250,000, respectively, among other qualifications.[18]

Within a few weeks, the IRS made a determination on this Form 1023-EZ application for Jennifer's corporate foundation. The IRS determined that this nonprofit corporation, which is the philanthropic initiative of Jennifer's dental practice, is a 501(c)(3)-public charity because of its educational and charitable purposes, as well as its proposed public support. Thus, the IRS issued a determination letter to Jennifer for this nonprofit corporation.

Jennifer was extremely excited to receive this determination letter in the mail because she could use this newly established 501(c)(3)-public charity to help additional underprivileged individuals while providing outstanding dental care. Based on this process of obtaining tax-exempt status from the IRS, Jennifer now understands the difference between a nonprofit corporation and a tax-exempt entity.

STATE LAW VS. FEDERAL LAW

The terms "nonprofit corporation" and "tax-exempt entity" are often used interchangeably. While many students and professionals in the nonprofit sector use these two terms interchangeably, they are in fact different. A nonprofit corporation does not necessarily have to seek federal tax-exempt status after it's created under state law. That is, a legal entity could be a nonprofit corporation but not classified under any subsection of Section 501(c) of the Code. Furthermore, a nonprofit corporation with tax-exempt status can lose that status after obtaining it, which is what occurred with TIAA. While this process of first creating a nonprofit corporation and then seeking tax-exemption for that legal entity is frequently followed, nonprofit leaders should understand that one is possible without the other. For instance, a limited liability company, which is *not* a nonprofit corporation, may seek tax-exemption under Section 501(c)(2) of the Code as a "title holding corporation." By understanding the difference between these two terms, you'll be able to use them correctly. Contrary to popular belief, they don't mean the same thing.

KEY PRINCIPLES

➜ A "nonprofit corporation" is a creature of state law.

➜ A "tax-exempt entity," such as a 501(c)(3)-public charity, is a product of federal law.

➜ After a nonprofit corporation has been created under state law, the leaders of that nonprofit corporation may then seek tax-exemption under federal law.

2

What's the Internal Affairs Doctrine?

■ ■ ■

Facebook was not originally created to be a company. It was built to accomplish a social mission—to make the world more open and connected.

—Mark Zuckerberg

THEFACEBOOK.COM LLC

Do you know that more than 66 percent of Fortune 500 companies are incorporated under the laws of the state of Delaware?[1] This fact leads to two questions: (1) what's so special about Delaware, and (2) how does this relate to nonprofit corporations? Let's examine Facebook's history to understand the answers to these two questions.

When Mark Zuckerberg and Eduardo Saverin started Facebook at Harvard University in 2004, they incorporated it under the laws of the state of Florida as a limited liability company (LLC).[2] Saverin had family in Miami, Florida, at the time of Thefacebook.com LLC's establishment.[3] Due to his Miami ties, setting up a Florida LLC was likely an easy move, and after Thefacebook.com LLC had been created, Saverin invested approximately $15,000 in the company.[4] In the movie *The Social Network*, the character played by Justin Timberlake famously said, "Drop the 'The.' Just 'Facebook.' It's cleaner."[5]

In 2004, Peter Thiel, PayPal's co-founder and former Chief Executive Officer, invested $500,000 in Facebook.[6] In his book *Zero to One*, Peter reflected on this early investment by stating, "Mark saw where he could take [Facebook] . . . [a] business with a good definite plan will always be underrated in a world where people see the future as random."[7] On July 29, 2004, around the time of Peter's investment, Facebook transitioned from a Florida LLC to a Delaware corporation.[8] Was it a coincidence that Facebook transitioned from a Florida LLC to a Delaware corporation around the time of Peter's investment, or is there some other explanation for this transition? While pure coincidence is certainly an option, a more likely explanation is that the internal affairs doctrine spurred this transition. Most corporate attorneys know it's beneficial to be a Delaware entity (i.e., a Delaware corporation) when raising capital from investors, and this presumption rests on the internal affairs doctrine.[9]

INTERNAL AFFAIRS DOCTRINE

The internal affairs doctrine applies to both for-profit corporations, such as Facebook, and nonprofit corporations. This doctrine is a choice of laws "principle which recognizes that only one State should have the authority to regulate a corporation's internal affairs."[10] The state that "regulate[s] a corporation's internal affairs," such as a nonprofit corporation, is the corporation's state of incorporation.[11] When Facebook was a Florida LLC, the laws of Florida dictated its internal affairs.[12] However, when Facebook transitioned to a Delaware corporation, the laws of Delaware began to govern its internal affairs.[13] Likewise, the American Heart Association, Inc. is a nonprofit corporation organized under the laws of New York.[14] It was incorporated under New York law in 1924; thus, New York law regulates its internal affairs.[15] The internal affairs doctrine is a common law doctrine, which means it's been developed over time by various courts.[16]

As applied to nonprofit corporations, the internal affairs doctrine dictates that issues *not* addressed in a nonprofit's articles of incorporation, such as (1) the number of board members a nonprofit must have, (2) the frequency with which those directors must meet, (3) the basis for a quorum, (4) whether those directors can act without a meeting, and (5) whether a nonprofit must have bylaws, may be addressed in a state's applicable nonprofit corporation act.[17] For example, the Model Nonprofit Corporation Act, developed by the Committee on Nonprofit Organizations by the American Bar Association, addresses similar issues.[18] The internal affairs doctrine in this sense acts as a safety net for nonprofit leaders, as certain issues not addressed in a nonprofit's governing documents might be addressed by the state's applicable nonprofit corporation act.

When nonprofit leaders select a state of incorporation, the internal affairs doctrine may not be top-of-mind. Amongst leaders in the for-profit sector, however, the internal affairs doctrine is typically well-known. For example, Delaware law is generally viewed as being favorable to a corporation's board and management.[19] Thus, it makes sense that approximately 66 percent of Fortune 500 companies are incorporated under Delaware law.[20] The applicable case law interpreting the Delaware General Corporation Law (DGCL) statute, which is the statute governing Delaware corporations, is also similarly viewed as being favorable to a corporation's leadership.[21] Accordingly, the internal affairs doctrine likely explains why Facebook transitioned from a Florida LLC to a Delaware corporation. Peter may have wanted the benefit of Delaware law, just like 66 percent of Fortune 500 companies, when he first invested in Facebook.

While the internal affairs doctrine also applies to nonprofit corporations, the state of incorporation for nonprofits is typically not as important as it is for for-profit corporations. Nonprofit corporation acts are generally the same from state to state, and the case law interpreting these acts is not necessarily more favorable to a nonprofit corporation's board or management.[22] For instance, state law governing the internal affairs of a Colorado nonprofit corporation will be similar to the state law governing the internal affairs of a Delaware nonprofit corporation. This is because many states have adopted a version of the Model Nonprofit Corporation Act.[23] As of 2002, for example, 23 states had adopted a version of this act.[24] Even though the state of incorporation may not be as important for nonprofit corporations, nonprofit leaders should understand what the internal affairs doctrine is and how it applies to nonprofits and other philanthropic initiatives, like The Chan Zuckerberg Initiative.

CASE STUDY: THE CHAN ZUCKERBERG INITIATIVE

In 2015, Mark Zuckerberg and Priscilla Chan started The Chan Zuckerberg Initiative to help formalize and solidify their philanthropic efforts.[25] According to The Chan Zuckerberg Initiative's website, this effort "is a new kind of philanthropic organization that brings together world-class engineering, grant-making, impact investing, policy, and advocacy work."[26] The Chan Zuckerberg Initiative focuses on the following priorities: (1) education, (2) justice and opportunity, and (3) science.[27]

Traditionally, most wealthy philanthropists start a nonprofit corporation that becomes exempt from federal income tax under Section 501(c)(3) of the Code as a private foundation.[28] Private foundations were the preferred vehicle for most philanthropists during the 20th century.[29] For example, the Bill and Melinda Gates Foundation is set up as a private foundation.[30] However, Zuckerberg faced a unique issue when he and Priscilla Chan set up their philanthropic initiative. Zuckerberg likely needed to maintain voting control over his shares in Facebook, but at the same time, both he and Chan desired to give away approximately 99 percent of their wealth, much of which is in Facebook stock, to philanthropic efforts during their lifetime.[31]

To accomplish both of these goals, the attorneys for Zuckerberg and Chan likely suggested creating a limited liability company organized under the laws of Delaware for their philanthropy.[32] This strategy allowed Zuckerberg and Chan to achieve their philanthropic goals, while at the same time providing other successful entrepreneurs an alternative to the 501(c)(3)-private foundation for accomplishing their charitable goals. Accordingly, The Chan Zuckerberg Initiative is a Delaware LLC as opposed to a Delaware nonprofit corporation.[33] Its internal affairs are governed by Delaware law because of the internal affairs doctrine.[34]

When Zuckerberg and Chan donate or transfer shares of Facebook to this Delaware LLC, they will *indirectly* hold these shares. The shares will be *directly* held by The Chan Zuckerberg Initiative. The key benefit related to this transfer is that Zuckerberg will maintain voting control over these Facebook shares.[35] Conversely, if Zuckerberg and Chan started a 501(c)(3)-private foundation and transferred Facebook shares to that foundation, the foundation would be able to vote those shares, assuming that Zuckerberg and Chan would want to obtain the full charitable deduction related to those donated shares.[36] By creating a Delaware LLC, however, Zuckerberg's ability to maintain voting power over any donated shares was achieved.

Second, LLCs are "pass-through" entities. This means that such entities don't pay federal income taxes. Thus, when The Chan Zuckerberg Initiative makes a donation to a public charity, for example, the charitable deduction related to that contribution flows through to the LLC's members.[37] In this case, if the members of this LLC are both Zuckerberg and Chan, they get the charitable deduction in equal proportions, which is also known as *pro rata*.[38] Therefore, the second objective related to their philanthropic goals was achieved by creating a Delaware LLC.

STATE OF INCORPORATION

The Chan Zuckerberg Initiative highlights the importance of the internal affairs doctrine and the way in which newer philanthropists are becoming more creative with their philanthropies than their 20th century predecessors. The internal affairs doctrine means the incorporating state's laws govern the internal affairs of an entity, whether that entity is an LLC, like The Chan Zuckerberg Initiative; a for-profit corporation, like Facebook; or a nonprofit corporation, like the American Heart Association. In the for-profit sector, Delaware is clearly the state of choice for most Fortune 500 leaders because Delaware law is generally viewed as being favorable to a corporation's leadership.[39] With nonprofit corporations, however, the state of incorporation is not as important because many states have adopted a version of the Model Nonprofit Corporation Act.[40] Since the internal affairs doctrine is a choice of laws principle, nonprofit leaders should understand that when they select an incorporating state they are also selecting the laws of that state to govern the nonprofit's internal affairs.

KEY PRINCIPLES

→ The internal affairs doctrine applies to nonprofit corporations.

→ This doctrine is a "choice of laws" principle.

→ The internal affairs doctrine means the incorporating state's laws govern the internal affairs of an entity.

3

What's a Dissolution Provision?

■ ■ ■

You have two choices in life: you can dissolve into the mainstream or you can be distinct. To be distinct, you must be different. To be different, you must strive to be what no one else but you can be.

—Alan Ashley-Pitt

WINDING UP AFFAIRS

An Italian proverb notes, "Once the game is over, the king and the pawn go back into the same box." While many of us might not like to think about this inevitable truth, have you ever considered what will happen to your assets when you pass away? Who will inherit your home, car, heirlooms, and all of the other assets you've accumulated over the course of your lifetime? Attorneys focusing on trusts and estates law help individuals and their families consider these important issues. An effective trusts and estates attorney can help plan for the event of death through the drafting of wills, trusts, and other estate planning documents.

If you haven't yet planned for this event, you should consider visiting an attorney specializing in trusts and estates law or make similar preparations with another expert to handle these affairs. For those of us who have lost loved ones and other close friends, we know how difficult such a time can be. Your family, friends, and other loved ones will be mourning your loss, and during that time, they shouldn't have to worry about affairs related to bereavement too. If you've adequately prepared for that moment, through the advice of a respected trusts and estates attorney, you'll help your family, friends, and loved ones get through a difficult time.

Just like we should prepare for our end-of-life affairs, the leaders of a nonprofit must consider similar issues. What will happen to a nonprofit's assets if and when that nonprofit corporation dissolves, or ceases to be a legal entity under applicable state law?[1] While most nonprofit corporations strive to exist in perpetuity, there are some that only plan to exist for a certain period of time and dissolve after that period. In those cases, the leaders who set up such nonprofits include a "sunset" provision in the nonprofit's governing documents, which solidi-fies the fact that it will cease to be a legal entity after a certain period of time.

Regardless of the initial intent, a board of directors for a nonprofit corpor-ation should—and in most cases are required to under state law—address what will happen to the assets of that nonprofit in the event of dissolution. This deci-sion is dictated in a dissolution provision.

DISSOLUTION PROVISION

What exactly is a dissolution provision? The dissolution provision is typically a paragraph or two included in a nonprofit's articles of incorporation when it's ini-tially formed.[2] In fact, several states, like the state of Colorado, require that a dissolution provision be included in a nonprofit's articles of incorporation when forming the nonprofit corporation.[3] That is, a nonprofit corporation cannot be validly formed unless its articles of incorporation includes a dissolution provision.[4] This dissolution provision addresses what will happen to a nonprofit's remaining assets (we'll learn later in this book that Net Assets = Total Assets – Total Liabilities) in the event that it dissolves. Most dissolution provisions are structured as a two-tiered provision. The first tier generally gives a nonprofit board the power to ear-mark assets if that nonprofit dissolves, and the second tier addresses what happens to those assets if the board fails to act.

A nonprofit may dissolve voluntarily, such as through the actions of its board or members, or involuntary, such as through the actions of its creditors, state attorneys general, or courts.[5] When a nonprofit dissolves, whether voluntarily or involuntarily, the dissolution provision usually dictates that the nonprofit's board of directors should earmark the remaining assets to another nonprofit. In this event, the board will typically earmark such assets to another nonprofit with a similar cause or mission. This strategy is consistent with the doctrine of *cy pres*, which simply notes that "donor intent" should be respected by a nonprofit board.[6]

When I was an attorney at the law firm of Davis Graham & Stubbs LLP, I advised the board of directors of a charter school in Denver, Colorado, that was dissolving. This charter school, which was also a 501(c)(3)-public charity, had numerous assets, including items like chairs, desks, computers, books, and school supplies. At the last board meeting for this charter school, the board earmarked all of those assets to another charter school in the Denver metro area. The charter school that received those assets had a similar mission and vision as the dissolving charter school, including a focus on serving students from low socioeconomic backgrounds. Thus, the board followed the doctrine of *cy pres*, which respects "donor intent,"[7] when it made this decision.

Furthermore, if the board of directors for a dissolving nonprofit corpor-ation fails to earmark the remaining assets to another nonprofit, then the typical dissolution provision notes that a "court of competent jurisdiction" must decide what will happen to those assets. Thus, if the board of directors for the dissolving nonprofit doesn't decide what to do with those assets, then a local district court judge will make a prudent decision regarding how to allocate them. The district court judge making this decision is generally in the same jurisdiction, or geographical area, where the dissolving nonprofit is headquartered. The local district court judge will also usually consider the doctrine of *cy pres*, so that the remaining assets of the dissolving nonprofit are transferred to another nonprofit with a similar mission.

CASE STUDY: LEVEL 3 FOUNDATION

Drafting a dissolution provision is straightforward when following the two-tiered structure. This two-tiered structure for the dissolution provision is reflected in the Level 3 Foundation, Inc.'s articles of incorporation.[8] This foundation was the philanthropic initiative of Level 3 Communications, Inc. (Level 3), which was a Fortune 500 company before being acquired by CenturyLink in 2017. This foundation raised hundreds of thousands of dollars each year from both Level 3 and its employees and then granted those monies to nonprofits.[9] I had the privilege of serving this foundation as its General Counsel. At the time of Level 3 Foundation's establishment, the following dissolution provision was included in its articles of incorporation:

> Upon any liquidation, dissolution, or winding up of the Level 3 Foundation, Inc. (the "Corporation"), the Board of Directors shall, after paying or adequately providing for the payment of all the obligations and liabilities of the Corporation, dispose of all the assets owned by the Corporation by transferring such assets exclusively to or for the benefit of such organization or organizations as shall at the time qualify under Section 501(c)(3) of the Internal Revenue Code of 1986, as amended, as the Board of Directors shall determine. Any of such assets not so disposed of shall be disposed of by the District Court for Denver County, Colorado, exclusively for such exempt purposes or to such organization or organizations which are organized and operated exclusively for such exempt purposes, as such Court shall determine.[10]

With this two-tiered dissolution provision, the foundation's board of directors decides where the remaining assets will go if and when this nonprofit dissolves under applicable state law. If the board fails to act, then a district court judge located in Denver County will decide where such assets should go. When CenturyLink acquired Level 3 in 2017 for approximately $34 billion, the board of directors of the Level 3 Foundation considered either merging this foundation with the Clarke M. Williams Foundation, (CenturyLink's corporate foundation), or dissolving it and transferring its assets to the Clarke M. Williams Foundation. Just like the charter school example above, this latter option would have been consistent with the Level 3 Foundation's dissolution provision.

TWO-TIERED STRUCTURE

Most nonprofits strive to exist in perpetuity because they are pursuing visions and fulfilling missions that require them to exist indefinitely, such as eradicating hunger, educating children, or finding cures to various diseases. Accordingly, the dissolution provisions for these nonprofits will likely never be invoked. Nonetheless, a well-thought-out dissolution provision typically follows a two-tiered structure. While nonprofit leaders may never have to think about a dissolution provision once a nonprofit's articles of incorporation have been filed, we don't have that same luxury on an individual basis. Eventually, all of us must metaphorically "wind up our affairs." For the good of our families, friends, and loved ones, we should determine where our remaining assets will go, just like a nonprofit must do with its dissolution provision, when that occurs.

KEY PRINCIPLES

→ The dissolution provision is typically a paragraph or two included in a nonprofit's articles of incorporation when it's initially formed.

→ This dissolution provision addresses what will happen to a nonprofit's remaining assets in the event that it dissolves.

→ Most dissolution provisions are structured as a two-tiered provision. The first tier generally gives a nonprofit board the power to earmark assets if that nonprofit dissolves, and the second tier addresses what happens to those assets if the board fails to act.

4

What Are Bylaws?

■ ■ ■

It is easier for a man to be loyal to his club than to his planet; the bylaws are shorter, and he is personally acquainted with the other members.

—E. B. White

RULES OF THE ROAD

Do you have guiding principles you won't compromise and that help you be the person you envision being? You've likely been exposed to some guiding principles throughout life, such as: live with integrity, treat others as you wish to be treated, don't tolerate intolerance, be inclusive, and pursue your passions. My favorite leadership professor, Dr. Ron Billingsley, emphasized this last principle by frequently stating, "Find your passion, but then more importantly, live a life that shows it." Dr. Billingsley also argued that the latter part, living a life that reflects your passion, is often more difficult than finding it. Having a set of guiding principles, such as living your passion, helps us lead the lives we want to lead. In a difficult situation, you can lean on such principles to help ensure you make the right decision and achieve your desired outcome. Just like we have "rules of the road" that help us in a variety of contexts, nonprofits with adopted bylaws have rules of the road to help them navigate various situations.

A nonprofit corporation is a legal entity, which essentially means that it's a collection of individuals who desire to pursue the same common goal.[1] With most nonprofits, this common goal is often a charitable one, such as improving educational outcomes for children, providing medical care to underserved populations, or supporting performing arts organizations. In their pursuit of a vision, it's helpful for those individuals to have a set of common principles. Accordingly, bylaws reflect the set of principles that are associated with the governance of the nonprofit. Taken together, these rules and procedures form the operating manual for the nonprofit's governance activities. When the nonprofit's annual meeting will be held, who the officers of the nonprofit will be, and when and how the directors of the nonprofit will be elected are typically addressed in

16

a nonprofit's bylaws. These "rules of the road" will guide a nonprofit's leaders as they fulfill the nonprofit's mission. Most nonprofit corporations exist in perpetuity, so it's important that they set this initial framework to be followed by the next generation of leaders.

Having taught both nonprofit law and nonprofit finance for nearly a decade at both the University of Colorado and the University of Denver, I've come to realize that nonprofit leaders don't always have a firm understanding of how bylaws differ from a nonprofit's articles of incorporation. Some individuals use these two terms interchangeably, when in fact they are distinct documents. Thus, this chapter is devoted to understanding the purpose of bylaws for a nonprofit, as Chapter 25 describes the purpose of a nonprofit's articles of incorporation.

BYLAWS

A nonprofit is governed by its articles of incorporation, or certificate of incorporation, and bylaws. A nonprofit's articles of incorporation allows it to exist as a legal entity under state law, whereas bylaws govern the internal affairs of a nonprofit. However, a nonprofit will only have bylaws if they've been implemented by its leaders, such as its incorporators who created the nonprofit corporation.[2] Under applicable state law, a nonprofit may not be required to adopt bylaws.[3] Under Colorado law, for example, a nonprofit isn't required to adopt bylaws.[4] While bylaws may be optional under applicable state law, it's certainly a best practice for nonprofits to adopt bylaws. On the Form 1023, the Internal Revenue Service (IRS) asks for a copy of the applicant's bylaws.[5] Nonprofit leaders file the Form 1023 when they are seeking 501(c)(3) status. Thus, the IRS also believes it's a best practice for nonprofits seeking exemption under Section 501(c)(3) of the Code to have bylaws.

Nonprofit bylaws address a myriad of governance issues.[6] Typically, they address: (1) the location of the nonprofit's corporate office; (2) requirements for board members' and officers' tenure, qualification, election, removal, and compensation; (3) whether board members will have "staggered terms," which means that not every board member is up for election during the applicable election period; (4) annual and special meeting requirements, including notices for such meetings; (5) quorum and voting requirements for annual and special meetings; (6) board committees; (7) whether the board may take action without a meeting; (8) conduct standards for the board and officers, including any conflict of interest issues; (9) officer positions, such as the president, executive director, vice president, secretary, and treasurer; (10) the powers and duties of those officers; (11) whether the nonprofit will indemnify the board and officers; and (12) who may engage in financial transactions on behalf of the nonprofit.[7]

As this comprehensive list demonstrates, nonprofit leaders typically want to address these governance matters when they create a nonprofit corporation. Additionally, such leaders may also address in the bylaws whether the non-profit will have "members."[8] Marion R. Fremont-Smith in her book, *Governing Nonprofit Organizations*, notes "Aside from determining the charitable purposes, the most important decision will be whether control of the [nonprofit] corpor-ation is to be in the board of directors or whether it will be divided between directors and members."[9] If the incorporators elect for the nonprofit to have "members," then they are giving those members certain powers that are similar to the powers possessed by shareholders of a for-profit corporation; however, unlike shareholders, members have no ownership interests.[10] Unlike for-profit corporations, the profits of a 501(c)(3) nonprofit cannot be distributed to members.[11] The decision of whether to have members may be reflected in the nonprofit's bylaws.[12] Because the leaders of a nonprofit will change over time, bylaws are set up to govern the internal affairs of the nonprofit long-term, regard-less of who's leading it.

CASE STUDY: GLOBAL ONE80

Over the course of my career as a lawyer, I've helped numerous leaders create and incorporate new nonprofits. Each time I assist those leaders, I recommend that the nonprofit they're creating adopt bylaws, even though those bylaws might not be required by the law of the incorporating state. That way everyone associated with that nonprofit can be aligned on the foregoing governance issues. For example, I assisted with the creation of Global One80, which is a Colorado nonprofit corporation. My graduate school classmate from the University of Colorado School of Public Affairs, Joaquin, created a nonprofit to inspire and promote the next generation of community leaders. The mission of Global One80 is to "identify commu-nity leaders that will implement charitable activities and initiatives in their respective communities that further public purposes."[13] Joaquin and I met over coffee to discuss the steps that must be taken in order to create both a Colorado nonprofit corporation and a 501(c)(3)-public charity.

During this discussion, I addressed the importance of adopting bylaws for this new nonprofit corporation, including the fact that the Form 1023 asks for an applicant's bylaws. As the founder of Global One80, Joaquin desired to lay the framework for various governance matters, including how this nonprofit would elect directors, which officer positions this nonprofit would have, how many meetings the board of directors would have per year, standards of conduct for both directors and officers, how the board would address conflicts of interest, and who would engage in financial transactions on behalf of the nonprofit. By establishing Global One80's bylaws, Joaquin was able to address these crucial administrative issues. Without bylaws, Global One80 would lack an operating manual that addresses these fun-damental governance matters that will inevitably arise as Global One80 pursues its vision.

As a nonprofit like Global One80 pursues its vision both its leaders and strategies will change over time. For this reason, bylaws should also change over time. Joaquin won't be able to lead this nonprofit—which helps promote community leaders who pursue charitable activities that further public purposes—forever. As the leaders of a nonprofit change, they can amend the nonprofit's bylaws to ensure that the "rules of the road" conform with the future practices of the nonprofit. In this sense, bylaws should be viewed as a living document. In fact, bylaws should be periodically amended by a nonprofit's board and/or its members. For example, some of the governance provisions that Joaquin and I drafted in Global One80's initial bylaws may not be applicable twenty years from now. Joaquin set the framework for Global One80's governance matters by adopting initial bylaws, and by periodically reviewing them, future leaders of this nonprofit will help ensure that Global One80 is meeting its objectives.

INTERNAL AFFAIRS

In the nonprofit sector, many people don't fully understand the difference between articles of incorporation and bylaws. Bylaws represent a set of rules that govern the internal affairs of the nonprofit. Just as you've likely adopted guiding principles that help you lead your life, so should nonprofits. Nonprofit leaders will look to the bylaws when they need to know which officers the nonprofit will have; how often the board needs to meet; who is qualified to serve on the board; whether the board can take action without a meeting; and who can engage in a financial transaction on behalf of the nonprofit, among other key governance issues. Because of their importance, bylaws should be viewed as a living document; one that should be reviewed each year by the leaders of a nonprofit to determine if any changes need to be made. As the leaders of a nonprofit change, these fundamental "rules of the road," as set forth in the bylaws, will help ensure that a nonprofit is both respecting its history and appreciating its future.

KEY PRINCIPLES

→ A nonprofit is governed by its articles of incorporation, or certificate of incorporation, and bylaws.
→ A nonprofit's articles of incorporation allow it to exist as a legal entity under state law, whereas bylaws govern the internal affairs of a nonprofit.
→ Nonprofit bylaws address a myriad of governance issues.

5

What's an Indemnification Provision?

■ ■ ■

Show business is my life. When I was a kid I sold insurance, but nobody laughed.

—Don Rickles

HOLD HARMLESS

If someone sues you, wouldn't it be nice if you had a contractual right to be "held harmless" for that lawsuit? In other words, wouldn't it be nice if another person or an entity paid for the legal costs associated with your defense of that lawsuit? The answer to these two questions likely depends on whether you're currently serving as a trustee, board member, or director of a corporation, including a nonprofit corporation. Many for-profit companies, especially those that are publicly traded on a major stock exchange, like the NASDAQ or the New York Stock Exchange, typically "hold harmless" their board members or directors in the event that they are sued in such capacities. This right to be "held harmless" in the event of a lawsuit, which is also known as an indemnification right, stems from a contractual right these board members or directors have with the companies for which they serve. This contractual right may arise from a standalone indemnification contract or from a legal provision found in a governing document, such as the articles of incorporation or bylaws.[1]

For example, let's assume that you're on the board of directors of Snap Inc. (Snap), a Delaware corporation that operates the popular "Snapchat" social media platform.[2] Snap is a publicly traded company on the New York Stock Exchange.[3] Let's further assume that Snap sells to Facebook because the board of directors of Snap believes it got the best possible sales price for the company. Finally, let's also assume that a few stockholders of Snap believe that the directors could have received an even *higher* sales price for the company. These stockholders sue the directors of Snap for allegedly breaching their fiduciary duties. One of the claims they allege in their lawsuit is that the directors of Snap did not receive a fair sales price for the company. When these stockholders sue the directors of Snap for allegedly breaching their fiduciary duties, the indemnity right these directors have with Snap kicks in.[4]

This example highlights that Snap itself would pay for its directors' legal defense costs related to this lawsuit. An indemnification right is a privilege that each board member or director possesses because of his or her role. In fact, many people would likely decline an invitation to serve on a board if this indemnity right was missing. Without an indemnification right, each board member or director might have to pay for legal defense costs out of his or her own pocket or hope that the company, in its discretion, picks them up. In the nonprofit sector, nonprofit corporations should also have this indemnification right with their board members or directors, who often serve voluntarily.

INDEMNIFICATION AND "D&O" INSURANCE

In the nonprofit sector, an indemnification provision is a contractual right a nonprofit corporation has with another entity, such as another corporation, or with an individual to hold that nonprofit or person harmless when some event occurs, such as a lawsuit.[5] For example, let's assume that I represent Stanford University, which is a 501(c)(3)-public charity, as one of its attorneys. Stanford decides to enter into a license agreement with Harvard University, which is another 501(c)(3)-public charity, to license certain intellectual property that it owns to Harvard. Most likely, an attorney for Harvard would include an indemnification provision in this contract related to the intellectual property it's licensing from Stanford. If a third party, such as Yale University, which is also a 501(c)(3)-public charity, sues both Stanford and Harvard alleging that Stanford and Harvard misappropriated its intellectual property, which Stanford is licensing to Harvard under this license agreement, then the indemnification provision would kick in.

Assuming that Harvard successfully negotiated for an indemnification right in the license agreement that it has with Stanford, then Stanford would have to "defend, indemnify, and hold Harvard harmless" when Yale sues both of them.[6] These magic words, "defend, indemnify, and hold harmless," are typically included in every indemnification provision.[7] For board members or directors of nonprofits, there is special insurance a nonprofit corporation may obtain once it decides to indemnify these individuals. This insurance is called "directors' and officers' liability insurance," or simply "D&O" insurance.[8] If a nonprofit corporation elects to indemnify its board members or directors, which it typically does through a provision that's found in the articles of incorporation, bylaws, or perhaps even a separate indemnity agreement, it should consider purchasing D&O insurance to cover that contractual right if and when it ever kicks in.

Nonprofits can usually get D&O insurance for an affordable price.[9] This affordability is due to the fact that only a few individuals, such as a state attorney general, or entities, such as the IRS, have "standing" to sue nonprofit board members or directors in such capacities.[10] For a lawsuit to be brought in a court of competent jurisdiction, an individual or an entity must have "standing" in that court, which simply means the ability of a plaintiff to properly bring that lawsuit.[11] By obtaining D&O insurance, a nonprofit does not have to create a reserve fund whereby certain assets of the nonprofit would be devoted to covering these indemnification provisions if they are ever implicated.[12] Instead, D&O insurance covers these indemnity rights, barring any exclusions set forth in such policies, such as a board member acting in "bad faith."[13] The coverage limits associated with D&O insurance for nonprofit corporations typically ranges from $1 million to $25 million.[14] With this strategy, the assets of a nonprofit can primarily be devoted to the nonprofit's mission. Additionally, by having D&O insurance, a nonprofit's board members or directors are typically covered if they are ever specifically sued and named in a lawsuit.

CASE STUDY: THE UNIVERSITY OF LOUISVILLE

Despite certain "standing" limitations related to nonprofit corporations, there are in fact times when board members, directors, and/or officers of nonprofits are sued. For example, certain directors and officers of the University of Louisville Foundation, a Kentucky nonprofit corporation and a 501(c)(3)-public charity, were sued because of alleged breaches of their fiduciary duties.[15] In the case of *The University of Louisville & The University of Louisville Foundation, Inc. v. James R. Ramsey et. al.*, the plaintiffs, including the University of Louisville Foundation, alleged that the defendants (1) breached their fiduciary duties; (2) breached certain provisions of the Kentucky Nonprofit Corporations Act; (3) aided and abetted breaches of fiduciary duties; (4) conducted fraudulent misrepresentation; (5) conducted fraudulent suppression and omissions; and (6) in the case of the law firm representing these two entities, even conducted legal malpractice.[16] David Grissom, a spokesperson for the University of Louisville, stated, "When certain activities occur that are so egregious and wrong for the future of the university and the foundation and our donors, you can't just sit back and let it go."[17]

If the University of Louisville, which is the other plaintiff, or the University of Louisville Foundation had indemnity provisions with the directors who are being sued, those indemnity provisions might require those two entities to cover the legal costs associated with these alleged claims, unless an exception such as a director or an officer "acting in bad faith" applies.[18] For example, the Amended and Restated Bylaws of the University of Louisville Foundation has an exception related to "acts or omissions not in good faith or which involved gross negligence or willful misconduct in the performance of such person's duties as a Director, officer, employee or committee member of the Foundation."[19] In such cases, the indemnity right of a director or an officer would *not* kick in. In this case, however, the Amended and Restated Bylaws further notes that "no Indemnified Person shall be indemnified . . . [where] such person shall have been *adjudicated liable*."[20] With an indemnity provision like this, the University of Louisville Foundation might need to cover the legal defense costs associated with its directors' and officers' alleged wrongdoing until there's a final adjudication by a judge or a jury. In this case, the legal fees associated with this lawsuit have totaled approximately $1.5 million to date.[21]

INDEMNITY PROVISION

When a nonprofit corporation is first formed, like the University of Louisville Foundation, an attorney representing that entity will likely include an indemnity provision in the articles of incorporation, bylaws, or in a separate indemnity agreement. When I served as the General Counsel for the Level 3 Foundation, for example, I included an indemnity provision in its articles of incorporation. The foundation's directors were distinguished leaders, as two of them served as C-suite executives for a Fortune 500 company. In turn, the foundation obtained D&O insurance from an insurance carrier to cover this indemnification right, which cost approximately $1,500 per year. Without D&O insurance, the foundation's assets would cover a director's contractual right to be "held harmless" in the event of a lawsuit brought against him or her. Since board members and directors often volunteer their time to serve on nonprofit boards, most of them require an indemnification right before they agree to serve in this capacity.

KEY PRINCIPLES

→ An indemnification provision is a contractual right a nonprofit corporation has with another entity, such as another corporation, or with an individual to hold that nonprofit or person harmless when some event occurs.

→ These magic words, "defend, indemnify, and hold harmless," are typically included in every indemnification provision.

→ There is special insurance a nonprofit corporation may obtain once it decides to indemnify another entity or individuals. This insurance is called "directors' and officers' liability insurance," or simply "D&O" insurance.

6

What's a Conflict of Interest Policy?

■ ■ ■

The harder the conflict, the more glorious the triumph.

—Thomas Paine

BROAD ART CENTER

The Eli and Edythe Broad Foundation based in Los Angeles, California (Broad Foundation), is one of America's largest private foundations. One of its founders, Eli Broad, grew up in Detroit, Michigan, graduated with honors from Michigan State University, became the state's then-youngest certified public accountant, and acquired SunLife Insurance Company (SunLife) in 1971 for $52 million.[1] Most of Eli and Edythe Broad's fortune came from the sale of SunLife to AIG Insurance for approximately $18 billion in 1999, which allowed them to then focus on their philanthropic initiatives, which included the Broad Foundation.[2] According to the Broad Foundation's most recent Form 990-PF, which is a private foundation's annual information return, it has total assets of approximately $1.75 billion and grants approximately $150 million each year to various charitable causes.[3] The Broad Foundation's mission is to "advance entrepreneurship for the public good in education, science and the arts."[4] One of its key objectives is to "expand public access to the arts," as both Eli and Edythe Broad share a passion for collecting contemporary artwork.[5]

If you've ever been to the main campus of the University of California, Los Angeles, (UCLA) in Westwood, California, you might have toured the Broad Art Center. The Broad Art Center houses "classrooms, galleries, studio space, auditoriums, and conference space for students and the general public," which helps the Broad Foundation accomplish its mission of advancing entrepreneurship in the arts.[6] The Broad Foundation gave a $23.2 million grant toward the construction of the new Broad Art Center at UCLA that opened in 2006, which also houses UCLA's School of Arts and Architecture.[7]

Let's imagine you're on the board of directors for the Broad Foundation, which is classified as a 501(c)(3)-private foundation.[8] During one of your board meetings, the senior managing director of the Broad Foundation, who is the equivalent of a nonprofit executive director, notes that the foundation would like to engage the services of a spouse of one of your fellow board members. This spouse of your fellow board member owns a very successful marketing firm in Los Angeles, and the Broad Foundation would like to hire that marketing firm to help it promote the Broad Art Center at UCLA.

During this board meeting, you learn that this spouse and your fellow board member collectively own 100 percent of this very successful marketing firm. You're not sure whether the Broad Foundation, which you owe your fiduciary duties to pursuant to California law, should hire this marketing firm since your fellow board member has a significant financial stake in it.[9] In this moment, you think to yourself: "should this board member benefit financially from this transaction?" One of the key reasons this marketing firm is being considered by the board is due to the relationship the spouse and your fellow board member have with the Broad Foundation.

This fact pattern, representing a potential conflict of interest transaction, frequently occurs within nonprofits. A nonprofit's board of directors or executive leadership team will likely encounter a potential conflict of interest transaction as a nonprofit conducts its business. For this reason, it's important for the leaders of a nonprofit corporation, like the board of directors for the Broad Foundation based on this hypothetical, to have a conflict of interest policy and also understand the purpose that such policy serves in effective corporate governance.

CONFLICT OF INTEREST POLICY

An effective conflict of interest policy for a nonprofit typically outlines the steps for disclosing and addressing a potential conflict of interest.[10] First, it helps those people subject to the policy, such as the nonprofit's board and senior staff, understand when and how they should disclose a potential conflict.[11] Without disclosure, such as the hypothetical potential hiring of the marketing firm by the Broad Foundation, a conflict of interest transaction could move forward. The headline for this transaction in the *Los Angeles Times* newspaper, if it were to occur, would not be favorable to the Broad Foundation, especially given the "self-dealing" rules related to private foundations.[12] A transaction like this one, which involves professional services rendered by a "disqualified person" (in this case, the spouse of a board member) to a private foundation, would constitute self-dealing unless an exception to the rules on self-dealing applies.[13]

For this reason, the first step to ensuring that a nonprofit has an effective conflict of interest protocol is to create a culture of disclosure. One way nonprofits can do this is by asking people who are subject to such policies to disclose, typically on an annual basis, any potential conflicts they may be aware of.[14] Disclosure of potential conflicts helps board members comply with their fiduciary duty of loyalty.[15] These periodic disclosures may include: (1) all of the boards of directors that the disclosing individuals serve on; (2) their current employment status with any applicable employers; (3) any groups, clubs, or professional societies that they are members of; and (4) any other groups or entities of which they are either members or owners, or otherwise have a financial stake in.[16] The goal of regular disclosure is to allow those who are disclosing these affiliations and those who are reviewing the disclosures to gain a sense of potential conflicts that may arise as the nonprofit conducts its business.[17]

Second, an effective conflict of interest policy also outlines how these potential conflicts of interest, once disclosed, should be handled.[18] The policy may note, for example, that a potential conflict should first be brought to a committee of the board of directors, such as the board's audit committee. If that committee determines that a potential conflict of interest indeed exists, then it may forward that potential transaction to the full board of directors for consideration. Along with disclosure practices, an effective conflict of interest policy should outline the steps a nonprofit will take to resolve potential conflicts.[19] For instance, when discussing potential conflicts, a board will likely address whether the transaction is "fair" to the implicated nonprofit. If the steps outlined in the policy are followed, the outcome of the board's discussion and its determination regarding a potential conflict of interest transaction, including its fairness to the nonprofit, will likely be the right outcome for those involved.

CASE STUDY: BROAD ART CENTER

The IRS places a high emphasis on conflict of interest policies for nonprofits, including 501(c)(3)-public charities and 501(c)(3)-private foundations. In fact, the Form 1023 application has a specific question related to whether the applicant has a conflict of interest policy in place.[20] Specifically, Question 5a of Part V of the Form 1023 asks, "Have you adopted a conflict of interest policy consistent with the sample conflict of interest policy in Appendix A to the instructions?"[21] If the answer to this question is "yes," then the IRS instructs the applicant to attach a copy of its conflict of interest policy to its application and explain how this policy was adopted.[22] If the answer to this question is "no," then the IRS wants the applicant to explain the procedures it will follow to help ensure that conflict of interest transactions will not occur.[23] Finally, the IRS notes at the end of Question 5a of Part V of the Form 1023 application that "A conflict of interest policy is recommended though it is not required to obtain exemption."[24] The IRS' Exempt Organizations Division likely recommends such policies because they help a nonprofit's board of directors avoid any potential breaches to the fiduciary duty of loyalty.

The duty of loyalty is typically invoked whenever a nonprofit's board faces a potential or an actual conflict of interest transaction.[25] For example, in the preceding hypothetical related to the spouse's marketing firm that might be engaged by the board of the Broad Foundation, the duty of loyalty is invoked in the director of the Broad Foundation who has a financial stake in this marketing firm. Since this director owes the Broad Foundation the duty of loyalty, along with other fiduciary duties imposed by California law, this director should first disclose that he or she has a significant ownership interest in this marketing firm. This director should also be recused from further discussions regarding this potential transaction. A recusal process would also typically be included in a nonprofit's conflict of interest policy. After disclosure and recusal, the remaining directors of the Broad Foundation would consider whether this proposed transaction, including the prices the marketing firm will charge the foundation for promoting the Broad Art Center at UCLA, is fair and reasonable.[26] If it is not, then the "fairness" exception to the self-dealing rules isn't available.[27] Since conflict of interest policies help nonprofit leaders navigate these issues, the IRS urges each 501(c)(3) applicants to adopt such a policy.[28]

EFFECTIVE CORPORATE GOVERNANCE

Every nonprofit corporation should aim to have a strong corporate governance structure and culture. To create this strong structure and culture, the leaders of nonprofits, including those classified as public charities and private foundations under Section 501(c)(3) of the Code, should adopt a conflict of interest policy. If an applicant for 501(c)(3) status does not have such a policy, then it has to explain to the IRS on its Form 1023 application how it deals with potential conflicts.[29] Rather than explaining how potential conflicts are addressed, it's easier for the nonprofit to affirmatively state it has adopted a conflict of interest policy. A conflict of interest policy for a nonprofit should address the importance of disclosing potential conflicts and the procedures for how to address those issues when they arise. When in doubt about a potential conflict, everyone associated with a nonprofit, including the nonprofit's board and senior staff, should err on the side of disclosure and have thoughtful deliberations related to that potential conflict. This way, any potential breaches to the duty of loyalty will be avoided.

KEY PRINCIPLES

➔ An effective conflict of interest policy for a nonprofit typically outlines the steps for disclosing and addressing a potential conflict of interest.

➔ The goal of regular disclosure is to allow those who are disclosing certain affiliations and those who are reviewing the disclosures to gain a sense of potential conflicts that may arise as the nonprofit conducts its business.

➔ The duty of loyalty is typically invoked whenever a nonprofit's board faces a potential or an actual conflict of interest transaction.

7

How Does a Nonprofit Corporation Become a 501(c)(3) Entity?

■ ■ ■

Good habits formed at youth make all the difference.

—Aristotle

SMOKEY THE BEAR

Countless people across the United States have started nonprofits that also become exempt from federal income tax under Section 501(c)(3) of the Code. These nonprofits might be classified as public charities or private foundations, but each has a goal of pursuing some charitable purpose. In 1980, US Customs Agent Tommy Austin met a seven-year-old boy named Chris Greicius.[1] Unfortunately, Chris had recently been diagnosed with leukemia.[2] Tommy's wife was friends with Chris' mom, which is how Tommy first learned about Chris' wish.[3] Chris wanted to be a police officer for the day to help Tommy and his colleagues "catch bad guys."[4] Tommy engaged his friend, Ron Cox, at the Arizona Department of Public Safety (DPS), with the hopes of eventually granting Chris' wish.[5] Tommy, who became a true champion for Chris' cause, even told Ron, "I'll rent [a] helicopter myself if I have to."[6] Ron ran this request up the chain of command at DPS and subsequently, the department's director, Ralph Milstead, gave a "carte blanche [check] to grant Chris' wish."[7]

While the DPS had no precedence for doing this, Ralph granted Chris' dream to help "catch bad guys." Shortly after learning about Chris' wish, the leaders of DPS met with Chris and his family. They gave Chris an officer badge and a Smokey the Bear hat and deemed Chris the "first and only honorary DPS officer."[8] Soon after spending the day with the DPS officers, Chris was readmitted to the hospital where he eventually passed away.[9] Chris was seven years, 269 days old when he died, but he had fulfilled his dream of serving as a DPS officer.[10] After Chris's passing, Ron remarked that he "didn't fear death anymore, because he knew Chris would be there waiting for him."[11] A few DPS officers and their families, led by Tommy and Ron, established Make-A-Wish in November 1980 based on their experience with Chris.[12] Today, Make-A-Wish "makes life better for kids with critical illnesses" by granting a new wish approximately every thirty-four minutes in the United States.[13] Make-A-Wish Foundation of America, an Arizona nonprofit corporation, received its 501(c)(3)-public charity status from the IRS.[14]

People establish nonprofit corporations, like Make-A-Wish, for a multitude of reasons. Usually, however, it's because they're passionate about a certain cause or issue. Tommy and Ron were likely deeply moved by their experience with Chris, and thus, established a nonprofit to give kids with critical illnesses an experience they'll never forget. Similarly, over the course of my tenure as a professor, I've had numerous students interested in starting nonprofit corporations that would also seek exemption under Section 501(c)(3) of the Code, just like the path followed by Make-A-Wish. These students who are interested in implementing their passions by starting 501(c)(3) organizations are all on a *need to know* basis, which any teacher knows is the best platform to teach from. Thus, we address the following key question: how does a nonprofit become exempt from federal income tax under Section 501(c)(3) of the Code?

FORM 1023

The Form 1023, entitled *Application for Recognition of Exemption Under Section 501(c)(3) of the Internal Revenue Code,* is the application that must be submitted by leaders of a nonprofit to the IRS in order to receive tax-exempt status under Section 501(c)(3) of the Code.[15] If an applicant is below certain thresholds, including (1) anticipated annual gross receipts of less than $50,000 over the next three years; (2) actual annual gross receipts of less than $50,000 in the preceding three years (if any); and (3) total assets of less than $250,000, then an applicant may file a shorter version of the full Form 1023 called the Form 1023-EZ.[16] If an applicant does not meet these financial thresholds, as well as certain other structural and history requirements, then the full Form 1023 must be submitted.[17] Regarding the sequence of events, nonprofit leaders first create a nonprofit corporation under applicable state law, then obtain an employer identification number (EIN) from the IRS for that nonprofit, and finally file the Form 1023, or the shorter Form 1023-EZ if certain eligibility requirements are met.

The full Form 1023 asks a variety of questions, but the key questions on the form relate to (1) the activities of the nonprofit; (2) the finances of the nonprofit; and (3) the leadership of the nonprofit, including its board of directors and management. First, Part IV, which is arguably the most important section of the Form 1023, asks about the nonprofit's past, present, and future activities. With Part IV, the IRS representative reviewing the application is trying to determine if the nonprofit meets the requirements of being a 501(c)(3) entity. Section 501(c)(3) of the Code lists eight categories that a nonprofit must fall under, such as "educational, charitable, or scientific," as well as requirements related to the flow of assets from the nonprofit to others, lobbying restrictions, and a prohibition on political campaign activities.[18] If these requirements are met by the nonprofit in its Form 1023 application, then the nonprofit will likely meet both the organizational and operational tests necessary for becoming a 501(c)(3) entity.[19]

Second, the full Form 1023 asks the nonprofit about its finances, or proposed finances if it's a new legal entity, including its balance sheet and income statement.[20] This financial information is important because a nonprofit that desires to be a public charity, as opposed to a private foundation, must eventually pass a public support test, including the "one-third" test or the facts and circumstances test, which are two frequently used public support tests.[21] Every nonprofit is presumed to be a 501(c)(3)-private foundation by the IRS until it can pass a public support test.[22] The one-third test is simply the "public support" of the nonprofit divided by its "total support."[23] If this ratio is at least 33 percent, then the nonprofit may qualify to be a 501(c)(3)-public charity.[24] If this ratio is between 10 percent and 33 percent, whereby the facts and circumstances test may be implicated, then a nonprofit can still qualify to be a public charity as long as it successfully explains its reasoning for this designation to the IRS.[25]

If a nonprofit doesn't have the requisite financial data at first, then the IRS gives that applicant five years to pass one of the public support tests.[26] During this time, the applicant may be classified as a 501(c)(3)-public charity, if such designation is sought by an applicant on its Form 1023 application.[27] Finally, the Form 1023 application asks about a nonprofit's leadership, including its board of directors, any conflicts of interest, or any related-party transactions.[28]

CASE STUDY: A TEACHER'S PASSION FOR DISADVANTAGED YOUTH

One of my former students has a passion for working with disadvantaged youth. Most recently, she worked for Denver Public Schools and its foundation, the Denver Public Schools Foundation. She pursued a graduate degree in order to fulfill her dream of starting a nonprofit to support disadvantaged youth. Accordingly, she wants to start a nonprofit corporation that will be exempt from federal income tax under Section 501(c)(3) of the Code as a public charity. After creating a Colorado nonprofit corporation by filing articles of incorporation with the Colorado Secretary of State, she must then obtain an EIN from the IRS. An EIN is simply a tax identification number, and the process for obtaining an EIN can be completed rather quickly. Once she obtains an EIN, she's ready to address the numerous questions listed in the Form 1023 application, all with the hopes of eventually obtaining tax exempt status under Section 501(c)(3) of the Code.

With this goal in mind, she must ensure that the activities of this nonprofit focusing on disadvantaged youth fall under at least one of the eight categories listed in Section 501(c)(3) of the Code. This connection between the nonprofit's activities and the categories listed in Section 501(c)(3) of the Code will be reflected in Part IV of the Form 1023 application. In this case, it's likely that her nonprofit will meet either the educational or the charitable categories, both of which are enumerated under Section 501(c)(3) of the Code. While only one category is needed for a nonprofit applicant to help meet the organizational and operational tests of being a 501(c)(3), it's best to include each category that a nonprofit might qualify for on its Form 1023 application. Attorneys frequently call this strategy a multi-pronged approach. If by chance the IRS agent reviewing the Form 1023 disagrees with one of those categories, then the nonprofit has another category that it can point to in order to justify its status as a 501(c)(3) entity.

Since this will be a new nonprofit corporation, there won't initially be sufficient financial data for it to pass a public support test, including the one-third test or the facts and circumstances test. Thus, this new nonprofit will be given five years to pass one of these tests. Finally, my former student will need to consider who will lead this nonprofit—including whether or not she will serve as its executive director and a board member—and address any potential conflicts of interest or related-party transactions in the Form 1023 application. Once she drops the completed Form 1023 in the mail, this new nonprofit can actually operate as a public charity until the IRS informs her otherwise.[29] While it may be hard to believe, the IRS actually trusts that a nonprofit applicant correctly meets the requirements for being a 501(c)(3)-public charity. Thus, until the IRS notifies a nonprofit that it doesn't meet those requirements, or it fails to pass one of the public support tests in a timely fashion, then it may receive tax-deductible contributions until that time.

SECTION 501(C)(3)

For many people, filing the Form 1023 can appear to be a daunting task. A completed application might be anywhere between twenty to thirty pages in length. Additionally, a few of the questions are highly technical, and those questions likely require a cross-reference to the Form 1023 instructions to ensure that an applicant is appropriately answering them. However, the IRS simply wants assurance that the nonprofit applying to be exempt under Section 501(c)(3) of the Code meets the requirements of that Code section. For example, the applicant should ensure that (1) its purpose and activities fall under one of the eight categories listed in Section 501(c)(3), such as being an "educational, scientific or charitable" organization; (2) the assets of the nonprofit will largely be used for its charitable purpose and won't "inure" to any private individual, except for any reasonable compensation and related exceptions to this private inurement doctrine; (3) the nonprofit won't engage in lobbying activities beyond what's allowed for 501(c)(3) entities; and (4) the nonprofit won't engage in any political campaign activities.

The IRS, through the Form 1023, appropriately engages each applicant on these key issues to ensure that it qualifies as either a 501(c)(3)-public charity or a 501(c)(3)-private foundation. Once the application is mailed to the Exempt Organizations Division of the IRS, it typically takes about four to six months to process and provide the applicant a definitive answer with respect to its 501(c)(3) status. The IRS issues such decisions through "determination letters." If the nonprofit meets the requirements for the shorter Form 1023-EZ, the IRS typically responds to those applications within one to two months. Regardless of which version of the Form 1023 is used, in order for a nonprofit to become a 501(c)(3), whether that's a public charity or a private foundation, an application must be filed with the IRS. Dropping a completed Form 1023 application in the mail can be exhilarating. Whether a nonprofit focuses on disadvantaged youth or makes life better for kids with illnesses, the work being conducted by 501(c)(3) organizations changes lives each day, just like the future leaders of Make-A-Wish did for Chris.

KEY PRINCIPLES

→ The Form 1023, entitled *Application for Recognition of Exemption Under Section 501(c)(3) of the Internal Revenue Code*, is the application that must be submitted by leaders of a nonprofit to the IRS in order to receive tax-exempt status under Section 501(c)(3) of the Code.

→ If an applicant is below certain thresholds, including (1) anticipated annual gross receipts of less than $50,000 over the next three years; (2) actual annual gross receipts of less than $50,000 in the preceding three years (if any); and (3) total assets of less than $250,000, then an applicant may file a shorter version of the full Form 1023 called the Form 1023-EZ.

→ The full Form 1023 asks a variety of questions, but the key questions on the form relate to (1) the activities of the nonprofit; (2) the finances of the nonprofit; and (3) the leadership of the nonprofit, including its board of directors and management.

8

What Does "Charitable" Mean under Section 501(c)(3) of the IRS Code?

■ ■ ■

The life of a man consists not in seeing visions and in dreaming dreams, but in active charity and in willing service.

—Henry Wadsworth Longfellow

PRINCETON UNIVERSITY

Do you know that the Ivy League, which includes Princeton University, is comprised of a series of 501(c)(3)-public charities? Section 501(c)(3) of the Code lists eight different exempt categories, and "educational" is one of those categories: (1) religious; (2) charitable; (3) scientific; (4) testing for public safety; (5) literary; (6) educational; (7) to foster national or international amateur sports competition; and (8) the prevention of cruelty to children or animals.[1] For a nonprofit corporation to become a 501(c)(3) organization, whether it's seeking status as a 501(c)(3)-public charity or a 501(c)(3)-private foundation, it must be "organized and operated" to further at least one of these eight enumerated exempt categories.[2] That is, it must be seeking 501(c)(3) status as a religious *or* charitable *or* scientific *or* educational organization.[3] For example, Princeton is classified as a 501(c)(3) organization largely because it's "organized and operated exclusively for . . . educational purposes."[4]

Princeton was founded in 1746 as the College of New Jersey and is the fourth oldest university in the United States.[5] In 1896, the college was renamed Princeton University after it received "university" status through expanded program offerings.[6] Today, Princeton has approximately 8,000 students between its graduate and undergraduate programs and is traditionally recognized as one of the nation's best educational institutions.[7] One of my classmates from the El Pomar Foundation Fellowship Program Carrie, graduated from Princeton in 2002. As a Princetonian, Carrie told me what graduates from Princeton hear each year at commencement: "Congratulations, now you know all that you don't know." I've frequently repeated that quote to my students, as it reminds us to pursue lifelong learning. I can't think of a better way to send off graduates. To become a 501(c)(3), like Princeton, a nonprofit corporation on its Form 1023 application must convince the IRS that it is "organized and operated exclusively" for one of those eight exempt categories.[8]

Part IV of the full Form 1023 application, which addresses the past, present, and future activities of the applicant, helps the IRS determine whether that applicant meets one of these eight exempt categories.[9] There's no doubt that Princeton meets the "educational" classification. However, does Princeton also meet the religious, scientific, or charitable classifications? Princeton operates the Princeton Theological Seminary; thus, does it also qualify as a "religious" organization?[10] Similarly, Princeton's professors, instructors, students, and other scholars conduct scientific research; so, does it also qualify as a "scientific" organization? Finally, Princeton issues numerous scholarships to its students each year. Does this also qualify it as a "charitable" organization?[11] The answer to these questions is likely "yes," but to qualify as a 501(c)(3), a nonprofit only needs to meet one of the eight exempt categories. Of those eight exempt purposes, "charitable" is the broadest of those noted in Section 501(c)(3) of the Code.

"CHARITABLE"

Since the word "charitable" under Section 501(c)(3) of the Code has been interpreted broadly, a nonprofit corporation seeking exempt status under Section 501(c)(3) should consider whether it's a "charitable" organization.[12] The IRS has interpreted the word "charitable" under Section 501(c)(3) to mean: (1) relief of the poor; (2) relief of the distressed; (3) provision of credit counseling; (4) provision of housing; (5) promotion of health; (6) lessening the burdens of government; (7) advancement of education; (8) advancement of science; (9) advancement of religion; (10) promotion of social welfare; (11) promotion of the arts; and (12) fundraising organizations.[13] Here, it's important to note that "educational" is its own separate category under Section 501(c)(3) of the Code, but the word "charitable," as interpreted by the IRS, also means the "advancement of education."[14]

In the case of Princeton, it's a 501(c)(3) organization because it's an "educational" nonprofit, but it's also a 501(c)(3) because it's a "charitable" organization. Given the broad interpretation of the word "charitable" by the IRS, there's no doubt that Princeton also advances education, advances science, advances religion, promotes the arts, and is even a fundraising organization through its development office.[15] Therefore, Princeton is a 501(c)(3) entity because it's both an "educational" and a "charitable" nonprofit. This broad definition of the word "charitable" dates back to 1601 and the Preamble of the Statutes of Charitable Uses under English common law.[16] In the United States, the term "charitable" was further expanded in 1959 when regulations were promulgated to encompass additional philanthropic activities.[17]

The IRS regulations and applicable case law interpreting the term "charitable" have both reaffirmed this broad definition.[18] First, the IRS regulations indicate that the word "charitable," as set forth under Section 501(c)(3) of the Code, "should be broadly applied in 'its generally accepted legal sense'."[19] Secondly, the broad definition of the term "charitable" has also been reaffirmed by numerous appellate courts, including the US Supreme Court, in their decisions.[20] For example, the US Supreme Court in 1877 in *Ould v. Washington Hospital* reaffirmed the principle that the term "charitable" is a broad term as it stated in its opinion: "charitable use, where neither law nor public policy forbids, may be applied to almost anything that tends to promote the well-doing and well-being of social man."[21] For these reasons, the term "charitable" has been interpreted by both the IRS and federal courts as being all-encompassing.

CASE STUDY: THE NEW YORK PUBLIC LIBRARY

Since the term "charitable" as set forth under Section 501(c)(3) of the Code has a broad legal definition, a nonprofit corporation seeking exemption under such section should consider whether it's a 501(c)(3) entity because it's a "charitable" organization. The leaders of a nonprofit seeking 501(c)(3) status should consider this classification in addition to any other category that it may fall under, such as "educational, religious or scientific." Princeton, as noted, is a 501(c)(3) entity because it meets more than one of these classifications. Like Princeton, the New York Public Library is also a 501(c)(3)-public charity.[22] The mission of the library, which also operates eighty-eight branch libraries, is to "inspire lifelong learning, advance knowledge, and strengthen our communities."[23] For the fiscal year ending June 30, 2016, the New York Public Library had total revenues of approximately $300 million and total expenses of approximately $335 million.[24] As of June 30, 2016, the net assets of the New York Public Library were approximately $1.26 billion, making it one of the largest 501(c)(3) nonprofits that's neither a university nor a healthcare organization.[25]

The New York Public Library is a 501(c)(3) entity for three main reasons. First, the New York Public Library meets the "literary" classification. Public libraries promote literature amongst their patrons, which meets the "literary" category. According to the New York Public Library's 2016 Form 990, it had approximately 50 million collection items and responded to more than 500,000 reference inquiries related to these collection items.[26] Secondly, the New York Public Library is a 501(c)(3) because it meets the "educational" classification. Like a college or a university, public libraries promote education; thus, a public library also qualifies as a 501(c)(3) because of this "educational" classification. Finally, the New York Public Library is a 501(c)(3) because it meets the "charitable" classification. The New York Public Library is charitable because it lessens the burdens of government; advances education; advances science; promotes social welfare; and promotes the arts.[27] While only one of the eight enumerated categories under Section 501(c)(3) of the Code is needed for a nonprofit to qualify for this exempt status, the New York Public Library qualifies because it meets at least three classifications.

"BELT AND SUSPENDERS"

This example highlights the fact that only one of the eight enumerated categories under Section 501(c)(3) of the Code is needed for a nonprofit to qualify as a 501(c)(3) entity, but every applicable classification should be noted on the Form 1023 application. Since the IRS and federal courts have interpreted the term "charitable" broadly, the leaders of a nonprofit seeking 501(c)(3) status should consider whether such nonprofit meets any of the charitable activities previously addressed, such as lessening the burdens of government.[28] The broad definition of the term "charitable" dates back hundreds of years to English common law.[29] If a nonprofit meets any one of these activities, then such nonprofit should qualify as a 501(c)(3) entity because it's a "charitable" organization, regardless of any other classifications that it may also fall under.[30] Metaphorically, the belt for 501(c)(3) status for Princeton may be its "educational" classification and the belt for the New York Public Library may be its "literary" classification; however, the suspender for each nonprofit may be its "charitable" classification. If one fails, not all is lost.

KEY PRINCIPLES

→ Since the word "charitable" under Section 501(c)(3) of the Code has been interpreted broadly, a nonprofit corporation seeking exempt status under Section 501(c)(3) should consider whether it's a "charitable" organization.

→ This broad definition of the word "charitable" dates back to 1601 and the Preamble of the Statutes of Charitable Uses under English common law.

→ In the United States, the term "charitable" was further expanded in 1959 when regulations were promulgated to encompass additional philanthropic activities.

9

What's a 501(c)(3)-Public Charity?

■ ■ ■

We look for people who demonstrate perseverance in the face of challenges, the ability to influence and motivate others—people who want to work relentlessly to ensure that kids who are facing the challenges of poverty have an excellent education.

—Wendy Kopp

WENDY KOPP'S VISION

Teach for America is one of the nation's most well-known 501(c)(3)-public charities. Teach for America's mission is to "find, develop, and support a diverse network of leaders who expand opportunity for children from classrooms, schools, and every sector and field that shapes the broader systems in which schools operate."[1] Teach for America was established by Wendy Kopp, who graduated from Princeton University, in 1989.[2] Like many other social entrepreneurs, Wendy had a vision for how to make her community, state, and nation better: to recruit recent college graduates and equip them with teaching skills so that they can teach in historically low-performing rural and urban schools.[3] At the time Wendy founded Teach for America, academic outcomes for "low-income kids . . . had not improved in a century."[4]

Leaders like Wendy are not satisfied with the status quo. If they were, there would be no need for leadership. Wendy's initial vision for Teach for America was aimed at changing the status quo for low-income students. In December 1989, Wendy worked with approximately one hundred recruiters across one hundred colleges and universities to recruit soon-to-be college graduates to work in historically low-performing rural and urban schools.[5] Based on these recruiting efforts, Teach for America placed 489 teachers, called "corps members," in 1990.[6] These first corps members were located in "New York, Los Angeles, eastern North Carolina, south Louisiana, and rural Georgia."[7] Today, Teach for America has approximately 7,000 corps members who commit to a two-year teaching assignment and are placed in one of 2,500 schools across the United

States.[8] These 7,000 corps members collectively impact and teach more than 400,000 students per year.[9] Since its inception, Teach for America has produced nearly 60,000 corps members who have collectively instructed millions of K–12 students.[10]

In 2007, Wendy established another 501(c)(3)-public charity called Teach for All to bring Teach for America's model to other countries facing educational inequity.[11] Today, Teach for All works in thirty-one countries in "Europe, Asia, the Americas, and the Middle East," to increase educational opportunities.[12] Between Teach for All and Teach for America, these two public charities spend approximately $315 million per year fulfilling their respective missions and pursuing their visions of educational justice for all, whether in the United States or abroad.[13] Both Teach for America and Teach for All, along with the millions of other public charities registered with the IRS, have impacted countless lives and causes. These public charities have changed our communities, states, nation, and world for the better. Thus, what exactly is a 501(c)(3)-public charity?

501(C)(3)-PUBLIC CHARITIES

Nonprofits seeking tax exemption under Section 501(c)(3) of the Code are either classified as public charities or private foundations. To become a 501(c)(3) entity, public charities and private foundations must pass both the "organizational and operational tests."[14] First, the organizational test notes that the entity seeking 501(c)(3) status, like a nonprofit corporation, must be organized "exclusively for one or more exempt purposes."[15] In this context, *exclusively* actually means *primarily*.[16] If a nonprofit pursues a non-exempt purpose, and if those non-exempt activities are "substantial in nature," then a nonprofit cannot qualify as a 501(c)(3) entity because its primary purpose is not related to its exempt purpose.[17] Whether any non-exempt activities are "substantial in nature" is a facts and circumstances analysis.

For a nonprofit corporation, whether it's organized primarily for one or more exempt purposes is typically reflected in its articles of incorporation.[18] Section 501(c)(3) of the Code lists eight enumerated categories, such as "charitable, educational, or scientific," that an applicant for 501(c)(3) status must fall under, as well as requirements related to a limitation on lobbying, a prohibition on political campaign activities, and a prohibition on private inurement.[19] The private inurement doctrine is related to the flow of the nonprofit's resources, including any net earnings, among others. As long as these requirements are met, which are typically noted in a nonprofit's articles of incorporation, a nonprofit will likely pass the organizational test.[20] As noted in the IRS regulations, a nonprofit with articles of incorporation stating that it's been created for "charitable purposes" will generally be able to pass the organizational test.[21]

With respect to the organizational test, it's also important to note that non-profit corporations created under applicable state law typically have broader powers than what's permitted under Section 501(c)(3) of the Code.[22] For example, under applicable state law, there's generally nothing that limits non-profit corporations from engaging in political campaign activities.[23] However, such political campaign activities are strictly prohibited by Section 501(c)(3) of the Code.[24] Thus, nonprofit corporations that desire to obtain 501(c)(3) status must limit those broader powers in their articles of incorporation, which may be permitted under applicable state law, to ensure that they comply with Section 501(c)(3) of the Code as well.[25] This constraint is commonly known as the "501(c)(3) limitation," and such limitation must be included in a nonprofit's articles of incorporation for it to qualify as a 501(c)(3) entity.

Second, a nonprofit corporation seeking 501(c)(3) status must pass the operational test.[26] The operational test focuses on the actual activities of the nonprofit and how the nonprofit utilizes its resources, including its assets, in order to further its exempt purpose(s).[27] That is, does it "[engage] primarily in activities that accomplish exempt purposes?"[28] Like the primary purpose test, if more than an insubstantial amount of its activities are not related to accomplishing its exempt purposes, then it will fail the operational test.[29] In this regard, an insubstantial non-exempt activity is permissible and has been accepted by the IRS, but a substantial non-exempt activity is *not* permissible.[30] Here, the IRS will consider the substance of the nonprofit's activities and whether those activities "[accomplish] an exempt purpose."[31] If an applicant fails the operational test, then it cannot qualify as a 501(c)(3) entity.

To become a 501(c)(3)-public charity as opposed to a 501(c)(3)-private foundation, a nonprofit corporation must show that it's supported by the general public. This support is demonstrated through the passage of either: (1) the one-third public support test; (2) the facts and circumstances test; or (3) the one-third/one-third test.[32] The one-third public support test is simply "public support" divided by "total support," which must be equal to or greater than 33 percent.[33] At first, a nonprofit has five years to accumulate financial data to pass this test, assuming that it has no such financial data when it initially applies to the IRS for 501(c)(3) status.[34] If this ratio is between 10 percent and 33 percent, then an entity must explain to the IRS why it's still supported by the general public through the facts and circumstances test.[35] The one-third/one-third test notes that an entity must show that at least 33 percent of its total support is from "public support," and that no more than 33 percent of its total support is from "gross investment income."[36] Finally, entities may also become 501(c)(3)-public charities if they support another 501(c)(3)-public charity, and these entities are known as "supporting organizations."[37] Typically, however, the one-third public support test is utilized by a nonprofit corporation to become a 501(c)(3)-public charity.

CASE STUDY: TEACH FOR AMERICA

Both Teach for America and Teach for All, as 501(c)(3)-public charities, have passed the organizational test, the operational test, and one of the foregoing public support tests.[38] First, the organizational test notes that both Teach for America and Teach for All must be organized primarily for one or more exempt purposes.[39] Both organizations are certainly organized for "educational" purposes, which is one of the eight exempt purpose classifications under Section 501(c)(3) of the Code.[40] Teach for All's mission, for example, is to "develop collective leadership to ensure that all children have the opportunity to fulfill their potential."[41] Additionally, both are likely "charitable" organizations, which is another exempt purpose classification under Section 501(c)(3) of the Code, because the word "charitable" has been interpreted to mean the advancement of education.[42]

Regarding the limitation on lobbying, a prohibition on political campaign activities, and a prohibition on private inurement, which also must be met for a nonprofit corporation to be a 501(c)(3) entity, those issues are likely addressed in the governing documents, including the articles of incorporation, of both Teach for America and Teach for All. Based on Teach for America's Form 990, it is a nonprofit corporation organized under the laws of the state of Connecticut and was incorporated in 1989.[43] Based on Teach for All's Form 990, it is a nonprofit corporation under the laws of the state of New York and was incorporated in 2007.[44] All of these additional requirements to be a 501(c)(3)-public charity are likely addressed in the governing documents of both organizations. For these reasons, both Teach for America and Teach for All have met the organizational test, which may also be viewed as the "magic words test" because the IRS is looking for very specific language in such governing documents.[45]

Secondly, both Teach for America and Teach for All have passed the operational test because their respective activities further their exempt purposes. For example, Teach for America spent approximately $117 million on the placement and professional development of corps members in urban and rural regions throughout the United States during the fiscal year ending May 31, 2017.[46] Likewise, Teach for All spent approximately $19.5 million on network partners to "accelerate impact in the areas of scale, network impact and learning, alumni leadership and organizational strength."[47] These expenditures help demonstrate that these two nonprofits are primarily engaged in activities that further their exempt purposes. Since "exclusively" means "primarily" under the operational test, both nonprofits may also pursue a non-exempt purpose so long as those non-exempt activities are not substantial in nature.[48]

Finally, both Teach for America and Teach for All are 501(c)(3)-public charities because they have passed a public support test. In this case, both nonprofits have passed the one-third public support test. For the fiscal year ending May 31, 2017, Teach for America's public support percentage was approximately 91 percent.[49] For the fiscal year ending September 30, 2017, Teach for All's public support percentage was approximately 78 percent.[50]

Both of these percentages are well above the required percentage of 33 percent to pass the one-third public support test. Accordingly, both Teach for America and Teach for All are 501(c)(3)-public charities because they have each passed the organizational test, the operational test, and the one-third public support test.

IMPACT OF 501(C)(3)-PUBLIC CHARITIES

Approximately one half of the registered exempt organizations with the IRS are 501(c)(3) entities, and most of those charitable organizations are 501(c)(3)-public charities.[51] These public charities help make our communities, states, nation, and world better places to live as they impact millions of lives every day. Teach for America and Teach for All are two excellent examples of public charities that have impacted the lives of millions since their establishment. Due to the collective impact that these public charities have on our communities, whether that's placing top-notch teachers in our schools, providing medical care to patients, or showcasing the latest theatrical play at a nonprofit performing arts center, our lives are much richer because of 501(c)(3)-public charities located throughout the country.

KEY PRINCIPLES

➔ Nonprofits seeking tax exemption under Section 501(c)(3) of the Code are either classified as public charities or private foundations.

➔ To become a 501(c)(3), both public charities and private foundations must pass the organizational and operational tests.

➔ To become a 501(c)(3)-public charity rather a 501(c)(3)-private foundation, an entity must pass a public support test or be classified as a "supporting organization."

10

What's a 501(c)(3)-Private Foundation?

■ ■ ■

When everything seems to be going against you, remember that the airplane takes off against the wind, not with it.

—Henry Ford

FORD FOUNDATION

The Ford Foundation, based in New York City, is one of the largest private foundations in the world. According to its most recently filed Form 990-PF with the IRS, entitled "Return of Private Foundation," the Ford Foundation had total revenues of approximately $700 million for the fiscal year ended December 31, 2016, and net assets of approximately $12 billion as of December 31, 2016.[1] Since "money equals mission" in the nonprofit sector, the Ford Foundation is able to use its financial resources to advance its various programs and activities, including its initiatives focusing on civic engagement, climate change, and internet freedom, just to name a few.[2] Today, the Ford Foundation's mission is "[T]o reduce poverty and injustice, strengthen democratic values, promote international cooperation, and advance human achievement," and in 2016, it spent approximately $535 million on these initiatives.[3]

Edsel Ford, the son of Henry Ford, established the Ford Foundation in 1936 with an initial donation of $25,000.[4] Henry Ford was the founder of the Ford Motor Company, which produced the successful Model T car in the early 20th century.[5] He derived most of his wealth from growing Ford Motor Company over the course of his career as an entrepreneur and as the company's key leader. A few Ford family members, including both Henry and Edsel Ford, developed the Ford Foundation's initial charter, which outlined its main purposes. This charter specified that the foundation should fund initiatives that focus on "scientific, educational, and charitable purposes, all for the public welfare."[6] These cause areas are all perfectly aligned with Section 501(c)(3) of the Code, which lists scientific, educational, and charitable purposes among its eight exempt purpose classifications.[7]

When both Henry and Edsel Ford passed away in the mid-1940s, and their wealth was transferred to the foundation, the Ford Foundation became the largest philanthropic organization in the world.[8] Today, the Ford Foundation is the second largest 501(c)(3)-private foundation behind the Bill and Melinda Gates Foundation, which had net assets of approximately $40 billion as of December 31, 2016.[9] Henry and Edsel Ford inspired many future philanthropists, such as Bill and Melinda Gates, to set up private foundations that are exempt from taxation under Section 501(c)(3) of the Code. Accordingly, what exactly is a 501(c)(3)-private foundation?

501(C)(3)-PRIVATE FOUNDATION

After a nonprofit corporation is incorporated under applicable state law, like the Ford Foundation, the leaders of that nonprofit must determine whether it should seek tax exempt status under Section 501(c) of the Code. Often, those leaders elect to pursue tax exempt status under Section 501(c)(3) of the Code, as approximately one-half of all registered 501(c) entities with the IRS are 501(c)(3) entities.[10] Nonprofits that are exempt under Section 501(c)(3) of the Code get two key tax benefits: (1) the 501(c)(3) nonprofit itself is exempt from paying federal income tax; and (2) donors to 501(c)(3) nonprofits get to deduct their contributions from their federal income taxes, assuming that they are able to itemize their tax deductions.[11] With the passage of the Tax Cuts and Jobs Act in 2017, fewer people will itemize their tax deductions since the standard deduction doubled. Nonetheless, this dual-benefit is only available for 501(c)(3) entities, as donations to other 501(c) entities, such as 501(c)(4)s or 501(c)(6)s, are not tax deductible.[12]

When applying for tax exempt status under Section 501(c)(3) of the Code, the leaders of a nonprofit must also determine whether that entity will be a 501(c)(3)-public charity or a 501(c)(3)-private foundation.[13] With the Form 1023 or the Form 1023-EZ, the applications filed with the IRS to obtain 501(c)(3) status, the IRS presumes that the applicant is a private foundation and not a public charity.[14] The key difference between a 501(c)(3)-public charity and a 501(c)(3)-private foundation is that a private foundation is not "publicly supported."[15] Rather, private foundations typically have one or two key donors who initially endow the foundation. Thus, a private foundation doesn't need to pass one of the three public support tests.[16] These tests are the one-third public support test, the facts and circumstances test, or the one-third/one-third test.[17] These tests all relate to a nonprofit being classified as a public charity.[18]

A nonprofit applying for 501(c)(3) status that neither passes one of these three tests nor is a "supporting organization" will be classified as a 501(c)(3)-private foundation.[19] A "supporting organization" is a 501(c)(3)-public charity because it supports another public charity. Private foundations, like public charities, need to pass both the organizational test and the operational test to become a 501(c)(3) entity.[20] That is, a private foundation must be organized for one or more exempt purposes, and its programs, activities, and resources must further those exempt purposes. Once a nonprofit obtains tax exempt status as a 501(c)(3)-private foundation, there are a few key rules that apply to that entity, including: (1) the 5 percent distribution requirement; (2) a prohibition on self-dealing; (3) a prohibition on excess business holdings; and (4) a prohibition on making "jeopardizing investments."[21] These four key rules will be examined through an analysis of the Daniels Fund.

CASE STUDY: THE DANIELS FUND

The Daniels Fund is a 501(c)(3)-private foundation with net assets of approximately $1.1 billion as of December 31, 2016.[22] Bill Daniels established the Daniels Fund in 2000, which was the same year that he passed away.[23] He was a cable television pioneer, a recipient of the Bronze Star for his heroism in World War II, and even a previous owner of the Los Angeles Lakers. Bill Daniels derived most of his wealth from his company, Daniels and Associates, a "cable television brokerage firm and investment bank."[24] Based on his successful career, he's one of a handful of inductees in the Cable Hall of Fame, which is a program of The Cable Center, a 501(c)(3)-public charity.[25] As a 501(c)(3)-private foundation, the Daniels Fund is subject to the four key rules related to private foundations noted above.

First, 501(c)(3)-private foundations, like the Daniels Fund, are subject to a minimum distribution amount each year. This amount is equal to 5 percent of the value of the private foundation's non-charitable assets, and such amount must be distributed for "charitable purposes."[26] Non-charitable assets include any assets held to produce income or for investment purposes, including "stocks, bonds, interest-bearing notes, endowment funds, and leased real estate."[27] A private foundation that fails to meet this minimum distribution requirement is "subject to an excise tax on its undistributed income."[28] Accordingly, private foundations strive to make "qualifying distributions," such as grants to 501(c)(3)-public charities, equaling at least 5 percent of its non-charitable assets per year to avoid excises taxes.[29] If a private foundation wants to distribute more than 5 percent per year, it can certainly elect to do that.

Second, 501(c)(3)-private foundations, like the Daniels Fund, are also subject to a prohibition on "self-dealing."[30] The self-dealing rules generally prohibit certain transactions, like a lease, between a 501(c)(3)-private foundation and its "disqualified persons."[31] All private foundations are led by disqualified persons, which include individuals or entities that have a close relationship with the foundation.[32] Section 4946 of the Code defines "disqualified persons" as the managers of a private foundation, including its board of directors and officers; substantial contributors; twenty-percent owners; certain family members of those individuals; and certain government officials.[33] Twenty-percent owners include those individuals who own more than 20 percent of an entity, where ownership may be either a voting interest or a financial interest, that is a substantial contributor to the private foundation.[34]

For example, former United States Senator Hank Brown, who is on the board of directors of the Daniels Fund, is a "disqualified person" as it relates to the Daniels Fund.[35] He's a disqualified person because he's a foundation manager, specifically a board member, of the foundation. If there's a financial transaction between a private foundation and a disqualified person, such as a sale of property, the rendering of services, or the payment of compensation that's not "reasonable and necessary," then the IRS may impose a two-tiered tax on that transaction.[36] The first tax is 10 percent of the transaction value imposed on the "self-dealer," and 5 percent of the transaction value imposed on any foundation manager "where the manager knowingly participated in the act."[37] If that self-dealing transaction is not corrected, then an additional tax of 200 percent may apply to the "self-dealer," and intentional violations of the self-dealing rules may lead to revocation of the private foundation's 501(c)(3) status.[38]

Third, a private foundation is subject to a prohibition on excess business holdings.[39] That is, a private foundation may not hold more than 20 percent of the voting shares or other interests in a business.[40] This limitation is invoked when the private foundation owns more than 2 percent of the value of the business.[41] The Daniels Fund, for example, is not permitted to own more than 20 percent of the voting shares or other interests in the Los Angeles Lakers, which is a business enterprise, if it owns more than 2 percent of the value of such enterprise.

Finally, the Daniels Fund, as a 501(c)(3)-private foundation, cannot make "jeopardizing investments."[42] This simply means that a private foundation cannot make any investments that would jeopardize its tax-exempt purpose.[43] A jeopardizing investment is one where foundation managers "[fail] to exercise ordinary business care and prudence, under the facts and circumstances prevailing at the time of making the investment, in providing for the long- and short-term financial needs of the foundation to carry out its exempt purpose."[44] If one of the goals of a private foundation is to give away 5 percent of its non-charitable assets per year in qualifying distributions, it should not make jeopardizing investments that might impact its ability to do that.

FIVE PERCENT DISTRIBUTION REQUIREMENT

Both private foundations and public charities are 501(c)(3) organizations. However, there are a few key differences between private foundations and public charities, most notably the 5 percent distribution requirement. Private foundations, like the Ford Foundation and the Daniels Fund, must distribute 5 percent of their non-charitable assets per year in "qualifying distributions." Public charities don't have this requirement. For example, the Ford Foundation distributes about $550 million per year, and the Daniels Fund distributes about $55 million per year based on its non-charitable assets.[45] Between these two private foundations alone, that's a huge influx of capital into various charitable causes. Because of the 5 percent distribution requirement, imagine the collective power of the philanthropic sector. The Bill and Melinda Gates Foundation, for example, distributes about *$2 billion* per year.[46] Nonprofit leaders should understand the key differences between public charities and private foundations so that when they file the application for the nonprofit to be exempt under Section 501(c)(3) of the Code, they can best determine whether that entity should seek exempt status as a public charity or as a private foundation.

KEY PRINCIPLES

→ Nonprofits that are exempt under Section 501(c)(3) of the Code get two key tax benefits: (1) the 501(c)(3) nonprofit itself is exempt from paying federal income tax; and (2) donors to 501(c)(3) nonprofits get to deduct their contributions from their federal income taxes, assuming that they are able to itemize their tax deductions.

→ When applying for tax exempt status under Section 501(c)(3) of the Code, the leaders of a nonprofit must also determine whether that entity will be a 501(c)(3)-public charity or a 501(c)(3)-private foundation.

→ 501(c)(3)-private foundations are subject to a minimum distribution amount each year. This amount is equal to 5 percent of the value of the private foundation's non-charitable assets.

11

What's the Private Inurement Doctrine?

■ ■ ■

If your only goal is to become rich, you will never achieve it.

—John D. Rockefeller

TWO SUPREME COURT JUSTICES

There are a multitude of differences between the nonprofit and for-profit sectors, but one of the primary differences is explained by the private inurement doctrine. This doctrine dictates how earnings from certain entities exempt under Section 501(c) of the Code may be distributed. Some scholars argue that the private inurement doctrine addresses the fundamental difference between the nonprofit sector and the for-profit sector.[1] In the for-profit sector, there are numerous legal entities, such as corporations, limited liability companies (LLCs), limited liability partnerships (LLPs), and limited partnerships (LPs), to name a few. The owners and employees of these entities in the for-profit sector hope to produce a profit, also known as net earnings or net income, so they can each benefit from the entity's success.

For example, after graduating from law school, I started as a Corporate Attorney at Davis Graham & Stubbs LLP, one of the oldest and most prestigious law firms in Denver, Colorado. Two United States Supreme Court justices have worked at Davis Graham & Stubbs LLP, the Honorable Byron "Whizzer" White and the Honorable Neil Gorsuch.[2] Davis Graham & Stubbs LLP is a limited liability partnership, and the "partners" of this law firm are its owners. When the partners and associate attorneys bill their clients for legal services, ideally the firm's revenues exceed its expenses, meaning the firm makes a profit. At Davis Graham & Stubbs LLP, those profits are distributed each quarter to the partners of the firm. In this sense, the profits of the firm "inure" or flow to its owners each quarter. Additionally, an associate attorney might win a big case, for example, and receive a bonus from the partners for this victory.

The flow of funds from the assets of this LLP to the associate attorney who excelled on a case, for instance, shows how the entity's assets, including its cash, may "inure" to an employee of the firm. In the for-profit sector, this flow of funds from the legal entity to its owners or employees occurs daily given the vast number of for-profits in the United States. In fact, it's extremely likely that you'll have a personal exchange with a for-profit entity on the same day that you read this chapter. Stockholders, partners, members, executives, board members, and employees may all personally benefit from the entity's assets or resources. In the for-profit sector there's no prohibition on the "inurement" of funds from the entity to those individuals, as generating and distributing profit is the purpose of a for-profit entity. In contrast, with certain tax-exempt nonprofits there is a general prohibition on the inurement of funds. This prohibition is called the private inurement doctrine.

PRIVATE INUREMENT DOCTRINE

The private inurement doctrine applies to many entities that are exempt from federal income tax under the Internal Revenue Code, including those that are exempt under Sections 501(c)(3), 501(c)(4), 501(c)(6), and 501(c)(7).[3] For 501(c)(3) entities, for example, the private inurement doctrine is reflected in the following provision of Section 501(c)(3) of the Code: "(3) Corporations, and any community chest, fund, or foundation, organized and operated exclusively for religious, charitable, scientific, testing for public safety, literary, or educational purposes, or to foster national or international amateur sports competition (but only if no part of its activities involve the provision of athletic facilities or equipment), or for the prevention of cruelty to children or animals, *no part of the net earnings of which inures to the benefit of any private shareholder or individual.*"[4] Because the private inurement doctrine is a statutory one, which means it comes directly from the Code, it's a test that must be passed for certain exempt entities.[5]

Similar to Section 501(c)(3) of the Code, Section 501(c)(6) of the Code notes: "(6) Business leagues, chambers of commerce, real-estate boards, boards of trade, or professional football leagues (whether or not administering a pension fund for football players), not organized for profit and *no part of the net earnings of which inures to the benefit of any private shareholder or individual.*"[6] Each provision, wherever found in an applicable 501(c) section, is referred to as the private inurement doctrine, and this doctrine simply states that the resources of the nonprofit corporation, such as its cash, cannot personally benefit any private shareholder or individual, such as an employee.[7] Rather, the resources of a nonprofit corporation that's also tax-exempt under a 501(c) section containing a prohibition on private inurement should generally be devoted to its mission and exempt purpose activities.[8] One court addressed this doctrine by stating, "A charity is not to siphon its earnings to its founder, or the members of the board, or their families, or anyone else fairly to be described as an insider."[9]

There is a key exception to the general rule against private inurement. A nonprofit corporation that's also subject to the private inurement doctrine may pay reasonable compensation to its employees, including its executives.[10] Reasonableness is a "question of fact, to be decided in the context of each case," but it's generally "[the] amount [that] would ordinarily be paid for like services by like enterprises under like circumstances."[11] If a nonprofit corporation that's also subject to the private inurement doctrine follows these three steps when it determines the compensation to be paid to its employees, including its executives, then the IRS bears the burden of proof to show that such compensation is not reasonable: (1) an independent committee, such as the independent directors of the nonprofit, determine the compensation; (2) such committee reviews compensation data from other entities, whether those entities are nonprofits or for-profits; and (3) such committee adequately and contemporaneously documents the basis for its compensation decisions.[12] These elements collectively comprise the "rebuttable presumption of reasonableness" test.[13] If these three elements are each followed, then there's a presumption in favor of the nonprofit that the compensation is reasonable.[14]

CASE STUDY: CESAR CHAVEZ ACADEMY

In the nonprofit sector, there are many examples of tax-exempt entities that violate the private inurement doctrine. For example, in Pueblo, Colorado, there is a charter school called the Cesar Chavez Academy that is both a nonprofit corporation and a 501(c)(3)-public charity.[15] Because the Cesar Chavez Academy is a 501(c)(3)-public charity, it must adhere to the private inurement doctrine. Today, the mission of the Cesar Chavez Academy is to "[prepare] our students for success as young scholars, productive citizens of the world, and community leaders. We do this by providing an ambitious college preparatory program in a supportive and challenging learning environment. Our curriculum is not only research based but research proven."[16] In 2010, however, the co-founders of the Cesar Chavez Academy faced public scrutiny, including from the state education commissioner, for the compensation that they received.[17]

During that time, top staff members of the Cesar Chavez Academy, including the school's co-founders, received more than $300,000 annually in salaries.[18] In response to these compensation packages, the then-Commissioner of

Education for the state of Colorado, Dwight Jones, noted: "The leaders of Cesar Chavez School Network squandered taxpayer money, ignored basic legal requirements, overcompensated senior staff, engaged in nepotism and failed to provide accountability over the resources entrusted to them."[19] If, for example, a typical executive for a charter school that's also a 501(c)(3)-public charity receives compensation around $160,000 per year for similar work under similar circumstances, then the "excess benefit" is approximately $140,000.[20] Because $300,000 minus $160,000 equals $140,000, the excess benefit in this hypothetical is approximately $140,000. The excessive part of the compensation arrangements that the top executives at the Cesar Chavez Academy received violates the private inurement doctrine, and this excessive amount would be subject to an initial 25 percent tax.[21]

In this case, public officials determined that the top staff of the Cesar Chavez Academy in 2010 used certain resources of this nonprofit, a 501(c)(3)-public charity, to personally benefit themselves. Representatives from "Pueblo City Schools, the Colorado Department of Education, and the state Charter School Institute" hired MGT of America to conduct an audit of the Cesar Chavez Academy.[22] Consultants from MGT of America concluded in this audit report that "The base pay alone of the [top executives] 'greatly exceeded the average' in a salary survey conducted by the Charter School Growth Fund."[23] Accordingly, the excessive part of the base pay, for example, would be subject to an excise tax.[24] Today, the Cesar Chavez Academy has moved on from these former executives and founders, continues to operate in Pueblo, Colorado, and strives to fulfill its mission and achieve its vision of producing productive citizens.

FLOW OF FUNDS

One of the key differences between the for-profit and nonprofit sectors relates to the flow of assets from the entity to any owners or individuals. In the for-profit sector, shareholders, members, partners, executives, board members, and employees can all "siphon off" the resources of that for-profit to personally benefit themselves. In many cases, that's the goal of for-profits. In the nonprofit sector, however, there's a limitation on how the flow of funds from a nonprofit that's subject to the private inurement doctrine may benefit any such individuals. This doctrine is a statutory one because it comes directly from the Code: "*no part of the net earnings of which inures to the benefit of any private shareholder or individual.*"[25] A nonprofit that's also exempt from federal income tax under a Code section that's subject to the private inurement doctrine may pay reasonable compensation. Doing so does not violate this doctrine. However, we expect that a majority of a nonprofit's resources will be used to further its exempt purposes. When that doesn't occur, a nonprofit may face public scrutiny for any excess benefits received by its leaders, just like the top executives of Cesar Chavez Academy experienced in 2010.

KEY PRINCIPLES

→ The private inurement doctrine applies to many entities that are exempt from federal income tax under the Internal Revenue Code, including those that are exempt under Sections 501(c)(3), 501(c)(4), 501(c)(6), and 501(c)(7).

→ The private inurement doctrine is derived from the following: "*no part of the net earnings of which inures to the benefit of any private shareholder or individual.*"

→ A nonprofit corporation that's also subject to the private inurement doctrine may pay reasonable compensation to its employees, including its executives.

12

What's the Private Benefit Doctrine?

■ ■ ■

Perhaps the truth depends on a walk around the lake.

—Wallace Stevens

A HOMEOWNERS ASSOCIATION (HOA)

Imagine that you own a 4,000-square-foot, custom-made home on a beautiful lake in Minnesota. The lake is surrounded by approximately fifty other charming homes and is in fact owned by the community's homeowners association, or HOA, which is exempt from taxation under Section 501(c)(7) of the Code.[1] Because the entire lake is owned by this HOA, only the homeowners can access it. A long time ago, the HOA's board of directors determined that the lake and the recreational facilities surrounding it, including a picnic area, two playgrounds, and a hiking trail, would not be available to the general public. The area surrounding this lake is very beautiful, and the HOA is concerned that access to the lake by the general public might cause the area to quickly deteriorate, which in turn could lower the value of these homes.

At the most recent HOA meeting, one of your neighbors suggested that the homeowners establish another Minnesota nonprofit corporation that would then seek exemption from federal income tax under Section 501(c)(3) of the Code as a public charity. Your neighbor contended that the purpose of this new public charity would be to maintain and beautify the lake and its surrounding natural habitats. Your neighbor is aware of other 501(c)(3)-public charities with similar environmental purposes, including the Minnesota Center for Environmental Advocacy.[2] Monies raised by this new public charity from your neighbors and other donors could be used to build a new boat dock for the lake, a picnic area covered by stylish pergolas, and even a nature center for the neighborhood kids allowing them to explore the lake's terrain and ecosystem. However, access to the lake will continue to be closed to the general public.

With a new nonprofit corporation that's exempt under Section 501(c)(3) of the Code as a public charity, you and other homeowners could make tax-deductible donations to this entity, as well as collect tax-deductible donations from other individuals, businesses, and private foundations.[3] Unfortunately, donations to the existing HOA that's exempt under Section 501(c)(7) of the Code are not tax-deductible. Thus, the neighbor who suggested creating a new 501(c)(3)-public charity is trying to maximize each homeowner's contributions, while also maintaining the beauty of the lake just like the current HOA does. Would this new nonprofit corporation, as suggested by your neighbor, qualify as a 501(c)(3)-public charity?

PRIVATE BENEFIT DOCTRINE

The answer to this question is "no" because of the private benefit doctrine. Unlike the private inurement doctrine, which is expressly stated in Section 501(c)(3) of the Code, the private benefit doctrine is *not* explicitly stated under that section.[4] Rather, the private benefit doctrine is derived from the fact that organizations that are exempt under Section 501(c)(3) of the Code must be both "organized and operated exclusively for" one or more exempt purposes.[5] The operational test notes that a 501(c)(3) entity must engage in activities that further its exempt purposes, or else it can't qualify for exemption under Section 501(c)(3).[6] Accordingly, the Treasury Department in Regulation § 1.501(c)(3)-1(d)(1)(ii) notes that a 501(c)(3) entity cannot be operated "for the benefit of private interests."[7] Similarly, a court in the case of *American Campaign Academy v. Commissioner* noted that "Prohibited private benefits may include an 'advantage; profit; fruit; privilege; gain; [or] interest.'"[8] These private benefits, if substantial in nature, will either prohibit or destroy an exemption under Section 501(c)(3) of the Code.[9]

If a 501(c)(3) entity may not substantially benefit private interests, then whom may it benefit? The Treasury Department's regulations related to this topic also note that "an organization is not organized or operated exclusively for exempt purposes unless it serves a *public* rather than a private interest."[10] Simply put, the private benefit doctrine notes that a 501(c)(3) organization must serve "a public . . . interest," and this pursuit of the public interest helps a nonprofit qualify as a 501(c)(3) entity.[11] The court in the *American Campaign Academy* case further noted that "Occasional economic benefits flowing to persons as an *incidental* consequence of an organization pursuing exempt charitable purposes will *not* generally constitute prohibited private benefits."[12] However, the US Supreme Court in 1945 also stated that "The presence of a single substantial non-exempt purpose destroys the exemption regardless of the number or importance of the exempt purposes."[13] Therefore, an insubstantial benefit to private interests is permissible, but a private benefit if substantial in nature will preclude an organization from being exempt under Section 501(c)(3) of the Code.[14] Whether an organization's activities serve private interests, and whether such benefits are substantial in nature, is determined by a facts and circumstances analysis with respect to that organization.[15]

CASE STUDY: A CAMPAIGN MANAGER SCHOOL AND A CLASSICAL RADIO STATION

The IRS has used the private benefit doctrine to preclude exemption under Section 501(c)(3) of the Code on numerous occasions. Unlike the private inurement doctrine, the private benefit doctrine may have nothing to do with the "flow of funds" from the 501(c)(3) organization to any person or entity.[16] Rather, the main inquiry with respect to the private benefit doctrine is whether the activities of the 501(c)(3) entity confer a substantial benefit on private interests.[17] In the *American Campaign Academy* case, for example, the Academy, which "operated a school to train individuals for careers as campaign managers," appealed a filing letter ruling from the IRS stating that the Academy "serve[d] the private interests of the Republican Party."[18] The vast majority of the Academy's graduates went on to work on Republican campaigns.[19] Thus, the court affirmed this determination by stating, "[W]e conclude that [the Academy] is operated for the benefit of private interests, a nonexempt purpose. Because more than an insubstantial part of petitioner's activities further this nonexempt purpose, petitioner has failed to establish that it operates exclusively for exempt purposes within the meaning of Section 501(c)(3)."[20]

Similarly, in another IRS revenue ruling, the IRS considered the exemption of an organization created to advance classical music in a certain community.[21] The IRS noted, "The organization carried on a variety of activities designed to stimulate public interest in the classical music programs of a for-profit radio station, and thereby enabl[ing] the station to continue broadcasting such music."[22] The IRS concluded that the activities of this new organization, which was formed to advance classical music in a certain broadcast area, primarily benefited this for-profit radio station.[23] In fact, the activities of this new organization allowed the for-profit radio station to increase its revenues from additional sponsors and subscriptions; thus, such activities conferred a substantial benefit on the for-profit radio station.[24] This revenue ruling demonstrates that the IRS is willing to either preclude or revoke the exempt status of a 501(c)(3) nonprofit whose activities confer more than an insubstantial benefit to private interests.

SUBSTANTIAL PRIVATE INTERESTS

While not expressly included under Section 501(c)(3) of the Code, the private benefit doctrine is derived from the fact that a 501(c)(3) organization must be "organized and operated exclusively for" one or more exempt purposes.[25] If a private benefit is substantial in nature, based on a facts and circumstances analysis related to the 501(c)(3) nonprofit in question, then exemption cannot be maintained or granted.[26] In our HOA hypothetical, you and your neighbors who own the homes surrounding the beautiful lake, which would continue to be closed to the general public, are the private parties that would substantially benefit from this proposed 501(c)(3)-public charity. Accordingly, this new non-profit corporation would not be granted exemption under Section 501(c)(3) of the Code because of the private benefit doctrine. Thus, nonprofit leaders should understand that this doctrine requires an exempt entity to confer no more than an insubstantial amount of private benefits. Being the owner of a custom-made home on a private lake in the land of ten thousand lakes has many benefits; but unfortunately, creating a 501(c)(3)-public charity that primarily benefits you and your neighbors isn't one of them.

KEY PRINCIPLES

→ Unlike the private inurement doctrine, which is expressly stated in Section 501(c)(3) of the Code, the private benefit doctrine is *not* explicitly stated under that section.

→ The private benefit doctrine is derived from the fact that organizations that are exempt under Section 501(c)(3) of the Code must be both "organized and operated exclusively for" one or more exempt purposes.

→ An insubstantial benefit to private interests is permissible, but a private benefit if substantial in nature will preclude an organization from being exempt under Section 501(c)(3) of the Code.

13

May a 501(c)(3) Nonprofit Engage in Lobbying?

■ ■ ■

Lobbying is the world's second oldest profession.

—Bill Press

THE SILENT SECTOR

Have you ever considered whether a nonprofit that's exempt from federal income tax under Section 501(c)(3) of the Code can engage in lobbying? Here we're not talking about political campaign activities such as a 501(c)(3) entity urging voters to either "vote for this candidate" or "don't vote for that candidate." These political campaign activities are strictly prohibited for 501(c)(3) entities because of the Johnson Amendment, which added the following provision to such section: "and which does not participate in, or intervene in (including the publishing or distributing of statements), any political campaign on behalf of (or in opposition to) any candidate for public office."[1] Rather, lobbying in this sense is related to the leaders of a 501(c)(3) nonprofit who wish to either directly lobby their elected officials on behalf of such nonprofit or encourage other individuals to talk to their elected officials about certain legislation. In the nonprofit sector there's a lot of confusion related to what 501(c)(3) nonprofits can and cannot do regarding lobbying.

With respect to nonprofits that are exempt from federal income tax under Section 501(c)(3) of the Code as a public charity, rather than as a private foundation, there's a remarkable book that outlines the history of lobbying by such nonprofits called *Seen But Not Heard*.[2] This book was published by the Aspen Institute, which is a 501(c)(3)-public charity, in 2007.[3] The Aspen Institute has operations in Aspen, Colorado; Washington, DC; and New York City.[4] This nonprofit frequently gathers world dignitaries and other thought-leaders to discuss various topics, including philanthropy and social enterprise, and aims to be a "nonpartisan forum for values-based leadership and the exchange of ideas."[5]

The main premise of *Seen But Not Heard* is that public charities typically do not engage in lobbying, even though they should.[6] The book's authors note, "[The book] is written from the perspective of one who believes it is right, proper, and beneficial for nonprofits to engage in the formation of public policy."[7]

If public charities are on the front lines of some of America's most pressing issues, such as education, healthcare, and the environment, to name a few, then who better to help advocate for effective policy positions than the professionals working day-in and day-out on these important issues? The authors of *Seen But Not Heard* advocate that more lobbying should be conducted by public charities.[8] However, they also discuss the confusion related to nonprofit lobbying, including the history of the applicable laws and regulations, and the default lobbying test that applies to public charities.[9] So, what exactly can a 501(c)(3) entity do with respect to lobbying?

NONPROFIT LOBBYING

There are different rules for lobbying depending on whether a nonprofit is exempt from federal income tax as a 501(c)(3)-public charity, a 501(c)(3)-private foundation, or a 501(c)(4)-social welfare organization. First, a public charity may engage in lobbying, but only to a point. Once the IRS approves a nonprofit to be exempt from federal income tax as a public charity, the default lobbying test that automatically applies to that public charity is called the "substantial part" test.[10] This substantial part test is derived directly from Section 501(c)(3) of the Code, which states: "[N]o substantial part of the activities of [the organization] is carrying on propaganda, or otherwise attempting, to influence legislation."[11] In the case *Haswell v. United States* the court addressed the substantial part test by stating, "A percentage test to determine whether the activities are substantial is *not* appropriate. Such a test obscures the complexity of balancing the organization's activities in relation to its objectives and circumstances in the context of the totality of the organization."[12]

A public charity that's subject to the substantial part test is also known as a "non-electing public charity" because it has elected to *not* make what's called "the 501(h) election."[13] The substantial part test simply affirms what's noted in Section 501(c)(3) of the Code, which is that a public charity cannot engage in lobbying activities that represent a "substantial part" of its activities.[14] As addressed in the *Haswell* case, there's no clear line with respect to what's "substantial."[15] For example, is "substantial" 60 percent, 50 percent, or 40 percent of a public charity's activities? Since there's no clear percentage threshold that a nonprofit can't cross, the facts and circumstances related to a public charity's lobbying activities must be reviewed to determine whether such activities are substantial in nature.[16] Since this test is an ambiguous one, public charities that engage in lobbying should make the 501(h) election.[17] This election, which is made by filing Form 5768 with the IRS, makes it clear to the electing public charity how much of its exempt purpose expenditures may be spent on lobbying.[18] As opposed to the substantial part test, making the 501(h) election, which only about 3 percent of public charities have done, subjects the electing public charity to a different test: the "expenditure test."[19] Under this test, there are clear limits for direct and grassroots lobbying expenditures, which are represented by table 13.1.

Table 13.1

Total Annual Exempt Purpose Expenditures	Direct Lobbying Limits (Nontaxable Amounts)	Grassroots Lobbying Limits (Nontaxable Amounts)
Up to $500,000	20%	5%
$500,000 to $1,000,000	$100,000 plus 15% of the excess over $500,000	$25,000 plus 3.75% of the excess over $500,000
$1,000,000 to $1,500,000	$175,000 plus 10% of the excess over $1,000,000	$43,750 plus 2.5% of the excess over $1,000,000
$1,500,000 to $17,000,000	$225,000 plus 5% of the excess over $1,500,000	$56,250 plus 1.25% of the excess over $1,500,000
Over $17,000,000	$1,000,000	$250,000

Sources: Gary D. Bass, David F. Arons, Kay Guinane, and Matthew F. Carter, *Seen But Not Heard: Strengthening Nonprofit Advocacy* (Washington, DC: The Aspen Institute, 2007), 191–92; Bruce Hopkins, *The Law of Tax-Exempt Organizations*, 11th ed. (Hoboken, NJ: John Wiley & Sons, 2016), 637.

Unlike public charities, 501(c)(3)-private foundations may only engage in "self-defense" lobbying.[20] As noted by Marion R. Fremont-Smith in her book *Governing Nonprofit Organizations*, the general rule is that "Section 4945(d) [of the Code] prohibits foundations from expending any amount on grassroots lobbying or attempting to influence legislation through communication with any member or employee of a legislative body or any other government official or employee who may participate in the formulation of legislation."[21] However, if there's a piece of legislation that directly attacks one of the purposes of that private foundation, then it may engage in lobbying.[22] Here, it should also be noted that neither nonpartisan studies nor responses to requests from governmental bodies constitute lobbying.[23] Finally, 501(c)(4)-social welfare organizations may engage in an unlimited amount of lobbying.[24] There is no restriction on the amount of lobbying that may be conducted by a 501(c)(4) entity so long as such lobbying activities are related to its exempt purposes.[25] For this reason, many public charities wishing to lobby above the foregoing limits affiliate with or launch a separate 501(c)(4) organization.

CASE STUDY: COMMON CAUSE AND AMENDMENT 41

During my tenure at the Boettcher Foundation, which is a 501(c)(3)-private foundation, we had to engage in self-defense lobbying. During the 2006 general election in Colorado, a nonprofit called Common Cause, which is also a 501(c)(3)-public charity, sponsored an amendment to the Colorado constitution called Amendment 41.[26] Amendment 41 was labeled the "ethics in government" amendment, as it prohibited certain Colorado government officials from receiving gifts in excess of $50.[27] There were exceptions to this general rule, but scholarships offered by the Boettcher Foundation to certain recipients didn't fall under any of those exceptions. The Boettcher Foundation scholarship is one of the most prestigious, merit-based scholarships a Colorado high school student can receive, and is arguably one of the nation's most prestigious scholarships. Other prominent scholarships include the Morehead-Cain scholarship, the Daniels Fund scholarship, and the Coca-Cola scholarship, among others.

Colorado high school students who are awarded the scholarship are called "Boettcher Scholars."[28] These Boettcher Scholars receive a full-tuition scholarship to any Colorado college or university that they're admitted to—including Colorado College, the University of Denver, or the University of Colorado—as well as expenses for books, lodging, and meals.[29] While the intent behind Amendment 41 was to create "ethics in government," it unintentionally swept in the Boettcher Foundation scholarship.[30] For example, if the foundation awarded a Colorado high school student with this prestigious merit-based scholarship, but that student had a parent that worked in state government, then it was uncertain whether that student could take the scholarship in the immediate aftermath of the passage of Amendment 41.[31] The Boettcher Foundation scholarship can be worth approximately $250,000 if a student elects to pursue his or her undergraduate studies at a private institution, such as the University of Denver.

Since the term "legislation," as it relates to lobbying for 501(c)(3) entities, includes constitutional amendments to be considered by the public, the Boettcher Foundation, as a 501(c)(3)-private foundation, would normally be prohibited from lobbying either for or against this amendment.[32] As noted by the IRS, "[The term] *Legislation* includes action by Congress, any state legislature, any local council, or similar governing body, with respect to acts, bills, resolutions, or similar items (such as legislative confirmation of appointive office), or by the public in referendum, ballot initiative, constitutional amendment, or similar procedure. It does not include actions by executive, judicial, or administrative bodies."[33] However, since Amendment 41 unintentionally swept in the Boettcher Foundation scholarship, which is one of the foundation's key programs, the foundation was allowed to lobby against this then-proposed constitutional amendment. This type of lobbying constituted self-defense lobbying.

EXPENDITURE TEST AND SUBSTANTIAL PART TEST

In the 2006 general election, the citizens of Colorado passed Amendment 41. Subsequently, however, a Denver District Court judge exempted the Boettcher Foundation scholarship from the amendment's reach.[34] While the foundation's lobbying efforts did not convince enough citizens to vote down Amendment 41, those lobbying efforts exemplified self-defense lobbying. At issue in this case was an amendment that would directly impact one of the foundation's key programs, and thus, the foundation was able to lobby against it without violating Section 501(c)(3) of the Code. On the other hand, public charities can engage in a certain amount of lobbying, even if it's not self-defense lobbying.[35] Public charities cannot, however, engage in a "substantial" amount of lobbying.[36] Since the "substantial part" test is not clear, public charities engaging in lobbying should make the 501(h) election. By filing IRS Form 5768, a 501(c)(3) will be subject to the expenditure test as opposed to the substantial part test.

The expenditure test gives nonprofit leaders clear thresholds with respect to lobbying expenses. So long as the public charity keeps its lobbying expenses below these thresholds for either direct or grassroots lobbying, the leaders of that nonprofit know that they won't be violating Section 501(c)(3) of the Code. While there has been significant confusion on this topic, nonprofits can and should engage in lobbying. Since nonprofit leaders are working on many of the same issues that our elected officials are addressing, they should work hand-in-hand to solve those issues. If a nonprofit professional has spent his or her entire career on education, who's better situated to help an elected official with education reform? The nonprofit sector should not operate in isolation. Rather, it should work closely with the government sector, and any policy solutions appearing to work in the nonprofit sector should be considered on a larger scale by the government sector. Effective lobbying by nonprofits will help turn these ideas into reality.

KEY PRINCIPLES

→ There are different rules for lobbying depending on whether a nonprofit is exempt from federal income tax as a 501(c)(3)-public charity, a 501(c)(3)-private foundation, or a 501(c)(4)-social welfare organization.

→ The default lobbying test that automatically applies to 501(c)(3)-public charities is called the "substantial part" test.

→ A 501(c)(3)-public charity making the "501(h) election" subjects the electing public charity to a different test: the "expenditure test."

14

What's the Johnson Amendment?

■ ■ ■

I'd rather give my life than be afraid to give it.

—Lyndon B. Johnson

RUNNING FOR PUBLIC OFFICE

Do you have any friends, colleagues, or acquaintances who have run for elected office? If so, you'll appreciate that it's typically an expensive endeavor. Their campaigns will likely call or email you at least once a month inviting you to an event such as a fundraiser or a "honk and wave," or asking you to make a donation to their campaign. In general, the campaigns that raise the most money have a greater chance of winning that campaign.[1] In addition to donations, however, campaigns are also looking for endorsements, especially endorsements that carry weight with the general public. If you visit a candidate's website, you'll likely see a page with all of the endorsements he or she has received.

With this in mind, let's presume that you're the executive director of a charter school, a 501(c)(3)-public charity, and you know that one of your friends running for Congress is a huge advocate for K–12 education. Let's further presume that your friend's views are perfectly aligned with the views of the charter school, including more pay for teachers, more technology in the classrooms, and a focus on standardized tests that actually track student achievement. These assessments can provide the leaders of the charter school with feedback they need to help ensure that the school's students are prepared for the next level, whether that's pursuing a post-secondary education at a college or pursuing an idea as a young entrepreneur.

Since the views of the charter school are perfectly aligned with the views of your friend running for Congress, it makes sense that your friend not only asks you for a personal endorsement, but also for a formal endorsement on behalf of the charter school. Your friend isn't familiar with the laws and regulations on what 501(c)(3) entities can and cannot do with respect to political campaign activities. Thus, as the executive director of the charter school, can you decide to have this 501(c)(3)-public charity formally endorse your friend who is running for Congress?

THE JOHNSON AMENDMENT

The answer to that question is "no," and that's because of the Johnson Amendment.[2] The Johnson Amendment, named after former United States Senator and President Lyndon B. Johnson, is the last part of Section 501(c)(3) of Code: "[a corporation] . . . which does not participate in, or intervene in (including the publishing or distributing of statements), any political campaign on behalf of (or in opposition to) any candidate for public office."[3] This provision prohibits a 501(c)(3) entity, whether that entity is a 501(c)(3)-public charity or a 501(c)(3)-private foundation, from engaging in "political campaign" activities, which are also known as "electioneering" activities, on behalf of a candidate running for public office.[4] A candidate may be running for office at any level of government, such as "a contestant . . . at the national, state, or local levels."[5]

Here, it's important to note that "political campaign" activities are different than lobbying activities; 501(c)(3)-public charities can engage in lobbying activities so long as such activities are not "substantial" in nature, and 501(c)(3)-private foundations may engage in self-defense lobbying.[6] "Political campaign" activities, on the other hand, are activities related to candidates running for elected office.[7] This restriction was added to Section 501(c)(3) of the Code in 1954.[8] At that time, then–United States Senator Lyndon B. Johnson was running for office in the state of Texas.[9] During this campaign, he was concerned that "funds provided by a charitable foundation were used to help finance the campaign of [his] opponent in a primary election."[10] When Senator Johnson made it to Washington, DC, he introduced a bill on July 2, 1954, to add this prohibition on "political campaign" activities to Section 501(c)(3) of the Code, which subsequently became the law of the land with the passage of the Revenue Act of 1954.[11]

Because of the Johnson Amendment, 501(c)(3) organizations are prohibited from telling their stakeholders or the general public to "vote for this person" or "don't vote for that person."[12] If a 501(c)(3) entity engages in this type of activity, then it's in jeopardy of losing its 501(c)(3) designation from the IRS.[13] If a nonprofit that's exempt from federal income tax under Section 501(c)(3) of the Code engages in "electioneering" activities, it may be classified as "an action organization and thus may be disqualified for exempt status" under such section.[14] Accordingly, 501(c)(3) organizations may not lawfully engage in "political campaign" activities because of the Johnson Amendment, and nonprofit leaders should be aware of any activities that may be deemed to be "favor[ing] or oppos[ing] a candidate for public office."[15] Such activities may lead to sanctions or even revocation of 501(c)(3) status.[16]

CASE STUDY: NATIONAL PRAYER BREAKFAST

The Johnson Amendment was not controversial when it passed in 1954 and was added to Section 501(c)(3) of the Code. However, it's recently become a subject of debate and controversy, especially in the 2016 presidential election. During the 2016 presidential campaign, then-candidate Donald Trump publicly denounced the Johnson Amendment and advocated for its repeal.[17] On February 2, 2017, then-candidate Trump noted at the National Prayer Breakfast in Washington, DC, that he would "totally destroy" the Johnson Amendment.[18] Specifically, then-candidate Trump stated: "That is why I will get rid of, and totally destroy, the Johnson Amendment and allow our representatives of faith to speak freely and without fear of retribution. I will do that remember."[19] In an attempt to deliver on this promise, an early version of the tax bill that was signed into law on December 22, 2017, contained a repeal of the Johnson Amendment.[20] However, the final version of that tax bill that was eventually signed into law by President Trump did not contain a repeal of the Johnson Amendment.[21]

Because President Trump has brought the Johnson Amendment to light, it will continue to be a topic that's debated at the federal level. Opponents of the Johnson Amendment, like President Trump, argue that 501(c)(3) entities should be free to either endorse or oppose candidates for public office.[22] United States Senator James Lankford from Oklahoma stated, "The federal government and the [Internal Revenue Service] should never have the ability, through our tax code, to limit free speech."[23] Conversely, proponents of the Johnson Amendment argue that its repeal from Section 501(c)(3) of the Code would lead to subsidized free speech, as donations to 501(c)(3) organizations are given the "deductibility benefit."[24] That is, not only are 501(c)(3) entities exempt from federal income tax, but donors to such 501(c)(3)s may also deduct those donations from their federal taxes under Section 170 of the Code: "There shall be allowed as a deduction any charitable contribution . . . payment of which is made within the taxable year."[25]

Accordingly, like all good policy debates, there's a tension in the debate over the Johnson Amendment between two competing interests, such as liberty and security or equity and efficiency.[26] For example, when you're in the security line at an airport, the tension in such situation is between liberty and security.[27] In this case, we sacrifice some of our individual liberties in exchange for additional security.[28] With the debate over the Johnson Amendment, the tension is between "free speech" and "subsidized free speech" by the federal government, namely the Internal Revenue Service.[29] Both President Trump and Senator Lankford from Oklahoma argue that the policy goal of "free speech" warrants the repeal of the Johnson Amendment.[30] If the Johnson Amendment was repealed, however, and the "deductibility benefit" under Section 170 of the Code was maintained, then donors could make a deductible contribution to a 501(c)(3) organization, which in turn could use those monies to advocate for certain candidates for public office. Opponents of repealing this provision argue that such a scenario would likely result in a "new dark-money channel for powerful donors to quietly funnel [tax-deductible] funds to political candidates."[31]

"POLITICAL CAMPAIGN" ACTIVITIES

The debate over whether to repeal the Johnson Amendment will surely continue, especially during President Trump's tenure in office. Since 1954, 501(c)(3) organizations, including both public charities and private foundations, have been prohibited from engaging in "political campaign" activities.[32] Even though a candidate for public office might have views or positions that perfectly align with a particular 501(c)(3)'s positions, that entity cannot tell its stakeholders or the general public to vote for that candidate. Certainly, the leaders of that 501(c)(3) entity, such as the executive director or a board member, may either endorse or oppose a candidate for elected office on an individual basis. However, they cannot endorse or oppose that candidate on behalf of the 501(c)(3) organization that they lead. Engaging in this type of activity would jeopardize that organization's 501(c)(3) status. Thus, while the leaders of the charter school, for example, might favor one candidate for public office over another candidate, that 501(c)(3)-public charity must remain silent, for now.

KEY PRINCIPLES

→ The Johnson Amendment, named after former United States Senator and President Lyndon B. Johnson, is the last part of Section 501(c)(3) of Code.

→ This provision prohibits a 501(c)(3) entity, whether that entity is a 501(c)(3)-public charity or a 501(c)(3)-private foundation, from engaging in "political campaign" activities, which are also known as "electioneering" activities.

→ "Political campaign" activities are activities related to candidates running for elected office.

15

May a 501(c)(3) Nonprofit Have a For-Profit Subsidiary?

■ ■ ■

Means must be subsidiary to ends and to our desire for dignity and value.

—Ludwig Mies van der Rohe

SUBSIDIARIES

Have you ever considered whether a nonprofit corporation that's exempt from federal income tax under Section 501(c)(3) of the Code may have a for-profit subsidiary? Before we address that question, let's briefly consider the opposite situation, which is whether a for-profit corporation may have a wholly-owned 501(c)(3) nonprofit corporation. "Wholly-owned" simply means that the for-profit corporation owns 100 percent of the "stock," or the ownership interests, of that nonprofit corporation. Because of the multitude of corporate foundations that exist, such as the Wells Fargo Foundation, the GE Foundation, and the Coca-Cola Foundation Inc., to name a few, many people think that a for-profit corporation may have a wholly-owned subsidiary that's both a nonprofit corporation and either a 501(c)(3)-public charity or a 501(c)(3)-private foundation.

These corporate foundations, like the one that I served as the general counsel for, conduct great work throughout our communities, nation, and the world. According to the Foundation Center, which is the "world's leading source of information on philanthropy, fundraising, and grant programs," the top fifty corporate foundations have approximately $12 billion in total assets.[1] While many for-profit corporations, such as Wells Fargo, GE, and Coca-Cola, desire to pursue charitable activities while also making a profit, these companies cannot have wholly-owned subsidiaries that are also exempt under Section 501(c)(3) of the Code. This arrangement would violate the private inurement doctrine.[2] This doctrine generally states that the assets of a 501(c)(3) entity should be devoted to its exempt purposes and not for private gain, such as the net earnings of the entity flowing to any entity or individual.[3] Additionally, many nonprofit corporation acts under various state laws, such as the Colorado Revised Nonprofit Corporation Act, do not allow nonprofit corporations to issue "stock."[4]

Between the private inurement doctrine and the inability to issue ownership interests, for-profit corporations should not have wholly-owned 501(c)(3) subsidiaries. Instead, for-profits that set up corporate foundations simply affiliate with these corporate foundations. In this sense, the relationship between for-profit corporations and their corporate foundations is more of a peer-to-peer relationship as opposed to a parent-subsidiary relationship. In sum, 501(c)(3) nonprofits cannot have private owners.[5] So, now that we've considered this threshold issue, we'll consider the opposite situation: can a 501(c)(3) nonprofit have a for-profit subsidiary?

FOR-PROFIT SUBSIDIARIES

The answer to that question is "yes." A nonprofit corporation that's exempt from federal income tax under Section 501(c)(3) of the Code may have a for-profit subsidiary.[6] There are many reasons that a 501(c)(3) nonprofit may want to have either a wholly-owned or partially-owned for-profit subsidiary.[7] Chief among these reasons is that a 501(c)(3) organization likely wants a steady source of revenues. Many nonprofit leaders strive to add revenue streams to accomplish more of that nonprofit's mission and vision. If a 501(c)(3) entity is able to generate a steady source of income through its own efforts, then that organization will be less reliant upon donations from individuals, foundations, and corporations. During a recession, those donations will likely decrease; however, the demand for that nonprofit's services may actually increase during the same economic downturn. For this reason, many 501(c)(3) nonprofits desire to have a steady source of income through the use of a for-profit subsidiary.[8]

Unrelated business taxable income, or "UBTI," is the second key reason a 501(c)(3) nonprofit many set up a for-profit subsidiary.[9] If a 501(c)(3) nonprofit creates an earned-income venture, like a trade or business, but that venture is both unrelated to the exempt purpose of that nonprofit and is regularly carried on, then such earned-income activity will be subject to UBTI.[10] Additionally, there's a risk that this venture becomes so substantial in nature that it actually threatens the 501(c)(3) status of that nonprofit.[11] To protect the 501(c)(3) status of a nonprofit, the leaders of that nonprofit or their attorneys may place that earned-income activity, which is unrelated to the exempt purpose of that 501(c)(3), in a for-profit subsidiary.[12] With this structure, the nonprofit "parent" of that for-profit subsidiary will continue to enjoy the benefits of having a stable source of income without the risk that this unrelated venture, which constitutes a "substantial portion of [that] exempt organization's income," will threaten its 501(c)(3) status.[13]

If the nonprofit "parent" is a 501(c)(3)-public charity, and its for-profit subsidiary makes a dividend payment to this 501(c)(3) parent, then the impact on the one-third public support test should also be considered. First, it's important to note that such dividend payment is not subject to UBTI when it's received at the 501(c)(3) parent level because the Code specifically exempts such dividend payments from UBTI.[14] This is because the subsidiary typically "pays taxes on earnings before distributing dividends to the exempt parent."[15] In addition, dividend income constitutes "gross investment income," which is used to help calculate the denominator of the one-third public support test.[16] The one-third public support test is simply "public support" divided by "total support."[17] Since dividends constitute "gross investment income," which is part of a public charity's "total support" number, the leaders of a 501(c)(3)-public charity need to be aware of the potential impact that such dividend payments could have on this calculation. Accordingly, the leaders of 501(c)(3)-public charities that have for-profit subsidiaries making dividend payments should monitor this ratio.

CASE STUDY: SHARE OUR STRENGTH AND COMMUNITY WEALTH PARTNERS

One of the best examples of a 501(c)(3) "parent" that has a wholly-owned, for-profit subsidiary is Share Our Strength, Inc. based out of Washington, DC ("Share Our Strength"). Share Our Strength's mission is "[t]o end hunger and poverty in the U.S. and abroad."[18] For the fiscal year ended June 30, 2016, Share Our Strength had total revenues of approximately $54.4 million and net assets of approximately $17.5 million, making it one of the nation's largest public charities.[19] The key initiative of Share Our Strength is "No Kid Hungry," which aims to connect hungry kids with resources that help alleviate that hunger.[20] To date, "No Kid Hungry" has served kids struggling with hunger with more than 500 million additional meals.[21] Each year, Share Our Strength spends approximately $22 million on the "No Kid Hungry" initiative.[22]

In 1997, Share Our Strength launched a wholly-owned, for-profit subsidiary called Community Wealth Partners (formerly Community Wealth Ventures).[23] Community Wealth Partners works with its clients on "capacity building, strategy, collaborations, and performance measurement and evaluation."[24] Since Community Wealth Partners is a wholly-owned, for-profit subsidiary of Share Our Strength, it strives to work with clients in the following areas, each of which has a role to play in alleviating hunger: (1) education; (2) health; (3) employment; and (4) community development.[25] The mission of Community Wealth Partners is to "offer leadership development and coaching, strategy and implementation, and community collaboration services," and to be "true partners focused on turning change agents' visions into bold goals, goals into plans, and plans into action."[26]

With Community Wealth Partners, one of Share Our Strength's likely goals is to have this earned-income venture generate a substantial dividend, which is ideally a stable source of revenue for this 501(c)(3)-public charity. In turn, Share Our Strength can use these financial resources from its subsidiary to fulfill its charitable mission and achieve its long-term vision of eradicating hunger and poverty.[27] For example, based on Share Our Strength's audited financial statements for the year ended December 31, 2012, Community Wealth Partners contributed approximately $2 million to Share Our Strength's revenues.[28] Accordingly, Share Our Strength is utilizing this for-profit subsidiary to both accomplish its charitable purpose, based on Community Wealth Partners' complimentary work, as well as provide it with a stable source of revenue. Share Our Strength's most recent "public support percentage" is approximately 89 percent, which means it still has room to receive additional dividend income.[29]

EARNED INCOME

The case study of Share Our Strength and Community Wealth Partners shows how a 501(c)(3)-public charity can operate a wholly-owned, for-profit subsidiary. Share Our Strength has been able to use Community Wealth Partners to generate approximately $2 million in annual revenues.[30] Since Share Our Strength is a 501(c)(3)-public charity, its leaders have been able to maintain its public charity status through its high "public support percentage," despite this additional revenue coming into the organization as "gross investment income." With the emergence of social entrepreneurship in the nonprofit sector, nonprofit leaders are being more creative when it comes to earned income activities.[31] A healthy nonprofit should have a diverse income stream, which might include revenues generated from a wholly-owned, for-profit subsidiary. Nonprofit leaders should understand the nuances related to this topic, including UBTI and the impact of dividend income on the one-third public support test, if they are interested in pursuing earned income activities, like operating a for-profit subsidiary.

KEY PRINCIPLES

→ A nonprofit corporation that's exempt from federal income tax under Section 501(c)(3) of the Code may have a for-profit subsidiary.

→ If a 501(c)(3) entity is able to generate a steady source of income through its own efforts, then that organization will be less reliant upon donations from individuals, foundations, and corporations.

→ A 501(c)(3) nonprofit may set up a for-profit subsidiary because of unrelated business taxable income (UBTI).

16

What Are the IRS Form 1024 and Form 1024-A?

■ ■ ■

Yeah! How [do] you like me now, F.E.C.? I'm rolling seven digits deep! I got 99 problems but a non-connected independent-expenditure only committee ain't one.

—Stephen Colbert

QUARTERLY FORUM

My friend and former colleague, Ashley, is a connector. If you've ever read *The Tipping Point* by Malcolm Gladwell, you know how a "connector" works.[1] Connectors are always trying to find a link, build a bridge, or establish a connection to you, whether that's through your friends, coworkers, background, profession, education, or experiences.[2] Connectors find great joy in making a connection, and this inclination to discover and reveal connections is simply how their brains are wired to operate. As scholars like Malcolm Gladwell and Wayne Baker have shown us, information flows through "connectors" or "linchpins."[3] This increased information flow means that communities with numerous connectors also typically have higher social capital, which is essentially the grease in the wheels of democracy.[4] When the board of directors of Quarterly Forum, which is a 501(c)(4) nonprofit based in Denver, Colorado, was looking to hire its next executive director, they knew they had found their perfect match with Ashley.

Quarterly Forum strives to bring together some of Colorado's most prominent business, nonprofit, and government sector leaders. Quite simply, it connects people, and Ashley, as a connector, relished the opportunity to lead this wonderful organization. Before Quarterly Forum was established, these business, nonprofit, and government sector leaders gathered together on an informal basis, but now they come together on a formal basis to help the state of Colorado reach its maximum potential. Quarterly Forum's mission is "[To] connect, educate, and inspire the state's best emerging community leaders."[5]

This begs the question, how was Quarterly Forum formally established? What exactly did the leaders of this idea and movement, like former Governor John Hickenlooper and Liberty Global's CEO Mike Fries, do to formally start this 501(c)(4) organization?

FORM 1024 AND FORM 1024-A

A person wishing to start a nonprofit that is exempt from taxation under most sections of Section 501(c) of the Code may file a Form 1024 with the IRS after the legal entity has been established under applicable state law.[6] For 501(c)(3) organizations, there's a different form, called the Form 1023 (or the shorter Form 1023-EZ, if applicable), that's filed with the IRS. Additionally, for 501(c) (4) entities, the applicable IRS form is now called the Form 1024-A, which was adopted by the IRS in January 2018.[7] This new form contains many questions that elicit similar information as the Form 1024.

The leaders of Quarterly Forum created a Colorado nonprofit corporation in 2015 and called it the "QF Group Inc."[8] They then filed a Form 1024 with the IRS to obtain exemption from federal income tax under Section 501(c)(4) of the Code. At the time, the Form 1024-A did not yet exist. The Form 1024 is only six pages, excluding its schedules.[9] The bulk of the Form 1024, as well as the new Form 1024-A, contains a series of questions related to the nonprofit's purpose, activities, and finances, including its latest income statement and balance sheet.[10] Depending on which 501(c) exemption is being sought by an applicant, such as exemption under Sections 501(c)(2), 501(c)(6), or 501(c)(7) of the Code, the Form 1024 may also contain an applicable schedule. For example, Schedule A relates to nonprofits seeking exemption under Section 501(c)(2) of the Code.[11] Schedule C relates to nonprofits seeking exemption under Section 501(c)(5) and Section 501(c)(6) of the Code.[12]

When thinking about whether to file the Form 1024, including the new Form 1024-A, it's important to note that certain nonprofits may "self-declare," as noted by Bruce Hopkins in his book, *The Law of Tax-Exempt Organizations*.[13] The ability to self-declare means that a nonprofit seeking exemption under certain sections of Section 501(c) of the Code may, but is not required to, file the Form 1024 or the new Form 1024-A.[14] This is because a nonprofit's tax-exempt status may result "by operation of law."[15] Nonprofits that may self-declare include 501(c)(4)s, 501(c)(5)s, and 501(c) (6)s.[16] While these self-declaring nonprofits are not required to file an application with the IRS, many of them voluntarily do to ensure that the IRS "recognizes [the] exemption."[17] Other than these self-declaring nonprofits, an application must be filed for nonprofits seeking tax exemption.

CASE STUDY: STEPHEN COLBERT'S "ANONYMOUS SHELL CORPORATION"

In addition to Quarterly Forum, another corporation that was exempt from federal income tax under Section 501(c)(4) of the Code was Stephen Colbert's "Anonymous Shell Corporation."[18] Yes, you read that correctly. Stephen Colbert, the current host of *The Late Show* on CBS, created a 501(c)(4) entity in 2011 with the help of his attorney, Trevor Potter.[19] Trevor Potter is the former chairman of the Federal Election Commission (FEC) and at Colbert's direction, he created a corporation called "Anonymous Shell Corporation," which subsequently sought exemption under Section 501(c)(4) of the Code.[20] When Colbert was the host of *The Colbert Report* on Comedy Central, he wanted to highlight the fact that donors to 501(c)(4) organizations didn't have to be publicly disclosed.[21]

This issue is known as "dark money" in political campaigns. Under certain circumstances, political leaders can utilize 501(c)(4) social welfare organizations for any donors who don't want to be publicly disclosed. In 2014, Trevor Potter noted:

> [Colbert] was able to show America the loopholes in the laws designed to regulate coordination between candidates and supposedly 'independent' groups. By having his own Super PAC and 501(c)(4), Stephen could evolve right alongside the campaigns—or often be a step ahead of them. His understanding of the possibilities inherent in the legal confusion was keen enough to discover and exploit absurd legalities before it became clear that actual candidates and political activists were doing the same thing.[22]

Colbert later changed the name of this 501(c)(4) corporation from "Anonymous Shell Corporation" to "Colbert Super PAC SHH Institute."[23] As Colbert comically noted on his previous show, *The Colbert Report*, the emphasis was on the "SHH."

In September 2018, Judge Beryl Howell of the United States District Court for the District of Columbia, in the *Citizens for Responsibility and Ethics in Washington vs. Federal Election Commission and Crossroads GPS* case, ruled that "politically active nonprofits organizations [like 501(c)(4)s] that make 'independent expenditures' will now be forced to disclose more of their donors."[24] An "independent expenditure" is defined as "an expenditure by a person . . . expressly advocating the election or defeat of a clearly identified candidate [and] that is *not* made in concert or cooperation with or at the request or suggestion of such candidate, the candidate's authorized political committee, or their agents, or a political party committee or its agents."[25] After this ruling by Judge Howell, 501(c)(4) social welfare organizations must disclose all contributions over $200 for the "purpose of advancing independent expenditures."[26]

However, as of the date of this book's publication, this ruling is under appeal before the United States Courts of Appeals for the District of Columbia Circuit.[27] Even if this ruling is upheld by this appellate court, or even the United States Supreme Court after that, there's an easy workaround solution for any politically-minded leaders who don't wish to disclose donors to 501(c)(4) entities.[28] This ruling only applies to nonprofits making "independent expenditures." Thus, instead of having the 501(c)(4) entity make the "independent expenditure" itself, politically-minded leaders could simply create a Super PAC to make those expenditures.[29] The 501(c)(4) organization could take in monies from donors wishing to remain anonymous, and then simply turn over those funds to the Super PAC making such expenditures. With this structure, "donors [to the 501(c)(4)] remain secret."[30]

PEABODY AWARD

Just like Quarterly Forum, Stephen Colbert and his attorney Trevor Potter established a corporation that subsequently obtained exemption from federal income tax under Section 501(c)(4) of the Code. They were successful in their efforts, and Stephen Colbert even won a Peabody Award in 2012 for his efforts to show the impact of "dark money" on political campaigns.[31] We can assume that "SHH" is a direct reflection of the fact that donors to 501(c)(4) organizations not making "independent expenditures" don't need to be publicly disclosed. When connectors come together, like they did with the creation of Quarterly Forum, or when politically-minded leaders come together, like they did with the creation of Stephen Colbert's 501(c)(4), the Form 1024-A is now the appropriate form that may be filed with the IRS to obtain tax-exempt status for 501(c)(4) social welfare organizations. This presumes that the leaders of those social welfare organizations don't want to self-declare the tax-exempt nature of that organization. Otherwise, the Form 1024 should be used to obtain tax-exempt status under most other 501(c) sections, such as 501(c)(2), 501(c)(6) or 501(c)(7).

KEY PRINCIPLES

→ A person wishing to start a nonprofit that is exempt from taxation under Section 501(c) of the IRS Code, except for Section 501(c)(3), will likely file the Form 1024 or Form 1024-A with the IRS.

→ The Form 1024 is only six pages, excluding the schedules. The Form 1024-A is only four pages.

→ When thinking about whether to file the Form 1024 or the Form 1024-A, it's important to note that certain nonprofits may "self-declare." The ability to self-declare means that the nonprofit seeking exemption under certain subsections of Section 501(c) Code may, but are not required to, file.

17

What's a 501(c)(2)?

■ ■ ■

The power of taxing people and their property is essential to the very existence of government.

—James Madison

PROPERTY TAX ASSESSMENTS

One of my friends and colleagues, Brittany, was in a sorority at the University of Colorado as an undergraduate student. She and I were having coffee one day to catch up, as she had recently changed jobs. During that meeting, she mentioned that one of her friends was serving as the president of that sorority's housing association. That housing association was a Colorado nonprofit corporation and was also exempt from federal income tax under Section 501(c)(2) of the Code. The night before that meeting I had just taught a nonprofit law class at the University of Denver College of Law, where we covered property tax exemptions. Since this topic was top-of-mind, I told my friend, "You know, if your sorority owns the building, it doesn't need to pay property taxes under Colorado law." One of my passions is teaching, so I couldn't resist sharing this bit of good news with Brittany. She wasn't sure whether her sorority owned the building, so she put me in touch with the president of that sorority's housing association.

Prior to my coffee meeting with that president, I checked the Boulder County Assessor's Office, which maintains an online property tax system, and determined that this sorority had been paying property taxes in Boulder County since its inception in the early 1900s. Most recently, this nonprofit had paid approximately $25,000 in property taxes, even though it met the qualifications for property tax exemption under Colorado law. After I conducted some further diligence on this nonprofit, I determined that it was exempt under Section 501(c)(2) of the Code, but that it wasn't set up properly under such section. Based on the governing documents that the president of the sorority's housing association had in her possession, this 501(c)(2) nonprofit lacked the proper "control" element. This control element is a requirement for a nonprofit to be properly recognized as a tax exempt entity under Section 501(c)(2) of the Code.[1]

If a nonprofit owns title to property, just like this sorority owed its chapter building in Boulder, Colorado, it should be aware of the rules regarding 501(c)(2) entities, which are also known as "title holding corporations."[2] Nonprofit leaders should also know that certain nonprofits are exempt from paying property taxes in the counties in which they own real property. In case you're wondering, yes, we saved this sorority's housing association from having to pay another property tax bill. Not only did it receive an exemption from Boulder County from paying property taxes in the future, it also received a check for approximately $25,000 back from Boulder County for property taxes previously paid in the prior tax year.

SECTION 501(C)(2)

Organizations that are exempt from federal income tax under Section 501(c)(2) of the Code are known as "title holding corporations" because they are created to hold title to property.[3] As noted in the Code, title holding corporations are "organized for the exclusive purpose of holding title to property, collecting income therefrom, and turning over the entire amount thereof, less expenses, to an organization which itself is exempt under [501(a)]."[4] According to the IRS, there are approximately 5,000 entities registered with the IRS that are exempt under Section 501(c)(2) of the Code, and the use of 501(c)(2) organizations by other tax exempt entities is on the rise.[5] If a 501(c)(3)-public charity owns an expensive piece of property, for example, then it may elect to have the title to that property held in a 501(c)(2) entity, which helps protect that valuable asset.[6] This same strategy, to use various legal entities in a parent-subsidiary relationship, is frequently used by for-profits to protect their valuable assets.

There are a few requirements for correctly setting up a 501(c)(2) organization. First, as noted in the Code, title holding corporations must be controlled or "owned" to some extent by another tax exempt entity, such as a 501(c)(3), 501(c)(4), 501(c)(6), or a 501(c)(7), because it's to function like a subsidiary of that other tax exempt entity.[7] If a 501(c)(2) is organized as a nonprofit corporation, and applicable state law allows for that nonprofit corporation to issue stock or shares, such as the state of Pennsylvania, then this control or ownership may be demonstrated by the parent tax-exempt entity owning all of the stock or shares of that 501(c)(2) entity.[8] If a 501(c)(2) entity is organized as a nonprofit corporation, but applicable state law does not allow for that nonprofit corporation to issue stock or shares, such as the state of Colorado, then control may be demonstrated by the parent tax-exempt entity being able to appoint all of the directors of the 501(c)(2).[9]

Additionally, if a 501(c)(2) is organized as a limited liability company, as opposed to a nonprofit corporation, then control or "ownership" may be demonstrated by the parent tax-exempt entity possessing all of the membership interests of the 501(c)(2) entity.[10] Without this control or ownership by another tax exempt entity, at least to some extent, exemption under Section 501(c)(2) cannot be achieved.[11] As noted by the IRS, "The absence of some control by the supported organization will be fatal to the exemption of the title-holding corporation."[12] Secondly, when a 501(c)(2) organization turns over its income, less expenses, to its parent tax-exempt entity, it must do so at least annually.[13] This is another requirement to be a proper 501(c)(2) organization. Finally, if the parent tax-exempt entity controlling or owning the title holding corporation "cease[s] to qualify for tax-exemption, the holding company would, in turn, lose its entitlement to tax exemption on this basis."[14]

CASE STUDY: A CHARTER SCHOOL

During my tenure as a Corporate Attorney at Davis Graham & Stubbs LLP, we represented a large charter school in the Denver metro area that was a 501(c)(3)-public charity. The board of directors and staff of this charter school did an excellent job of generating revenues that exceeded expenses since the school's inception. Thus, its leadership team enabled the school to save a significant amount of money (e.g., net assets) since inception, and they wanted to use those funds toward the purchase of a new school building. After searching for nearly a year, they found an old, unused school building being sold by the local school district. After conducting diligence on this property, the board of directors of this charter school decided to purchase the old, abandoned building for a few million dollars.

This purchase was by far the largest asset that the school had ever acquired. Previously, the school operated out of a less-than-ideal leased facility. They wanted to protect this valuable asset, and accordingly, my colleague from Davis Graham & Stubbs LLP and I told them about the advantages of placing the title to this expensive piece of property into a 501(c)(2) title holding corporation. If, for whatever reason, a claim was brought against the school, such as a slip-and-fall claim after a large snowfall, this asset would likely be protected. The for-profit sector frequently utilizes various corporate entities, including those that are structured in a parent-subsidiary relationship, in order to protect its valuable assets. The nonprofit sector, as demonstrated by the rise in the number of registered 501(c)(2) organizations with the IRS, is starting to do the same with its valuable assets.

For this charter school, we first created a Colorado limited liability company. Then we filed the Form 1024 with the IRS to obtain tax exempt status under Section 501(c)(2) of the Code. To obtain the requisite control and "ownership" over this 501(c)(2), all of the membership interests of that limited liability company were held by the charter school. Since the charter school was exempt from federal income tax under Section 501(c)(3) of the Code as a public charity, the requirement that a title holding corporation

serves another tax-exempt entity was also met.[15] Thus, the corporate structure for this new 501(c)(2) title holding corporation, including the control or
ownership element, met the requirements as outlined by the IRS.

"TITLE HOLDING CORPORATIONS"

Based on my experience, not many professionals working in the nonprofit sector,
or even the board members directing those nonprofits, are aware of 501(c)(2)
title holding corporations. If a nonprofit that's exempt from federal income tax,
such as a 501(c)(3), 501(c)(4), 501(c)(6), or 501(c)(7), has a valuable piece of
property that it desires to protect, then the use of a 501(c)(2) should be considered. The benefits from utilization of a 501(c)(2) entity include: "protect[ing]
the nonprofit from liability, enhanc[ing] the organization's ability to borrow
against property, and simplify[ing] management and accounting."[16] Both the
charter school, which is a 501(c)(3)-public charity, and the sorority's housing
association, which is a 501(c)(7), utilized 501(c)(2) entities to protect the valuable assets that they owned.

For the sorority housing association, property tax exemption under Colorado
law was the initial goal. This objective was achieved, thereby saving this nonprofit approximately $50,000 in property taxes in one year. Moving forward,
this housing association will no longer have to pay property taxes on its property.
A review of the corporate structure for this nonprofit revealed that the control
element for this 501(c)(2) had to be implemented as well, and it was achieved
by giving the 501(c)(7) housing association the power to appoint the board of
directors of the 501(c)(2).[17] By understanding the purpose behind 501(c)(2)
entities, board members and other nonprofit leaders may decide to create a corporate structure that helps protect a nonprofit's property. In the nonprofit sector,
"money equals mission"; thus, it's imperative that these leaders do everything in
their power to protect the valuable assets owned by the nonprofits they direct.

KEY PRINCIPLES

→ Organizations that are exempt from federal income tax under Section 501(c)
   (2) of the Code are known as "title holding corporations."
→ Title holding corporations are "organized for the exclusive purpose of holding
   title to property, collecting income therefrom, and turning over the entire
   amount thereof, less expenses, to an organization which itself is exempt."
→ If a 501(c)(3)-public charity owns an expensive piece of real property, then it
   may elect to have the title to that property held in a 501(c)(2) entity, which
   helps protect that valuable asset.

18

What's a 501(c)(4)?

■ ■ ■

The great thing about getting older is that you don't lose all the other ages you've been.

—Madeleine L'Engle

DR. ETHEL PERCY ANDRUS AND LEONARD DAVIS

Reaching age fifty is certainly a time of reflection and celebration. By then, you've accomplished and experienced so much in life, perhaps graduations, births, marriages, vacations, and professional achievements, to name a few; and you'll likely take this moment to reflect upon what you still want to accomplish in the future. Do you want to ride a bicycle across America or Europe? Now's the time to do it. Do you want to visit Africa for the first time? Now's the time to do it. Do you want to jump out of an airplane and parachute for the first time? Now's the time to do it. Do you want to start a nonprofit? There's no time like the present, and after reading this book, you can surely do it!

Along with this time of reflection, I've been told that a routine walk back from the mailbox will become a memorable event because of an invitation that you'll receive around this time. Walking to your mailbox is normally not a memorable event. However, around age fifty, a certain tax-exempt organization will send you an invitation to become part of this nonprofit's membership base, and that invitation will be delivered directly to your mailbox by the United States Postal Service. Which tax-exempt organization will make a walk to your mailbox around your fiftieth birthday a memorable event? AARP of course. The "American Association of Retired Persons," which is now officially called AARP, was established in 1958 by Dr. Ethel Percy Andrus and Leonard Davis.[1] AARP came out of the National Retired Teachers Association (NRTA), which Dr. Andrus had also established in 1947.[2]

Today, the mission of AARP is "to empower people to choose how they live as they age."[3] As people age, it provides various benefits to its members, such as medical, travel, and entertainment discounts.[4] AARP's vision is "A society in which all people live with dignity and purpose, and fulfill their goals and dreams."[5] To fulfill this mission and achieve its vision, AARP elected to be exempt from federal income tax under Section 501(c)(4) of the Code when it was established in 1958. So, what exactly is a 501(c)(4) organization?

SECTION 501(C)(4)

A 501(c)(4) entity is a "social welfare organization."[6] More specifically, Section 501(c)(4) of the Code notes: "(A) Civic leagues or organizations not organized for profit but operated exclusively for the promotion of social welfare, or local associations of employees, the membership of which is limited to the employees of a designated person or persons in a particular municipality, and the net earnings of which are devoted exclusively to charitable, educational, or recreational purposes. (B) Subparagraph (A) shall not apply to an entity unless no part of the net earnings of such entity inures to the benefit of any private shareholder or individual."[7] Here, we see that Section 501(c)(4) of the Code sets forth three key elements.

First, Section 501(c)(4) of the Code addresses the concept of "social welfare."[8] A social welfare organization must be operated primarily for such exempt purpose.[9] In this context, the IRS has interpreted the phrase "social welfare" to mean furthering the "common good and general welfare of those in a community," promoting the "welfare of mankind," and providing "civic betterments and social improvements," among other interpretations.[10] For example, combatting deterioration within a community, such as gentrifying a neighborhood, is a form of "civic betterments and social improvements."[11] As these example interpretations demonstrate, "social welfare" in this context has been interpreted broadly and "has been defined liberally to include virtually any charitable or educational cause that does not violate the law."[12]

Second, Section 501(c)(4) of the Code notes that social welfare organizations must benefit the community as a whole and not just a specific set of individuals.[13] For example, a social welfare organization must bestow at least one "benefit" to a larger community: "if the beneficiary class is too small, as for example, where organizations benefit only their members, it will be difficult, if not impossible, to find the required community benefit."[14] Finally, Section 501(c)(4) of the Code notes that the private inurement doctrine, which prohibits siphoning off a nonprofit's assets to personally benefit any individual or entity, applies to these social welfare organizations, just like it does to 501(c)(3) tax-exempt organizations.[15] Unlike a 501(c)(3) entity, a 501(c)(4) organization may engage in "political campaign" activities, such as endorsing a candidate for public office, so long as such activities are not its primary purpose.[16]

CASE STUDY: AARP

AARP is exempt from federal income tax under Section 501(c)(4) of the Code as a social welfare organization because it meets these three key elements. First, AARP promotes "social welfare" since its programs and activities both further the "common good and general welfare" and provide "civic betterments and social improvements."[17] According to AARP's audited financial statements for the fiscal year ended December 31, 2017, this nonprofit spent approximately $1.2 billion on its programs and activities, including: (1) community engagement, education, and outreach; (2) publications and communications; and (3) member engagement.[18] Thus, AARP's expenditures related to its programs and activities demonstrate that it's primarily engaged in promoting "social welfare," as defined by Section 501(c)(4) of the Code.

Second, the IRS has determined that AARP's programs and activities benefit a sufficiently large enough community as opposed to just a specific set of individuals.[19] Today, AARP has approximately 40 million members, which is certainly a broad enough "beneficiary class" to demonstrate that this nonprofit benefits the "community as a whole."[20] Finally, the IRS has determined that AARP meets the requirements set forth by the private inurement doctrine.[21] While AARP compensates its leadership team, as demonstrated by the Form 990 for the fiscal year ended December 31, 2016, reasonable compensation may be paid to such executives without violating this doctrine.[22] If AARP didn't meet the private inurement doctrine's requirements, then its 501(c)(4) exempt status would be revoked by the IRS. For these reasons, AARP is an excellent example of a 501(c)(4) social welfare organization.

Finally, it should be noted that since approximately 2008, the role that social welfare organizations have played in our elections has skyrocketed.[23] While 501(c)(4) organizations must primarily be engaged in activities that promote "social welfare," such as "civic betterments and social improvements," they can also engage in "political campaign" activities.[24] These political campaign activities, if any, should be secondary to the promotion of "social welfare" to maintain status as a 501(c)(4) entity.[25] A key reason that 501(c)(4) organizations have played a role in our elections is due to the fact that donors to such organizations *not* making "independent expenditures" do not need to be publicly disclosed.[26] This makes 501(c)(4) entities the vehicle of choice for any political donors who do not wish to be disclosed.[27] The practice of donating to 501(c)(4) organizations to remain anonymous is referred to as "dark money."[28] A donor who wishes to remain anonymous can make a contribution to a 501(c)(4) organization not making "independent expenditures" and in turn, that 501(c)(4) entity will likely use those monies to support a Super PAC created to support the choice candidate's campaign.[29]

PROMOTION OF "SOCIAL WELFARE"

Due to the fact that social welfare organizations play an increasing role in our elections and that they promote "social welfare" within our communities, such as increasing the general welfare of people aged fifty and older like AARP, it's important for the leaders of the nonprofit sector to understand the three key elements of a 501(c)(4) organization. First, 501(c)(4)s are primarily engaged in the promotion of social welfare.[30] Second, they must benefit a broad class of the community and not just a few individuals.[31] Finally, they need to adhere to the private inurement doctrine just like 501(c)(3) entities.[32] While some politically-minded leaders may walk the line on whether their utilization of 501(c)(4) entities, including the use of "dark money" in political campaigns, entirely complies with these three key elements, the majority of social welfare organizations, like AARP, benefit our communities. As long as AARP continues to qualify for exemption under Section 501(c)(4) of the Code, its mailings will continue to show up in mailboxes across the country.

KEY PRINCIPLES

→ A 501(c)(4) entity is a "social welfare organization."
→ A social welfare organization must be operated primarily for such exempt purpose.
→ In this context, the IRS has interpreted the phrase "social welfare" to mean furthering the "common good and general welfare of those in a community," promoting the "welfare of mankind," and providing "civic betterments and social improvements," among other interpretations.

19

What's a 501(c)(6)?

■ ■ ■

Change before you're forced to change.

—Roger Goodell

CHAMBERS OF COMMERCE

Do you know that your local chamber of commerce is likely a tax-exempt organization? One of my friends, Ross, served on the board of directors of the Louisville Chamber of Commerce for three years. Now, most of you are likely thinking about Louisville, Kentucky. However, as Lee Corso from ESPN's College GameDay frequently says, "Not so fast my friends!" Instead of Louisville, Kentucky, it's the chamber of commerce for Louisville, Colorado, a town of approximately 19,000 that's adjacent to Boulder, Colorado.[1] *Money Magazine* has ranked this Louisville as the number one "Best Places to Live" *twice*.[2] Since Boulder is starting to resemble Palo Alto, California, with numerous technology companies like Google, CA Technologies, and NetApp moving to town, adjacent Louisville has experienced a nearly decade-long economic boom. Arguably, the last time Louisville experienced this type of popularity, it was primarily occupied by miners who were mining the surrounding foothills.

The goal of the Louisville Chamber of Commerce, like most other chambers of commerce, is to both support and expand the vibrancy of the business sector located in and around Louisville. Specifically, the mission of the Louisville Chamber of Commerce is "To advance the economic, business, cultural and civic welfare of the City of Louisville and its citizens."[3] Businesses that become members of the Louisville Chamber of Commerce receive various benefits, including access to events, sponsorship opportunities, and networking opportunities.[4] My friend Ross, who served on this nonprofit's board of directors, is an entrepreneur and a local business owner. He wanted to give back to the city where he's raising a family and to the business community that has meant a lot to his career. A chamber of commerce, like this local one, is an example of the nonprofit sector supporting the for-profit sector.

In the United States, we have three economic sectors: the for-profit, government, and nonprofit sectors. If you think about three sectors in terms of a Venn diagram, you can imagine that in certain situations, like when a nonprofit chamber of commerce supports and advances a local business community, there are overlapping goals between these three sectors (figure 19.1).

Figure 19.1 Venn Diagram: The Three Sectors

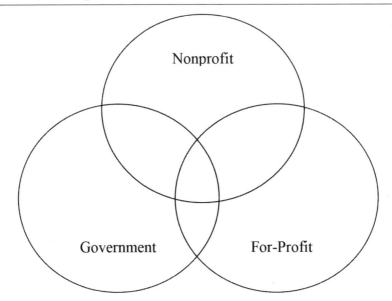

An exemplary program, activity, or initiative, regardless of the sponsoring organization, is one that both meets and advances the objectives of all three sectors. Given this interplay between the three sectors, the IRS allows trade associations, business leagues, and chambers of commerce to be exempt from federal income tax under Section 501(c)(6) of the Code. Thus, what does a 501(c)(6) look like and how does a nonprofit become one?

SECTION 501(C)(6)

Trade associations, business leagues, and chambers of commerce are all exempt from federal income tax under Section 501(c)(6) of the Code.[5] Like a few other 501(c) entities, 501(c)(6) organizations are not required to file a Form 1024 with the IRS since they may "self-declare" their status.[6] Regardless of whether a nonprofit self-declares or files a Form 1024, it must meet the following requirements to be a 501(c)(6), as noted in *The American Automobile Association* case: "(1) it must be an association of persons having a common business interest; (2) its purpose must be to promote that common business interest; (3) it must not be organized for profit; (4) it should not be engaged in a regular business of a kind ordinarily conducted for a profit; (5) its activities should be directed toward the improvement of business conditions of one or more lines of business; and (6) its net earnings, if any, must not inure to the benefit of any" individual.[7] This last requirement is known as the private inurement doctrine, and like 501(c)(3) entities, 501(c)(6) organizations are also subject to it. If an applicant files the Form 1024 and the IRS determines that it meets these qualifications, then it will recognize such applicant's tax-exempt status under Section 501(c)(6) of the Code.[8]

While there is no "deductibility-benefit" for 501(c)(6) entities like there is for a 501(c)(3) organization, the 501(c)(6) entity is itself still exempt from federal income tax. Additionally, trade associations, business leagues, and chambers of commerce are all typically supported by their "members" sharing a common business interest and, in turn, these 501(c)(6) organizations either support, advance, or promote such business interests. More specifically, each "member" likely pays membership dues to the applicable trade association, business league, or chamber of commerce of which they are a member, and the revenues from this key funding source is how these organizations typically raise a substantial amount of their operating budget. With this support from membership dues, 501(c)(6) entities are not as reliant on donations, especially given the fact that donations to 501(c)(6) entities are not tax deductible.

By way of example, members of the Louisville Chamber of Commerce pay membership dues to this 501(c)(6) organization.[9] For the fiscal year ended December 31, 2016, the Louisville Chamber of Commerce raised approximately $92,000 of its $218,000 in total revenues from membership dues, which represents 42 percent of such total revenues. Similarly, the Boulder Chamber of Commerce, which has approximately 1,300 paying members, raised approximately $1 million of its $4 million in total revenues from membership dues for the fiscal year ended December 31, 2016.[10] Accordingly, membership dues for the Boulder Chamber of Commerce constituted approximately 25 percent of its total revenues for this fiscal year. For any nonprofit, raising anywhere between 25 percent and 42 percent of its total revenues from one funding source is significant.

CASE STUDY: NATIONAL FOOTBALL LEAGUE (NFL), AMERICAN DENTAL ASSOCIATION, AND THE BITCOIN FOUNDATION

Both the Louisville and Boulder Chambers of Commerce demonstrate how 501(c)(6) entities are primarily supported by their members, and each share a common business interest. However, there are numerous other examples of trade associations, business leagues, and chambers of commerce across the United States, and you may not have realized that a few of these entities are 501(c)(6) organizations. Most notably, the National Football League (NFL) was once exempt under Section 501(c)(6) of the Code.[11] In 1944, the NFL first obtained tax-exempt status, and in 1966, it was granted status as a 501(c)(6) organization.[12] In fact, Section 501(c)(6) of the Code notes, "or professional football leagues (whether or not administering a pension fund for football players), not organized for profit and no part of the net earnings of which inures to the benefit of any private shareholder or individual."[13]

While the NFL enjoyed tax-exempt status as a 501(c)(6) organization for over seventy years, it voluntarily gave up its exempt status in April 2015.[14] As you can imagine, the NFL was criticized for being a tax-exempt entity, as it had millions of dollars in net income each year but didn't pay federal income tax on such earnings.[15] To be clear, however, the various teams within the NFL are taxable organizations; it's just the league office, known as the "NFL," that was tax-exempt.[16] Because the NFL was exempt under Section 501(c)(6) of the Code, it was required to file Form 990s, which showed the compensation paid to Commissioner Roger Goodell.[17] The NFL's last Form 990 filed with the IRS showed that Commissioner Goodell's compensation "placed him among the ranks of America's most highly paid executives."[18]

Another example of a 501(c)(6) entity is the American Dental Association.[19] The mission of this nonprofit is to "[serve] as the professional association for dentists committed to the public's oral health, ethics, science, and professional advancement, leading a unified profession through initiatives in advocacy, education, research, and the development of standards."[20] Based on its Form 990 for the fiscal year ended December 31, 2016, the American Dental Association had total revenues of approximately $123 million, of which approximately $54 million came from membership dues.[21] These members share a common business interest, as noted by the mission, and the American Dental Association's activities advance at least "one line of business," as required by Section 501(c)(6) of the Code. Similarly, the Bitcoin Foundation is a 501(c)(6) entity, and its mission is to "standardize, protect and promote the use of bitcoin cryptographic money for the benefit of users worldwide."[22] The Bitcoin Foundation supports its members' common business interest and its activities promote this "line of business," thereby passing the "line of business" test.[23]

MEMBERSHIP SUPPORT

You may not have realized that your local chamber of commerce is exempt from federal income tax under Section 501(c)(6) of the Code, or that the NFL was also once a 501(c)(6) organization. The overarching goal of these trade associations, business leagues, and chambers of commerce is to support their members sharing a common business interest that, in turn, typically support such organizations through membership dues. Such membership dues typically constitute a large proportion of the yearly total revenues earned by these organizations. For example, the American Dental Association's membership dues constituted approximately 44 percent of the total revenues earned by this nonprofit corporation during the fiscal year ended December 31, 2016.[24] Similarly, both the Louisville and Boulder Chambers of Commerce raised a significant amount of yearly total revenues from membership dues. Since most of these members are in the for-profit sector, like my friend's business, 501(c)(6) entities are examples of the non-profit sector supporting the for-profit sector. This interplay between the nonprofit and for-profit sectors occurs daily with the programs and activities of 501(c)(6) organizations that support at least one common business interest.

KEY PRINCIPLES

→ Trade associations, business leagues, and chambers of commerce are all exempt from federal income tax under Section 501(c)(6) of the Code.

→ Like a few other 501(c) entities, 501(c)(6) organizations are not required to file a Form 1024 with the Internal Revenue Service (IRS) since they may "self-declare" their status.

→ While there is no "deductibility-benefit" for 501(c)(6) entities like there is for a 501(c)(3) organization, the 501(c)(6) entity is itself still exempt from federal income tax.

20

What's a 501(c)(7)?

■ ■ ■

If it is not possible for me to go somewhere and to be willing to encounter people with different views, then I'm really not doing my job.

—Condoleezza Rice

KYLE FROM OMAHA

During the summer of 2002, right after graduating from college, I had the opportunity to participate as a cyclist in the *Journey of Hope*. The *Journey of Hope* is a 4,000 mile cross-country bicycle ride from the Golden Gate Bridge in San Francisco, California, to the US Capitol Building in Washington, DC. The ride raises funds and awareness for people with disabilities. Each day during this sixty-two-day event, my team and I cycled approximately seventy-five miles— typically from one small American town to the next—showered, ate lunch, and then volunteered with a local nonprofit serving people with disabilities.

The *Journey of Hope* is known for changing lives, which is one of the reasons I was eager to participate in this monumental event. My most memorable day of the ride took place in Omaha, Nebraska. It was around the 4th of July, and we had cycled approximately seventy miles from Lincoln, Nebraska. In Omaha, we volunteered with a local nonprofit serving children with physical and mental disabilities. Such visits were called "friendship visits," and we conducted more than fifty of these visits on our trek across the country. During our friendship visit in Omaha, I met a boy named Kyle. Kyle had severe mental retardation, and his mom dropped him off for this particular friendship visit so that he could hang out with us for the afternoon.

As a cyclist on the *Journey of Hope*, I quickly learned that everyone has abilities, and that we should focus on those abilities instead of any particular disability that a person may have. During my friendship visit with Kyle, we focused on all of his abilities, which included swimming and playing basketball. That afternoon with Kyle forever changed my life. After spending that time with him, I had a simple yet powerful epiphany. I realized that I *get to* do things in life, like ride a bike and serve others. I don't *have to*, but I *get to*. I've never lost that mindset.

The *Journey of Hope* is the flagship program of The Ability Experience, which is a nonprofit exempt from federal income tax as a public charity under Section 501(c)(3) of the Code.[1] Based in Charlotte, North Carolina, The Ability Experience's mission is to "[use] shared experiences to support people with disabilities."[2] It's the philanthropic initiative of Pi Kappa Phi Fraternity, a nonprofit exempt from federal income tax under Section 501(c)(7) of the Code.[3] While approximately one-half of the registered exempt entities with the IRS are exempt under Section 501(c)(3) of the Code, there's a multitude of 501(c)(7) entities in our communities, such as fraternities, sororities, country clubs, homeowners associations, and similar social clubs.[4] In fact, organizations exempt under Section 501(c)(7) of the Code are generally referred to as "social clubs."[5]

As an undergraduate student at the University of Colorado, I was a member of Pi Kappa Phi Fraternity, which is how I learned about and then eventually participated in the *Journey of Hope*. During the summer of 2002, I also met Bruce Rogers, who started the *Journey of Hope* in 1987 when he decided on his own to bike across the country to raise funds and awareness for people with disabilities. Each year since then, Pi Kappa Phi and The Ability Experience have recruited members of the fraternity to participate in the *Journey of Hope*. Participating in this cross-country bike ride was one of the best decisions I've ever made. Like others who have completed this unforgettable experience, my life is forever change for the better because of it.

SECTION 501(C)(7)

For a nonprofit like Pi Kappa Phi to become exempt under Section 501(c)(7) of the Code, it must be primarily organized for one or more exempt purposes.[6] In particular, Section 501(c)(7) of the Code notes that a "social club" must be organized and operated for the "provision of pleasure and recreation to [its] members."[7] Thus, the "social club" exemption allows people who share a common interest to come together and interact with one another.[8] Section 501(c)(7) of the Code affirms this common interest requirement by stating: "Clubs organized for pleasure, recreation, and other nonprofitable purposes, substantially all of the activities of which are for such purposes and no part of the net earnings of which inures to the benefit of any private shareholder."[9]

Accordingly, along with being organized and operated for the "pleasure, recreation, and other nonprofitable purposes" of its members, a nonprofit desiring to be exempt from federal income tax under Section 501(c)(7) of the Code must also meet the following two requirements: (1) substantially all of its activities must further such exempt purposes; and (2) it must adhere to the private inurement doctrine, just like 501(c)(3) entities.[10] Since social clubs primarily benefit their members and *not* the general public, they are typically supported by membership dues or fees, or in the case of homeowners associations, membership assessments.[11] Examples of social clubs include: "athletic clubs, golf clubs (including country clubs), garden clubs, fraternities, sororities, diving clubs, book clubs, and chess clubs," among others.[12]

Additionally, since social clubs primarily benefit their members, they cannot maintain their exempt status under Section 501(c)(7) of the Code if they make their facilities available to the public.[13] Social clubs should have members who commingle, interact, or have fellowship with one another.[14] Because social clubs serve their members, one that has recreational facilities generally may not solicit the general public to use such facilities.[15] If they do, then the IRS may either revoke or deny exemption under Section 501(c)(7) of the Code.[16] For example, "a tennis club was held not to be entitled to tax exemption because it received more than one-half of its income from the conduct of national championship tennis matches" for non-members.[17] Infrequent use of such recreational facilities by the public is permitted, which means that "no more than 15 percent of the gross receipts" may be derived from the general public.[18]

CASE STUDY: AUGUSTA COUNTRY CLUB

One of the best examples of a nonprofit that is exempt under Section 501(c)(7) of the Code that you've likely heard of is The Augusta Country Club Inc. ("Augusta Country Club").[19] The Augusta Country Club, based in Augusta, Georgia, was incorporated as a nonprofit in the state of Georgia in 1899.[20] Each year in the month of April, the Augusta Country Club hosts the Masters Golf Tournament, one of the four major professional golf tournaments, along with the US Open, the PGA Championship, and the British Open. Thousands of golf fans flock to Augusta each April to see one of the world's most well-maintained and beautiful courses, including its iconic 12th hole. Based on the Augusta Country Club's Form 990 for the fiscal year ended December 31, 2016, it had approximately $21 million in net assets.[21]

As noted in this Form 990, the mission of the Augusta Country Club is to "provide its *members* and guests with the highest quality dining, entertainment, and recreational experience."[22] Since the Augusta Country Club is exempt under Section 501(c)(7) of the Code, and it has been able to maintain this status, it meets the following requirements for being a tax-exempt entity under this section of the Code: (1) it's organized and operated primarily for the pleasure and recreation of its members, and it may pursue other related-exempt purposes; (2) substantially all of its activities further such exempt purposes; and (3) it adheres to the private inurement doctrine.[23] Today, the Augusta Country Club has approximately 300 members, and Condoleezza Rice, a fellow graduate of the University of Denver, is one of them.

Most nonprofits that are exempt from federal income taxes, like those that are exempt under Section 501(c)(3) of the Code as public charities, primarily benefit a certain charitable class. This group of beneficiaries should be sufficiently large enough to help justify a nonprofit's public charity status. Thus, these 501(c)(3)-public charities are primarily engaged in promoting charitable causes and serving others. On the other hand, social clubs that are exempt from federal income tax under Section 501(c)(7) of the Code must be organized and operated primarily for the pleasure and recreation of their members.[24] The Augusta Country Club, for example, is organized and operated primarily for the pleasure and recreation of its members, including Condoleezza Rice, Warren Buffett, Bill Gates, and Roger Goodell, among others.[25]

BENEFITTING MEMBERS

Like the Augusta Country Club, Pi Kappa Phi is organized and operated primarily for the pleasure and recreation of its members, a few of whom elect to participate in the *Journey of Hope*. The Augusta Country Club, Pi Kappa Phi, and similar social clubs exempt under Section 501(c)(7) of the Code, like sororities or homeowners associations, pursue activities that further their exempt purposes, but that don't violate the private inurement doctrine. These three requirements must be met for a nonprofit to be exempt under Section 501(c)(7) of the Code, whether that nonprofit "self-declares" such status or files the Form 1024 to be recognized as such. Personally, I'm very thankful that Pi Kappa Phi was established in 1904 in Charleston, South Carolina, because it eventually led to my friendship visit with Kyle and the *get to* mindset I developed from our brief yet life-changing visit. In fact, writing this book is something that I *get to* do, and I hope to make Kyle proud as I continue to carry this mindset throughout my life.

KEY PRINCIPLES

→ Section 501(c)(7) of the Code notes that a "social club" must be organized and operated for the "provision of pleasure and recreation to [its] members."
→ Along with being organized and operated for the "pleasure, recreation, and other nonprofitable purposes" of its members, a nonprofit desiring to be exempt from federal income tax under Section 501(c)(7) of the Code must also meet the following two requirements: (1) substantially all of its activities must further such exempt purposes; and (2) it must adhere to the private inurement doctrine.
→ Since social clubs primarily benefit their members, they cannot maintain their exempt status under Section 501(c)(7) of the Code if they make their facilities available to the public on a frequent basis.

21

What Are the IRS Form 990 and Form 990-PF?

■ ■ ■

I think the currency of leadership is transparency. You've got to be truthful. I don't think you should be vulnerable every day, but there are moments where you've got to share your soul and conscience with people and show them who you are, and not be afraid of it.

—Howard Schultz

A PASSION FOR NONPROFIT LAW

In 2005, I was deciding whether I should attend law school or continue my academic pursuits as a public affairs student by pursuing a PhD. At that time, I had many wonderful mentors, including William J. Hybl, the author of this book's foreword, and his son, Kyle Hybl, who both offered me insightful advice for this pivotal decision. Both of them attended law school at the University of Colorado. Another one of my mentors at the time was my friend Monica, who attended law school at Georgetown University and served as a board member with me for the University of Colorado Alumni Association Board of Directors. At one of our board meetings, which was held on campus at the foot of the majestic flatirons in Boulder, Colorado, Monica gave me great insight into what it's like being a law school student. She also addressed the pros and cons of pursuing this demanding and intellectually stimulating profession.

Because of the insights and advice I received from my mentors, including Bill, Kyle, and Monica, I decided to enroll in law school. In retrospect, this decision was the perfect one for me. Accordingly, I'm forever grateful to my mentors, as they allowed me to find a passion for nonprofit law and to then share that passion with others in hopes that they too will find and pursue their passions for nonprofits. This book, of course, is a manifestation of that passion. At the time Monica shared her advice with me, she served as an in-house attorney at the World Wildlife Fund, which is one of America's largest 501(c)(3)-public charities.[1]

The World Wildlife Fund is based in Washington, DC, and its mission is to "conserve nature and reduce the most pressing threats to the diversity of life on Earth."[2] The World Wildlife Fund accomplishes this mission by focusing on six key program areas: (1) food; (2) climate; (3) fresh water; (4) wildlife; (5) forests; and (6) oceans.[3] Today, this nonprofit has operations in approximately one hundred countries and more than one million members supporting its mission.[4] As of June 30, 2017, the World Wildlife Fund had net assets of approximately $350 million to spend on its mission, programs, and initiatives.[5] Additionally, for the fiscal year ended June 30, 2017, the World Wildlife Fund had revenues of approximately $306 million, and operating expenses of approximately $320 million.[6]

The World Wildlife Fund's operating expenses of approximately $320 million for this particular fiscal year demonstrate that this 501(c)(3)-public charity is fulfilling its mission through its focus on these six distinct areas of conservation. For example, of this $320 million in operating expenses for the fiscal year ended June 30, 2017, the World Wildlife Fund spent approximately $270 million on its programs, including conservation, public education, and international programs, among others.[7] How and on what a tax-exempt organization, whether it's a 501(c)(3)-public charity, a 501(c)(3)-private foundation, or another tax-exempt organization, spends its financial resources to accomplish its mission and fulfill its vision is reflected on either its Form 990 or Form 990-PF. Thus, what are the Form 990 and the Form 990-PF?

FORM 990 AND FORM 990-PF

The Form 990, which must be filed annually with the IRS unless an exception applies, is the publicly available annual information return for entities that are exempt from federal income tax under certain 501(c) sections of the Code, like 501(c)(3)-public charities.[8] The Form 990 was drastically revamped by the IRS in 2007 to focus on various governance issues, among other changes.[9] The Form 990-PF, which should also be filed annually with the IRS, is the publicly available annual information return for 501(c)(3)-private foundations.[10] Organizations that are exempt from federal income tax under Section 501(c)(3) of the Code as public charities should annually file either a Form 990, Form 990-EZ, or Form 990-N, depending on certain financial thresholds.[11]

The version of the Form 990 that an exempt organization must file depends on its gross receipts for a particular year as well as its total assets.[12] If the exempt entity's gross receipts are normally less than $50,000 in a given year, then the Form 990-N is the appropriate annual information return for such organization.[13] The Form 990-N is typically referred to as the "postcard filing," as it's a simple postcard-size return that must be completed and returned online to the

IRS.[14] The Form 990-N is the easiest annual information return to file due to its size. It's due by "the 15th day of the 5th month after the close of the tax year" the tax-exempt entity selected, like December 31.[15]

If the exempt organization's gross receipts are less $200,000 in a given year and its total assets are less than $500,000, then the Form 990-EZ is the appropriate annual return to file.[16] The Form 990-EZ, called the "Short Form Return of Organization Exempt from Federal Income Tax," is only four pages long.[17] If the exempt organization's gross receipts in a given year are equal to or greater than $200,000 and its total assets are equal to or greater than $500,000, then the Form 990 is the appropriate annual return for such organization to file.[18] If an exempt entity is allowed to file a Form 990-EZ in one particular year because it meets the "less than $200,000 in gross receipts" and the "less than $500,000 in total assets" thresholds, then it may do so even if it filed the full Form 990 in previous years.[19]

The Form 990 is twelve pages long and contains twelve sections: (1) summary of the exempt organization, including its mission; (2) a signature block; (3) statement of program service accomplishments; (4) checklist of required schedules; (5) statements regarding other IRS filings and tax compliance; (6) governance, management, and disclosure; (7) compensation of officers, directors, trustees, key employees, highest compensated employees, and independent contractors; (8) statement of revenue; (9) statement of functional expenses; (10) balance sheet; (11) reconciliation of net assets; and (12) financial statements and reporting.[20] Based on these sections, the IRS is most interested in a tax-exempt entity's governance, finances, and programs.

Regarding the "checklist of required schedules" section, there are a few key schedules to the Form 990 and Form 990-EZ that an exempt entity may also have to file, including (1) "Schedule A: Public Charity Status and Public Support," which addresses the public support percentage, if applicable; (2) "Schedule B: Schedule of Contributors," which addresses the key donors to the exempt organization; and (3) "Schedule C: Political Campaign and Lobbying Activities," which addresses whether the exempt organization engaged in either political campaign or lobbying activities.[21] The various schedules to the Form 990 run from A to R, but Schedules A, B, and C are the three key schedules related to 501(c)(3)-public charities.

Finally, the Form 990-PF is the annual information return that must be filed by 501(c)(3)-private foundations, regardless of its gross receipts or total assets.[22] Like the Form 990-N, each of the Form 990, Form 990-EZ, and Form 990-PF are "due on or before the 15th day of the 5th month following the close of the tax-exempt organization's tax year."[23] Because of the Pension Protection Act of 2006, if an exempt organization fails to file the applicable Form 990 for three consecutive years, then its exempt status is automatically revoked by the IRS.[24] In fact, after the passage of the Pension Protection Act of 2006, many exempt organizations have failed to file an applicable Form 990 for at least three consecutive years. Since 2011, approximately 500,000 exempt organizations have lost their exempt status because of this requirement.[25]

Certain tax-exempt entities are not required to file a Form 990, Form 990-EZ, or Form 990-N, including: "(1) churches and other religious organizations, including their integrated auxiliaries and conventions or associations; (2) small organizations, including those that don't normally receive more than $5,000 in gross receipts each year; and (3) governmental units, including affiliates of governmental units."[26] Tax-exempt organizations that are also a part of a "group return," which means that it's affiliated with another tax-exempt organization, don't need to file their own separate annual information return since these "subordinate organizations" may be included in the group return. In this case, "a group return must contain a schedule identifying the subordinate organizations included in the return" and those that are not included.[27]

CASE STUDY: WORLD WILDLIFE FUND

Here, the World Wildlife Fund's Form 990 filed with the IRS for its fiscal year ended June 30, 2017, will be examined. This 501(c)(3)-public charity filed the Form 990 for this fiscal year because its gross receipts and total assets exceeded the thresholds required to file either the Form 990-N or the Form 990-EZ.[28] As noted above, the Form 990 contains twelve different sections, and individuals who review an annual information return for a particular exempt organization are able to learn a lot about such organization based upon a review of these twelve sections.

For example, under Part I of the Form 990, which is entitled "Summary," we're able to see an exempt organization's revenues, expenses, total assets, total liabilities, and net assets for its most recently completed fiscal year.[29] The World Wildlife Fund had net assets of approximately $350 million as of June 30, 2017.[30] Under Part II of the Form 990, entitled "Signature Block," we see that the Chief Financial Officer of the World Wildlife Fund signed this annual information return, and that this nonprofit's external auditors, BDO USA LLP, prepared the Form 990.[31] Under Part III of the Form 990, entitled "Statement of Program Service Accomplishments," we're able to see how much the World Wildlife Fund spent on its key programs and activities.[32] For example, this 501(c)(3)-public charity spent approximately $200 million on its program services during the fiscal year covered by this Form 990.[33] Under Part IV of the Form 990, entitled " Checklist of Required Schedules," we're able to see that the World Wildlife Fund is required to file Schedules A, B, and C, among others.[34] Under Part V, entitled "Statements Regarding

Other IRS and Tax Compliance," we see that the World Wildlife Fund had 605 employees for the calendar year covered by this annual return.[35] Under Parts VI and VII of the Form 990, which deal with governance, management, and compensation, we're able to see the number of directors that led the World Wildlife Fund during the fiscal year covered by this annual return and the compensation related to this nonprofit's management team, including its directors and executive officers.[36]

Indeed, one of the most popular sections of the Form 990 is the section that deals with compensation. If the leaders of a nonprofit want to include additional information related to compensation paid to its management team, then they can state "See Additional Data Table," or something similar, under Part VII of the Form 990.[37] With this strategy, the compensation data related to the exempt entity's leaders will be included as an exhibit to the Form 990. With the passage of the Tax Cuts and Jobs Act of 2017, nonprofit leaders should be aware of the fact that this act imposes a 21 percent excise tax on any compensation that's above $1 million, subject to a few exceptions.[38] Prior to the passage of this act, there was no such threshold amount.

Parts XIII, IX, X, and XI of the Form 990 all deal with an exempt organization's finances, including revenues, expenses, assets, liabilities, and net assets.[39] Part XII of the Form 990 indicates whether the exempt organization utilized cash-basis or accrual-basis accounting, as well as whether the exempt organization engaged an independent auditor to audit its financial statements.[40] For example, the World Wildlife Fund utilized accrual-basis accounting and its financial statements were reviewed by an independent auditor.[41]

PUBLIC ANNUAL REPORTING

A Form 990 will indicate: (1) the type of 501(c) entity; (2) the state of incorporation; (3) the year of formation; (4) total revenues and expenses; (5) total assets and liabilities; (6) net assets; (7) the number of employees; (8) the number of directors; (9) the compensation related to management; (10) whether the exempt organization utilizes cash-basis or accrual-basis accounting; (11) the additional schedules that an exempt organization needs to file; and (12) whether the exempt organization used an independent auditor to review its financial statements.[42] Given the fact that all of this information is publicly available through Guidestar.org, nonprofit leaders should accept and embrace the themes of transparency and accountability. These two themes are also present for 501(c)(3)-private foundations because Form 990-PFs are also publicly available. Given the publicly available nature of both forms, exempt organizations should carefully complete their annual information returns. In many ways, both forms are marketing tools. They convey what the exempt organization is all about and how it hopes to fulfill its mission and achieve its vision based upon its financial resources.

KEY PRINCIPLES

→ The Form 990, which must be filed annually with the IRS unless an exception applies, is the publicly available annual information return for entities that are exempt from federal income tax under certain 501(c) sections of the Code.

→ There are three different versions of the Form 990: (1) Form 990-N; (2) Form 990-EZ; and (3) Form 990.

→ The Form 990-PF is the annual information return that must be filed by 501(c)(3)-private foundations, regardless of its gross receipts or total assets.

22

Who Are Independent Contractors?

■ ■ ■

The secret of my success is that we have gone to exceptional lengths to hire the best people in the world.

—Steve Jobs

SUBJECT MATTER EXPERTS

Have you ever considered what makes contractors "independent"? The leaders of a nonprofit will inevitably need to engage independent contractors at some point. There are a myriad of subject matter experts, such as accountants, lawyers, insurance brokers, and consultants—each of whom are all typically independent contractors—that these leaders typically need to rely upon to help the nonprofit fulfill its mission and achieve its vision. For example, when I served as the General Counsel of the Level 3 Foundation, we engaged an independent auditor to produce this public charity's financial statements. In this case, the board of directors of the Level 3 Foundation relied on an external accountant, who is a subject matter expert on "Generally Accepted Accounting Principles," to produce audited financial statements. While this external accountant performed audit work, he was not an "employee" of the foundation. If he was an employee, then the foundation would have a multitude of responsibilities, such as the need for it to pay payroll taxes.[1]

For this reason, it's important that the leaders of a nonprofit appropriately determine whether someone is an independent contractor or an employee. Such leaders should not label someone as an "independent contractor" when in fact that person should be labeled as an employee due to his or her responsibilities and the manner in which those responsibilities are carried out with the nonprofit. For example, the board of directors of the Level 3 Foundation could have relied solely on external legal counsel rather than having an in-house attorney represent the foundation. If this board of directors decided to only rely upon external legal counsel, then that attorney would also typically be an independent contractor, just like the external accountant that was hired by the foundation. In this scenario, the board of directors of the Level 3 Foundation would not oversee the legal services that this attorney would provide to the foundation. Rather, that attorney would be able to conduct his or her work independently.

When determining whether someone is an independent contractor or an employee, there are various guidelines and principles that employers, including nonprofits, can use to help make this determination.[2] Because of the importance of correctly applying independent contractor status to a person or an entity, such as a law firm or an audit firm, these guidelines, including a two-step analysis developed by the IRS, help us determine whether such contractor is truly independent.

INDEPENDENT CONTRACTORS

Independent contractors must meet two key elements. First, independent contractors are typically engaged in an occupation, trade, business, or profession.[3] Independent contractors typically sell their services or expertise, like legal, consulting, or accounting services, to the general public.[4] Second, independent contractors must be able to carry out their work in a manner that is free from oversight from the nonprofit hiring such independent contractors.[5] If someone or some entity, such as a nonprofit hiring a person, has the ability to both control and direct the outcome of that person's work, as well as the manner in which that work will be conducted, then it's more likely than not that this person is not an independent contractor.[6]

The IRS calls this second element "what will be done" and "how it will be done."[7] If both "what will be done" and "how it will be done" are controlled by someone else, then a person selling their services or expertise is likely not an independent contractor.[8] Whether someone is an independent contractor is based on a "facts and circumstances" test.[9] That is, the facts and circumstances related to a person selling his or her services are examined to determine whether that person is in fact an independent contractor based largely on "how [something] will be done."[10] Typically, "how" something is accomplished is determined by the contractor.[11] When conducting this analysis, the IRS is focused on the "evidence of the degree or control and the degree of independence."[12]

To help with this "facts and circumstances" analysis, both the IRS and applicable state agencies, such as a state's department of labor, examine a series of factors. For example, under Colorado law the following factors are examined, which are typical factors for most other states, and if most of these factors are present, then a person selling his or her services is likely not an independent contractor:

> (1) require the individual to work exclusively for the person for whom the services are performed; except that the individual may choose to work exclusively for the said person for a finite period of time . . . ; (2) establish a quality standard for the individual; except that such person can provide plans and specifications regarding the work but cannot oversee the actual work or instruct the individual how the work will be performed; (3) pay a salary . . . ; (4) terminate the work during the contract period unless the individual violates the terms of the contract or fails to produce a result that meets the specifications of the contract; (5) provide more than minimal training for the individual; (6) provide tools or benefits to the individual . . . ; (7) dictate the time of performance; except that a completion schedule and a range of mutually agreeable work hours may be established; (8) pay the individual personally . . . ; and (9) combine business operations in any way with the individual's business.[13]

Similarly, the US Department of Labor's "economic realities test," which is used by the department to determine whether someone is an independent contractor or an employee, examines the following factors: "(1) whether the worker provides services that are part of the employer's regular business; (2) whether management retains control over the work performed; (3) whether the worker has a permanent or extended relationship with the employer; (4) whether the worker has an investment in the work facilities and equipment; (5) whether the worker can make a profit or incur a loss; and (6) whether the work requires unique skills or judgment."[14] The first three factors weigh in favor of a "finding that the worker is an employee," and the latter three factors "weigh in favor of a finding that the worker is *not* an employee."[15] These factors, whether derived from state or federal law, will be weighed against each other to determine if someone is an independent contractor or an employee. In general, not one factor is dispositive to this analysis. All of these factors are weighed to make an appropriate conclusion.

CASE STUDY: ACCOUNTANTS, LAWYERS, AND CONSULTANTS

For a person who is selling his or her services or expertise to be correctly labeled as an independent contractor, most of the factors noted above should weigh in favor of such a finding. In this scenario, "how [something] will be done" should be determined by the contractor. For example, when my colleague from graduate school called on me to help him create a new nonprofit, he did not have oversight over "how it [would] be done." Rather, he had a clear goal: to create a Colorado nonprofit corporation that would be exempt from federal income tax as a 501(c)(3)-public charity. With that clear direction in mind, I was able to utilize my knowledge of both nonprofit law and finance to accomplish this goal.

First, I created a Colorado nonprofit corporation by drafting and then filing the articles of incorporation with the Colorado Secretary of State. My colleague from graduate school did not dictate how this would be done. Rather, because I'm an attorney possessing subject matter expertise in nonprofit law, he left it to me to draft articles of incorporation that would comply with state law, and which would allow that Colorado nonprofit corporation to then obtain tax-exempt status under Section 501(c)(3) of the Code.

Secondly, my colleague did not dictate how the IRS Form 1023 should be completed. Just like the articles of incorporation, he deferred to me, because of my expertise in nonprofit law, with respect to the responses to the questions set forth in the IRS Form 1023. Thus, in this case, none of the factors weighing in favor of an "employee" status were met. Rather, while I'm an attorney that's engaged in the practice of law, thereby satisfying the first element of the independent contractor analysis, my colleague neither had control nor direction over how my assigned tasks would be completed. Because this second element was missing, I was not his employee.

TWO-STEP ANALYSIS

This example personifies the typical independent contractor engagement. When nonprofit leaders need assistance with a particular objective, whether that objective is to obtain tax-exempt status under Section 501(c) of the Code or to produce audited financial statements, they may need to engage a subject matter expert, such as an attorney, an accountant, or a consultant. It's imperative that these leaders understand the nature of this engagement, such that they can correctly label the relationship as either an "independent contractor" engagement or an "employer-employee" engagement. In general, this two-step inquiry hinges on the second element: whether such contractor is able to carry out his or her work in a manner that is free from oversight. Because this inquiry is a highly fact-specific one, applicable state and federal law address a series of factors that should be weighed to help reveal the true nature of the engagement. Nonprofit leaders should have a general awareness of this two-step analysis and these various factors that are used to determine whether a contractor is indeed "independent."

KEY PRINCIPLES

→ Independent contractors typically meet two key elements.

→ First, independent contractors are generally engaged in an occupation, trade, business, or profession.

→ Second, independent contractors must be able to carry out their work in a manner that is free from oversight from the nonprofit hiring such independent contractors.

23

What Are Low-Profit Limited Liability Companies (L3Cs) and Program-Related Investments (PRIs)?

■ ■ ■

An investment is deemed an investment only through its returns.

—Lamine Pearlheart

SOCIAL CAPITAL

During the summer of 2018, I had the opportunity to attend a roundtable discussion in downtown Denver featuring the Executive Director of Conscious Venture Lab, Jeff Cherry, a former hedge fund manager and entrepreneur.[1] Jeff and the other leaders of Conscious Venture Lab are focused on answering a key question: what would happen if businesses around the world started caring as much about people as they do about profit?[2] Based on this premise, Conscious Venture Lab, which is based in Baltimore, Maryland, strives to "[develop] companies and leaders who embrace capitalism as a powerful catalyst for good in society."[3] Conscious Venture Lab is a business accelerator program that raises funds from various investors, including venture capital firms, institutional investors, and wealthy individuals, among others, and then makes investments in companies that share in its mission.[4] For example, one of its portfolio companies is Hungry Harvest, which aims to "end food waste and eliminate hunger in the [United States]."[5]

Erik Mitisek, the state of Colorado's former Chief Innovation Officer, organized this roundtable discussion during which Jeff shared his vision to develop a cadre of "conscious" companies through this business accelerator program.[6] Attendees at the discussion included representatives from the Colorado Impact Fund, University of Denver, Zayo Group, Leaf Global Fintech, and Frosh Philanthropy Partners, to name a few. Prior to the discussion, Jeff sat down with the then-Governor of Colorado, John Hickenlooper, to discuss the possibility of establishing a Denver chapter of Conscious Venture Lab. To establish a Denver chapter, Conscious Venture Lab needs to raise funds from various investors so it can, in turn, use those financial resources to make investments ranging from $25,000 to $50,000 in "purpose driven startups."[7]

At this meeting, I asked Jeff if he's ever heard of the terms "low-profit limited liability company" and "program-related investments." As a social entrepreneur he had, but not many people fully understand the nuances related to low-profit limited liability companies and program-related investments. A low-profit limited liability company, which is a relatively new form of entity, is also known as an "L3C." For example, if Conscious Venture Lab, which is a for-profit company with a socially beneficial purpose, wants to raise funds from private foundations that are exempt from taxation under Section 501(c)(3) of the Code, then it might want to create an L3C. By establishing an L3C, Conscious Venture Lab, and any similar for-profit company desiring to raise funds from 501(c)(3)-private foundations, will likely increase its chances of securing investments from such foundations. Thus, social entrepreneurs should understand the purpose of both low-profit limited liability companies and program-related investments.

L3Cs AND PROGRAM-RELATED INVESTMENTS

A private foundation that is exempt from taxation under Section 501(c)(3) of the Code must distribute at least 5 percent of its noncharitable assets per year.[8] These 501(c)(3)-private foundations are largely in the business of making "qualifying distributions" that can count toward this 5 percent payout requirement, which is also known as the "minimum investment return."[9] In general, investments in for-profit companies, like Conscious Venture Lab, by 501(c)(3)-private foundations don't count toward this 5 percent payout requirement.[10] In this scenario, a 501(c)(3)-private foundation may make a financial investment as a limited partner (LP) in the new fund that Conscious Venture Lab is establishing for startups in Denver; however, this investment doesn't count toward the foundation's 5 percent payout requirement. Accordingly, if a for-profit company wants to give a 501(c)(3)-private foundation the option to make an investment that counts toward its 5 percent payout requirement, then it's important to understand both low-profit limited liability companies and program-related investments.

A low-profit limited liability company is a relatively new form of entity that takes its form from the tax code provision related to program-related investments, otherwise known as "PRIs."[11] Like nonprofit corporations, L3Cs are creatures of state law. Under applicable state law that permits this form of entity, like the laws of Utah or Michigan, an L3C may be established.[12] Private foundations exempt from federal income tax under Section 501(c)(3) of the

Code may not make "jeopardizing investments."[13] A jeopardizing investment is one that may threaten a 501(c)(3)-private foundation's ability to fulfill its charitable purpose.[14] However, a private foundation's investment in a program-related investment is not considered to be a jeopardizing investment.[15] This is due to the fact that a program-related investment should further the private foundation's charitable purposes.[16]

An investment in a program-related investment counts toward a 501(c)(3)-private foundation's 5 percent payout requirement as long as the PRI's "primary purpose is to accomplish one or more charitable purposes and no significant purpose of which is the production of income or the appreciation of property."[17] Additionally, the applicable Treasury Department regulations note that neither "substantial legislative [nor] political campaign activities" are permitted.[18] A program-related investment may be made in a nonprofit corporation, like a 501(c)(3)-public charity, or in a for-profit corporation.[19] However, if the investment is in a for-profit company, then the private foundation must exercise "expenditure responsibility" for that investment to count as a qualifying distribution.[20] Since L3Cs were created from the tax code provision related to program-related investments, which notes that the PRI's "production of income" is secondary to its pursuit of some charitable purpose, an investment in an L3C may count towards a private foundation's 5 percent distribution requirement.[21]

CASE STUDY: CONSCIOUS VENTURE LAB AND THE FLEXIBLE CAPITAL FUND

Based on the foregoing summaries, if Conscious Venture Lab created a low-profit limited liability company somewhere within its corporate organizational structure, it might be able to secure additional financial investments from 501(c)(3)-private foundations. For example, Conscious Venture Lab could create a wholly-owned subsidiary that's a low-profit limited liability company, which in turn could be used to raise funds from 501(c)(3)-private foundations desiring to make only qualifying distributions. Such L3C should have a primary objective aimed at "accomplishing one or more charitable purposes."[22]

With this scenario, a 501(c)(3)-private foundation would be presented with two options for investing in the mission of Conscious Venture Lab. First, it could invest as a traditional limited partner (LP) in Conscious Venture Lab's latest fund, just like all of the other LP investors. Alternatively, a 501(c)(3)-private foundation could make a potential qualifying distribution, which would count toward that foundation's 5 percent payout requirement, through program-related investment that's structured as a low-profit limited liability company created by Conscious Venture Lab. In this latter case, the 501(c)(3)-private foundation would need to exercise "expenditure responsibility" for such investment to count as a qualifying distribution.

For example, the Flexible Capital Fund, L3C (Flex Fund) is a low-profit limited liability company incorporated under the laws of the state of Vermont.[23] The mission of the Flex Fund is to "[provide] creative financing in the form of near equity capital (subordinated debt and royalty financing) to Vermont's growth-stage companies in sustainable agriculture and food systems, forest products, and clean technology sectors."[24] The Flex Fund was launched in 2011 by the Vermont Sustainable Jobs Fund, which is a 501(c)(3)-public charity devoted to "[accelerating] Vermont's green economy."[25] The Flex Fund is "supported by 38 members committed to helping small and innovative growth-stage companies in the green economy stay and grow in Vermont."[26] The Flex Fund is an excellent example of how an L3C may be utilized, whether by a nonprofit or a for-profit, to accomplish one or more charitable purposes through various investments.

QUALIFYING DISTRIBUTIONS

The Flex Fund demonstrates how both nonprofit corporations and for-profit companies, like Conscious Venture Lab, can utilize program-related investments and low-profit limited liability companies to advance their missions and visions. Private foundations that are exempt from federal income tax under Section 501(c)(3) of the Code need to make qualifying distributions that count toward their 5 percent payout requirement. Since 501(c)(3)-private foundations should not make jeopardizing investments, program-related investments are a viable option because such investments are not deemed to be jeopardizing investments.[27] 501(c)(3)-private foundations may make program-related investments in both 501(c)(3)-public charities and for-profit companies. Since the state statutes creating low-profit limited liability companies typically mirror the tax code provision related to program-related investments, there's a good chance that an investment in a low-profit limited liability company by a 501(c)(3)-private foundation may count as a qualifying distribution.[28] Thus, social entrepreneurs should understand how to utilize both L3Cs and PRIs to help them accomplish their visions, just as the Vermont Sustainable Jobs Fund did by creating the Flex Fund.

KEY PRINCIPLES

→ A low-profit limited liability company (L3C) is a relatively new form of entity that takes its form from the tax code provision related to program-related investments, otherwise known as "PRIs."

→ Like nonprofit corporations, L3Cs are creatures of state law.

→ An investment in a program-related investment counts toward a 501(c)(3)-private foundation's 5 percent payout requirement as long as the PRI's "primary purpose is to accomplish one or more charitable purposes and no significant purpose of which is the production of income or the appreciation of property."

24

What Are Benefit Corporations?

■ ■ ■

To do good, you actually have to do something.

—Yvon Chouinard

"GO WHEN THE WAVES ARE BIG"

The founder of the apparel company Patagonia, Yvon Chouinard, wrote both an autobiography and a business book called *Let My People Go Surfing*.[1] Based on the various philosophies covered in his book, Yvon clearly wants what's best for Patagonia's employees. For example, he states, "If you care about having a company where employees treat work as play and regard themselves as ultimate customers for the products they produce, then you have to be careful [who] you hire, treat them right, and train them to treat other people right."[2] Since these employees share a "passion for something outside [of] themselves," like surfing, Patagonia has always had a flexible work schedule.[3] Yvon mentions that surfers don't surf at a certain time on the same day of the week; rather, they go when the "waves, [the] tide and wind are right."[4] This premise, in turn, led Yvon to create and maintain a flexible work schedule for his employees.

Yvon also asserts that companies have a duty to act responsibly. He states, "At Patagonia the protection and preservation of the natural environment aren't just something we do after hours or when we finish our regular work; they're the reason we are in business."[5] Thus, Yvon wants Patagonia to be an archetype of a company that acts responsibly by "[using] business to inspire and implement solutions to the environmental crisis."[6] As these two examples demonstrate, working flexible hours and creating a responsible company, *Let My People Go Surfing* addresses Yvon's personal and business philosophies. In turn, these philosophies likely led Patagonia to seek status as a benefit corporation.[7] Patagonia was one of the first companies to convert to a benefit corporation in the state of California once the state passed legislation creating a new type of corporation desiring to "pursue a positive impact on society."[8]

While a benefit corporation is still a for-profit corporation, under applicable state law it may pursue goals and objectives other than simply maximizing shareholder value. Typically, maximizing shareholder value is the ultimate objective for most for-profit companies. On the day that Patagonia converted to a benefit corporation under California law, Yvon issued a press release noting: "Patagonia is trying to build a company that could last 100 years. Benefit Corporation legislation creates the legal framework to enable mission-driven companies like Patagonia to stay mission-driven through succession, capital raises, and even changes in ownership, by institutionalizing the values, culture, processes, and high standards put in place by founding entrepreneurs."[9]

A social entrepreneur like Yvon may have faced the following dilemma before the creation of benefit corporations: either (1) create a tax-exempt nonprofit that can pursue charitable purposes but which cannot take on private shareholders who expect a return on their investment, thereby limiting sources of capital; or (2) create a for-profit corporation that can take on private shareholders, but the interests of those shareholders, including maximizing shareholder value, must come above all other goals and objectives of the company.[10] If a social entrepreneur desires to build a company that makes money and pursues a social purpose, without the fear of a shareholder lawsuit alleging that the company is not maximizing shareholder value, then a benefit corporation is a viable option to consider.

BENEFIT CORPORATIONS

A benefit corporation is first and foremost a for-profit enterprise. Thus, one of its key objectives is to make money, including net earnings. Patagonia cannot pursue any of its socially beneficial objectives without its ability to make a sustained profit. Because benefit corporations are for-profit enterprises where shareholders expect some form of financial return on their investment, they cannot qualify for tax-exemption because of the private inurement doctrine that's found in numerous 501(c) sections, like 501(c)(3) of the Code.[11] However, given the fact that numerous states, including California, New York, Hawaii, Virginia, Maryland, Vermont, New Jersey, and Colorado, among others, have enacted legislation creating benefit corporations, these for-profit enterprises can both make money and pursue a social purpose without the fear of a shareholder derivative suit.[12]

In general, the various state statutes related to benefit corporations require these entities to have at least a "general public benefit."[13] These "general public benefits" could be "pursuing ends such as environmental preservation, promotion of health, and promotion of the arts and sciences," among others.[14] In

Colorado, for instance, a "general public benefit" is defined as: "A material, positive impact on society and the environment, taken as a whole, as measured by a third-party standard, from the business and operations of a benefit corporation."[15] The most prominent "third-party standard" is B Lab, a nonprofit based in Berwyn, Pennsylvania.[16] B Lab created the "B Certified" standard. The "B Certified" process is a voluntary process that any entity may pursue, whether that entity is a benefit corporation, limited liability company, corporation, or nonprofit.[17] It's important to note that receiving "B Certified" status is different than being an actual benefit corporation under applicable state law.

CASE STUDY: PATAGONIA

Benefit corporations generally must pursue at least one socially beneficial purpose. Patagonia, in its *Annual Benefit Corporation Report* for the fiscal year ended April 30, 2017, notes that it is pursuing six "specific benefit purpose commitments."[18] These six general public benefits include: "(1) [give] 1% for the Planet®; (2) build the best product with no unnecessary harm; (3) conduct operations causing no unnecessary harm; (4) [share] best practices with other companies; (5) [be] transparent; and (6) [provide] a supportive work environment."[19]

Because of this first objective, the "1% for the planet campaign," Patagonia donates 1 percent of its "annual net revenues to nonprofit charitable organizations that promote environmental conservation and sustainability."[20] Second, the goal of "build[ing] the best product with no unnecessary harm" means, for example, that Patagonia strives to "[design and fabricate] products that . . . are made from materials that can be reused or recycled."[21]

Third, the goal of "conduct[ing] operations causing no unnecessary harm" means that Patagonia will strive to "reduce the environmental footprint and impact of [its] operations in water use, water quality, energy use, greenhouse gas emissions, chemical use, toxicity and waste."[22] Fourth, Patagonia will share its best practices with other companies "when the board of directors determines that doing so may produce a material positive impact on the environment."[23]

Fifth, with respect to transparency, Patagonia will "provide information through [its] website and print catalogs that describes the environmental impact of representative items across [its] different product lines."[24] Finally, Patagonia strives to "provide a supportive work environment and high-quality healthcare" to its employees, which includes on-site child care.[25] These six commitments likely reaffirmed Yvon's decision to seek benefit corporation status for Patagonia.

PUBLIC BENEFITS

As these six distinct "public benefits" demonstrate, a benefit corporation must pursue a purpose beyond simply maximizing shareholder value.[26] Many social entrepreneurs, like Yvon, desire to both "do good" and make money at the same time. With a benefit corporation, the board of directors and management can feel more assured that shareholders will not be able to bring a lawsuit alleging that the corporation is not maximizing shareholder value, as the state statute governing that corporation likely gives them some protection. Partly because of this reason, other for-profit companies, like Kickstarter, Ripple Foods, and Allbirds Inc., have all elected to become benefit corporations.[27] Given the rise of both millennials and xennials in the workforce, who care about making a positive impact in the communities where they live and work, it's likely that this trend of companies desiring to pursue both profits and public benefits will continue.

KEY PRINCIPLES

→ A benefit corporation is first and foremost a for-profit enterprise.

→ However, these for-profit enterprises can both make money and pursue a social purpose, largely without the fear of a shareholder derivative suit.

→ In general, the various state statutes related to benefit corporations require these entities to have at least a "general public benefit."

25

What Are Articles of Incorporation?

■ ■ ■

In a truly great company profits and cash flow become like blood and water to a healthy body: They are absolutely essential for life but they are not the very point of life.

—Jim Collins

MILLENNIALS

In 2014, Level 3 Communications' (Level 3) Chief Administrative Officer Laurinda Pang and Senior Director of Corporate Social Responsibility Sondra Smith asked me to help the company start a corporate foundation. Prior to attending law school, they knew I had worked at two prominent foundations in the state of Colorado, Boettcher and El Pomar Foundations, and had obtained a master of public administration with an emphasis in nonprofits. My nonprofit background had adequately prepared me for this task. At the time, Level 3 was a Fortune 500 company but had not yet formalized its corporate giving program. As millennials ascended through the ranks, both Laurinda and Sondra had the foresight to know that Level 3 needed to formalize its corporate giving program in order to both recruit and retain these millennials.

Research on millennials shows that this generation, in particular, desires to work for "socially-minded" companies.[1] According to a *Forbes* article, citing Phase 1 of the *Millennial Impact Report*, "Millennials are becoming even more engaged in philanthropic causes in 2017 than they were in late 2016."[2] Some of the most successful companies in the United States, including Wells Fargo, Google, and Salesforce, have formal corporate giving or corporate social responsibility programs.[3] Over the past decade, there's been a strong movement for companies to not only have a profit-motivation, but also a socially-driven purpose.[4] The creation of low-profit limited liability companies (L3Cs), benefit corporations, and B-Lab's "Certified B Corporation" process for nonprofits and for-profits, all reflect this movement towards a dual bottom line: money and mission.[5] Certain companies, like Level 3, desire to maximize shareholder value while improving the communities in which they operate.

Since I was tasked with the important job of creating a corporate foundation for Level 3, I reviewed the corporate giving programs at other Fortune 500 companies, including Wells Fargo and Salesforce. Based on this review of best practices in the field of corporate philanthropy, Laurinda, Sondra, and I decided to create a new Colorado nonprofit corporation, called the "Level 3 Foundation, Inc." This new foundation aimed to "give back to the communities in which Level 3 and its affiliates have operations."[6] So, just how did Laurinda, Sondra, and I start this new corporate foundation? We started by filing articles of incorporation.

ARTICLES OF INCORPORATION

From a legal perspective, filing either articles of incorporation or a certificate of incorporation in a particular state kick-starts the legal entity known as a nonprofit corporation.[7] All entities, including corporations, limited liability companies, limited liability partnerships, L3Cs, and benefit corporations, to name a few, are created by filing a document with a certain state agency or department. For example, to create a nonprofit corporation in the state of Oregon, articles of incorporation must be filed with the Oregon Secretary of State and a filing fee must also be paid to that department.[8] In most states, the filing fee to create a nonprofit is nominal. This nominal fee is likely due to the fact that it's in each state's best interest to promote a culture of service, volunteerism, and philanthropy in that state.

The rules outlining how a nonprofit corporation is created in a particular state typically flow from a state's nonprofit corporation act or statute. For instance, in Colorado the relevant act is called the "Colorado Revised Nonprofit Corporation Act."[9] This act outlines the process for creating a Colorado nonprofit corporation.[10] This act also dictates what must be included in the articles of incorporation.[11] These mandatory provisions may include, for example, the name of the incorporator of the nonprofit, whether the nonprofit has "members," the principal office address of the nonprofit, the registered agent of the nonprofit, and what happens to the net assets of the nonprofit if and when it dissolves.[12] This last requirement is known as the "dissolution provision," which is an issue that must be addressed by an applicant in its IRS Form 1023 application when that applicant is seeking tax-exempt status as a 501(c)(3) entity.[13]

While the relevant nonprofit act or statute under applicable state law specifies what must be included in a nonprofit's articles of incorporation, like the examples mentioned above, there are also optional provisions that may be included, such as an indemnification provision.[14] An indemnification provision is a contractual right that a director or an officer of a nonprofit corporation may have because of the nonprofit's articles of incorporation. In sum, this indemnity right notes that the legal entity, which is the nonprofit corporation itself, may "stand in the shoes" of that director or officer for certain issues, thereby holding that director or officer harmless for certain alleged claims.[15] Additionally, a nonprofit's articles of incorporation may include the names of the nonprofit's initial directors.[16] After filing articles of incorporation, the legal entity known as the nonprofit corporation has been created.

CASE STUDY: THE MILLENNIAL WORKFORCE AND A CORPORATE FOUNDATION

When Laurinda and Sondra came to me with the idea of formalizing the company's giving program, I knew that establishing a nonprofit corporation would be the first step. To create the legal entity known as the "Level 3 Foundation, Inc.," I drafted articles of incorporation for a Colorado nonprofit corporation. Those articles of incorporation contained all of the required provisions pursuant to the Colorado Revised Nonprofit Corporation Act, including whether the foundation would have "members," the principal office address, the registered agent, and the "dissolution provision."[17] In addition, the articles of incorporation for this foundation contained many optional provisions, including the initial directors' names, an indemnification provision, and what's known amongst nonprofit lawyers as the "501(c)(3) limitation."

When drafting articles of incorporation for a 501(c)(3) entity, such as the Level 3 Foundation, Inc., it's important to include the "501(c)(3) limitation" in the articles of incorporation.[18] Under applicable state law, nonprofit corporations can typically undertake various activities that are beyond the scope of the activities that may be pursued by 501(c)(3) organizations. Thus, these broader powers must be limited by a reference to Section 501(c)(3) of the Code. For instance, state law may not prohibit a nonprofit corporation from engaging in "political campaign" activities (e.g., endorsing or opposing a candidate for public office). However, Section 501(c)(3) of the Code explicitly prohibits such political campaign activities.

Accordingly, well-drafted articles of incorporation for a nonprofit corporation seeking to be a 501(c)(3) organization should state that the corporation is allowed to pursue "any lawful activity as permitted under applicable state law *and* Section 501(c)(3) of the Code."[19] This latter provision is known as the "501(c)(3) limitation." Without it, leaders of a nonprofit corporation desiring for that entity to be exempt under Section 501(c)(3) of the Code may not be able to obtain such status.[20] This is a detailed drafting point that many practitioners in the nonprofit field may miss; thus, a nonprofit's articles of incorporation should "expressly limit the organization's purpose to those described" in Section 501(c)(3) of the Code.[21]

For the Level 3 Foundation, Inc., I included the "501(c)(3) limitation" in the articles of incorporation. Subsequently, we were able to successfully obtain exempt status under Section 501(c)(3) of the Code, in part because the articles of incorporation contained the requisite provisions. After filing the articles of incorporation with the Colorado Secretary of State, the legal entity known as the Level 3 Foundation, Inc. was created. Just like every other nonprofit corporation, filing the articles of incorporation kick-started the foundation's formal existence. Since inception, the board of directors of the Level 3 Foundation has been able to both raise and grant monies to various charitable organizations where Level 3 and its affiliates have operations. This socially-minded aspect of Level 3 surely made its millennial employees proud.

NONPROFIT CORPORATIONS

Every semester, I teach numerous students who are interested in pursuing careers in the nonprofit sector, whether as a lawyer, fundraiser, program director, or executive. When they begin my course, it's clear to me they often confuse the differences between articles of incorporation, bylaws, nonprofit corporations, and tax-exempt entities. To help address this confusion, I clarify that nonprofit corporations are created by someone filing articles of incorporation, or what some states call a certificate of incorporation. That person or group of individuals, known as the incorporators, must take action with a state agency or department to create a nonprofit corporation. Hopefully those leaders include some of the key provisions in the nonprofit's articles of incorporation, such as the "501(c)(3) limitation" or an indemnification provision. After explaining this process to my students, they begin to understand that articles of incorporation and nonprofit corporations go hand in hand. You can't have one without the other.

KEY PRINCIPLES

→ From a legal perspective, filing either articles of incorporation or a certificate of incorporation in a particular state kick-starts the legal entity known as a nonprofit corporation.

→ All entities, including corporations, limited liability companies, limited liability partnerships, L3Cs, and benefit corporations, to name a few, are created by filing a document with a certain state agency or department.

→ In most states, the filing fee to create a nonprofit is nominal.

26

Why Is a Board of Directors Legally Responsible for a Nonprofit's Finances?

■ ■ ■

Education, especially business education will only give you tools. What you do with these tools is all that matters. Life and business isn't paint by numbers. You have to think for yourself. You have to invent yourself. You have an inferred fiduciary mandate to yourself.

—Gene Simmons

PARENT-TEACHER ASSOCIATION (PTA)

If you serve as a board member for a nonprofit corporation or desire to serve as a board member in the future, you should be aware that this leadership position comes with certain fiduciary—including fiscal—responsibilities. By stepping into a board member position, which is typically an important, prestigious, and personally fulfilling role, you have entered into a realm that's primarily governed by state law. Since board members help nonprofits fulfill their missions and achieve their visions, it's critically important that you understand these legally imposed responsibilities. The sooner you learn about and understand these fiduciary duties, the better prepared and effective you'll be as a board member.

For example, let's presume you've just been elected to the board of directors of the parent-teacher association (PTA) for your neighborhood elementary school. You're very enthusiastic about this new leadership position because you get to help the school with various initiatives, including new supplies and equipment that will benefit the teachers and students. You're also eager to impress your fellow board members. At your first PTA board meeting, you learn that the PTA is a nonprofit corporation that's also been classified as a 501(c)(3)-public charity by the IRS. Like many nonprofit board meetings, one of the first agenda items at this meeting is to review the PTA's audited financial statements.

The PTA's objectives, which include procuring new computers, books, gym equipment, and musical instruments for the benefit of the school's teachers and students, are all linked to this nonprofit's financial resources. Accordingly, the board's treasurer distributes the PTA's audited financial statements to you and to every other board member in attendance at the meeting. After spending a few minutes reviewing the audited financial statements, the PTA president initiates a conversation about this topic by looking directly at you and asking, "Based on your review of our financial statements, what do you think about our financial situation?"

There is actually a legal rationale for asking this question. Each board member of a nonprofit corporation, like the board members of the PTA, must adhere to certain fiduciary duties. These fiduciary duties are imposed by state law, and one of the responsibilities that flows from these duties is the board's role in overseeing a nonprofit's finances. Thus, nonprofit leaders should understand the three key fiduciary duties, and in turn, the importance of their fiscal oversight role.

DUTIES OF CARE, LOYALTY, AND OBEDIENCE

A nonprofit's board of directors, just like the board of directors for the PTA, should exercise fiscal oversight over that nonprofit's finances because of its three fiduciary duties. State law imposes certain fiduciary duties on a nonprofit's board of directors as soon as the nonprofit corporation is created. Typically, a nonprofit is created, which is also known as "being incorporated," as soon as an individual files articles of incorporation under applicable state law. At the moment of incorporation, the following fiduciary duties are imposed on a nonprofit board member under most state laws: (1) duty of care; (2) duty of loyalty; and (3) duty of obedience.[1]

First, the duty of care requires that a nonprofit board member act in good faith and as a reasonable person would under the same or similar circumstances.[2] When assessing whether a board member adhered to the duty of care, courts will apply a standard known as the business judgment rule.[3] So long as a board member of a nonprofit: (1) assesses all available and pertinent information when making a decision; (2) acts in good faith to further the nonprofit's interests; and (3) acts as a reasonable person would under the same or similar circumstances, then such board member will likely meet the business judgment rule under the duty of care.[4]

Second, the duty of loyalty requires a nonprofit board member to act in the nonprofit's best interests.[5] The duty of loyalty is often implicated in a "conflict of interest" situation, where competing interests may arise.[6] For instance, if a board member of a nonprofit has a significant financial interest in a vendor a nonprofit might use to supply certain goods or services to it, this situation could create a potential conflict of interest for that board member. Here, that board member may have conflicting loyalties, as the vendor wants to sell its goods or services for the highest possible price and the nonprofit wants to purchase those goods and services for the lowest possible price. A nonprofit will likely have a conflict of interest policy to address such situations. Thus, the nonprofit's board of directors will adhere to the procedures set forth in such policy to resolve any potential or actual conflicts of interest.

Finally, the duty of obedience requires a board member to adhere to both the nonprofit's mission and to applicable law, including both state and federal law.[7] Given the importance of adhering to a nonprofit's mission, or the reason a non-profit exists, this fiduciary duty is unique to nonprofit corporations.[8] Combined, these three fiduciary duties create the framework for the board's role in over-seeing a nonprofit's finances.

CASE STUDY: A UNIVERSITY ALUMNI ASSOCIATION

Nonprofit leaders must understand the duties of care, loyalty, and obedi-ence because they provide a framework for how to address certain issues that may arise during the course of conducting a nonprofit's business. For example, during my tenure as a board member for the El Pomar Foundation located in Colorado Springs, Colorado, the duty of loyalty was implicated during one of our board meetings. This foundation was established by Julie and Spencer Penrose in 1937 with an initial gift of $21 million, and today, it has assets of approximately $500 million.[9]

During this time, I not only served as a board member for the El Pomar Foundation, but I also served on the board of directors and executive committee for the University of Colorado Alumni Association. At the time, this alumni association primarily operated under the University of Colorado Foundation, Inc., which is a 501(c)(3)-public charity.[10] As a board member for both organizations, I owed the duties of care, loyalty, and obedience to the El Pomar Foundation as well as to the University of Colorado Alumni Association.

When I served on both boards of directors, the University of Colorado began construction on a new building for its highly regarded law school. Before passing away, the former dean of the law school, David Getches, launched a capital campaign to raise funds for this construction project. As part of this effort, the Development Office for the University of Colorado applied for a significant grant from the El Pomar Foundation. When the foundation's staff presented this grant proposal to the board of directors, I knew to recuse myself from the deliberations because of the duty of loyalty that I owed to both organizations.

In this situation, it's arguable whether I could have acted in the best interests of both the El Pomar Foundation and the University of Colorado. To avoid any potential or actual conflict of interest, I removed myself from the deliberations on this grant proposal altogether. The other board members of the El Pomar Foundation, and only such board members, determined if the University of Colorado should be awarded a grant for this project.

FIDUCIARY DUTIES OF THE BOARD

Through a firm comprehension of the duty of care, duty of loyalty, and duty of obedience, a nonprofit board will likely be an engaged board that assesses all pertinent information, acts in the best interests of the nonprofit, avoids conflict of interest transactions, and adheres to the nonprofit's mission when making a decision.[11] If a particular situation arises implicating one of these fiduciary duties, then each board member will be able to effectively address that issue and act in an appropriate manner. Without this knowledge, however, a nonprofit board member may inadvertently breach one of these fiduciary duties. Since the objectives of a nonprofit are intrinsically tied to its finances, just like the PTA's goals, each nonprofit board member must also understand that his or her fiscal oversight role flows directly from these three fiduciary duties.

KEY PRINCIPLES

→ The board's role in overseeing the nonprofit's finances stems directly from its fiduciary duties.

→ The three key fiduciary duties are: (1) duty of care; (2) duty of loyalty; and (3) duty of obedience.

→ The duty of care requires a board member to act (1) in good faith to further the nonprofit's interests; and (2) as a reasonable person would under similar circumstances. The duty of loyalty requires a board member to act in the best interests of the nonprofit. The duty of obedience requires a board member to adhere to the nonprofit's mission and applicable law.

27

What Are a Nonprofit's
Two Bottom Lines?

■ ■ ■

My mission in life is not merely to survive, but to thrive; and to do so with some passion, some compassion, some humor, and some style.

—Maya Angelou

NONPROFIT HOSPITALS

One of the benefits of living in Colorado is our access to the majestic and rugged Rocky Mountains. One weekend, I decided to take our two young kids to Vail, Colorado, so we could enjoy a few summer activities that the Vail area has to offer, including biking, hiking, swimming, and of course ice cream! The first activity on our list was a bike ride. The greater Vail area has some incredible bike paths, and the one between Frisco and Copper Mountain is particularly well-suited for young children. There are no cars, and the path is completely paved and runs along a beautiful mountain stream. I was well on my way to being named "Dad of the Week" with this idea. During one of our snack breaks, however, my son attempted to climb a large rock—as any adventurous five-year-old boy would do—just off the bike path. Unfortunately, a piece of that rock immediately came loose as he attempted to climb, and it fell directly on his little thumb. That rock caused a compound fracture of his small thumb, and blood started to flow out of the tiny little hole in his skin where the bone had pierced through it.

In a matter of seconds, we went from enjoying a snack on a lovely and relaxing bike ride to figuring out how we could get my injured son to the closest emergency room. Thankfully, we weren't too far from the parking lot, so we were able to get my son in the car within minutes of breaking his thumb. From there, we were only minutes away from the Vail Health Center, which is a 501(c)(3)-public charity. Because of my tenure at the Boettcher Foundation, where we awarded the Vail Health Center a capital grant for a construction project, I knew that medical center was one of the best in the area. We quickly drove my son there, where he was rushed off for emergency surgery with a hand trauma doctor from the world-renowned Steadman Clinic. He repaired my son's compound fracture with a screw and two pins.

As a concerned father, the last thing on my mind that particular Saturday was the medical bill related to this accident. In that moment, I just wanted the doctor and his team to help my son. When we did receive that bill in the mail, however, it certainly wasn't cheap, but at the same time it wasn't overly expensive. Vail Health Center, like numerous nonprofits, was able to balance its two bottom lines: mission and money.[1]

TWO BOTTOM LINES

The mission of a nonprofit represents the reason that it exists. Drawing upon the conclusions reached by Simon Sinek in his book, *Start with Why*, a nonprofit's mission is equivalent to its *why*.[2] It conveys to the world why the nonprofit exists in the first place. A nonprofit's mission could be to help alleviate homelessness, educate K–12 students, provide healthcare to underserved communities, or raise money and awareness for people with disabilities, just to name a few examples. A nonprofit's purpose is typically reflected in its mission statement. By way of example, the mission of Imagine Charter School is both clear and compelling: "[T]o positively shape the hearts and minds of our students by providing them with a classical, core knowledge curriculum that is academically rigorous and content rich, a safe environment in which character is modeled and promoted, and a community in which to build trusting relationships with others."[3] A mission statement reflects a nonprofit's "unifying force."[4]

A vision statement, on the other hand, conveys how a nonprofit wants to impact its community, state, nation, or even the world, generally over the next three to five years. That is, which outcomes does the nonprofit want to accomplish during this timeframe? This is detailed in a strategic plan, which outlines how the nonprofit will achieve three to five key objectives throughout this time period.[5] While these goals or objectives may change, a nonprofit's mission generally remains the same and sets the foundation for any vision that the nonprofit may pursue. For example, Imagine Charter School's vision is: "[students] develop a foundation of wisdom [to] be life-long learners, positive role models, and virtuous citizens."[6] Since the mission and vision of a nonprofit convey why it exists, nonprofit leaders must consider both the nonprofit's mission and vision when making decisions for the nonprofit. For this reason, the mission, including its then-current vision, represents one of the nonprofit's bottom lines.

The other bottom line is money.[7] In the nonprofit sector, "money equals mission."[8] The more financial resources a nonprofit has, the more mission it can produce, which in turn help it achieve its vision. Accordingly, nonprofits must balance these two bottom lines.[9] Some nonprofit scholars argue that between the two bottom lines of money and mission, nonprofit leaders should first focus on a nonprofit's finances, or at least pay special attention to such finances.[10] This assertion is based on the premise that "poor financial performance" by a nonprofit can be recognized by outsiders.[11] Financial statements, like balance sheets and income statements, are generally the same between for-profits and nonprofits, which means that outsiders can easily spot financial issues with a nonprofit.[12] In the for-profit sector, there's typically one bottom line: money. With nonprofits, however, both bottom lines must be considered.

CASE STUDY: VAIL HEALTH CENTER

Vail Health Center, like other nonprofits, has a dual bottom line. First, the mission of the Vail Health Center is "[to] provide superior health services with compassion and exceptional outcomes."[13] This is the reason that the Vail Health Center exists. This mission conveys the *why* of the Vail Health Center. Vail Health Center fulfills its mission by focusing on the following values: compassion, integrity, stewardship, teamwork, safety, and excellence.[14] My son and countless other patients and their families have experienced these key objectives first-hand, including the fact that the Vail Health Center has some of the world's best orthopedic surgeons.

Second, the Vail Health Center also has a vision for how it will impact the larger Vail-area. The vision of the Vail Health Center is "[to] continue its development as an independent, nonprofit health care system, providing superior health services aligned to the needs of Eagle County residents and visitors, world-renowned orthopedic services, regional cancer services and emergency services."[15] The Vail Health Center achieves this vision by focusing on three initiatives: (1) "flexibility and responsiveness to patient needs; (2) excellence in specialized care supported by comprehensive research and education; and (3) continuous quality improvement through investment in technology, facilities, and staff development."[16] After a nonprofit has formulated its purpose, it should then set a course for how it can impact its beneficiaries, including the communities where it operates.

Along with its mission and vision, the Vail Health Center must also focus on its finances. Without financial resources, the Vail Health Center would not be able fulfill its mission or vision. According to the Vail Health Center's latest IRS Form 990, it had revenues of approximately $216 million and expenses of approximately $165 million.[17] This means that the Vail Health Center spent approximately $165 million on fulfilling its mission and pursuing its vision. The Vail Health Center also has net assets of approximately

$426 million.[18] These net assets have been accumulated since the Vail Health Center's establishment in 1965, when it was just a small clinic with only one full-time doctor.[19] The board of directors of the Vail Health Center balances the two bottom lines of mission and money, as it provides outstanding healthcare services to residents and visitors of the Eagle County area in an affordable manner.

MONEY AND MISSION

In the for-profit sector, money is generally the only bottom line, but there is a movement for for-profits to focus on other goals besides just making money. That's why benefit corporations and low-profit limited liability companies (L3Cs) are gaining momentum. Many entrepreneurs in the for-profit sector want to "do good" while also making money. In the nonprofit sector, however, there has always been a dual bottom line, which consists of both money and mission. Because financial performance is easily understood by outsiders, such as donors reviewing the financial statements of a particular nonprofit, it must also be a focal point.[20] The world's most compelling mission and vision cannot be fulfilled unless that nonprofit has the appropriate financial resources to accomplish its objectives. Accordingly, there are two bottom lines that the leaders of a nonprofit must focus on. Not only did my son benefit from this dual focus, but countless others have also benefitted from the nonprofit sector.

KEY PRINCIPLES

→ The mission of a nonprofit represents the reason that it exists.
→ The mission, including its then-current vision, represents one of the nonprofit's two bottom lines.
→ The other bottom line is money.

28

What's a Balance Sheet?

■ ■ ■

One of the great responsibilities that I have is to manage my assets wisely, so that they create value.

—Alice Walton

"100 & CHANGE"

One of the largest 501(c)(3)-private foundations in the world is the John D. and Catherine T. MacArthur Foundation (MacArthur Foundation) located in Chicago, Illinois. John and Catherine MacArthur earned most of their fortune through their company, Bankers Life and Casualty Company of Chicago, as well as through their real estate holdings in Florida, New York, and Illinois.[1] On October 18, 1970, the MacArthurs started a private foundation after their attorney, William Kirby, convinced them that a foundation would "allow [their] money to go to good use long after [they] were gone."[2] On January 6, 1978, when John MacArthur died of cancer, the MacArthur Foundation inherited approximately $1 billion from his estate.[3] During that year, the MacArthur Foundation also made its first two grants, totaling $50,000 each, to Amnesty International and the California League of Cities.[4]

Today, the MacArthur Foundation awards approximately $250 million in "qualifying distributions" per year, which represent about 5 percent of this foundation's noncharitable assets.[5] The MacArthur Foundation focuses on the following five priorities, which it calls its "big bets": (1) climate change; (2) criminal justice; (3) impact investments; (4) nuclear challenges; and (5) Nigeria, including "good governance in the country."[6] Additionally, the MacArthur Foundation operates the prestigious MacArthur Fellows Program, which is more commonly known in the nonprofit and academic fields as the "genius grant."[7] Each genius grant recipient currently receives a five-year grant totaling $625,000.[8] In 2017, the MacArthur Foundation launched the *100 & Change* initiative, which is a "competition for a $100 million grant to fund a single proposal that promises real and measurable progress in solving a critical problem of our time."[9] With the *100 & Change* program, the MacArthur Foundation's board of directors wants to make a significant difference in a problem facing our world. This type of impact investing is inspiring, and other private foundations should consider similar impact investing initiatives. The MacArthur Foundation can implement all of these programs and initiatives, including the genius grants and *100 & Change*, because of its strong balance sheet. Philanthropic leaders desiring to improve the world need a strong understanding of balance sheets.

BALANCE SHEET

The balance sheet, which is a component of a nonprofit's audited financial statements, shows what a nonprofit owns and what it owes as of a particular date. This date is typically at the end of the applicable accounting period, such as December 31 or June 30.[10] The balance sheet sets forth a nonprofit's assets, or what it owns; its liabilities, or what it owes; and the difference between the two, which is the nonprofit's net assets.[11] The balance sheet derives its name from the fact that it should always *balance* based on the following accounting formulas:

$$\text{Net Assets} = \text{Total Assets} - \text{Total Liabilities, or}$$
$$\text{Total Assets} = \text{Total Liabilities} + \text{Net Assets}[12]$$

In fact, as reflected by the latter equation, the balance sheet is generally organized from top to bottom in the following manner: total assets, followed by total liabilities, followed by net assets.

On the balance sheet, assets are typically organized in order of descending liquidity. A nonprofit's "liquid" assets refer to cash or other assets that are easily convertible into cash in the short-term.[13] Since cash is the most liquid asset, the top of the balance sheet displays a nonprofit's "cash and cash equivalents" holdings. After cash and cash equivalents, it lists the nonprofit's other current assets. Current assets are those assets that may generally be converted into cash or used over the next twelve months.[14] Along with cash, current assets include: cash equivalents, such as money market funds or short-term certificates of deposit (CDs), accounts receivable, pledges receivable, grants receivable, inventories, and prepaid expenses.[15] After current assets, the balance sheet lists the nonprofit's non-current assets, which are assets that cannot be easily converted into cash. Non-current assets include: investments, such as publicly traded stock; land, buildings, and equipment; and intangible assets, such as intellectual property (e.g., patents, copyrights, or trademarks).[16]

Like assets, liabilities are also organized on the balance sheet as both current and non-current. Current liabilities, which are typically due within the next twelve months, include: accounts payable, accrued expenses, grants payable (e.g., for grantmaking nonprofits, such as private foundations), and deferred revenue.[17] Non-current liabilities, which are generally *not* payable within the next twelve months, include bond liabilities and mortgages or other notes payable (e.g., loans).[18] Finally, a nonprofit's net assets equal the difference between its total assets and total liabilities (Net Assets = Total Assets – Total Liabilities), and this number represents the "net worth" of the nonprofit.[19] If the nonprofit were to cease operations and dissolve, for example, then the dissolution provision in that nonprofit's articles of incorporation likely states that the net assets must be used for some other charitable purpose. With for-profit entities, such as publicly-traded companies, net assets are the equivalent of "stockholders' equity."[20]

CASE STUDY: THE MACARTHUR FOUNDATION

The MacArthur Foundation is able to impact the world through its programs and initiatives because of its assets, both current and non-current. In the nonprofit sector, money equals mission. The more financial resources a nonprofit has, the more mission it can accomplish. The MacArthur Foundation's balance sheet as of December 31, 2017, shows it had net assets of approximately $6.3 billion.[21] This same balance sheet shows it had total assets of approximately $6.9 billion.[22] This growth shows the power of "time value of money," as $1 billion has grown to more than $6.9 billion in forty years. The MacArthur Foundation's assets included cash and cash equivalents of $20.4 million, investments of $6.8 billion, program-related investments of $132 million, and assets held for charitable uses of $28.6 million.[23]

The MacArthur Foundation also had liabilities as of December 31, 2017, but those liabilities were negligible compared to its total assets of approximately $6.9 billion and net assets of approximately $6.3 billion, respectively.[24] The foundation's balance sheet as of December 31, 2017, shows that it had total liabilities of approximately $660 million, which was comprised of grants payable of $534 million, other liabilities of $104 million, and excise and income taxes of $22 million.[25] Given the accounting formula for the balance sheet (Net Assets = Total Assets – Total Liabilities), the foundation's net assets on this date were approximately $6.3 billion.[26] I would take that balance sheet, wouldn't you? These net assets are unrestricted, meaning that the foundation's board of directors has the power to allocate these financial resources to purposes they deem appropriate.[27] If the MacArthur Foundation ceased operations and dissolved, this $6.3 billion in net assets would likely be distributed to another nonprofit, and that nonprofit would use those resources to fulfill its mission and achieve its vision. This scenario is highly unlikely, of course, but it shows the impact of a nonprofit's net assets.

The MacArthur Foundation's key programs, including its genius grants and *100 & Change*, are all made possible by its assets. Accordingly, it has both internal staff members and external investment advisors who are devoted to increasing the value of these assets.[28] With more assets, the

MacArthur Foundation can accomplish more of its mission, which certainly reaffirms the MacArthurs' initial desire of "allowing those funds to go to good use."[29] By reviewing the MacArthur Foundation's balance sheet, we can see the makeup of its assets, liabilities, and net assets, and this same analysis can be conducted for any nonprofit balance sheet.

SNAPSHOT IN TIME

The balance sheet is a snapshot in time. Each balance sheet for a nonprofit contains its assets, liabilities, and net assets as of a particular date, which is typically the end of the applicable accounting period. Based on the following accounting formula, Total Assets = Net Assets + Total Liabilities, the balance sheet should always balance. From top to bottom, it should start with total assets, move to total liabilities, and then conclude with net assets, which is the difference between total assets and total liabilities. Based on these numbers, we can assess the fiscal health of a nonprofit by running various financial ratios, including the current ratio, working capital, debt ratio, equity ratio, and debt-equity ratio. Doing so will reveal a nonprofit's capital structure, or how it acquired its assets, and fiscal health. The MacArthur Foundation, for example, has an outstanding capital structure based on its makeup of assets, liabilities, and net assets. Any nonprofit leader would love to inherit a balance sheet like this one, and to eventually get to that point, it's important to have a firm understanding of the various components of the balance sheet.

KEY PRINCIPLES

→ The balance sheet, which is a component of a nonprofit's audited financial statements, shows what a nonprofit owns and what it owes as of a particular date.

→ The balance sheet derives its name from the fact that it should always *balance* based on the following accounting formula: Net Assets = Total Assets – Total Liabilities.

→ The balance sheet sets forth a nonprofit's assets, or what it owns; its liabilities, or what it owes; and the difference between the two, which is the nonprofit's net assets.

29

What's an Income Statement?

■ ■ ■

American capitalists, enthralled by the doctrines of finance, have put their income statements in service of the balance sheet.

—Clayton Christensen

AUDITED FINANCIAL STATEMENTS

When a nonprofit receives its audited financial statements from its external auditors, those financial statements contain six key sections: (1) the auditor's opinion letter; (2) balance sheet; (3) income statement; (4) statement of functional expenses; (5) statement of cash flows; and (6) the notes section.[1] The two most important financial statements are the balance sheet and the income statement. The balance sheet indicates the nonprofit's assets, liabilities, and net assets as of a particular date.[2] Accordingly, the balance sheet is a "snapshot in time" of what the nonprofit owns, or its assets, and what it owes, or its liabilities, as of that date.[3] The balance sheet also reveals the nonprofit's capital structure by showing how the nonprofit acquired its assets, including whether those assets were acquired through donations, loans, or savings (e.g., net assets). A nonprofit's capital structure generally refers to its blend of debt and net assets.[4]

The income statement, which is the other key financial statement, shows the nonprofit's revenues, expenses, and changes in net assets over a certain period of time. The income statement also further classifies the nonprofit's nets assets by placing such funds into one of the following three classes: (1) unrestricted; (2) temporarily restricted; or (3) permanently restricted.[5] These classifications are needed because a donor may impose a condition on his or her donation to a nonprofit. The income statement is also called the "statement of activities" or the "statement of revenues, expenses, and changes in net assets." On an individual basis, you're already very familiar with the income statement whether you realize it or not. Each month you generally know your revenues, or how much income you bring in from your job(s), and your expenses, or how much you spend on your mortgage or rent, car payment(s), student loan(s), credit card(s), and other expenses that you may have in any given month. As you know from this monthly routine, when your revenues exceed your expenses, you'll generate savings.

Over time, you might accumulate enough savings to acquire another asset, such as a house, car, land, or publicly-traded stocks, among others. Such an exchange is known as an asset exchange transaction because you'll be using one asset, likely cash, to acquire another asset. All of these assets would show up on your personal balance sheet, but the savings you used to acquire these assets would first be reflected on your income statement. Similarly, a nonprofit's savings are reflected in its net assets. That is, when revenues exceed expenses in a given period, this excess is reflected in the nonprofit's net assets. A nonprofit ideally accumulates enough net assets over time to acquire additional assets that help it fulfill its mission and achieve its vision. It's good to have savings or net assets, both for you as an individual and for nonprofits.

INCOME STATEMENT

The income statement shows a nonprofit's revenues, expenses, and changes in net assets over a certain period of time, which is typically one year, every quarter, or every month.[6] For example, when a nonprofit receives its audited financial statements from its external auditors, the income statement is typically for the accounting period beginning on January 1 and ending on December 31.[7] This fiscal year is used by most nonprofits. If the nonprofit is a charter school or private school, then it might use the accounting period commencing on July 1 and ending on June 30. This fiscal year may be more appropriate for a school since it mirrors the school's academic year. Regardless of the accounting period that's chosen, the income statement reflects all revenues and expenses occurring over that period.

Revenues for a nonprofit may include: (1) gifts, contributions, and grants; (2) investment income, such as revenues from dividends or rental income; (3) gross amounts received from fundraising or special events; (4) gross amounts from earned income, including either related or unrelated business activities, or program service revenue; (5) membership dues; or (6) donated services, goods, or facilities.[8] For donated goods and services, such contributed items must be recorded at their "fair [market] value at the time of receipt."[9] Expenses for a nonprofit may include a multitude of items, such as: (1) salaries; (2) benefits; (3) utilities; (4) supplies, including office supplies; (5) equipment; (6) advertising; (7) legal, accounting, and lobbying expenses; (8) insurance; (9) licenses and permits; (10) grants (e.g., if the nonprofit awards grants); (11) payroll taxes; (12) information technology; (13) travel; and (14) depreciation.[10]

Depreciation is an expense that shows up on the income statement, but unlike most of the other expenses, it's a non-cash event.[11] For example, when a nonprofit pays for an employee's salary, it typically uses its asset known as *cash* to pay for that expense. With depreciation, however, a nonprofit doesn't use any of its cash for the expense category on the income statement listed as "depreciation." Rather, a nonprofit has purchased a tangible asset, elected to capitalize that asset, and then depreciates that asset over time.[12] When an asset is capitalized, which generally occurs when it has a useful life greater than one year and its cost is material to the nonprofit, it's placed on the balance sheet as an asset and then depreciated over time on the income statement.[13] The depreciation cost related to that asset during the applicable accounting period shows up on the nonprofit's income statement under the expense line item, "depreciation."

If a nonprofit's revenues exceed its expenses, which may include expenses related to depreciation, then the nonprofit runs a surplus for that given period of time.[14] This surplus or net income is added to the nonprofit's existing net assets, and that number is reflected on the nonprofit's balance sheet.[15] For example, if a nonprofit has a surplus of $500,000 during a certain accounting period, and its existing net asset number is $5 million, then its new net asset number is $5,500,000. This new net asset number of $5,500,000 is reflected on the nonprofit's balance sheet. On the other hand, if a nonprofit's expenses exceed its revenues for a given period of time, then the nonprofit runs a deficit or net loss. If a nonprofit runs a deficit, then that deficit is subtracted from the nonprofit's existing net assets. For example, if the nonprofit has a deficit of $250,000 in a given period, and its existing net asset number is $5 million, then its new asset number is $4,750,000. These examples show how these two financial statements are connected.

CASE STUDY: NATIONAL COUNCIL OF NONPROFITS

It's critically important for the leader of any nonprofit to understand what's in the income statement as well as how the balance sheet is linked to the income statement. In fact, these two issues are both fundamental principles of nonprofit finance. To highlight these two principles, let's review the audited financial statements of the National Council of Nonprofits.[16] The National Council on Nonprofits, headquartered in Washington, DC, was founded in 1990 as a nonprofit corporation that's also tax-exempt as a 501(c)(3)-public charity.[17] The mission of the National Council of Nonprofits is to "advance the vital role, capacity, and voice of charitable nonprofit organizations through state and national networks."[18] The National Council of Nonprofits works with the various state nonprofit associations, such as the state nonprofit associations located in California, Colorado, Minnesota, and Florida, just to name a few.[19]

For the fiscal year ended December 31, 2017, the National Council of Nonprofits had revenues of $1,981,355 and expenses of $1,713,662, which means that it had net income.[20] The fiscal year for this accounting period was between January 1, 2017, and December 31, 2017.[21] Revenues for this accounting period included: (1) contributions; (2) membership dues; (3) fees for services; (4) sponsorships; (5) contributed goods and services; (6) investment earnings; and (7) net assets released from restrictions.[22] Expenses for this accounting period included: (1) public policy/advocacy; (2) network support; (3) communications; (4) lobbying activities; (5) general and administrative services; and (6) fundraising services.[23]

Since revenues were greater than expenses for this period, the National Council of Nonprofits had a surplus of $267,693.[24] That is, if we take the revenue number of $1,981,355 and subtract the expense number of $1,713,662, we get a difference of $267,693.[25] Since the National Council of Nonprofits had net assets of $958,813 at the beginning of this accounting period, the total net assets at the end of this period is now $958,813 plus $267,693, or $1,226,506.[26] Accordingly, the National Council of Nonprofits' balance sheet as of December 31, 2017, shows total net assets of $1,225,506, which reaffirms how these two financial statements are linked.[27] Since the balance sheet is a snapshot in time, how we get from net assets at the beginning of the period to net assets at the end of the period is reflected on the income statement, just as this example from the National Council of Nonprofits shows us.

SURPLUS OR DEFICIT?

The balance sheet and the income statement are the two most important financial statements. The income statement shows a nonprofit's revenues, expenses, and changes in net assets over a certain period of time. If a nonprofit's revenues exceed its expenses, then the nonprofit will run a surplus for that period. On the other hand, if a nonprofit's expenses exceed its revenues, then the nonprofit will run a deficit for that period. Ideally, a nonprofit runs a surplus year over year such that it's adding to its net assets, or simply its savings. If this occurs for a few fiscal years, then the leaders of that nonprofit must determine what to do with those net assets. For example, should they take those net assets and increase employee salaries? Conversely, perhaps the nation is facing an economic downturn and those leaders need to use the nonprofit's net assets to produce more mission-related activities. In this regard, it may make sense for expenses to exceed revenues during this time. In fact, many nonprofit leaders decide to save in good times, or accumulate net assets, as they know that an economic downturn is around the corner and they'll need to use those net assets to continue the good works of the nonprofit.

KEY PRINCIPLES

→ The income statement shows a nonprofit's revenues, expenses, and changes in net assets over a certain period of time, which is typically either one year, every quarter, or every month.

→ If a nonprofit's revenues exceed its expenses, then the nonprofit runs a surplus for that given period of time.

→ If a nonprofit's expenses exceed its revenues, then the nonprofit runs a deficit for that given period of time.

30

How's the Balance Sheet Linked to the Income Statement?

■ ■ ■

We are led by lawyers who do not understand either technology or balance sheets.

—Thomas Friedman

PROGRAM OFFICERS

After completing a two-year leadership development fellowship at the El Pomar Foundation, I transitioned to the Boettcher Foundation to serve as its Grants Program Officer. In this capacity, I helped ensure that the Boettcher Foundation was achieving its "distributable amount" every year.[1] The "distributable amount" is at least 5 percent of a 501(c)(3)-private foundation's "net investment assets."[2] All private foundations, including El Pomar Foundation and the Boettcher Foundation, are required to give away this 5 percent each year to grantees like 501(c)(3)-public charities. As the Grants Program Officer, I processed grants requests, conducted due diligence on potential grantees, and then summarized the grants proposals for the foundation's board. Program officers also frequently make recommendations to the foundation's board as to which grant proposals should receive funding and which ones should not.

During my first week at the Boettcher Foundation, the then–vice president Katie Kramer, who is now the foundation's president and chief executive officer, gave me a stack of grant proposals from various 501(c)(3)-public charities. She asked me to process and summarize the grant requests for the foundation's board and, in doing so, evaluate the fiscal health of each nonprofit applying for funding. The foundation's board members received these summaries in advance of their meetings, which allowed them to have a thorough discussion on each potential grantee, including conversations about their fiscal health. At the time, this was a challenging task for me because I had only completed one semester of graduate school, and a course on how to understand financial statements wasn't in my first semester curriculum!

Given my limited background on this topic, I had to quickly learn how to both read and understand financial statements to be effective in my new role. As I examined this topic, I learned that the link between the balance sheet and the income statement is one of the most crucial concepts of nonprofit finance. In addition to helping evaluate a nonprofit's fiscal health, this link allows us to better understand certain financial concepts we deal with on a daily basis, such as assets, liabilities, revenues, and expenses.

LINKED BY NET ASSETS

Understanding how the balance sheet is linked to the income statement is one of the most important aspects of analyzing a set of nonprofit financial statements. On Wall Street, for example, investment bankers frequently review both the audited and interim financial statements of Facebook, Google, Apple, Snap, Microsoft, Amazon, Netflix, and other large publicly traded companies. They review these financial statements to determine whether assets, liabilities, net assets, revenues, expenses, net income, or net loss, among other items, are increasing or decreasing. This information, which they determine from a review of balance sheets and income statements, helps them make calculated investment decisions.

Just like these investment bankers on Wall Street, nonprofit leaders should also know whether a nonprofit's net assets are increasing or decreasing. To understand these trends, however, it's important to first understand that a balance sheet for a nonprofit has three key components: (1) assets; (2) liabilities; and (3) net assets.[3] The balance sheet, also known as a statement of financial position, derives its name from the fact that it *balances*, which is due to the following accounting equation: Net Assets = Total Assets − Total Liabilities.[4] By rearranging this equation (remember your high school math class), the formula becomes: Total Assets = Total Liabilities + Net Assets. This equation makes intuitive sense, as whatever you have left over (e.g., net assets) is based on what you "own" (e.g., assets) and what you "owe" (e.g., liabilities).[5]

You should also think of the balance sheet as a snapshot in time.[6] For example, it's whatever the nonprofit "owns and owes" as of a particular date.[7] In fact, most balance sheets are prepared as of either December 31 or as of June 30. Because the balance sheet is a "snapshot," reflecting its assets, liabilities, and net assets as of a certain date, we don't have a clear picture of what may cause a nonprofit's net assets to either increase or decrease between two different balance sheets. For example, if I had $100 last December 31, and I now have $50 this December 31, what happened over the course of this year? This is where the income statement comes in.

The income statement, which contains revenues, expenses, and net income, or net loss depending how the nonprofit did that year, tells us what happened between two different balance sheets.[8] If revenues exceed expenses in a given year, then the nonprofit had *net income*, and that net income number is added to the then-existing net asset number (think "net worth") on the previous balance sheet.[9] This resulting number shows up on the subsequent balance sheet, like the following example.

Net Assets Reflected on the Balance Sheet as of December 31, 2017:	Net Income from the Income Statement:	Net Assets Reflected on the Balance Sheet as of December 31, 2018:
$1,000,000	$200,000	$1,200,000

Conversely, if expenses exceed revenues in a given year, then the nonprofit had a *net loss*, and that net loss number is subtracted from the then-existing net asset number on the previous balance sheet.[10] Just like the previous scenario, this resulting number shows up on the subsequent balance sheet. This process explains how the balance sheet is linked to the income statement, and is reflected in the next example.

Net Assets Reflected on the Balance Sheet as of December 31, 2017:	Net Loss from the Income Statement:	Net Assets Reflected on the Balance Sheet as of December 31, 2018:
$1,000,000	($100,000)	$900,000

CASE STUDY: CLINICA TEPEYAC

Explaining how the balance sheet is linked to the income statement is a topic I address every semester in my nonprofit finance course at the University of Colorado School of Public Affairs. Due to the fact that it's one of the most important concepts for nonprofit leaders to understand when studying nonprofit finance, we cover numerous examples in class to highlight the link between these two financial statements. For instance, my graduate students will review a particular nonprofit's Form 990, which is the annual information return for a 501(c)(3)-public charity, because each Form 990 contains both a balance sheet and an income statement for the latest fiscal year (e.g., as of June 30, 2018, or as of December 31, 2018).

The website www.guidestar.org is a public repository for Form 990s, and accessing all of these publicly available tax returns only requires a simple enrollment with Guidestar.[11] After enrolling, you may review Form 990s from various tax-exempt organizations. For example, in my class I show my students a Form 990 for Clinica Tepeyac. Clinica Tepeyac is a healthcare facility for medically underserved patients in the Denver metro area that is also a 501(c)(3)-public charity.[12] Established in 1994, the mission of Clinica Tepeyac is "to provide culturally competent health care and preventive health services for the medically underserved."[13]

Clinica Tepeyac's sample Form 990 that I distribute to my students shows that this nonprofit had net assets of $2,334,957 at December 31, 2014.[14] This same Form 990 also shows that it had net assets of $3,251,138 at December 31, 2015.[15] This is a difference of $916,181 (e.g., $3,251,138 – $2,334,957 = $916,181). Thus, what happened between these two balance sheets to account for this gain of approximately $916,000 in net assets in one year?

The income statement for the fiscal year ending December 31, 2015, which is also in the Form 990 for 2015, shows that this nonprofit had revenues exceeding expenses totaling $916,181.[16] This net income number of $916,181 for the fiscal year ending December 31, 2015, added to the net asset number of $2,334,957 at December 31, 2014, yields a result of $3,251,138, which is the net asset number at December 31, 2015. This 2015 Form 990 for Clinica Tepeyac clearly shows my students how the balance sheet is linked to the income statement.

INCREASE OR DECREASE IN NET ASSETS?

Your understanding of the equation for the balance sheet, which is Net Assets = Total Assets – Total Liabilities, combined with your understanding of the equation for the income statement, which is Net Income (or Net Loss) = Revenues – Expenses, will allow you to review any set of nonprofit financial statements. The income statement will reflect whether a nonprofit is increasing (think "net income") or decreasing (think "net loss") its net assets year over year, just like the income statement for Clinica Tepeyac demonstrated. In turn, a nonprofit's subsequent balance sheet will also reflect this increase or decrease in net assets, as net income *increases* a nonprofit's net assets and a net loss *reduces* a nonprofit's net assets.

In this regard, the balance sheet for a nonprofit is like a holiday card you receive in the mail from your good friend. One year your friend sends you a holiday card showing you the awesome ski vacation she had in Aspen. The next year she sends you a card reflecting the fantastic surfing vacation she took to Maui. You don't know what happened to your friend between those two vacations, but a movie about your friend's life would show you what happened between those two vacations. The income statement is like the movie that shows you what occurred in your friend's life between those two points in time.[17]

Just like the investment bankers on Wall Street, your comprehension of how the balance sheet is linked to the income statement is crucial for understanding a nonprofit's finances. Based on this knowledge, you'll be able to quickly assess the fiscal health of any nonprofit, which is a lesson I had to learn quickly during my first week as a Grants Program Officer.

KEY PRINCIPLES

→ The equation for the balance sheet is: Net Assets = Total Assets – Total Liabilities. Or, Total Assets = Total Liabilities + Net Assets.

→ The balance sheet is a snapshot in time; it represents whatever a nonprofit "owns and owes" as of a particular date.

→ The income statement, which contains revenues, expenses, and net income or net loss, tells us what happened between two different balance sheets.

31

What's the Statement of Cash Flows?

■ ■ ■

If I had to run a company on three measures, those measures would be customer satisfaction, employee satisfaction, and cash flow.

—Jack Welch

MARY GOODWIN, ALICE GOODWIN, AND ELIZABETH HAMMERSLEY

The Boys and Girls Clubs of America (BGC) is a 501(c)(3)-public charity based in Atlanta, Georgia.[1] In 1860, three women who lived in Hartford, Connecticut, Mary Goodwin, Alice Goodwin, and Elizabeth Hammersley, decided that children living in their area deserved a better after-school option than "roaming the streets."[2] Accordingly, these three women created the first club in Hartford, Connecticut, which focused on character development.[3] In 1906, several clubs in the northeast decided to affiliate with one another; thus, the "Federated Boys Clubs in Boston" was established with fifty-three affiliate organizations.[4] For this reason, 1906 is the official establishment year recognized by BGC, and this nonprofit celebrated its 100th year of serving youth throughout the nation in 2006.[5]

Today, the mission of BGC is to "enable all young people, especially those who need us most, to reach their full potential as productive, caring, responsible citizens."[6] BGC's vision is to "provide a world-class club experience that assures success is within reach of every young person who enters our doors, with all members on track to graduate from high school with a plan for the future, demonstrating good character and citizenship, and living a healthy lifestyle."[7] Since the first club in Hartford, Connecticut, the number of clubs has grown to 4,300, which collectively impact more than 4 million youth per year.[8] Among those 4,300 clubs, BGC operates 481 clubs on military bases, 990 clubs in rural areas, and approximately 1,600 school-based clubs.[9] To fulfill its mission and achieve its vision, BGC needs financial resources, including cash, to operate those 4,300 clubs.

Because BGC, like other nonprofits, needs financial resources to achieve its vision, it's important that its Board of Governors as well as its executive leadership team understand how to review a statement of cash flows. Nonprofit leaders should be educated consumers of the information in the statement of cash flows, just as they should be educated consumers of the information in the balance sheet, income statement, and the statement of functional expenses.

STATEMENT OF CASH FLOWS

The statement of cash flows is a financial statement included in a nonprofit's audited financial statements because of the requirements set forth in Generally Accepted Accounting Principles (GAAP).[10] The statement of cash flows for any nonprofit is broken down into three different sections: (1) cash flows from operating activities; (2) cash flows from investing activities; and (3) cash flows from financing activities.[11] The first section, cash flows from operating activities, shows how the nonprofit either received cash or used cash related to its activities, including cash fluctuations related to membership dues, grants, contributions, or accounts payable.[12] The second part, cash flows from investing activities, shows the "purchases and sales of assets, such as investments and property and equipment."[13] The last section, cash flows from financing activities, shows any cash inflows or outflows related to investments, such as repayments on bonds, leases, or similar borrowings.[14]

The income statement, which is another financial statement included in a nonprofit's audited financial statements, is over a certain period of time such as January 1 to December 31 or July 1 to June 30. Similarly, the statement of cash flows is over the same period of time as the income statement, and it shows how a nonprofit both generated cash and used cash during this period.[15] Since most nonprofits utilize accrual-basis accounting, which is required by GAAP, the statement of cash flows utilizes cash-basis accounting to record transactions under the nonprofit's operating, investing, and financing activities.[16] That is, it converts these transactions to cash-basis accounting.[17] By doing this, nonprofit leaders can determine cash inflows and cash outflows for the same period of time as the income statement.

CASE STUDY: BOYS AND GIRLS CLUBS OF AMERICA

BGC issued consolidated financial statements for the fiscal year ended December 31, 2016, for all of its 4,300 clubs located throughout the world.[18] It used KPMG LLP, one of the world's largest accounting firms, as its external auditors for these consolidated financial statements.[19] KPMG LLP, in the notes section of these consolidated financial statements, noted that BGC utilizes the "accrual basis of accounting."[20] This means that "revenue is recognized when earned and expenses are recognized when incurred."[21] For example, if BGC enters into a contract with a vendor for $1 million, this expense is recognized because it's been incurred.

From a cash-basis of accounting perspective, the statement of cash flows helps the leaders of this nonprofit understand how this nonprofit both used and generated its cash during the period between January 1 and December 31, 2016. For example, the balance sheet for BGC as of December 31, 2015, shows that this nonprofit had cash and cash equivalents of $29,508,891 as of this date.[22] As of December 31, 2016, the balance sheet for this nonprofit shows that it had cash and cash equivalents of $15,543,350, representing a decrease of $13,965,541 in its cash and cash equivalents number over this one-year period.[23]

The statement of cash flows for the fiscal year commencing on January 1, 2016, and ending on December 31, 2016, shows us how BGC used approximately $14 million in cash during this period. The statement of cash flows breaks down this cash usage from its operating, investing, and financing activities.[24] First, the statement of cash flows shows us that BGC used $28,744,853 of its cash on operating activities.[25] Operating activities are generally related to the nonprofit's exempt purposes, like operating the various 4,300 clubs of the BGC.

Secondly, the statement of cash flows shows us that BGC generated $14,872,790 in cash from its investing activities during this period.[26] This nonprofit generated $73,231,303 in cash by selling various investments during this timeframe; however, it used $57,960,649 of its cash to purchase new investments and used $397,864 of its cash to purchase property and equipment during this same period.[27] Thus, this nonprofit's investing activities led to a net increase in cash of $14,872,790 during this period.

Proceeds from sales of investments	$73,231,303
Purchase of investments	($57,960,649)
Purchases of property and equipment	($397,864)
Net cash provided by investing activities	$14,872,790

Finally, the statement of cash flows for BGC shows us that it used $93,478 of its cash from its financing activities.[28] By combining this nonprofit's operating, investing, and financing activities, we see that BGC had a net decrease in its cash and cash equivalents of $13,965,541 during this period.

Net cash used in operating activities	($28,744,853)
Net cash provided by investing activities	$14,872,790
Net cash used in financing activities	($93,478)
Net decrease in cash and cash equivalents	($13,965,541)

This net decrease in cash and cash equivalents of $13,965,541, in turn, represents the difference in cash and cash equivalents of $29,508,891 and $15,543,350, respectively, as represented on the two balance sheets for this nonprofit: (1) the balance sheet as of December 31, 2015; and (2) the balance sheet as of December 31, 2016.[29]

EDUCATED CONSUMERS OF FINANCIAL STATEMENTS

This example highlights the importance of understanding how to review a statement of cash flows. External auditors, like KPMG LLP, produce audited financial statements for nonprofits. However, the goal for nonprofit leaders is not to become producers of financial statements like these external auditors, but rather to become educated consumers of such financial statements. These leaders have to make decisions impacting the nonprofit they're leading based upon the information conveyed in these financial statements, including the statement of cash flows. As a nonprofit accumulates cash, those leaders can determine what should be done with that cash. For example, let's presume that BGC doubled its cash holdings, from approximately $15 million to $30 million. If this nonprofit had approximately $30 million of cash on hand, those resources could be used to build more clubs, which would positively impact the communities where such clubs would be located. Building more clubs would certainly make Mary Goodwin, Alice Goodwin, and Elizabeth Hammersley proud.

KEY PRINCIPLES

→ The statement of cash flows for any nonprofit is broken down into three different sections: (1) cash flows from operating activities; (2) cash flows from investing activities; and (3) cash flows from financing activities.

→ The statement of cash flows is over the same period of time as the income statement, and it shows how a nonprofit both generated cash and used cash during this period.

→ Since most nonprofits utilize accrual-basis accounting, which is required by GAAP, the statement of cash flows utilizes cash-basis accounting to record transactions under the nonprofit's operating, investing, and financing activities.

32

How's the Balance Sheet Linked to the Statement of Cash Flows?

■ ■ ■

In the Great Depression, you bought something if you had the cash to buy it.

—S. Truett Cathy

LIQUIDITY

Finance and accounting professionals frequently focus on an entity's liquidity. For example, my good friend Braden is a partner at KPMG LLP, which is one of the world's largest accounting firms. Venture capital and private equity firms pay him to determine, among other things, the liquidity of certain assets from companies they may invest in, such as the next promising start-up. In this sense, "liquidity" has nothing to do with a liquid. As a chemistry minor at the University of Colorado, I was disappointed to first learn this fact! Rather, liquidity in this context simply means the amount of cash and cash equivalents an entity has on-hand, and how quickly that entity's other assets can be turned into cash in the near-term, which is typically over the next year.[1] As we've all heard before, "cash is king," and this frequently repeated phrase is due to cash being the most liquid asset on the balance sheet.

On the balance sheet, assets are organized in order of descending liquidity. If you look at any balance sheet, including one for a nonprofit, you'll see that assets are divided into "current" and "non-current" assets, with current assets located at the top of the balance sheet and non-current assets located right after those current assets. Current assets are those assets that can likely be converted into cash or consumed within the next year.[2] Non-current assets, on the other hand, are any assets that, in general, cannot be converted "into cold cash on short notice."[3] Real estate, for example, is typically a non-current asset because it is not very liquid.[4] When someone decides to sell a house, it might be a few months before that asset is turned into cash. Only then can the cash proceeds from the sale of that property be used for another purpose.

When the 2008 financial crisis hit, "many nonprofits found they had underestimated [their] liquidity needs."[5] In fact, "2008 taught many investors painful lessons about managing liquidity needs," including their cash positions.[6] For any nonprofit seeking to accomplish its mission and fulfill its vision, it's important for the leaders of that nonprofit to understand how the balance sheet is linked to the statement of cash flows. Cash can't be "king" until we first understand how it got to the throne, or in this case, the top of the balance sheet.

BOTTOM LINE OF THE STATEMENT OF CASH FLOWS

The bottom line of the statement of cash flows is the "cash and cash equivalents" number located at the bottom of that financial statement. For example, the statement of cash flows for the Rockefeller Foundation for the fiscal year ended December 31, 2017, might show a "cash and cash equivalents" number of $5 million. This same "cash and cash equivalents" number is found at the top of the balance sheet. Thus, the top of balance sheet for the Rockefeller Foundation as of December 31, 2017, will also show $5 million. This example shows how these two financial statements are connected. The "cash and cash equivalents" number found at the bottom of the statement of cash flows is also located at the top of the balance sheet.

In a given accounting period, like the fiscal year commencing on January 1, 2018, and ending on December 31, 2018, a nonprofit's "cash and cash equivalents" holdings will likely fluctuate. Thus, the statement of cash flows breaks down cash inflows and outflows from a nonprofit's operating, financing, and investing activities. For example, a nonprofit may generate cash from its investing activities. If the Rockefeller Foundation purchased one share of Facebook stock for $50 in November 2018 and then sold that share in December 2018 for $100, the statement of cash flows for that period will show a gain of $50 in cash from that investing activity, assuming we ignore any fees, costs, or expenses related to that sale. The Rockefeller Foundation's statement of cash flows for this transaction would look like this:

Statement of Cash Flows for the Year Ended December 31, 2018

Cash flow from investing activities	
Facebook stock sale proceeds	$50
Total cash flows from investing activities	$50

Additionally, let's assume that the Rockefeller Foundation depreciated one of its computers, an asset it elected to capitalize, during this same period. Let's further assume that the depreciation cost related to this asset during this period totaled $40. The Rockefeller Foundation's statement of cash flows for this transaction would also look like this:

Statement of Cash Flows for the Year Ended December 31, 2018

Cash flow from operating activities	
Depreciation expense	($40)
Total cash flows from operating activities	($40)

Finally, let's assume that the Rockefeller Foundation elected to withdraw $200,000 from a line of credit that it has with a bank. This transaction impacted its financing activities. The Rockefeller Foundation's statement of cash flows for this transaction would look like this:

Statement of Cash Flows for the Year Ended December 31, 2018

Cash flow from financing activities	
Net borrowings from line of credit	$200,000
Total cash flows from financing activities	$200,000

If we put these three transactions together, we're able to see the aggregate impact that the foregoing investing, operating, and financing transactions have on the Rockefeller Foundation's "cash and cash equivalents number" for the period ending December 31, 2018:

Statement of Cash Flows for the Year Ended December 31, 2018

Cash flow from investing activities	
Facebook stock sale proceeds	$50
Total cash flows from investing activities	$50

Cash flow from operating activities	
Depreciation expense	($40)
Total cash flows from operating activities	($40)

Cash flow from financing activities	
Net borrowings from line of credit	$200,000
Total cash flows from financing activities	$200,000

Net increase in cash	$200,010

This "net increase in cash" number, combined with the cash the Rockefeller Foundation had at the beginning of the accounting period, which was $5 million, shows up on its balance sheet dated as of December 31, 2018. In this case, $5,200,010 would show up on the "cash and cash equivalents" line item of this balance sheet dated as of December 31, 2018.

CASE STUDY: DAVID AND LUCILE PACKARD FOUNDATION

The David and Lucile Packard Foundation, based in Los Altos, California, is one of the nation's largest 501(c)(3)-private foundations. David Packard, originally from Pueblo, Colorado, was the co-founder of Hewlett-Packard Company, based in Palo Alto, California.[7] The emergence of Hewlett-Packard set the stage for Silicon Valley as we know it today, as it became one of the "world's leading technology companies," thereby paving the way for other technology companies to be headquartered there.[8] David met his wife Lucile at Stanford University.[9] He was a student in electrical engineering there and Lucile was volunteering at the Stanford Convalescent Home, a facility that treated children diagnosed with tuberculosis.[10]

In 1964, David and Lucile established the David and Lucile Packard Foundation.[11] In 1996, after David's passing, the foundation inherited most of the estate.[12] Approximately twenty years later, as of December 31, 2016, the David and Lucile Packard Foundation had "cash and cash equivalents" of $78,148,000.[13] This cash number appeared on the foundation's balance dated as of December 31, 2016.[14] However, for that fiscal year, did the foundation's cash increase or decrease? The statement of cash flows will show us the answer. For the fiscal year ending December 31, 2016, the foundation's statement of cash flows looked like this:

Statement of Cash Flows for the Year Ended December 31, 2016[15]

Cash flows from operating activities	($327,100,000)
Cash flows from investing activities	$361,568,000
Cash flows from financing activities	$0
Net increase in cash	$34,468,000
Cash at the beginning of the year	$43,680,000
Cash at the end of the year	$78,148,000

In this statement of cash flows, we see that the David and Lucile Packard Foundation experienced a net increase in cash of $34,468,000 for the fiscal year ending December 31, 2016. This cash number, combined with the cash of $43,680,000 that the David and Lucile Packard Foundation had on-hand at the beginning of the year, totals $78,148,000. This new total is the "cash and cash equivalents" number that showed up on the foundation's balance sheet as of December 31, 2016. As this example demonstrates, we can determine how any nonprofit either increased or decreased its "cash and cash equivalents" number just by reviewing its statement of cash flows. As demonstrated by the financial statements for the David and Lucile Packard Foundation, the bottom line of the statement of cash flows, which is the "cash and cash equivalents" number, shows up on the top of the balance sheet. This is how these two financial statements are linked.

CASH ON HAND

As a fellow Coloradoan, I'm extremely proud of what both David and Lucile Packard have been able to accomplish from their success. As of December 16, 2016, the David and Lucile Packard Foundation's assets totaled approximately $7.1 billion.[16] These assets allow the foundation to award approximately $300 million in grants per year to various charitable causes. These grants and other "qualifying distributions" each year create a tremendous impact on the nonprofit sector. In a given fiscal year, the cash and cash equivalents number for a nonprofit, like the David and Lucile Packard Foundation, fluctuates because of its operating, financing, and investing activities. For example, for the fiscal year ended December 31, 2016, this foundation's cash number increased by approximately $34 million.[17] This cash number, combined with the cash that the foundation previously had on hand, appears on its balance sheet. By understanding how the statement of cash flows is linked to the balance sheet, nonprofit leaders can help ensure that the nonprofit they're leading has enough cash on hand to accomplish that nonprofit's vision and fulfill its mission.

KEY PRINCIPLES

→ The bottom line of the statement of cash flows is the "cash and cash equivalents" number located at the bottom of that financial statement.

→ This same "cash and cash equivalents" number is found at the top of the balance sheet.

→ This is how these two statements are linked: the "cash and cash equivalents" number found at the bottom of the statement of cash flows is also located at the top of the balance sheet.

33

What's the Statement of Functional Expenses?

■ ■ ■

Beware of little expenses. A small leak will sink a great ship.

—Benjamin Franklin

REVENUES, EXPENSES, AND MONTHLY BUDGETS

Do you know exactly where your money goes every month? Do you have a monthly budget that helps you keep track of those expenses? If so, does your monthly budget contain line items for a "rainy day" fund, an annual or a quarterly vacation fund, or a "fun money" fund that can be used for any discretionary purpose? Finally, do you periodically think about what could be cut from your monthly budget, like cable television, a music streaming subscription, or perhaps subscriptions to apps you hardly ever use? From a personal finance perspective, it's certainly a best practice to have a monthly budget showing all of your income and expenses. In fact, the two authors of the best-selling book *The Millionaire Next Door*, Thomas Stanley and William Danko, contend that the ability to reign in expenses is a key tactic to generating wealth over the long-term.[1]

In this book, the authors argue that how much you spend is arguably more important than how much you make.[2] For example, a doctor may make a lot of money each year, but since money is an easily renewable resource for that doctor, he or she may spend a lot too, which makes wealth generation more difficult.[3] Similarly, it's important for the leaders of a nonprofit to understand how much the nonprofit they are leading spends, including on its programs and activities. This is what the statement of functional expenses, which is included in a nonprofit's audited financial statements, tells those leaders.

For example, one of nation's largest 501(c)(3)-public charities is St. Jude Children's Research Hospital (St. Jude).[4] You're likely familiar with its commercials, which feature various celebrities like Jennifer Aniston, Sofia Vergara, Michael Strahan, and Jimmy Kimmel, to name a few.[5] St. Jude was established in 1959 in the state of Tennessee.[6] The entertainer Danny Thomas, who was a key visionary behind the nonprofit, helped open the first St. Jude Children's Research Hospital a few years later on February 4, 1962.[7]

Today, the mission of St. Jude is "to advance cures, and means of prevention, for pediatric catastrophic diseases through research and treatment."[8] During one of the St. Jude's Thanks and Giving® Campaigns, which are held every holiday season, actress Jennifer Aniston stated, "St. Jude holds a special place in my heart, and I am honored to lend my voice in raising awareness to support St. Jude's life-saving mission of finding cures and saving children in communities across America and around the world."[9]

Through the Thanks and Giving® Campaign, and similar fundraising activities, St. Jude generates hundreds of millions of dollars each year in contributions and grants.[10] For example, during the fiscal year ended June 30, 2017, the hospital actually raised approximately $1 billion from various donations and contributions.[11] The way this nonprofit spends these monies to accomplish its mission of advancing cures and preventing catastrophic diseases for children is reflected on its statement of functional expenses.

STATEMENT OF FUNCTIONAL EXPENSES

The statement of functional expenses is a financial statement included in a nonprofit's audited financial statements. Both the income statement and the statement of functional expenses show a nonprofit's expenses over the same accounting period, which is typically every year. While the income statement contains a nonprofit's revenues and expenses, the statement of functional expenses only contains its expenses.[12] Additionally, unlike the income statement, the statement of functional expenses categorizes a nonprofit's expenses for a particular fiscal year into different categories.[13] These categories are commonly referred to as either "functions" or "functional areas," which is how the statement of functional expenses derives its name.[14] These functions or categories include, for example, both program services and supporting services.[15]

Program services are those programs, initiatives, and activities that are related to the nonprofit's exempt purpose. For example, with a nonprofit educational institution, like a college or a university, these categories might include: (1) educational programming; (2) public policy; (3) community outreach; or (4) research. As this example demonstrates, these functional areas are all related to the mission of a nonprofit educational institution. Thus, the statement of functional expenses will show the expenses related to these various program services.

Second, the statement of functional expenses also lists the different functional areas related to the nonprofit's supporting services. Supporting services, as the name indicates, support the programs, initiatives, and activities that help the nonprofit fulfill its exempt purpose. For example, such supporting services may include administrative or fundraising expenses.[16] With a nonprofit college or university, for example, the fundraising department supports each of the following programs and activities of this nonprofit: (1) educational programming; (2) public policy; (3) community outreach; and (4) research. Thus, the statement of functional expenses will also show the expenses related to the various supporting services.

Finally, the statement of functional expenses further classifies these expenses by their type, such as salaries, depreciation, or rent.[17] These different types of expenses are shown on the vertical axis of the statement of functional expenses, whereas the expenses related to both program services and supporting services are shown on the horizontal axis of this statement. Table 33.1 provides an example solely for the educational programming functional area.

Table 33.1

	Program Services: Educational Programming Expenses	*Supporting Services:* General and Administrative Expenses	*Supporting Services:* Fundraising Expenses	Total Program and Supporting Services Expenses
Salaries	$250,000	$100,000	$75,000	$425,000
Depreciation	$75,000	$25,000	$15,000	$115,000
Rent	$100,000	$10,000	$5,000	$115,000

As noted by authors Peter Konrad and Alys Novak in their book, *Financial Management for Nonprofits: Keys to Success*, the statement of functional expenses "is of great help in determining how much is spent on the various functions of the [nonprofit] organization."[18] The Form 990, under Part IX, requests a statement of functional expenses, including: (1) total expenses; (2) program services expenses; (3) management/general expenses; and (4) fundraising expenses.[19]

CASE STUDY: ST. JUDE CHILDREN'S RESEARCH HOSPITAL

The statement of functional expenses for St. Jude for the fiscal year ended June 30, 2017, shows its expenses related to both program services and supporting services.[20] The program services for St. Jude include: (1) patient care services; (2) research; and (3) education, training, and community service.[21] In sum, these are the three key programs related to St. Jude's mission of advancing cures and preventing catastrophic diseases for children. For the fiscal year ended June 30, 2017, St. Jude spent approximately $428 million on patient care services; $368 million on research; and $126 million on education, training, and community service.[22] Combined, this 501(c)(3)-public charity spent approximately $922 million during this fiscal year on its key programs, activities, and services.[23]

Second, St. Jude also had expenses related to support services, including both (1) general and administrative expenses and (2) fundraising expenses. In sum, these two support services, commonly referred to as "G&A" expenses and fundraising expenses, help each of the programs, activities, and services operated by St. Jude. For the fiscal year ended June 30, 2017, St. Jude spent approximately $211 million on its "G&A" expenses and approximately $144 million on its fundraising expenses, for a combined total of $355 million.[24] The statement of functional expenses shows that this 501(c)(3)-public charity, between its program services and support services, spent approximately $1.277 billion in total expenses during this fiscal year.[25]

Additionally, the statement of functional expenses also shows how much this nonprofit spent on salaries and benefits, supplies, and professional fees, among other expenses.[26] This total expenses number of $1.277 billion for the fiscal year ended June 30, 2017, also appears on the income statement for St. Jude under "total expenses."[27] Given the fact that the hospital spent nearly $1.277 billion on advancing its mission of helping sick children, it's no wonder so many celebrities get behind the fundraising efforts for this influential nonprofit.

PROGRAM SERVICES AND SUPPORTING SERVICES

Whether you're reviewing your own monthly budget or a nonprofit's budget, it's important to understand how revenues are being spent. Financial resources are limited, so it's key to determine the mix of these various expenses. The statement of functional expenses provides the necessary level of detail with respect to a nonprofit's expenses. It breaks down a nonprofit's expenses into both program services and supporting services. Program services are directly related to the purpose of the nonprofit. Supporting services, which typically include "G&A" expenses and fundraising expenses, benefit each of the programs, activities, and services that the nonprofit operates. Finally, the statement of functional expenses also shows the different types of expenses, such as salaries, depreciation, or rent. By reviewing this financial statement, nonprofit leaders can gain a firm understanding of a nonprofit's various expenses and make well-informed decisions regarding the limited resources of that nonprofit.

KEY PRINCIPLES

→ The statement of functional expenses is a financial statement included in a nonprofit's audited financial statements.

→ Both the income statement and the statement of functional expenses show a nonprofit's expenses over the same accounting period, which is typically every year.

→ Unlike the income statement, the statement of functional expenses categorizes a nonprofit's expenses.

34

How's the Income Statement Linked to the Statement of Functional Expenses?

■ ■ ■

"How did you go bankrupt?" Bill asked. "Two ways," Mike said. "Gradually and then suddenly."

—Ernest Hemingway, *The Sun Also Rises*

NONPROFIT BANKRUPTCIES

Do you know that nonprofits can file for bankruptcy? In February 2009, Stephanie Strom from *The New York Times* wrote an article entitled, "Charities Now Seek Bankruptcy Protection."[1] This article highlighted various nonprofits that have filed for bankruptcy under the United States Bankruptcy Code, including the Baltimore Opera Company located in Baltimore, Maryland; the American Musical Theater located in San Jose, California; and Glass Youth and Family Services located in Los Angeles, California.[2] Diana Aviv, the then-president of the Independent Sector, a 501(c)(3) trade association for the nonprofit sector, stated in the article, "Our expectation is that this [trend] is just the tip of the iceberg."[3] This article further noted that Michael Miller, the then-CEO of the American Musical Theater, took over this nonprofit when it was operating at a $2 million per year deficit.[4] Given this significant yearly deficit, the American Musical Theater elected to file for bankruptcy because "it had loans it could not repay."[5]

A nonprofit's board of directors can hopefully avoid this situation when properly fulfilling their fiduciary duties, including the duties of loyalty, care, and obedience.[6] These duties help ensure that the nonprofit will operate effectively from a financial perspective, and ideally not in a situation where it's running an annual deficit. A nonprofit can only operate with a deficit for so long before having to dissolve, merge, or declare bankruptcy. To prevent this outcome, nonprofit leaders need to understand the connection between the statement of functional expenses and the income statement. By understanding a nonprofit's various expenses, its leaders will be able to put it in a good financial position, such that dissolving, merging, or declaring bankruptcy aren't even considerations.

LINKED BY TOTAL EXPENSES

The statement of functional expenses is linked to the income statement through the "total expenses" number. An income statement notes both the revenues and the expenses of a nonprofit over a certain period of time, typically one year. For example, the American Musical Theater's income statement may have noted revenues of $1 million and expenses of $3 million, thereby leading to the $2 million deficit noted in *The New York Times* article.[7] On the income statement, both revenues and expenses are further broken down into various categories, such as revenues from "gifts, contributions, and grants" or expenses related to "salaries and wages." Like the income statement, the statement of functional expenses also lists the nonprofit's total expenses; however, it may break down those expenses into either two or three key categories, including: (1) program service expenses; (2) management and general expenses; and (3) fundraising expenses.[8] In fact, these are the three expense categories noted on the Form 990 under Part IX.[9]

Conversely, the statement of functional expenses may only have two main expense categories: (1) program services and (2) supporting services. Those categories may be further broken down into program service expenses, management and general expenses, and fundraising expenses. For example, if a nonprofit operates three key programs, then the "program services" category will show the expenses related to those three key programs. Similarly, the "supporting services" category will show the expenses related to (1) management and general expenses and (2) fundraising expenses. While both the income statement and the statement of functional expenses break down expenses into specific categories, the bottom line of the statement of functional expenses is the total expenses number. This total expenses number is also found on the income statement, which is how these two financial statements are linked. Nonprofit leaders should understand this relationship so that they can maintain control over those expenses.

CASE STUDY: INDEPENDENT SECTOR

The Independent Sector is one of the leading trade associations for nonprofit professionals. Its mission is to "lead and catalyze the charitable community [to] advance the common good."[10] Its Form 990 for the fiscal year ended December 31, 2016, shows us the connection between the income statement and the statement of functional expenses.[11] From the first page of the Form 990, we see that it had total expenses of $10,469,858 for this fiscal year.[12] On the statement of functional expenses, which is found under Part IX of the same Form 990, we see that the total expenses also equaled $10,469,858.[13] Accordingly, the bottom line of the statement of functional expenses, which is the total expenses number, also shows up on the income statement. This example demonstrates how these two financial statements are linked.

The statement of functional expenses, however, shows us another level of detail with respect to these expenses that the income statement does not. For example, the statement of functional expenses shows us that of this total approximately $7.5 million was spent on "program service expenses."[14] This statement also shows that of this total approximately $1 million was spent on "fundraising expenses," and approximately $1.9 million was spent on "management and general expenses," giving us an aggregate of $10.4 million in expenses.[15]

If we look at the prior year's Form 990 for the Independent Sector, we're also able to see the connection between the income statement and the statement of functional expenses.[16] For the fiscal year ended December 31, 2015, it had total expenses of $9,483,426.[17] On the statement of functional expenses, the total expenses also totaled $9,483,426.[18] Thus, the income statement is linked to the statement of functional expenses through the total expenses number. This relationship can be seen by reviewing any Form 990 or a set of audited financial statements for a nonprofit, both of which include these two financial statements needed to conduct this analysis.

"ADVANCING THE COMMON GOOD"

As a general rule, we don't want nonprofits to file for bankruptcy. Regardless of its size, each nonprofit has a mission, or a reason for its existence, and hopefully a vision for how it hopes to impact its community, state, nation, or perhaps even the world. For a nonprofit to fulfill its mission and achieve its vision, it must be able to obtain financial resources, whether that's through donations, loans, or earned income. When a nonprofit obtains these financial resources, it can deploy them to implement its programs, services, or activities. For example, the Independent Sector spent approximately $7.5 million in 2016 on program service expenses that "advanc[ed] the common good."[19] Program service expenses demonstrate that a nonprofit is making a difference from its operations. Thus, nonprofit leaders should have a firm understanding of a nonprofit's expenses so that they can make informed decisions about those expenses and ensure that their nonprofit is operating effectively from a financial perspective. In turn, hopefully only a few, if any, nonprofits will ever have to file for bankruptcy.

KEY PRINCIPLES

→ The statement of functional expenses is linked to the income statement through the "total expenses" number.

→ An income statement notes both the revenues and the expenses of a nonprofit over a certain period of time, typically one year.

→ While both the income statement and the statement of functional expenses break down expenses into specific categories, the bottom line of the statement of functional expenses is the "total expenses" number. This total expenses number is also found on the income statement, which is how these two financial statements are linked.

35

What Are Unrestricted, Temporarily Restricted, and Permanently Restricted Funds?

■ ■ ■

A loose horse is any horse sensible enough to get rid of its rider at an early stage and carry on unencumbered.

—Clive James

EARMARKING DONATIONS

Big Brothers Big Sisters of Metropolitan Chicago (BBBS) is an Illinois nonprofit corporation that is exempt from federal income tax under Section 501(c)(3) of the Code as a public charity.[1] The overarching goal of this nonprofit is to provide at-risk youth in the Chicagoland area with one-on-one mentoring so that they can achieve lifelong success.[2] The mission of BBBS is to "provide children facing adversity with strong and enduring, professionally supported one-to-one relationships that change their lives for the better, forever."[3] These one-on-one mentoring programs may occur in schools, including elementary, middle, and high schools; clubs, like various Boys and Girls Clubs; and workplace settings.[4] This nonprofit's mentees have achieved a 100 percent high school graduation rate.[5] Because of its compelling case for support, it receives donations from the government sector, corporations, foundations, and individual donors.[6]

Based on BBBS' audited financial statements for fiscal year ended June 30, 2018, it brought in revenues of $4,273,780, most of which came from corporations ($930,779), foundations ($1,358,556), and individuals ($823,146), among other revenue sources.[7] BBBS also brought in $986,024 in revenues from special events, which was net of any costs incurred by BBBS to put on such events.[8] Now, let's assume that at a fundraising dinner for BBBS, someone moved by both the mission and vision of this nonprofit decides to make a $50,000 donation. However, such donor elects to earmark that donation for the one-on-one mentoring program that occurs at a specific elementary school located near that

151

donor's home. How does BBBS appropriately reflect, or "book," that donation on its financial statements?

Because donors may earmark their donations for specific causes or purposes, nonprofits have to appropriately book such earmarked donations on their financial statements. In addition to purpose conditions, donors may impose time conditions on their donations. For example, a donor may contribute $150,000 to BBBS, but that donation is payable at $50,000 over the next three years. For these reasons, the rules governing nonprofit financial statements address the concepts of "unrestricted, temporarily restricted, and permanently restricted" funds.[9]

UNRESTRICTED, TEMPORARILY RESTRICTED, AND PERMANENTLY RESTRICTED

Understanding the difference between unrestricted, temporarily restricted, and permanently restricted net assets is key for any nonprofit leader. This type of "fund accounting" represents a major difference between nonprofit and for-profit accounting. First, it's important to understand that only a donor has the power to impose either a time or purpose condition on his or her donation.[10] When a donor does so, the nonprofit must account for that purpose or time condition on its financial statements.[11] Those donations, depending on the purpose or the time condition, are either temporarily restricted or permanently restricted funds.[12] For example, in the foregoing hypothetical where the donor contributed to the one-on-one mentoring program at a specific elementary school, such donation would be booked as "temporarily restricted."[13]

In this hypothetical, the donor placed a purpose condition on his or her $50,000 donation. This donation is restricted because it must be used for the one-on-one mentoring program at a specific elementary school. To appropriately reflect that purpose condition on BBBS' financial statements, those funds are booked as "temporarily restricted" funds.[14] If and when BBBS uses those funds for the donor's intended purpose, the income statement for the fiscal year in which those funds were used will show movement from the "temporarily restricted" column to the "unrestricted" column.[15] This movement shows that such funds were used for the purpose identified by that donor, and thus, the nonprofit met the donor-imposed condition.

	Unrestricted	Temporarily Restricted	Permanently Restricted
Net assets released: Satisfaction of condition(s)	$50,000	($50,000)	—

On the other hand, if the donor at that fundraising dinner was so moved by the mission and vision of BBBS that he or she elected to create a permanent endowment for this nonprofit, then that donation would be booked as "permanently restricted."[16] A permanent restriction means that the nonprofit will never be able to fulfill either the time or purpose condition, such that the funds will always be booked as "permanently restricted" funds on its financial statements: "For an asset to be permanently restricted, there needs to be a condition imposed by the donor that can never be met or that simply does not expire with the passage of time."[17]

If a donor neither imposes a time nor a purpose condition on his or her donation, such donation will be booked as "unrestricted."[18] This means that a nonprofit's board of directors may use those funds however they see fit to accomplish the mission and vision of the nonprofit. Thomas McLaughlin in *Streetsmart Financial Basics for Nonprofit Managers* affirms the importance of unrestricted donations by referring to them as follows: "[The] portion of net assets [that are] unencumbered by any restrictions placed by donors and can therefore be used freely by the nonprofit."[19] As a result, nonprofit leaders like to receive unrestricted donations. If the board then subsequently earmarks those unrestricted donations for a specific purpose, those funds are still booked as "unrestricted" funds because only a donor has the power to impose a condition.[20]

CASE STUDY: BIG BROTHERS BIG SISTERS OF METROPOLITAN CHICAGO

The financial statements for BBBS for fiscal year ended June 30, 2018, shows that this nonprofit has unrestricted, temporarily restricted, and permanently restricted net assets.[21] The balance sheet, or statement of financial position, as of June 30, 2018, for BBBS shows that it had net assets of $3,410,909.[22] Of this amount, only $838,473 was unrestricted net assets.[23] The rest of its net assets were temporarily restricted, totaling $2,446,924, and permanently restricted, totaling $125,512.[24]

In fact, most of these temporarily restricted funds were "site-based" restrictions to various schools, just like the hypothetical donor's contribution above.[25] Of the $2,446,924 in temporarily restricted funds as of June 30, 2018, only $117,218 was temporarily restricted due to "time restrictions."[26] This nonprofit also has one permanently restricted endowment fund, which "consists of one permanently restricted fund established to act as an operating reserve fund for the Organization."[27] The notes section to the financial statements states, "As required by generally accepted accounting principles, net assets associated with endowment funds are classified and reported based on the existence or absence of *donor-imposed restrictions*."[28]

In turn, this means that BBBS' board of directors as of June 30, 2018, only has the power to direct $838,473, even though the aggregate net assets for this nonprofit total $3,410,909.[29] The unrestricted net assets totaled

$838,473 as of June 30, 2018.[30] This example shows the significance of a nonprofit receiving unrestricted donations. BBBS has over $3.4 million in net assets, which is equivalent to the "net worth" of the nonprofit; however, all but $838,473 of those funds are tied up in donor imposed conditions.[31]

If BBBS runs into financial trouble, for example, and needs to use some or all of the temporarily restricted or permanently restricted funds, then its board of directors would have to go back to its respective donors and ask them to remove their conditions. If that wasn't possible, then BBBS would have to ask a judge of a court of competent jurisdiction for the power to use those funds for another purpose, under either the *cy pres* doctrine or the doctrine of equitable deviation.[32] For this reason, receiving unrestricted donations is preferable for any nonprofit.

FUND ACCOUNTING

Fund accounting, which shows how a nonprofit's net assets are broken down into either unrestricted, temporarily restricted, or permanently restricted funds, is unique to nonprofits. When a donor elects to impose either a time or a purpose condition, the nonprofit must account for that condition on its financial statements. With fund accounting it's important to remember that only a donor has the power to impose a condition. If you don't do this already, you'll start to analyze the breakdown between unrestricted, temporarily restricted, and permanently restricted funds. A nonprofit might have $10 million in net assets, for example, but the board of directors might only have power over $100,000, as the rest of those funds are either temporarily restricted or permanently restricted. Understanding this nuance in financial statements for nonprofits is important, as it's one of the key differences between nonprofit and for-profit accounting.

KEY PRINCIPLES

→ Only a donor has the power to impose either a time or purpose condition on his or her donation.

→ When a donor does so, the nonprofit must account for that purpose or time condition on its financial statements.

→ Those donations, depending on the purpose or the time condition, are either temporarily restricted or permanently restricted funds.

36

What Are the Current Ratio and Working Capital?

■ ■ ■

Liquidity is oxygen for a financial system.

—Ruth Porat

CURRENT ASSETS AND CURRENT LIABILITIES

If you've ever purchased a home and had to obtain a loan from a bank to finance that home, you were either knowingly or unknowingly subject to both the current ratio and working capital calculations by that bank's underwriter. The underwriter determines whether you'll be approved for the loan. Your bank, like all other banks, is hopefully in the business of making loans that will be repaid. Otherwise, that bank won't be in business very long! Even though your bank takes a "security interest" in your home when it makes the loan, which just means that your home is used as collateral for the loan, the bank still wants assurance from the onset of the loan that you'll be able to make the first few payments. With this security interest in your home, the bank can foreclose on your house if you can't make the monthly loan payments.

Accordingly, the bank protects itself in two key ways. First, for home purchases most banks typically request a down payment of at least 20 percent of the purchase price of the home. This protects the bank from any potential downturn in the economy. During an economic recession, for example, your house value may decrease by 20 percent. During the Great Recession, many housing markets, such as those located in the Las Vegas and Phoenix metro areas, experienced a decrease of this magnitude.[1] In fact, between September 2007 and September 2008, the Las Vegas and Phoenix markets were down 31.1 percent and 31.9 percent, respectively.[2] Second, when you close on your home loan at the title company, many banks require that you have cash on hand equal to at least six months of your new monthly mortgage payment, inclusive of property taxes, homeowners insurance, and homeowners association (HOA) fees, if any.

For example, if your new monthly mortgage payment is $1,500, inclusive of property taxes, homeowners insurance, and HOA fees, then your lender may require that you have at least $9,000 of available cash when you close on the loan, which is six months of this payment amount. This amount of cash helps to ensure you'll be able to make your first few mortgage payments to your lender. In turn, having this cash reserve on hand also increases both your current ratio and working capital number. So, what are the current ratio and working capital?

CURRENT RATIO AND WORKING CAPITAL

Both the current ratio and working capital measure liquidity. A nonprofit's liquidity is a reflection of its ability to pay its short-term obligations once they become due. In this context, "short-term" means those obligations that are due by the nonprofit within the next twelve months, otherwise known as its current liabilities.[3] The current ratio is measured by dividing a nonprofit's current assets by its current liabilities.[4] Ideally, the result of this calculation is at least 2:1, which means that a nonprofit has at least twice as many current assets to pay its current liabilities.[5] If the current ratio is not at least 2:1, hopefully it's at least 1:1, which means that a nonprofit has at least enough current assets on hand to pay its current liabilities.[6] You can imagine what happens when this ratio drops below 1:1; short-term liquidity will quickly become an issue.

Your liquidity is exactly what the bank is concerned about when it requires that you have at least six months of cash on hand when you close on your home loan. If your personal current ratio is below 1:1, this is obviously a red flag for your lender. Similarly, if a nonprofit's current ratio is below 1:1, this is a red flag for such nonprofit's board of directors. In both scenarios, the ability to pay any short-term obligations in a timely manner is in question. Here, "current assets" include both cash and any assets that may be converted into cash within the next twelve months.[7] A key exception to current assets is securities, more commonly known as stocks, which are not included in current assets.[8] With stocks, the expectation is that a nonprofit would hold those securities for more than twelve months. Thus, while publicly-traded stock may easily be converted into cash over a twelve-month period, they are excluded from current assets for this reason.[9]

Just like the current ratio, working capital also measures a nonprofit's liquidity.[10] However, working capital is the *difference* between current assets and current liabilities.[11] Here, the result of this computation should show that a nonprofit has at least three months of operating expenses on hand.[12] If, for whatever reason, a nonprofit's revenues are completely cutoff, then it would at least be able to cover three months of operating expenses with this reserve. For example, if a nonprofit has operating expenses of $1,000,000 over the course of a year, then it has expenses of approximately $83,333 per month or $250,000 over three months. The working capital number for this nonprofit should be at least $250,000, which means that it has three months of operating expenses on hand. If a nonprofit doesn't have at least three months of operating expenses on hand, this too is a red flag for the nonprofit's board of directors to consider.

CASE STUDY: HABITAT FOR HUMANITY

Many people are familiar with the nonprofit, Habitat for Humanity International ("Habitat for Humanity"), which is a 501(c)(3)-public charity.[13] Habitat for Humanity operates in all fifty states, focusing on approximately 1,400 communities throughout the United States and in about seventy countries around the world.[14] Habitat for Humanity's vision is "[A] world where everyone has a decent place to live."[15] Habitat for Humanity has numerous local affiliates, such as Habitat for Humanity of Utah County, which focuses on home building in that geographical area.[16]

Habitat for Humanity of Utah County is a nonprofit corporation that was incorporated in 1991 under the laws of the state of Utah.[17] As a separate nonprofit corporation, Habitat for Humanity of Utah County is operated by an independent board of directors. In addition to home building activities, it operates two home improvement stores called "ReStore," which are located in Orem, Utah, and Spanish Fork, Utah, respectively.[18] Operating these two stores is an earned-income activity for Habitat for Humanity of Utah County. Just like Habitat for Humanity of Utah County, many nonprofits engage in earned-income activities to bolster their liquidity.

Based upon a review of the audited financial statements for fiscal year ended June 30, 2017, Habitat for Humanity of Utah County is in a strong financial position with respect to both its current ratio and working capital. At June 30, 2017, Habitat for Humanity of Utah County had current assets of $1,025,308 and current liabilities of $185,362.[19] Accordingly, the current ratio for this nonprofit is 5.53:1, or $1,025,308 divided by $185,362, which is a sign of good fiscal health. This result means that Habitat for Humanity of Utah County has more than enough current assets, to the tune of five times what's needed, to take care of its current liabilities.

Similarly, the working capital number for this nonprofit is $839,946, or $1,025,308 minus $185,362. Based upon a review of Habitat for Humanity of Utah County's statement of functional expenses, this nonprofit has monthly operating expenses of approximately $302,000.[20] Thus, Habitat for Humanity of Utah County needs approximately $906,000 of current assets on hand for three months of operating expenses. With $839,946, Habitat for Humanity of Utah County has nearly enough working capital to meet this three month rule. From a short-term liquidity perspective, Habitat for Humanity of Utah County's current ratio and working capital number demonstrates that it has enough current assets to meet its current liabilities.

2:1 AND THREE MONTHS

Short-term liquidity is important for both individuals and nonprofits. Individuals and nonprofits likely have liabilities, such as mortgage payments or accounts payable, and those liabilities must be paid. If those liabilities are not fulfilled or satisfied when they're due, then lenders or vendors will likely have various recourse options available to them to ensure that those liabilities are paid. Banks are not in the business of making loans that cannot be repaid, and likewise, vendors are not in the business of selling goods or services that cannot be paid in a timely manner. For these reasons, both the current ratio and working capital are key liquidity measurements for nonprofits. Ideally, a nonprofit has at least twice as many current assets to satisfy its current liabilities. Similarly, a nonprofit ideally has at least three months of operating expenses on hand to ensure that it has adequate short-term liquidity.

KEY PRINCIPLES

→ Both the current ratio and working capital measure liquidity.
→ The current ratio is measured by dividing a nonprofit's current assets by its current liabilities.
→ Working capital is the *difference* between current assets and current liabilities.

37

What Are the Debt Ratio, Equity Ratio, and Debt-to-Equity Ratio?

■ ■ ■

Every nonprofit—no matter how small or young—has a capital structure.

—Clara Miller

CAPITAL STRUCTURE

Do you periodically analyze your personal balance sheet? That is, do you systematically think about how much you own as opposed to how much you owe to others? A balance sheet is comprised of assets and liabilities, and your net worth is the difference between the two. Your house, car, and computer are all assets, and you acquire the assets you possess in one of three different ways. First, you can acquire assets with cash you've accumulated over time by having your revenues exceed your expenses. When revenues exceed expenses in a given month or year, you have savings, which are part of your "net assets," and those savings are added to the savings that you've accumulated over time. Whether your revenues exceed your expenses for a particular month, quarter, or year can be reflected on your personal income statement.

Second, you can acquire assets by having someone, such as a parent, grandparent, or another relative, gift you money or another asset without any strings attached. That parent, grandparent, or relative, for example, might donate or gift you money or another asset out of the goodness of their hearts. Gifts like this are a terrific way to build up your savings, and don't we all wish that we got these kinds of gifts more often! Finally, you can acquire assets by taking out a loan. Incurring debt is a common way to acquire an asset, such as taking out a mortgage on a new home or a loan on a new car. The manner in which you've acquired your assets is reflected on your personal balance sheet, which shows your assets, liabilities, and net worth.

Similarly, a nonprofit also has its own balance sheet showing its assets, liabilities, and net assets. The leaders of a nonprofit use this information to guide large decisions, like constructing a new building. Should they use some or all of the nonprofit's net assets, should they try to secure enough donations to cover the cost of the new building, or should they take out a loan for some or all of the cost of that new building? The "capital structure," or the distribution of assets, liabilities, and net assets you have on an individual basis and that a nonprofit has on an entity basis, reflects how acquisition decisions were made over time.[1] We can look to the debt ratio, the equity ratio, and the debt-to-equity ratio to help us make these determinations regarding the nonprofit's capital structure.

DEBT RATIO, EQUITY RATIO, AND DEBT-TO-EQUITY RATIO

The capital structure you personally have or that a nonprofit has is reflected upon a review of the (1) debt ratio; (2) equity ratio; and (3) debt-to-equity ratio.[2] These three ratios may be calculated by reviewing a nonprofit's balance sheet for a particular point in time. Balance sheets are a "snapshot in time," and they show a nonprofit's assets, liabilities, and net assets as of a certain date.[3] For example, December 31 is a common date if the nonprofit has a fiscal year end that coincides with the end of the calendar year, and June 30 is another common date for nonprofit schools since it coincides with the end of the academic calendar. By reviewing a nonprofit's balance sheet, you can calculate a nonprofit's debt, equity, and debt-to-equity ratios.

First, the debt ratio is simply a nonprofit's total liabilities divided by its total assets:

$$\text{Debt Ratio} = \text{Total Liabilities/Total Assets}$$

The debt ratio reveals the percentage to which "outsiders," such as banks, credit unions, or other lenders, have a claim against a nonprofit's assets.[4] Ideally, this ratio should be less than 50 percent, which means that the nonprofit itself has a greater claim to its assets than outsiders.[5] Conversely, a debt ratio that's higher than 50 percent means that these outsiders have a higher claim to the assets of a nonprofit than the nonprofit itself, which is certainly not ideal.

Secondly, the equity ratio is simply the flip side of the debt ratio. That is, the equity ratio is a nonprofit's net assets divided by its total assets:

$$\text{Equity Ratio} = \text{Net Assets/Total Assets}[6]$$

Unlike the debt ratio, the equity ratio should be higher than 50 percent because this result shows that the nonprofit itself has a greater claim to its assets than outsiders.[7] Because the equity ratio is the opposite of the debt ratio, these two ratios add up to 100 percent. For example, if a nonprofit has an equity ratio of 60 percent, then we immediately know that the debt ratio is 40 percent. This fact is due to the formula for the balance sheet: Total Assets = Total Liabilities + Net Assets.[8] These two ratios will tell us if a nonprofit acquired its assets through either gifts, savings, or loans.

A ratio that's related to both the debt ratio and the equity ratio is the debt-to-equity ratio. This ratio is simply the debt ratio divided by the equity ratio.[9] If you remember your high school math class, the debt ratio divided by the equity ratio is simply total liabilities divided by net assets, as the denominator of "total assets" from both such ratios cancel each other out:

Debt-to-Equity Ratio	Total Liabilities/Total Assets*
	Net Assets/Total Assets*

* Total Assets from each formula cancel each other out.

Accordingly, the result of the debt ratio divided by the equity ratio is:

$$\text{Debt–to–Equity Ratio} = \text{Total Liabilities/Net Assets}^{10}$$

Ideally, the result of the debt-to-equity ratio calculation is less than one-to-one.[11] This means that the nonprofit itself has a greater claim to its assets than outsiders. If this ratio rises past one-to-one, this means that outsiders are increasing their claims (e.g., total liabilities are increasing) to the nonprofit's assets. A review of the debt-to-equity ratio will also reveal the capital structure of a nonprofit, just like the debt ratio and the equity ratio.

CASE STUDY: YMCA OF THE USA

YMCA of the USA is an Illinois nonprofit corporation based in Chicago, Illinois, that is exempt from federal income tax as a 501(c)(3)-public charity.[12] This nonprofit, like many, makes its audited financial statements publicly available for review on its website.[13] YMCA of the USA operates approximately 2,700 YMCAs throughout the United States, and each one is focused on "youth development, healthy living, and social responsibility."[14] Accordingly, by reviewing its audited financial statements for the fiscal year ended December 31, 2017, we can determine the debt ratio, equity ratio, and debt-to-equity ratio as of that date. An analysis of these three ratios will reveal the capital structure of this well-known nonprofit.

First, the balance sheet of the YMCA of the USA shows that it has the following assets, liabilities, and net assets as of December 31, 2017:[15]

Total assets	$175,680,000
Total liabilities	$23,037,000
Net assets	$152,643,000

With this example, note that the balance sheet balances because the total assets of $175,680,000 equal the total liabilities of $23,037,000 plus the net assets of $152,643,000.

The balance sheet allows us to determine the debt, equity, and debt-to-equity ratios as of December 31, 2017. First, the debt ratio of the YMCA of the USA as of this date is equal to the total liabilities of $23,037,000 divided by the total assets of $175,680,000, or about 13 percent. This result is a good sign of fiscal health because outsiders only have claim to 13 percent of the YMCA of the USA's assets. Since the equity ratio is the flip side of the debt ratio, we immediately know that the equity ratio of the YMCA of the USA as of December 31, 2017, is 87 percent. These two percentages, 13 percent and 87 percent, add up to 100 percent. However, we can also obtain this result by computing the equity ratio itself. Accordingly, the equity ratio for the YMCA of the USA as of December 31, 2017, is equal to the net assets of $152,643,000 divided by the total assets of $175,680,000, or approximately 87 percent. This result is an outstanding equity ratio because it shows that the YMCA of the USA itself has a claim to about 87 percent of its total assets.

Finally, we can also review the debt-to-equity ratio to reveal this nonprofit's capital structure. For the debt-to-equity ratio as of December 31, 2017, this result is equal to the total liabilities of $23,037,000 divided by the net assets of $152,643,000. This calculation yields a result of 0.15, or 0.15:1 if we convert it to a ratio. Here, note that we can get the same result of 0.15 if we divide the debt ratio of 13 percent by the equity ratio of 87 percent. Since this result is less than 1:1 (it's actually much lower), this ratio is also a sign of strong fiscal health, as the YMCA of the USA has a much greater claim to its assets than outsiders. Since the YMCA of the USA has approximately $175 million in total assets, these three ratios show us the capital structure of the YMCA of the USA as of December 31, 2017, is not a risky one. Rather, its distribution of assets, liabilities, and net assets, and the magnitude of each, reveals a very healthy capital structure.[16]

ANALYZING THE BALANCE SHEET

If you're looking to quickly assess the fiscal health of a nonprofit like the YMCA of the USA, first review its debt ratio, equity ratio, and debt-to-equity ratio. The debt ratio, which is total liabilities divided by total assets, will reveal the percentage of claims that outsiders have on the nonprofit's assets. Ideally, this ratio is *less* than 50 percent, which means that the nonprofit has a greater claim to its assets than outsiders. The flip side of the debt ratio is the equity ratio. Accordingly, the equity ratio reveals the percentage to which the nonprofit itself has a claim to its assets. Unlike the debt ratio, this percentage should be *higher* than 50 percent. Finally, for the debt-to-equity ratio, ideally the result is *less* than one-to-one. This also means that the nonprofit itself has a greater claim to its assets than outsiders. Reviewing each of these three ratios will reveal the capital structure of a nonprofit which reflects how a particular nonprofit acquired its assets since inception. You can also use these ratios to determine how you've acquired your assets.

KEY PRINCIPLES

→ The Debt Ratio is a nonprofit's Total Liabilities divided by its Total Assets

→ The Equity Ratio is a nonprofit's Net Assets divided by its Total Assets.

→ The Debt-to-Equity Ratio is a nonprofit's Total Liabilities divided by its Net Assets.

38

What's So Important about the "Notes" Section in Audited Financial Statements?

■ ■ ■

Misery is the company of lawsuits.

—Francois Rabelais

AUDITED FINANCIAL STATEMENTS

During my tenure as a Grants Program Officer at the Boettcher Foundation, a potential grantee submitted a grant request for a capital campaign to renovate a building. At the time, the Boettcher Foundation focused primarily on nonprofit capital campaigns, so receiving a submission like this one was a routine occurrence. As part of Boettcher's diligence process, its Trustees required that each potential grantee submit its latest audited financial statements. The other staff members and I reviewed these audited financial statements, including the "notes" section within them. We knew that the notes section contained important and material information about the nonprofit that could only be found in that particular section. Reviewing only a nonprofit's financial statements, including the balance sheet, income statement, statement of functional expenses, and statement of cash flows, would not give us a full picture of the applicant. When this applicant submitted its grant proposal to the foundation, however, it failed to include its latest audited financial statements.

When we inquired about this potential grantee's failure to submit its latest audited financial statements, a representative from the nonprofit said there was a significant lawsuit settlement summarized in the notes section of the audited financial statements. In sum, this potential grantee was sued, it settled that lawsuit for a large sum of money, and the liability related to that lawsuit was addressed in the notes section of its audited financial statements. Thus, this nonprofit did not want to submit its latest audited financial statements to the foundation because its board of directors and the executive leadership team were embarrassed about the settlement. Since this potential grantee did not submit audited financial statements, it was not eligible to receive a grant from the foundation.

THE "NOTES" SECTION

This example highlights the significance of the type of information contained in the notes section of a set of audited financial statements. When reviewing a nonprofit's audited financial statements, one should always review the notes section in addition to the financial statements. While a set of audited financial statements can reveal both the capital structure and the fiscal health of a nonprofit, including its allocation of assets, liabilities, net assets, revenues, and expenses, those statements don't always tell the entire story. Along with any lawsuit settlements, for example, there's a myriad of other important information that can only be found in the notes section.[1]

In accordance with Generally Accepted Accounting Principles (GAAP), a nonprofit must address any "material disclosures" along with its financial statements.[2] These disclosures are typically addressed in the notes section.[3] First, the notes section frequently starts with a brief summary of the nonprofit, including its mission and key programs and activities, whether it's a 501(c) entity, and whether it's a subsidiary of another organization.[4] Second, the notes section then summarizes the accounting practices of the nonprofit, such as whether: (1) it's using the cash-basis or the accrual-basis accounting method; (2) it's utilizing a deduction for uncollectible accounts or bad debts, including any deductions for either pledges or grants receivable that likely won't be collected by the nonprofit; (3) the financial statements were prepared in accordance with GAAP; and (4) the nonprofit's assets have been listed at their historic cost.[5]

Third, the notes section to a set of audited financial statements may also contain an explanation regarding the fair value of various financial instruments, such as fixed income funds, assets held in trust, equity funds, and beneficial interests in perpetual trusts, and whether such instruments have been "marked down" or reduced in value.[6] If they have been so reduced, the notes section will explain the reason.[7] Finally, the notes section may also contain information about: (1) insurance held by the nonprofit; (2) retirement plans operated by the nonprofit, such as deferred compensation or defined contribution plans; (3) in-kind contributions received by the nonprofit; (4) operating lease obligations or other commitments; (5) temporarily restricted or permanently restricted funds held by the nonprofit; and (6) subsequent events occurring between the end of the nonprofit's fiscal year and prior to the audited financial statements being issued.[8]

CASE STUDY: ALZHEIMER'S ASSOCIATION

A review of the audited financial statements for the Alzheimer's Association reaffirms the importance of reviewing the notes section to the financial statements. The Alzheimer's Association, based in Chicago, Illinois, is one of America's largest 501(c)(3)-public charities.[9] Its mission is to "eliminate Alzheimer's disease through the advancement of research; to provide and enhance care and support for all affected; and to reduce the risk of dementia through the promotion of brain health."[10] As of June 30, 2017, the Alzheimer's Association had net assets of approximately $270 million.[11] In the notes section to its audited financial statements, we're able to review this nonprofit's *material* disclosures, which can only be found in that section.

For example, on July 1, 2016, the notes section addresses the fact that forty-six independent chapters of the Alzheimer's Associated merged with the Alzheimer's Association to "create a unified Alzheimer's Association."[12] The notes section also addresses the fact that the total assets associated with these acquired chapters, along with one chapter that dissolved as part of this consolidation, totaled approximately $152 million.[13] This merger is a significant development for this nonprofit, and this important disclosure is only addressed in the notes section.

Second, the notes section discloses that the Alzheimer's Association operates a voluntary political action committee, called the Alzheimer's Impact Movement Political Action Committee (AIMPAC), that's exempt from federal income tax under Section 527 of the Code.[14] This initiative shows that this nonprofit is likely involved in politics. Third, the notes section addresses that the Alzheimer's Association as of June 30, 2017, had pledges receivable of approximately $57.2 million.[15] However, because of a discount factor associated with perceived uncollectible amounts, the aggregate amount of pledges receivable was reduced to $54.9 million.[16] This discount factor for pledges receivable ranges from 1.492 percent to 2.514 percent.[17]

Fourth, the notes section discloses that the Alzheimer's Association had a thirteen-year operating lease for office space in Chicago, Illinois, a ten-year operating lease for office space in Washington, DC, and 232 leases for its various chapters.[18] The aggregate rental expenses related to these lease commitments totaled $11.7 million for the year ended June 30, 2017.[19] Finally, the notes section addresses that the Alzheimer's Association received $5.5 million in contributed services and gifts-in-kind for the fiscal year ended June 30, 2017.[20] These examples all demonstrate that certain key information can only be found in the notes section of the audit, and typically this information helps us better understand a nonprofit's full financial position.

"ISSUE SPOTTING"

When I teach both law school and graduate school students about the importance of reviewing the notes section, I introduce them to the concept of "issue spotting." Because the notes section contains material information that can only be found in that section, such as any in-kind contributions, discount factors related to grants or pledges receivable, or lawsuit settlements, reviewing this section can reveal significant issues facing that nonprofit. The process of identifying issues is known as "issue spotting." Any discovered issues might lead a reviewer, such as a potential donor, to ask follow-up questions. For example, if you reviewed the notes section to the Alzheimer's Association's audited financial statements, you might inquire about the integration process related to the merger of the forty-six chapters, including any leadership issues related to a consolidation of this magnitude.[21] If the notes section is ignored, then the full operational and financial story related to that nonprofit might be missed.

KEY PRINCIPLES

➔ When reviewing a nonprofit's audited financial statements, one should always review the notes section in addition to the financial statements.

➔ A myriad of important information can only be found in the notes section.

➔ In accordance with Generally Accepted Accounting Principles (GAAP), a nonprofit must address any "material disclosures" along with its financial statements, and such disclosures are typically found in the notes section.

39

What's Time Value of Money?

■ ■ ■

Not money, not skills, but time is the biggest lever for massive wealth creation.

—**Manoj Arora**

EXPONENTIAL GRAPHS

If you don't yet know what an exponential graph looks like, now's the time to learn. An understanding of exponential graphs has the power to change your life and your family's life for the better. The leaders of Harvard University's endowment, for example, have an understanding of exponential graphs, which is one of the reasons it's close to $40 billion.[1] For its most recently completed fiscal year, Harvard's endowment grew by approximately 10 percent, and most of this financial return was likely from interest earnings off of the endowment's existing corpus. This "interest money," once earned, is reflected on an exponential graph.[2]

Here's a quick story to highlight the impact of an exponential graph. Let's presume that we know a brother and sister, Fred and Susan, who are twins. Fred decides *not* to go to college. Instead, he obtains a job at age eighteen and invests $15,000 in an individual retirement account (IRA) that year. Susan, on the other hand, goes to college at age eighteen, graduates at the top of her class, and then goes to medical school after that. Susan starts her post-residency medical practice at age thirty, at which point she contributes $40,000 to her IRA.

Assume that both Fred and Susan receive an annual rate of return of 10 percent with monthly compounding interest, they do not invest any more money in their respective IRAs, and they both decide to retire at age sixty-five. Thus, what has Fred's $15,000 investment grown to at age sixty-five, and what has Susan's $40,000 investment grown to at age sixty-five? At age sixty-five, Fred's $15,000 investment has grown to $1,617,400 and Susan's $40,000 investment has grown to $1,305,546. The initial difference between these two investments was only $25,000, but that's grown to a difference of approximately $311,000 at age sixty-five! This example shows the power of an exponential graph.

TIME VALUE OF MONEY

The concept of "time value of money" is directly related to an exponential graph. Time value of money is the idea that a dollar invested today can be used to earn interest, and thus, will be worth more in the future, even after accounting for inflation.[3] Time value of money is one of the key reasons that individuals and nonprofits, like Harvard University, should invest their discretionary income today. At first, most of the savings that a person has, like a 401(k) plan, are related to principal contributions and only a little bit comes from interest. In this context, the principal amount is the amount that a person contributes to his or her savings vehicle.

Over time, however, an exponential graph slowly but surely flips that premise, and either an individual or an entity—like a nonprofit—making investments will make most of his, her, or its financial gains from interest as opposed to principal contributions.[4] This inflection point in an exponential graph is where you, or a nonprofit that's investing its net assets, wants to get to as quickly as possible. It represents the point in time when "interest money" in a given year becomes greater than principal contributions. In our example, Fred got to this inflection point on the graph sooner than Susan, despite the fact that he invested less principal.

After reaching its inflection point, an exponential graph really starts to take off. At this point, a person who's investing his or her savings or a nonprofit investing its net assets will start to see the rewards of investing a dollar today rather than one tomorrow. The formula for time value of money is reflected by $FV = PV \times [1 + (i/n)]^{(n+t)}$, where (1) "FV" = Future Value; (2) "PV" = Present Value; (3) i = the interest rate; (4) n = the number of compounding interest periods per year; and (5) t = the number of years.[5] Of all the subjects I teach graduate school and law school students, the power of time value of money, including exponential graphs and this formula, is one of the most important concepts for them to understand.

Figure 39.1 An Exponential Graph

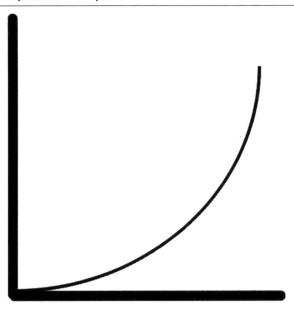

CASE STUDY: THE CAPITAL AREA FOOD BANK

If "money equals mission" in the nonprofit sector, nonprofit leaders must understand that additional financial resources, or what we've been referring to as "interest money," come from an understanding of time value of money, exponential graphs, and this formula. Arguably, "interest money" is the best way to earn a dollar, and who knows that better than a bank? For example, if we examine the balance sheet of the Capital Area Food Bank, which is a nonprofit that is also exempt from federal income tax under Section 501(c)(3) of the Code, we can see what leaders of a nonprofit can do with that nonprofit's net assets.[6]

The Capital Area Food Bank was established in 1979.[7] Its mission is to "feed those who suffer from hunger in the Washington, D.C. metropolitan area by acquiring food and distributing it directly and through our network of member agencies."[8] The Capital Area Food Bank is one of the largest food banks serving this area.[9] Based on its Form 990 for the fiscal year ended June 30, 2017, the Capital Area Food Bank had total assets of approximately $48 million and total liabilities of about $35 million; thus, its net assets were approximately $13 million.[10]

A nonprofit's net asset number is equivalent to its "net worth" because it represents what's left over after all of a nonprofit's liabilities are accounted for. Unless some of these net assets are either temporarily or permanently restricted, which means that a donor imposed a condition on such donation, a nonprofit's board of directors or management can invest such net assets so that they begin to work for the nonprofit. These leaders may invest some or all of those unrestricted net assets into a multitude of different investment vehicles, such as: (1) equity or stock, either private or publicly-traded equity, whether domestic or international; (2) fixed income, bonds, and related-debt instruments; (3) property, buildings, or other real estate holdings; or (4) money market funds or certificates of deposit.

For example, the Capital Area Food Bank had approximately $8 million in "investments" as of June 30, 2017, which were reported at their fair market value on the balance sheet.[11] The Capital Area Food Bank received approximately $800,000 in "interest income" from such investments during that fiscal year.[12] That's not entirely free money, as fees were likely paid to money managers, but it's pretty close. Those 800,000 additional dollars can now be devoted to the nonprofit's mission. Ideally, the leaders of a nonprofit will consider its "asset allocation" when making investment decisions so that these net assets are diversified across various investment vehicles, including those noted above. Also, as one investment vehicle performs well, like real estate, then the leaders may rebalance the nonprofit's invested assets across these different investment vehicles to maintain the nonprofit's appropriate "asset allocation."

"INTEREST MONEY"

By investing unrestricted net assets that don't need to be readily available, the leaders of a nonprofit can put those net assets to work for the nonprofit. The concept of time value of money rests on the assumption that a dollar invested today will be worth more in the future.[13] For instance, let's presume the Capital Area Food Bank needs to purchase a new van in five years. At that time, it expects to pay $10,000 for a new van. How much does this nonprofit need to invest today to ensure that it will have $10,000 in five years, assuming an annual rate of return of 10 percent? Based on the foregoing formula, the answer is $6,209.[14] Without this investment, the Capital Area Food Bank would need to use $10,000 of its unrestricted net assets in five years to make this purchase.

With time value of money, however, the leaders of the Capital Area Food Bank only need to invest $6,209 today, make good "asset allocation" decisions, and then let an exponential graph do its work to get a new van valued at $10,000 in five years. Time is of the essence when considering when to invest, and nonprofit leaders should determine how they can best utilize "interest money," along with donations from individuals, foundations, and corporations, to further the nonprofit's mission. On a much larger scale, this is exactly what the leaders of the Harvard endowment have been doing since inception. After all, 10 percent of $40 billion is *$4 billion*. Their knowledge of exponential graphs has enabled them to maximize the endowment's ability to grow.

KEY PRINCIPLES

→ The concept of "time value of money" is directly related to an exponential graph.

→ Time value of money is the idea that a dollar invested today can be used to earn interest and thus will be worth more in the future, even after accounting for inflation.

→ The formula for time value of money is reflected by $FV = PV \times [1 + (i/n)]^{(n+t)}$, where (1) "FV" = Future Value; (2) "PV" = Present Value; (3) i = the interest rate; (4) n = the number of compounding interest periods per year; and (5) t = the number of years.

40

What's the Difference between an Audit, a Review, and a Compilation?

■ ■ ■

Creativity is great, but not in accounting.

—Charles Scott

PHILANTHROPIC BANKS

Most 501(c)(3)-private foundations require audited financial statements when a nonprofit applies for a grant. In many ways, private foundations are like banks that make everyday investments. These private foundations, however, function more like philanthropic banks because they typically invest in various charitable causes, programs, or initiatives. When a nonprofit applies for a grant from a private foundation, it's hopefully conveying to the foundation's board of directors and executive leadership team through its grant proposal that it will be able to deliver on its proposed project, programs, or activities. Based on my experiences at two large private foundations, that's what we looked for in a potential grantee: its ability to deliver.

For example, if a potential grantee is requesting a grant to help it build a new headquarters facility, it's ideally conveying to the foundation's board of directors and executive leadership team that it will be able to successfully complete that construction project. If the foundation's board of directors eventually issues a grant to this potential grantee, they are conveying that they too believe the potential grantee can in fact complete a new headquarters facility. A foundation's financial resources are limited, so its leadership team wants to make wise and prudent investments. Since the leaders of private foundations want assurance that a potential grantee will be able to successfully deliver on its proposed project, programs, or activities, they typically require a nonprofit to submit audited financial statements.

After a nonprofit has been established, it might take a few years before the leaders of that nonprofit obtain audited financial statements. This delay is largely due to the fact that the cost to obtain audited financial statements from an audit firm can run anywhere from $5,000 to $50,000, or even higher, depending on the complexity of a nonprofit's activities, financial statements, or transactions. The amount that a 501(c)(3) entity spends on accounting and audit fees, whether that entity is a public charity or a private foundation, is reflected on its Form 990 or Form 990-PF, respectively.[1] If you review a few Form 990s or Form 990-PFs, you'll see that costs related to accounting and audit fees vary from one 501(c)(3) entity to the next.

A nonprofit generally won't have audited financial statements until it has a need for them, such as applying for a grant from a private foundation or registering under a state's charitable solicitations laws.[2] Until that time, those monies can be devoted to that nonprofit's mission. An audit, however, will likely be required at some point. For instance, when I served as a Grants Program Officer for the Boettcher Foundation, I counseled numerous nonprofits, especially recently established ones, on the importance of having audited financial statements as part of the application process. As those nonprofit leaders approached the accounting marketplace, they likely learned not only about audits, but also about reviews and compilations. So, what's the difference between an audit, a review, and a compilation?

AUDITS, REVIEWS, AND COMPILATIONS

When leaders of a nonprofit engage external auditors, they face a choice of whether to obtain an audit, a compilation, or a review. In general, these three reports, which are each prepared by an audit firm, give both internal and external stakeholders of a nonprofit assurance with respect to that nonprofit's financial statements and the transactions underlying such statements.[3] This level of assurance varies depending on the type of report being prepared.[4] An audit performed under Generally Accepted Accounting Principles (GAAP) represents the highest level of assurance.[5] With an audit, the external auditors conduct testing, like testing of internal controls and financial transactions, to ensure that a nonprofit's financial statements "present fairly, in all material respects, the financial position of the nonprofit" without any exceptions.[6]

This "presents fairly in all material respects" statement, or something similar, is found in the opinion letter prepared by the external auditors as part of the audit. This opinion letter precedes the financial statements. It gives both internal and external stakeholders assurance that these financial statements reflect the financial position of the nonprofit in all *material* respects.[7] While the auditors may make a mistake here or there, these mistakes are not material in nature.

Second, a "review" involves no testing by the nonprofit's external accountants; rather, only inquiries are conducted by the external auditors.[8] In a review, the accountants affirm to both internal and external stakeholders that the nonprofit's financial representations appear to make sense, thereby providing some, but not full, assurance.[9] Finally, a "compilation" doesn't provide any testing or assurance to stakeholders regarding the nonprofit's financial statements.[10] Instead, the external accountants are just collecting and reformatting the financial statements.[11]

CASE STUDY: A CORPORATE FOUNDATION

During my tenure as the General Counsel for the Level 3 Foundation, the board of directors had to determine when it would first obtain audited financial statements. Even though the Level 3 Foundation was a 501(c)(3)-public charity, pursuing both charitable and educational objectives, it was also a grantmaking public charity. It primarily collected contributions from both the entity known as Level 3 Communications, Inc., a Fortune 500 company, and the thousands of employees that worked for that entity. In turn, it granted the funds it collected to various other 501(c)(3)-public charities. Because of this structure, the Level 3 Foundation did not seek grants from 501(c)(3)-private foundations, which would likely have required it to obtain audited financial statements.

In our case, the need to obtain audited financial statements came from various states under their charitable solicitations laws and acts. Several states require a nonprofit that anticipates raising over a certain amount in that state, like $25,000 for instance, to obtain audited financial statements.[12] Submitting audited financial statements may be required before that nonprofit can be registered in that state to conduct fundraising activities.[13] Since the Level 3 Foundation exceeded this anticipated threshold in a few states, and each of those states required audited financial statements to be registered in that state under its charitable solicitations act, the board of directors had to obtain audited financial statements. The initial cost of that first audit was around $7,500.

ASSURANCE

After a nonprofit has been established, its leaders must decide whether to obtain an audit, a compilation, or a review. Typically, a nonprofit first obtains an audit once it applies for a grant from a private foundation. Since private foundations are like philanthropic banks, the leaders of these entities want assurance that their investment in a nonprofit will be a successful one. Accurately presented financial statements are a key start to this grantor-grantee relationship, as they help a nonprofit show that it will be able to deliver on the promises contained in its grant request. An audit provides the highest level of assurance that a nonprofit's financial statements, in all material respects, are presented fairly.[14]

A review, which is less expensive than a full audit, provides limited assurance.[15] Finally, a compilation, which is generally the least expensive option, provides no assurance that the financial statements are presented fairly.[16] Additionally, a state's charitable solicitations act might require a nonprofit to obtain an audit.[17] A nonprofit in this scenario must submit its audited financial statements before it can raise funds in that state, assuming there's no minimum threshold.[18] In this regard, states are serving as philanthropic watch dogs to help both the philanthropic banks located in that state as well as its citizenry.

KEY PRINCIPLES

→ An audit performed under Generally Accepted Accounting Principles (GAAP) represents the highest level of assurance.

→ With an audit, the external auditors conduct testing, like testing of internal controls and financial transactions, to ensure that a nonprofit's financial statements "present fairly, in all material respects, the financial position of the nonprofit" without any exceptions.

→ A "review" involves no testing by the nonprofit's external accountants; rather, only inquiries are conducted by the external auditors. A "compilation" doesn't provide any testing or assurance to stakeholders regarding the nonprofit's financial statements.

41

What's the Difference between Cash-Basis and Accrual-Basis Accounting?

■ ■ ■

Humanitarian action is more than simple generosity, simple charity. It aims to build spaces of normalcy in the midst of what is abnormal.

—Dr. James Orbinski, Doctors Without Borders

PASS-THROUGH ENTITIES

When Congress passed the Tax Cuts and Jobs Act of 2017, which was subsequently signed into law by President Donald J. Trump on December 22, 2017, owners of pass-through entities, like limited liability companies (LLCs), S Corporations, and limited liability partnerships (LLPs), likely rejoiced in the creation of the "pass-through deduction."[1] The pass-through deduction, which is now codified under Section 199A of the Code, allows owners of these pass-through entities to deduct from their federal income taxes an amount equal to 20 percent of their "qualified business income" from such entities, subject to various exceptions and limits.[2] For federal income tax purposes, a pass-through entity itself doesn't pay any such taxes; instead, the profits from the pass-through entity, if any, flow through to its owner(s).[3]

This tax structure for pass-through entities is why nearly all major law firms are organized as pass-through entities, such as LLCs or LLPs. The law firm where I used to work, Davis Graham & Stubbs LLP, is organized as a limited liability partnership.[4] The profits from such firm, if any, flow through to its owners, as the entity itself doesn't pay any federal income taxes. With the adoption of the new pass-through deduction, if a pass-through entity's qualified business income is $1 million, for instance, then the owner of that entity may deduct up to $200,000 from his or her federal income taxes (e.g., 20 percent of $1 million), subject to certain exclusions and caps for some professional services.[5] If a taxpayer is in the 24 percent marginal tax bracket, for instance, then this equates to a tax savings of $48,000. This pass-through deduction took effect on January 1, 2018, and will run through December 31, 2025, unless it's extended.[6]

With the addition of Section 199A to the Code, there's certainly an incentive to create a pass-through entity for any of your independent contractor work. By way of example, a driver for either Uber or Lyft, as an independent contractor, might be well-served to create a pass-through entity for this work.[7] In general, the applicable federal income tax deduction for such driver would be equal to 20 percent of any qualified business income from the ride-sharing business that he or she operates through a pass-through entity.[8] If the qualified business income is equal to $20,000, for example, then the deduction under Section 199A could be as great as $4,000.[9] Assuming the 24 percent marginal tax bracket again, the driver's tax savings equals $960. When an independent contractor, such as a driver for either Uber or Lyft, is engaged to perform services, when should that contractor "book" the revenues associated with those services?

CASH VS. ACCRUAL

An independent contractor has two options for when he or she "books" the revenues associated with the engagement of his or her services. Similarly, non-profit leaders have the same two options when considering at what point to book a nonprofit's revenues or expenses. These two options are: (1) cash-basis accounting, and (2) accrual-basis accounting.[10] First, cash-basis accounting means that revenues or expenses are booked at the time they are actually received or paid.[11] That is, a nonprofit records the transaction when cash comes in or goes out of the organization.[12] For example, when I worked at the Boettcher Foundation it used cash-basis accounting, and based on its most recent Form 990-PF it still does.[13] For a private foundation primarily engaged in making grants, cash-basis accounting might be the preferred option.

On the other hand, nonprofit leaders can book a nonprofit's revenues when they are *earned* and its expenses when they are *incurred*, even before any cash has been received or paid.[14] This method is known as accrual-basis accounting, and it differs from cash-basis accounting in terms of *timing*.[15] Accrual-basis is a more reliable method because a transaction is recorded when an obligation, such as a payment obligation, is either earned or incurred, regardless of the timing of cash inflows or outflows.[16] Accordingly, a nonprofit's use of the accrual-basis method gives a more complete financial picture with respect to that nonprofit. For this reason, it's the method required by Generally Accepted Accounting Principles (GAAP).[17] The accounting method a nonprofit utilizes is reflected on its Form 990 or Form 990-PF.[18]

CASE STUDY: DOCTORS WITHOUT BORDERS

The vast majority of nonprofits, including both public charities and private foundations, utilize accrual-basis accounting due to the fact that it gives both internal and external stakeholders a more complete financial picture of a nonprofit's financial position. For example, let's presume that you're the executive director of Doctors Without Borders USA, Inc. (Doctors Without Borders), which is a 501(c)(3)-public charity.[19] The mission of this nonprofit is to "provide independent medical humanitarian emergency aid to people affected by armed conflict, epidemics, malnutrition, natural disasters and exclusion from health care."[20] According to its most recent Form 990, Doctors Without Borders completed more than 92,500 surgical procedures in 2016, which reaffirms that this nonprofit is fulfilling its mission.[21]

Let's also presume you've negotiated a contract with a medical supply vendor for various surgical supplies totaling $5 million. For cash flow purposes, you negotiated ninety-day payment terms. Once the contract has been executed by both parties, this $5 million payment isn't due to the vendor for ninety days. If Doctors Without Borders utilizes accrual-basis accounting, this $5 million obligation is booked once the contract has been executed by both parties, as this is the point in time when this expense has been incurred by this nonprofit.[22] On the other hand, if Doctors Without Borders utilizes cash-basis accounting, then this transaction isn't recorded until the $5 million is actually paid.[23] The payment reflects when cash actually leaves the nonprofit. This example highlights the difference between cash- and accrual-basis accounting.

A MORE COMPLETE FINANCIAL PICTURE

According to its most recent Form 990, Doctors Without Borders utilizes accrual-basis accounting.[24] Like many other nonprofits, accrual-basis accounting is the preferred accounting method, not only because it is required by GAAP, but also because it gives a more complete picture of the financial condition of a nonprofit.[25] In the Doctors Without Borders example, the fact that you successfully negotiated a $5 million contract for various surgical supplies should be reflected on this nonprofit's financial books and records once the contract has been executed, not simply when this $5 million has been issued. Cash-basis accounting would reflect this transaction only when the $5 million payment is actually paid, and not when it is incurred.[26]

Similarly, if you have any independent contractor work and you've decided to create a pass-through entity to potentially take advantage of the pass-through deduction from the Tax Cuts and Jobs Act of 2017, then you would also probably want to know when revenues are earned and expenses are incurred. For this reason, accrual-basis accounting is preferred. Cash-basis accounting and accrual-basis accounting are significant concepts that all nonprofit leaders should comprehend. Based on this hypothetical, it could mean the difference of $5 million over a ninety-day period.

KEY PRINCIPLES

→ There are two accounting methods: (1) cash-basis accounting, and (2) accrual-basis accounting.

→ Cash-basis means that revenues or expenses are booked at the time they are actually received or paid.

→ Accrual-basis means a nonprofit books revenues when they are *earned* and its expenses when they are *incurred*, even before any cash has been received or paid.

42

What Does It Mean to Capitalize an Asset and Then Depreciate That Asset?

■ ■ ■

Today people who hold cash equivalents feel comfortable. They shouldn't. They have opted for a terrible long-term asset, one that pays virtually nothing and is certain to depreciate in value.

—Warren Buffett

MAYO CLINIC

When you purchase an asset, such as a computer, refrigerator, or car, do you think about how many years of use you'll get out of that asset? If you don't think about an asset's "useful life," don't worry because you're not alone. Most people are so excited about a purchase, such as a new car, that they don't think about what happens to that asset down the road. In other words, what happens to that asset once its useful life has come to an end? Just like you, nonprofits purchase assets to help them fulfill their missions and achieve their visions. For example, the Mayo Clinic, based in Rochester, Minnesota, and a 501(c)(3)-public charity, has one of the best healthcare systems in the world. In fact, *U.S. News and World Report* recently ranked the Mayo Clinic as the "No. 1 hospital overall."[1] To deliver on its mission of "provid[ing] comprehensive medical care and education in clinical medicine and medical sciences," including at its hospitals and clinics, the Mayo Clinic has various assets.[2]

Based on the Mayo Clinic's audited financial statements for the fiscal year ended December 31, 2017, it has numerous assets, including: (1) land; (2) buildings and improvements; and (3) furniture and equipment, among others.[3] The Mayo Clinic has principal healthcare facilities in Minnesota, Arizona, and Florida, and between these three locations and others, it has approximately $4.489 billion in "property, plant, and equipment" assets.[4] Since the Mayo Clinic's total assets were approximately $16.307 billion as of December 31, 2017, its "property, plant, and equipment" assets comprised about one-fourth of its total assets.[5] This makes intuitive sense, as nonprofit hospitals need assets like land, buildings, and equipment to fulfill their healthcare purposes. Similarly, nonprofit hospitals typically spend a lot of money on software. Storage of "personally identifiable information" under HIPAA needs to be both secure and accessible for healthcare professionals. The Mayo Clinic's costs associated with "capitalized software" totaled approximately $891 million as of December 31, 2017.[6] Of this amount, the Mayo Clinic depreciated approximately $57 million in software during this fiscal year.[7]

Most assets, like software, are only good for a certain period of time, which is known as the asset's "useful life." Entrepreneurs in Silicon Valley work hard every day to ensure that software will have more features and functionality. When this new software is introduced to the marketplace by such entrepreneurs, potential customers, like the Mayo Clinic, may want to upgrade their software to obtain those new features and functionality. However, it's likely that an asset such as software will be used for more than one year once it's purchased. Thus, what does it mean to both capitalize an asset and then depreciate it over time?

CAPITALIZATION AND DEPRECIATION

Since most assets are only useful for a certain period of time, nonprofit leaders may elect to capitalize and then depreciate an asset over its useful life. When a nonprofit chooses to capitalize an asset, that means it's spreading the cost of that asset out over its useful life, which is also known as amortization. The other option would be to expense the entire cost of that asset in one fiscal period.[8] For example, if the leaders of a nonprofit capitalize a car used to deliver goods or services for that nonprofit, that means that the cost of that car is first placed on the nonprofit's balance sheet as an asset and then depreciated over that asset's useful life on the income statement as an expense.[9] If that asset is not capitalized, then the entire cost of that car is put on the income statement as an expense.[10] Thus, whether or not to capitalize an asset is a key decision that nonprofit leaders or their accountants must make when they first acquire an asset.

As a general rule, nonprofits should capitalize any assets in accordance with Generally Accepted Accounting Principles (GAAP) that meet the following two requirements: (1) have a useful life greater than one year, and (2) are a material or significant cost to that nonprofit.[11] If both of these elements are met, then an asset is typically capitalized because it more accurately reflects how the cost of that asset should be distributed each fiscal period.[12] If the leaders of a nonprofit capitalize an asset, the next issue they must consider is how that asset should be depreciated over time.[13] Accordingly, it's important to note that capitalization and depreciation "go hand in hand"; a capitalized asset placed on the balance sheet must then be depreciated.[14]

Depreciation simply means that the usage costs or expenses related to that asset are allocated over a certain period of time, which is typically one year because an income statement is usually prepared for a one-year period.[15] The Internal Revenue Service in Publication 946 has outlined the useful life for many assets.[16] For example, nonresidential rental property must be depreciated over 27.5 years.[17] If that rental property costs $275,000, exclusive of land, then each year $10,000 is depreciated using the straight-line depreciation method and expensed on the income statement.[18] The straight-line depreciation method is one method for depreciating an asset, which is simply taking the cost of that asset and dividing it by its useful life.[19] Some other depreciation methods include the double-declining balance method, sum-of-the-years' digits method, and 150 percent declining balance method.[20] Nonprofit leaders typically look to their accountants to determine the depreciation method that should be implemented for a certain asset.

CASE STUDY: RONALD MCDONALD HOUSE

If you picked up this book, it's likely that you've either attended a fundraising event for a nonprofit at some point or are generally aware that nonprofits often hold fundraising events. In 2018, I attended a fundraising event for the Ronald McDonald House of Denver. One of my good friends is on the board of directors and is passionate about this nonprofit's mission to provide "comfortable, low-cost housing to out-of-town families needing to be near hospitalized children."[21] Thus, if a child is receiving treatment at Children's Hospital of Colorado, for example, then his or her family may be housed at Ronald McDonald House during that treatment period.

At this fundraising event, the mother of a teenage cancer survivor was the guest speaker, and she spoke about the impact that this nonprofit made on her family during her daughter's treatment. Ronald McDonald House of Denver has two separate locations, one in Denver and one in Aurora. Between these two houses, Ronald McDonald House can serve up to 118 families at any given time.[22] Let's presume that the executive director of Ronald McDonald House of Denver decides to purchase twenty new computers, ten computers for each house, so that family members can have access to a computer during their stay. Let's further presume that (1) each computer costs $3,000, and (2) for the purposes of this hypothetical, this nonprofit does *not* obtain audited financial statements. Should this executive director expense the full $60,000 on the income statement, or should these computers be capitalized and then annually depreciated?

On these facts, there's no right or wrong answer, but the latter option is a better financial choice as these computers all have a useful life greater than one year, and the aggregate cost of $60,000 (based on a per item cost of $3,000) is likely a material cost to this nonprofit. Here, the key issue is whether $3,000 per item is a *material* cost to this nonprofit, and thus, such assets should be capitalized in accordance with GAAP.[23] Ronald McDonald House of Denver typically has expenses of approximately $3.5 million per year.[24] In this example, purchasing these new computers at an aggregate cost of $60,000 would represent about 2 percent of the nonprofit's annual expenses.[25] The "material cost" element noted above is likely met on these facts. If this nonprofit adopts a capitalization policy, then its leaders would also need to review that policy to determine if the computers should be capitalized.[26] Smaller nonprofits typically have a $1,000 per item capitalization threshold, while larger nonprofits usually have a $5,000 per item threshold.[27] Since these two elements are likely met on these facts, the executive director of Ronald McDonald House of Denver should capitalize these assets by placing them on the balance sheet and then depreciating them over time as an annual expense on the income statement.

For this hypothetical, let's further presume that these computers have a useful life of five years. Thus, using the straight-line depreciation method, and assuming no salvage or residual value at the end of this five-year period, these new computers will be depreciated at $600 per year: $3,000 divided by five years equals $600 per year. Each year, the accumulated depreciation for these new computers will also show up on the balance sheet. Accordingly, after two years, this portion of the balance sheet would look something like this:

Equipment (computers)	$60,000
Less accumulated depreciation	$24,000 (representing two years of depreciation for 20 computers)
Equipment (computers), net of depreciation	$36,000

USEFUL LIFE OF AN ASSET

Most assets depreciate over time, with the key exception being land. Land does not depreciate.[28] Each year that depreciating assets are used, they get closer to needing to be replaced. That's why nonprofit leaders should recognize and understand the impact of depreciation. For instance, the leaders of Ronald McDonald House of Denver, after purchasing the new computers for its two houses, should include a line item in the annual budget to account for depreciation so that in five years they'll have enough money saved to replace those computers. It's much easier to save $12,000 per year, which represents the annual, aggregate depreciation costs related to those sixty new computers, as opposed to finding $60,000 in year five. If the leaders of Ronald McDonald House of Denver implement the former strategy rather than the latter strategy, they'll know the impact that depreciation costs have on this nonprofit's budget.

KEY PRINCIPLES

→ Since most assets are only useful for a certain period of time, nonprofit leaders may elect to capitalize and then depreciate an asset over its useful life.

→ When a nonprofit chooses to capitalize an asset, that means that it's spreading the cost of that asset out over its useful life.

→ If an asset is not capitalized, then the entire cost of that asset is put on the income statement as an expense.

43

What's the Difference between Fixed Costs and Variable Costs?

■ ■ ■

On the Internet, companies are scale businesses, characterized by high fixed costs and relatively low variable costs. You can be two sizes: you can be big, or you can be small. It's very hard to be medium.

—Jeff Bezos

BOSTON CENTER FOR THE ARTS

Many nonprofits, including 501(c)(3)-public charities, are engaging in earned income activities to reduce their reliance on contributions from individuals, corporations, and foundations. These earned income activities typically contain both fixed costs and variable costs. A study conducted by the Bridgespan Group noted that "half of [nonprofit executive respondents] said they believed earned income would play an important or extremely important role in bolstering their organizations' revenue in the future."[1] For example, the Boston Center for the Arts (BCA), which is a 501(c)(3)-public charity, derives approximately 60 percent of its operating expenses from earned income.[2] The mission of BCA is to "[support] working artists, to create, perform and exhibit new works; [develop] new audiences; and [connect] arts to [the] community."[3] Despite its significant earned income, in 2005 BCA ran into about $3 million of deferred maintenance issues and engaged consultants from the Nonprofit Finance Fund to help.[4]

The Nonprofit Finance Fund analyzed BCA's situation and provided various recommendations to overcome these deferred maintenance issues.[5] The Nonprofit Finance Fund recommended that BCA should leverage its existing assets to generate additional earned income.[6] The then-CEO and President of BCA, Lisa Giuffre, stated: "This plan focuses on generating [additional] earned revenue while maintaining our arts programs and services as is."[7] Based on the Nonprofit Finance Fund's recommendations, BCA "rent[ed] more of its spaces for private events, consider[ed] short-term property leases, and launch[ed] an on-site retail concept, all to achieve the goal of generating operating surpluses of 25–30% each year."[8] These surpluses, in turn, helped address BCA's deferred maintenance issues totaling approximately $3 million.[9] Each of these earned income solutions, like the on-site retail store, contained both fixed and variable costs.

FIXED COSTS AND VARIABLE COSTS

To successfully implement earned income activities, nonprofit leaders must understand the difference between fixed costs and variable costs. This is because the break-even equation, which is X(Variable Costs) + Fixed Costs = X(Unit Price) + G, relies on both variable costs and fixed costs to determine the break-even point for an earned income activity.[10] Here, "X" equals the number of units or hours sold (depending on the earned income activity), and "G" equals any grants or other philanthropic support that the nonprofit might procure for its earned income activity.[11] If a nonprofit receives philanthropic support for an earned income activity, then it lowers the break-even point.

To determine the break-even point for an earned income activity, as evidenced by the foregoing equation, nonprofit leaders need to determine both the fixed costs and the variable costs for that potential activity. By understanding the break-even point, those leaders can determine whether to engage in or move forward with that activity. First, fixed costs generally do not vary with changes in volume.[12] For example, if a nonprofit sells vaccines as part of its mobile healthcare clinic, the cost of the van that helps it deliver this earned income activity is a fixed cost because it does not vary with changes in volume.[13] Regardless of how many vaccines this nonprofit sells, the cost of the van is fixed.[14] Similarly, the rent that a charter school pays for its facilities generally does not vary with the number of students it enrolls.

Variable costs, on the other hand, do increase or decrease in direct proportion to changes in volume.[15] For instance, with the mobile healthcare clinic, the aggregate cost of the vaccines either rises or falls based on the number of units, or vaccines, that it sells to consumers. If this nonprofit sells 1,000 or 10,000 vaccines, or even 100,000 vaccines, then its aggregate costs related to these vaccines will proportionately change. Here, the vaccine is the "unit," which has both a quantity and a price.[16] In general, fixed costs are indirect costs, like rent, and variable costs are direct costs of operating an earned income idea, like vaccines in this example.[17]

CASE STUDY: A MOBILE HEALTHCARE CLINIC

In the mobile healthcare clinic example, let's presume that the fixed costs related to this earned income activity total $20,000. Let's also assume that the unit cost of the vaccine is $10, the variable cost is $5, and that this nonprofit did not receive any grants to support this earned income activity. How many units, or vaccines, does this nonprofit have to sell in order to break-even on this earned income activity? Using the break-even equation, which is X(Variable Costs) + Fixed Costs = X(Unit Price) + G, we can determine the break-even point. With the foregoing information, we get the following:

$$X(\$5) + \$20,000 = X(\$10) + \$0$$

If we rearrange X to one side of the equation, then we get the following formula:

$$\$20,000 = 5X$$

Thus, X = 4,000. This means that this nonprofit must sell at least 4,000 vaccines for this earned income activity to break-even.

When using the break-even equation, you can always check your math to ensure you're obtaining the correct break-even point. For example, if we plug 4,000 back into the original equation, we get:

$$4,000(\$5) + \$20,000 = 4,000(\$10) + \$0$$

In turn, this equates to:

$$\$20,000 + \$20,000 = \$40,000, \text{ or simply } \$40,000 = \$40,000$$

Because these two numbers match, $40,000 = $40,000, you know that the break-even point of 4,000 vaccines is correct. If this nonprofit secured a grant or other philanthropic support for this earned income idea, then the break-even number would decrease. For example, a grant of $10,000 for this earned-income activity means that the break-even number is now 2,000:

$$X(\$5) + \$20,000 = X(\$10) + \$10,000, \text{ or}$$
$$5X = \$10,000, \text{ or}$$
$$X = 2,000 \text{ vaccines}$$

BREAK-EVEN ANALYSIS

Nonprofits with earned income activities don't have to rely solely on donations to achieve their visions. The Boston Center for the Arts, for instance, derives more than 60 percent of its operating expenses from earned income activities.[18] When BCA encountered an issue with its deferred maintenance expenses, it turned to its existing assets to determine how to generate more earned income. If nonprofit leaders desire to either implement or grow an earned income activity, they need to know both the fixed costs and the variable costs related to that activity. Fixed costs generally don't change with volume; variable costs do. In our mobile healthcare clinic example, the aggregate cost related to selling this vaccine either rises or falls based upon the number of vaccines it sells. When both fixed costs and variable costs are known, then the break-even point can be determined for any earned income idea. If the break-even point appears to be attainable, non-profit leaders can prudently move forward with that earned income idea.

KEY PRINCIPLES

→ Fixed costs generally do not vary with changes in volume.

→ Variable costs, on the other hand, do increase or decrease in direct proportion to changes in volume.

→ The break-even equation, which is X(Variable Costs) + Fixed Costs = X(Unit Price) + G, relies on both variable costs and fixed costs to determine the break-even point for an earned income activity. "X" equals the number of units or hours sold, and "G" equals any grants or other philanthropic support.

44

What's Zero-Based Budgeting?

■ ■ ■

Objectives are not fate; they are direction. They are not commands; they are commitments. They do not determine the future; they are means to mobilize the resources and energies of the business for the making of the future.

—Peter Drucker

PETER DRUCKER

When you create your personal monthly budget, do you start from scratch or do you build off of your last budget? Have you ever thought of the pros and cons of each method? For example, if you start from scratch, you can look at each expenditure to determine if you really need that expense. Do you need Netflix, Comcast, and Hulu? Or, can you get by with just Netflix? Do you need two cars? Or can you get by with just one and purchase a bus pass and ride a bike? My wife and I did the latter for ten years, even though it wasn't our kids' preference. Picking up dad from the Park-n-Ride wasn't their favorite way to spend fifteen minutes at the end of their day! Building a monthly budget from scratch means that you'll critically examine each expenditure in your life and make a deliberate assessment as to whether that expense is needed. If it isn't, it can be eliminated. On the other hand, if you build a new monthly budget based on your last one, you might assume that all listed expenses are still valid.

For example, why would you need a bus pass or a bike when you already have two cars? The fact that you currently have two cars might eliminate the need to think about whether you need a second car in the first place. This line of reasoning helps explain the purpose behind Zero-Based Budgeting (ZBB). Peter Drucker, a former scholar and professor at Claremont University, helped develop the concept of ZBB.[1] The purpose of ZBB is to not make any assumptions when building a budget.[2] Rather, by using the ZBB method, each expense is questioned.[3] Peter Drucker helped develop ZBB as an alternative to incrementalism, whereby a budget is incrementally changed from its prior version, whether that prior budget was a monthly, quarterly, or yearly budget. ZBB is a more time consuming method, as it questions each expense, but it can be well worth the effort and stress. For this reason, nonprofit leaders should be aware of ZBB.

ZERO-BASED BUDGETING

ZBB has many pros and cons, but if implemented effectively by the leaders of a nonprofit, it can help ensure that the limited resources of a nonprofit are used effectively and efficiently. First, let's state its two main downfalls: (1) it's time consuming; and (2) it may lead to angst amongst the staff of a nonprofit because it has the potential to evoke stress and negative emotions.[4] During the budgeting process, if each program or activity is evaluated as to whether or not it should continue, that's certainly going to take some time. To determine whether a program should continue, the leaders of a nonprofit need a great deal of information when making their decision. They need to know the program's direct costs, number of individuals impacted or served by that program, and indirect costs allocated to that program.[5]

Second, if each program or activity of a nonprofit is reviewed during each budgeting cycle, it can create a culture of uncertainty within that nonprofit. If a staff member is assigned to a particular program or initiative, there's no assurance that his or her program or initiative will continue into the future.[6] Accordingly, the leaders of a nonprofit need to consider the impact that ZBB might have on both the culture and the staff of a nonprofit.[7]

While ZBB has two major downfalls, there are also numerous benefits of this budgeting method. ZBB requires leaders of a nonprofit to build the nonprofit's budget from scratch, whereby each expense is justified. Since financial resources of a nonprofit can often be scarce, ZBB helps ensure that those resources are being devoted to their highest and best use. One of the goals of ZBB is to eliminate inefficiencies within a nonprofit, such as a program or an activity that maybe no longer has as great of an impact as it once did.[8] By reevaluating each program or activity annually through the use of ZBB, such inefficiencies can be identified and eliminated if necessary.[9] As stated by Peter Drucker in his book *Managing for Results*, "If this product (activity or unit) were not here today, would we start it?"[10] Asking fundamental questions like this one helps eliminate a nonprofit's inefficient programs.

CASE STUDY: EL POMAR FOUNDATION

Rob Hilbert is one of the best chief financial officers I've ever been around, and he implemented ZBB at El Pomar Foundation during my tenure there. At that time, I was both a senior fellow and a program director for the foundation. The El Pomar Fellowship Program is one of the nation's best leadership development fellowships for recent college graduates interested in public service. My classmates hailed from Princeton, Rice, Yale, and Brown, among other tier-one institutions. During their first year of the fellowship, fellows are assigned to various operating programs within the foundation, such as the American Council of Young Political Leaders (ACYPL), the Forum for Civic Advancement, and the El Pomar Youth in Community Service Program (EPYCS), to name a few.

During the second year of the fellowship, most fellows are asked to lead one of those operating programs, and I was asked to lead EPYCS. At that time, EPYCS was the nation's second-largest youth grantmaking program behind a similar program operated by the Kellogg Foundation. We distributed $1 million annually to approximately 125 high schools so their students could make grants to various nonprofits in their communities. Working on EPYCS for two years was so much fun that I never really viewed it as work. When I led the program as a senior fellow, I had a team of twelve staff members and an operating budget of approximately $250,000. When it was time to consider the EPYCS' program budget, Rob Hilbert asked me, and every other program director, to use ZBB.

Because of this directive, we had to build the EPYCS' budget from scratch. It was definitely a time-consuming task, as I recall having numerous Excel spreadsheets as well as flip-chart notes from our team meetings up on my office wall. However, after we completed this thorough review of the EPYCS' budget, we were able to eliminate certain inefficiencies and actually lower the program's operating budget. We accomplished this goal without impacting the quality of the education we delivered to those high school students, which included sessions on philanthropy, leadership, and grantmaking. Rob Hilbert didn't want to impact the quality of the programming either, and by using ZBB, we not only identified some inefficiencies, but also reaffirmed key aspects of the program. Working without any assumptions has its benefits.

NO ASSUMPTIONS

ZBB is the main alternative to incremental budgeting. When nonprofit leaders need to build a budget, whether that's a monthly, quarterly, or yearly budget, they need to determine whether they'll use incremental budgeting or ZBB. With incremental budgeting, the new budget is reviewed in light of the previous budget, and incremental changes are made based on that last iteration. Using this method means that built-in assumptions related to the prior budget are typically carried forward. With ZBB, on the other hand, no assumptions are made. Each program or activity must be justified during the budgeting process. Questions that nonprofit leaders may ask when using ZBB include:

1. Do we need this program or activity?
2. Is this program or activity achieving the impact that we want it to?
3. What are the expenses related to this program or activity, and are all of those expenses necessary to achieve this impact?[11]

With no built-in assumptions, everything must be questioned. Accordingly, ZBB helps nonprofit leaders ensure that a nonprofit's limited resources are being allocated to their highest potential, which allows a nonprofit to achieve its greatest impact. Donors and potential donors would likely be impressed with this thoughtful and detailed-oriented approach to budgeting.

KEY PRINCIPLES

➜ ZBB has many pros and cons, but if implemented effectively by the leaders of a nonprofit, it can help ensure that the limited resources of a nonprofit are used effectively and efficiently.

➜ The purpose of ZBB is to not make any assumptions when building a budget.

➜ Peter Drucker helped develop ZBB as an alternative to incrementalism, whereby a budget is incrementally changed from its prior version, whether that prior budget was a monthly, quarterly, or yearly budget.

45

What's Unrelated Business Taxable Income (UBTI)?

■ ■ ■

In a number of instances a mysterious tax known as UBIT or UBTI, or the Unrelated Business Taxable Income, could be triggered and could cause financial havoc and turn a potential tax-free investment into a very tax-inefficient investment.

—Adam Bergman

GOODWILL INDUSTRIES

Goodwill Industries International, Inc. (Goodwill) is a 501(c)(3)-public charity based in Rockville, Maryland.[1] It was established in Boston, Massachusetts, in 1902 by Rev. Edgar Helms.[2] At that time, Rev. Helms received various donated items, such as clothes and other household items, and employed underprivileged individuals to repair those items before they were resold to the public.[3] This history continues to influence Goodwill's current mission, which is "[t]o enhance the dignity and quality of life of individuals and families by helping people reach their full potential through education, skills training and the power of work."[4] One way that Goodwill accomplishes its mission is by employing people with disabilities in its retail stores located the United States and Canada.[5] In 2017, Goodwill employed approximately 288,000 individuals and served more than 38.6 million people—which are impressive statistics.[6]

Collectively, Goodwill has 3,300 retail stores and outlets that have generated approximately $4.29 billion in sales since its inception in 1902.[7] Goodwill has generated approximately $5.87 billion in total revenues since inception, which includes grants, fees for contract work, and donations.[8] Due to its retail stores and outlets, Goodwill is among the top nonprofits in terms of dollars generated because of earned income activities. Whether this income is taxed by the IRS largely hinges on whether such income is *related* to the exempt purposes of Goodwill. In fact, every 501(c)(3)-public charity generating earned income should analyze this issue. The outcome of this analysis could allow a nonprofit to keep the unrestricted monies generated from earned income rather than having to give some of it to the IRS as a tax.[9] For this reason, nonprofit leaders should have a firm understanding of unrelated business income and the tax associated with that income under Section 512 of the Code.

UNRELATED BUSINESS INCOME TAX

Whether income is *unrelated* business income, and hence subject to the unrelated business income tax under Section 512 of the Code, or *related* income, and hence *not* subject to this tax, hinges on three elements. Those elements are whether an activity is: (1) a trade or business; (2) regularly carried on; and (3) *not* substantially related to a nonprofit's exempt purposes.[10] These three elements must *all* be met for income generated by a nonprofit to be classified by the IRS as "unrelated business income."[11] Accordingly, if any one of the foregoing elements is *not* met, then such income is *not* unrelated business income. For instance, if a trade or business is not "regularly carried on," then the income generated from an activity conducted by the nonprofit is not unrelated business income and thus, not subject to this tax.

Each year, Girl Scouts of the USA (Girl Scouts) sells millions of cookies.[12] During "cookie season," you've likely been asked to purchase these cookies by a Girl Scout troop as you enter a local supermarket. After all, who can resist a box of Thin Mints®? However, the income generated from the sales of these cookies is not subject to the unrelated business income tax because it is related to the charitable purposes of Girl Scouts.[13] The volunteers who help sell these cookies learn important business and leadership skills, both of which are related to the charitable purposes of Girl Scouts. Also, there's an exception to UBTI, which is one of many, for any trade or business carried on by volunteers who perform work "without compensation."[14]

An activity is "substantially related" to a nonprofit's charitable or exempt purpose if it "contributes importantly" to that mission.[15] This analysis is conducted on the facts and circumstances of each case.[16] Typically, the UBTI analysis hinges on whether an activity "contributes importantly" to the nonprofit's charitable or exempt purpose. The first two elements under this analysis, a "trade or business" that is "regularly carried on," are more straightforward. Thus, if an activity does "contribute importantly" to the nonprofit's charitable or exempt purpose, then the income from such activity is *not* subject to the unrelated business income tax.[17]

Because of the Tax Cuts and Jobs Act of 2017, which was signed into law on December 22, 2017, a nonprofit can no longer aggregate all of its trade or business activities when it's calculating its unrelated business income tax.[18] Because of this change in the law, nonprofits must track each trade or business that is subject to the unrelated business income tax on its own.[19] Additionally, the Tax Cuts and Jobs Act of 2017 treats certain "fringe benefits" offered by a nonprofit as UBTI, such as an on-site employee cafeteria, an on-site employee gym, or commuting benefits for its employees. Therefore, such activities are now subject to UBTI.[20] This change in the law resulting from this Act caught many nonprofit leaders by surprise.

CASE STUDY: A FINANCIAL LITERACY PROGRAM

The IRS frequently issues Private Letter Rulings (PLRs) on the issue of unrelated business taxable income. For example, on June 6, 2014, the IRS issued PLR 201423030 regarding potential unrelated business taxable income for a 501(c)(3)-public charity providing financial literacy and counseling programs to various colleges and universities.[21] At issue in this PLR was whether the income derived from the financial literacy and counseling programs offered in connection with nonprofit colleges and universities at no cost to the individual beneficiaries, including students and recent graduates, was unrelated business taxable income.[22]

The mission of this 501(c)(3)-public charity is "to aid and assist students to fulfill a program of higher education."[23] The activities of this nonprofit include, among other initiatives, public education, outreach, and community services.[24] Accordingly, one of the programs that this nonprofit operates is a financial literacy course offered through its website that student borrowers or recent graduates may sign up for at no cost.[25] The nonprofit colleges and universities "pay a fixed fee that constitutes approximately 15% to 20% of the actual cost to provide [the program] to their students and alumni."[26]

The IRS determined that these fixed fees are not unrelated business income and therefore, are not subject to the unrelated business income tax.[27] The IRS reasoned that the financial literacy and counseling programs furthered both the charitable and educational purposes of this 501(c)(3)-public charity.[28] Thus, the fees paid by the nonprofit colleges and universities so that their students and recent graduates could enroll in these courses is "excludible from . . . unrelated business taxable income within the meaning of [Section] 512."[29] Section 512 of the Code addresses UBTI.[30]

The IRS held that "since the fees you will be paid by schools to provide [the financial literacy and counseling programs] to their students is income from the conduct of a trade or business that is substantially related to your exempt purposes, such fees will *not* be considered gross income from an unrelated trade or business and would be excludible from your unrelated business taxable income."[31] Thus, the third element of the unrelated business income tax analysis was not satisfied. Rather, the fees generated from the financial literacy and counseling programs "contribute importantly" to this 501(c)(3)-public charity's exempt purposes.[32]

EARNED INCOME ACTIVITIES

Throughout the past few decades, nonprofit leaders have become more aware of whether income derived from a nonprofit's trade or business is subject to

UBTI. During this time, social entrepreneurs have thought of creative ways for nonprofits to earn revenue. If a nonprofit is entirely reliant upon donations from individuals, foundations, and corporations, then its programs and activities may be at risk during a downturn in the economy. Thus, earned revenue has many advantages, the main one being that it adds a stable source of revenue for the nonprofit. When a nonprofit engages in an earned income activity, the leaders of that nonprofit must be cognizant of whether the income derived from that activity is subject to the unrelated business income tax. Typically, this analysis depends on whether a trade or business is "substantially related" to the nonprofit's exempt purposes, just as it did in the foregoing private letter ruling. Based on this key element, nonprofit leaders should strive to implement earned income activities that are indeed "substantially related" to a nonprofit's exempt purposes. If that trade or business "contributes importantly" to a nonprofit's exempt purpose, it will be able to avoid UBTI. Consequently, a nonprofit will be able to hold on to additional unrestricted monies that can be used to accomplish its mission.

KEY PRINCIPLES

→ Whether income is unrelated business income, and hence subject to UBTI, hinges on three elements.

→ Those elements are whether an activity is: (1) a trade or business; (2) regularly carried on; and (3) *not* substantially related to a nonprofit's exempt purposes.

→ For income to be subject to UBTI, all three elements must be met.

46

What Are Internal Controls?

■ ■ ■

People don't buy what you do, they buy why you do it.

—Simon Sinek, *Start with Why* & TEDxPuget Sound

"IDEAS WORTH SPREADING"

My classmate from the El Pomar Foundation Fellowship Program, Jeremy, is the founder and curator of TEDxMileHigh. TEDxMileHigh is the Denver affiliate of TED. TED helps communities from across the world, like Denver, Puget Sound, or Portland, to name a few, produce independent "TED-like" talks known as "TEDx" events.[1] The mission of TED is simply "[to] spread ideas worth spreading."[2] TED is a nonprofit that was established in 1984 as a four-day conference held in Monterey, California, where "technology, entertainment and design converged."[3] Now, "TED Talks," as they are commonly referred to, cover a wide-range of topics, ideas, and subjects. On the TED website, the non-profit notes: "We believe passionately in the power of ideas to change attitudes, lives and, ultimately, the world."[4]

For example, TEDxMileHigh recently organized an event around the topic of "uncommon ideas," where leaders and experts from various industries addressed unconventional ideas.[5] A private-practice doctor in the Denver metro area who only treats refugees presented his uncommon idea for how to build a lucrative medical practice that serves a historically underserved population.[6] At the same TEDxMileHigh event, an artist who is passionate about using technology to help people understand each other's views, thoughts, and perspectives presented his uncommon idea of using virtual reality to help bridge these differences.[7] This technology would allow anyone willing to spend five to ten minutes in the vir-tual reality simulation to learn from others and build upon their commonalities, rather than on their differences or perceived differences.

Like TED, TEDxMileHigh is a nonprofit corporation. My friend incorpo-rated TEDxMileHigh as a Colorado nonprofit corporation in 2010.[8] Because TEDxMileHigh is a nonprofit corporation and brings in thousands of dollars in annual ticket sales, its board of directors should implement effective internal controls. Such controls would help ensure that TEDxMileHigh's financial resources are devoted to its charitable causes. The importance of implementing effective internal controls is reflected by certain publicly-traded companies. In those companies, the chief executive officer and the chief financial officer must periodically attest to the effectiveness of internal controls.[9] Just like their for-profit peers, nonprofit leaders should also understand the purpose and significance of implementing effective internal controls.

INTERNAL CONTROLS

Effective internal controls are important because they help the leaders of nonprofits avoid fraud, mismanagement, errors, misstatements, and related mistakes, abuses, and issues. In the nonprofit sector, "money equals mission." Accordingly, nonprofit leaders need to implement an effective internal controls scheme to ensure that a nonprofit's limited and valuable financial resources are devoted to its exempt purposes. For example, a nonprofit should pursue a policy that emphasizes segregation of duties.[10] This manifests itself, for instance, by having two people process donation checks to the nonprofit as opposed to one person.[11] It's harder to commit fraud when someone is looking over another person's shoulder. In this regard, nonprofit leaders should also strive to create a culture whereby everyone associated with that nonprofit knows that those leaders value the internal controls system.[12] This means that those leaders have adopted policies and procedures, such as a conflict of interest policy or a document destruction and retention policy, which help reaffirm their culture of strong internal controls.[13]

Just like the federal government's system of checks and balances, an effective internal controls program also implements certain checks and balances. An effective risk management program for a nonprofit, which includes a strong internal controls system, will both help: (1) a nonprofit retain its assets, as opposed to those assets being siphoned off from the nonprofit because of either intentional misconduct or gross negligence; and (2) save money down the road.[14] According to scholars Peter Konrad and Alys Novak in their book, *Financial Management for Nonprofits: Keys to Success*, an effective internal controls system is comprised of the following objectives: "(1) provide reliable data, (2) safeguard assets, (3) promote [the nonprofit's] operational efficiency, and (4) encourage adherence to [the nonprofit's] polic[ies]."[15] A nonprofit can achieve these outcomes if it maintains financial books and records tracking all financial transactions; keeps adequate board minutes; has its board periodically review its financial statements; and has external auditors audit its financial statements.[16] If the leaders of a nonprofit engage external auditors to produce a nonprofit's audited financial statements, and those auditors identify a material deficiency in the nonprofit's internal control system, then those auditors may reflect that deficiency in their management letter to the board of directors.[17] A management letter is simply a letter written by a nonprofit's external auditors to the leaders of that nonprofit, including the board of directors, which outlines various recommendations for improving certain aspects of that nonprofit's activities.[18] A material weaknesses in a nonprofit's internal control system could be one of the issues that these auditors identify, while also recommending ways to improve that system.[19]

CASE STUDY: TED AND TEDX

Let's presume that TEDxPortland, the TED affiliate for the Portland metro area, engages external auditors to produce its audited financial statements. TEDxPortland is an Oregon nonprofit corporation that is also exempt from federal income tax under Section 501(c)(3) of the Code as a public charity.[20] For the fiscal year ended December 31, 2016, TEDxPortland had revenues of approximately $840,000 and expenses of approximately $816,000.[21] Because TEDxPortland's revenues and expenses for the fiscal year ended December 31, 2016 generally match, this is an excellent example of "money equaling mission." That is, each year TEDxPortland uses nearly all of its financial resources to fulfill its mission through its speakers, who include former *Today* show correspondent Ann Curry, among other speakers.[22]

Let's further presume that TEDxPortland only uses one person to process checks related to ticket sales for its speaker events. In this scenario, TEDxPortland's external auditors may note that this process is a material weakness in its internal controls system. With only one person processing those checks, as opposed to two people, that person can more easily commit fraud against the nonprofit.[23] Finally, let's also presume that TEDxPortland does not have a document destruction and retention policy. This policy outlines the documents and records that must be maintained by a nonprofit and for how long. Not having a document destruction and retention policy might be another material deficiency in this nonprofit's internal controls system.[24] If TEDxPortland did in fact have these two material deficiencies, its external auditors may note such weaknesses in its management letter to the board of directors and executive leadership team.

REDUCING RISK AND DETERRING FRAUD

It's imperative that the financial resources of nonprofits are devoted to their charitable causes. Whether that charitable cause is feeding the homeless, educating K–12 students, or providing medical care to historically underserved populations, those resources must be protected. For this reason, nonprofit leaders should strive to implement an effective internal controls system for their nonprofits. An effective internal controls system helps to both reduce the risk of financial errors and deter fraud. Nonprofit leaders, such as the leaders of TEDxMileHigh or TEDxPortland, should also strive to create a culture that values effective internal controls. This top-down strategy will likely influence everyone associated with that nonprofit. A nonprofit's donors will appreciate it because an effective internal controls system will likely inspire a sense of trust and confidence among those donors. Just like TED, TEDxMileHigh, and TEDxPortland strive to do every day, implementing a strong internal controls system is an "idea worth spreading" amongst all nonprofit leaders.

KEY PRINCIPLES

→ Effective internal controls are important because they help the leaders of nonprofits avoid fraud, mismanagement, errors, misstatements, and related mistakes, abuses, and issues.

→ Nonprofit leaders need to implement an effective internal controls scheme to ensure that a nonprofit's limited and valuable financial resources are devoted to its exempt purposes.

→ Just like the federal government's system of checks and balances, an effective internal controls program also implements certain checks and balances.

47

What's a Capital Campaign?

■ ■ ■

I deem it the duty of every man to devote a certain portion of his income for charitable purposes; and that it is his further duty to see it so applied and to do the most good for which it is capable.

—Thomas Jefferson

BUTTERFLY PAVILION

The Butterfly Pavilion is one of the nation's largest 501(c)(3)-public charities devoted exclusively to invertebrates.[1] Invertebrates don't develop backbones, and include crabs, spiders, and butterflies, among others. If you visit the Butterfly Pavilion you'll get to experience these species on a first-hand basis, including Rosie, a famous tarantula visitors can hold if they so choose. The Butterfly Pavilion was the first stand-alone nonprofit invertebrate zoo accredited by the Association of Zoos and Aquariums.[2] It opened in 1995, and today strives "[t]o foster an appreciation of invertebrates by educating the public about the need to protect and care for threatened habitats globally, while conducting research for solutions in invertebrate conservation."[3] Each year, thousands of school-aged children, families, and other patrons visit the Butterfly Pavilion to learn more about invertebrates.

Based on the Butterfly Pavilion's most recent Form 990, it has approximately $4 million in revenues each year and net assets of approximately $3.5 million.[4] Over the past decade, the Butterfly Pavilion has experienced tremendous growth, and as a result, has outgrown its current facility. Accordingly, its board of directors and chief executive officer launched a multi-million dollar capital campaign to raise funds to build a new facility that can meet its growing demand. A capital campaign is typically initiated when a nonprofit has a major project or two it would like to complete. All over the United States, nonprofits conduct similar capital campaigns to raise funds for either endowments, buildings, or other significant mission-related purposes.

During my tenure at the Boettcher Foundation, we funded numerous capital campaigns, just like the one launched by the Butterfly Pavilion. The foundation's key donors, Charles and Claude Boettcher, made a substantial portion of their wealth from Ideal Cement Company, which they established in 1924.[5] Charles served as its president and Claude as its vice president.[6] Because a large portion of their wealth was made from selling cement, they directed the foundation's board of directors to primarily fund capital campaigns related to buildings.

At any given time, thousands of nonprofits will be conducting capital campaigns. Thus, every nonprofit leader should understand the basic elements of a capital campaign and how he or she might be able to help that nonprofit raise a significant amount of money, typically for one or two special purposes. In fact, there are numerous consultants who help nonprofits do just that.

CAPITAL CAMPAIGNS

If a nonprofit needs to raise a substantial amount of money for a particular purpose, they typically launch a capital campaign. A new building, for example, is an expensive endeavor, and a nonprofit can attempt to acquire this asset in one of three ways. First, it can take out a loan for either the full or partial cost of that new building. Second, it can use some of its net assets to help with construction costs. For example, the Butterfly Pavilion's board of directors could use some or all of its approximately $3.5 million in net assets to help build its new building.[7] Third, it can launch a capital campaign to bring in donations to cover either the full or partial cost of that new building. Ideally, that nonprofit is able to raise the full cost of the new building through donations. By doing so, the nonprofit's net assets increase by the value of that new building.

When a nonprofit launches a capital campaign, it typically follows one of three fundraising strategies to achieve its fundraising goal: (1) the triangle method; (2) the inverse triangle method; or (3) the hourglass method (figure 47.1).[8]

Figure 47.1 Capital Campaign Fundraising Models

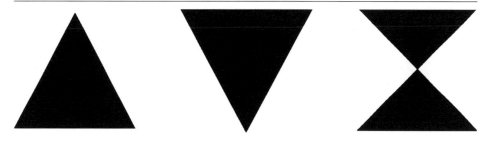

First, a nonprofit using the triangle method targets a large number of small donations, a few midsize donations, and even fewer large donations to achieve its fundraising goal (see Figure 47.1).[9] Given this makeup of donors, this fundraising strategy is shaped like a triangle.[10] In contrast, the inverse triangle method targets a significant number of larger donations, a few midsize donations, and even fewer small donations (see Figure 47.1).[11] Given this makeup of donors, this fundraising strategy is shaped like an upside down triangle.[12] Finally, the hourglass method is a blend of these two triangle methods. With the hourglass method, a nonprofit targets a significant number of larger donations, a small number of midsize donations, and a large number of small donations (see Figure 47.1).[13] The fundraising strategy a nonprofit chooses to implement will depend primarily on its donor base.

CASE STUDY: BOSTON UNIVERSITY

Most nonprofits utilize the triangle method when launching capital campaigns. This is because they generally have a large number of donors who can give smaller amounts, a few who can give midsize amounts, and a small number who can give larger amounts. One of my alma maters, Boston University, launched a capital campaign in 2010 to raise funds to renovate its law school building, and it likely utilized the triangle method.[14] To stay competitive in the law school market, the leaders of Boston University knew that they had to raise millions of dollars to enhance the law school's existing building, the Redstone Building.[15] This building is named after Sumner Redstone, the former chairman of both CBS and Viacom.[16]

Accordingly, the Boston University School of Law launched a $45 million capital campaign in 2010 to raise much-needed funds to renovate this building.[17] As the chair of the capital campaign committee, Richard Godfrey, noted in a letter to the Boston University School of Law alumni and community, a renovated building is necessary for "vibrant and flexible spaces to teach" as well as a "more connected student experience."[18] Statements like this one reinforce a nonprofit's "case for support" for its capital campaign. An effective "case for support," which fundraisers frequently use, helps a nonprofit reach its fundraising goal by conveying to donors and other stakeholders the key reasons for the capital campaign. When a nonprofit, like Boston University, launches a capital campaign it typically does so in two different phases.

The first phase is called the "silent phase," in which a nonprofit lines up a few large gifts so that when it publicly announces the capital campaign it can show that the campaign already has significant momentum. In turn, this reinforces the likelihood that a nonprofit will reach its fundraising goal. During the silent phase, a nonprofit generally aims to raise at least one-third of its fundraising goal from its closest donors. For Boston University, the silent phase goal was likely $15 million, representing one-third of the campaign's total fundraising goal of $45 million. After the silent phase, a nonprofit publicly announces the capital campaign, which is known as the "public phase." The goal of the public phase is to raise the remaining amount of the capital campaign's fundraising goal by utilizing one of the aforementioned three fundraising methods.[19]

"MOVES MANAGEMENT"

As a nonprofit grows, it's likely that its leaders will need to launch a capital campaign at some point. A capital campaign aims to raise a significant amount of money for a particular purpose or set of purposes. These purposes may include a new building, an endowment, or another large asset purchase, such as land or equipment. During the two phases of a capital campaign, a nonprofit will likely utilize the "moves management" framework for fundraising, which involves: (1) identifying and cultivating potential donors; (2) soliciting those potential donors; (3) stewarding those donors; and (4) attempting to move those donors up the metaphorical giving ladder.[20] This "moves management" framework aims to have a donor's second gift be larger than his or her first gift, and it's typically the backbone of an effective capital campaign. Some people may, in jest, assert that both the Butterfly Pavilion and the Boston University School of Law launched their respective capital campaigns to benefit spineless species: invertebrates and lawyers. As a member of the latter group, I certainly hope that's not the case! Effective lawyering, including nonprofit representation, can also be used as a force for good.

KEY PRINCIPLES

→ If a nonprofit needs to raise a substantial amount of money for a particular purpose, they typically launch a capital campaign.

→ When a nonprofit launches a capital campaign, it typically follows one of three fundraising strategies to achieve its fundraising goal: (1) the triangle method; (2) the inverse triangle method; or (3) the hourglass method.

→ The fundraising strategy a nonprofit chooses to implement will depend primarily on its donor base.

48

What Are Donor-Advised Funds, Charitable Remainder Trusts, and Charitable Lead Trusts?

■ ■ ■

Jazmyne's goal in life was to become a doctor. That was her goal since she was three years old, [and] when you would ask why her answer was simple, she would say "I want to make the world a better place."

—Bobbette Davis

THE SEVENTH FLOOR

When our daughter was three years old, we noticed that she would wake up from a night's sleep gasping for breath and with damp hair. My wife, with her motherly instincts, understood this was not normal midnight behavior for a three-year-old. When we took our daughter to her pediatrician to talk about these symptoms, he recommended that we visit an ear, nose, and throat (ENT) specialist. We met with an ENT doctor at Children's Hospital Colorado (Children's Hospital), who ordered a sleep study to determine if our daughter had sleep apnea. At the time, we had no idea what sleep apnea was, but sure enough, the sleep study concluded that our daughter had "severe obstructive sleep apnea."

We learned she was sweating while she slept because her little body was working so hard to overcome the airway blockage caused by enlarged tonsils and adenoids. After the ENT doctor confirmed she had sleep apnea, our daughter had a successful tonsillectomy, to remove her enlarged tonsils, and a successful adenoidectomy, to remove her enlarged adenoids. As the three of us walked into Children's Hospital the morning of surgery, we saw that the lobby is now called the "Boettcher Atrium," in honor of the foundation's grantmaking legacy to this hospital. When I worked at the Boettcher Foundation, it rarely occurred to me that a grant made by the foundation might personally benefit me or my family one day. That morning, I felt a sense of pride that I had worked at a place whose daily work was devoted to improving the lives of others.

Children's Hospital and several hospitals like it throughout the country impact the lives of thousands of patients and their families every day. There's no better example of this impact, however, than the experience of my former colleague, Bobbi, and her family. Bobbi and her family had to visit the seventh floor of Children's Hospital for nearly two years because her daughter had a rare form of cancer called Ewing's Sarcoma. The seventh floor is where the hospital's incredible team of doctors and nurses treat pediatric cancer patients.

Words are insufficient to describe all that Bobbi and her family endured throughout this experience, but Bobbi's perspective on life is unique and beautiful because of it. She cherishes and seizes each day, as all of us should. In our house, we have a daily reminder to follow Bobbi's lead because of what she taught us about life. Due to these life-changing experiences, which my friend, her family, and countless others have experienced, numerous donors contribute annually to nonprofit hospitals serving children. They do this through various giving vehicles, like donor-advised funds, charitable remainder trusts, and charitable lead trusts.

DONOR-ADVISED FUNDS, CHARITABLE REMAINDER TRUSTS, AND CHARITABLE LEAD TRUSTS

If a philanthropist does not want to establish his or her own private foundation but still wants to contribute to public charities, a donor-advised fund (DAF) is a viable option for accomplishing this goal. The legal structure related to DAFs was formalized with the passage of the Tax Reform Act of 1969.[1] With a DAF, another 501(c)(3) entity, called the "sponsoring organization," deals with the administrative tasks related to donations, such as IRS reporting.[2] Once a DAF is established, that organization has legal control over those funds.[3] However, an individual creating a DAF is able to make grant recommendations to the sponsoring organization, which are typically adopted by that organization.[4] Thus, a DAF allows a donor to take an immediate tax deduction once the fund is established, make grant recommendations to the sponsoring organization, and avoid dealing with any administrative tasks.

Along with DAFs, both charitable remainder trusts and charitable lead trusts are great options for individuals wishing to make a significant impact on a nonprofit grantee. To understand trusts, whether it's a charitable remainder trust or a charitable lead trust, it's important to first note that trusts are either *revocable* or *irrevocable*.[5] A revocable trust means that the grantor, or the individual who created the trust, may alter or terminate the trust after it has been established.[6] An irrevocable trust, on the other hand, means that the trust may not be altered, revoked, or terminated after it's been established unless its beneficiary consents to such action.[7]

With this background in trusts, both charitable remainder trusts and charitable lead trusts are *irrevocable* trusts. First, a charitable remainder trust allows a donor to identify one or more charitable organizations to receive a donation once the trust terminates.[8] During the lifespan of the charitable remainder trust, which cannot exceed twenty years with a beneficiary that's a charity, the grantor or another designee receives an income stream.[9] Pursuant to Section 664 of the Code, this income stream cannot be less than 5 percent or more than 50 percent of the initial assets in the trust.[10] At the end of the trust's lifespan, the assets remaining in the charitable remainder trust will be given to the charity designated by a grantor when he or she created it.[11] A grantor may receive a tax deduction on his or her federal income taxes for creating a charitable remainder trust.[12]

Second, a grantor may also create a charitable lead trust. Like a charitable remainder trust, a charitable lead trust is also *irrevocable*.[13] However, with a charitable lead trust, a grantor will designate one or more charitable organizations to receive an income stream during the lifespan of the trust.[14] This lifespan may vary, depending on the grantor's wishes, as there's no maximum or minimum period.[15] When the trust terminates, one or more individuals, such as the grantor's children or grandchildren, will receive the assets remaining in the trust.[16] Thus, with a charitable lead trust, a grantor may receive a partial tax deduction for creating the trust, and then one or more beneficiaries will receive the assets that are remaining in the trust once it terminates.[17] A grantor may also designate a DAF as the beneficiary for a charitable lead trust.

CASE STUDY: CHILDREN'S HOSPITAL

My friend Ashley worked as a fundraising professional for Children's Hospital. Frequently, she's asked to speak at national conferences devoted to fundraising excellence. Because she's an expert on fundraising techniques and best practices, I frequently ask her to serve as a guest lecturer in my nonprofit courses. Her insights into donor cultivation, solicitation, and stewardship greatly benefit my students, as many of them desire to become fundraising professionals like Ashley. During Ashley's presentations she always discusses DAFs, charitable remainder trusts, and charitable lead trusts. Her premise is simple: if a nonprofit leader has an understanding of the various giving vehicles a donor may take advantage of, such as DAFs, charitable remainder trusts, and charitable lead trusts, it's more likely that a donor will make a significant contribution to the nonprofit cultivating and soliciting him or her. For instance, Ashley cultivated a large donor for the hospital that utilized a charitable remainder trust.

With this thesis, it's no coincidence that Children's Hospital has been the beneficiary of various DAFs.[18] The website for Children's Hospital states, "Currently, donors can recommend grants to Children's Hospital Colorado Foundation from Fidelity® Charitable, Schwab® Charitable, and [the] Greater Kansas City Community Foundation [and] more sponsoring charities may be added in the future."[19] As Ashley frequently tells my students, each donor situation is unique, especially when donors are considering significant gifts. Accordingly, it's important for nonprofit leaders who are part of the fundraising process to understanding these various giving vehicles. Throughout this process, the goal is to find a match between a donor's needs or desires and the nonprofit's needs, programs, and activities. Utilizing a DAF, charitable remainder trust, or charitable lead trust might help nonprofit leaders find an appropriate match.

THE GREATEST 10 PERCENT

As you progress in life, it's extremely likely that a nonprofit, like a 501(c)(3)-public charity or a 501(c)(3)-private foundation, will positively impact either you or your loved ones. In fact, perhaps this impact has already occurred. For my family, Children's Hospital and its doctors, nurses, and staff members positively affected our lives, including the daily well-being of our daughter. On an infinitely larger scale, and with a clear understanding that any words I place on this page are insufficient to describe Bobbi's experiences with Children's Hospital, the doctors, nurses, and staff members devoted to the seventh floor of this hospital forever impacted her life. Because of her family's experiences with Children's Hospital, they annually raise funds and awareness for Ewing's Sarcoma patients.

Millions of donors have supported the missions of nonprofit hospitals due to the life-changing work they conduct each day. Donors may choose to provide support through DAFs, charitable remainder trusts, or charitable lead trusts. With each giving vehicle, donors may earmark financial support for causes or issues they're passionate about. When nonprofit leaders and fundraising professionals have a firm understanding of the various giving vehicles available to donors, they're likely to generate more resources. In turn, they're able to produce more mission. When that mission is related to cancer treatment and research, especially pediatric cancer, there's no ceiling with respect to how much money could potentially be donated.

I sincerely hope that Bobbi and Jazmyne's story in particular, and every other story highlighted in this book, demonstrate the tremendous impact of the nonprofit sector. While the nonprofit sector may only make up 10 percent of the

American economy, it represents the greatest 10 percent of our economy. I'm sure of it. If you ever visit the seventh floor, you'll be sure of it too.

KEY PRINCIPLES

→ With a DAF, another 501(c)(3) entity, called the "sponsoring organization," deals with the administrative tasks related to donations, such as IRS reporting.

→ A charitable remainder trust allows a donor to identify one or more charitable organizations to receive a donation once the trust terminates.

→ With a charitable lead trust, a grantor will designate one or more charitable organizations to receive an income stream during the lifespan of the trust.

Notes

■ ■ ■

FOREWORD

[1] Ron Chernow, *Alexander Hamilton* (New York: Penguin Books, 2004), 36–40.
[2] Ibid.
[3] Ibid.
[4] Ibid.
[5] Ibid.
[6] Ibid.
[7] Ibid.

INTRODUCTION

[1] Simon Sinek, *Start With Why: How Great Leaders Inspire Everyone To Take Action* (New York: Penguin Group, 2009), 41.
[2] Simon Sinek, "How Great Leaders Inspire Action," TEDx, accessed December 1, 2018, https://www.youtube.com/watch?v=qp0HIF3SfI4&t=41s.
[3] Sinek, *Start With Why*, 11–225.
[4] Ibid.
[5] Ibid.
[6] Ibid.
[7] Ibid.
[8] Abraham Lincoln, "The Gettysburg Address," Abraham Lincoln's Speeches and Writings, accessed January 13, 2019, http://www.abrahamlincolnonline.org/lincoln/speeches/gettysburg.htm.
[9] Alexis de Tocqueville, *Democracy in America*, 1st ed., trans. Henry Reeve, Esq. (New York: Adlard and Saunders, 1838), 595.

1. WHAT'S THE DIFFERENCE BETWEEN A NONPROFIT CORPORATION AND A TAX-EXEMPT ENTITY?

[1] "Who We Are," TIAA, accessed November 11, 2018, https://www.tiaa.org/public/why-tiaa/who-we-are.
[2] Gretchen Morgenson, "The Finger-Pointing at the Finance Firm TIAA," *The New York Times*, October 21, 2017, https://www.nytimes.com/2017/10/21/business/the-finger-pointing-at-the-finance-firm-tiaa.html.
[3] Ibid.

4   "Who We Are," TIAA, https://www.tiaa.org/public/why-tiaa/who-we-are.

5   Ibid.

6   Ibid.

7   "Teachers Insurance and Annuity Association," Encyclopedia.com, accessed November 11, 2018, https://www.encyclopedia.com/books/politics-and-business-magazines/teachers-insurance-and-annuity-association; Irving S. Schloss and Deborah V. Abildsoe, *Understanding TIAA-CREF: How to Plan for a Secure and Comfortable Retirement* (New York: Oxford University Press, 2000), 19.

8   Schloss and Abildsoe, *Understanding TIAA-CREF*, 19.

9   Paul Arnsberger, Melissa Ludlum, Margaret Riley, and Mark Stanton, "A History of the Tax-Exempt Sector: An SOI Perspective," Internal Revenue Service, accessed November 11, 2018, https://www.irs.gov/pub/irs-soi/tehistory.pdf.

10   Schloss and Abildsoe, *Understanding TIAA-CREF*, 19; Arnsberger, Ludlum, Riley, and Stanton, "A History of the Tax-Exempt Sector," https://www.irs.gov/pub/irs-soi/tehistory.pdf.

11   "When TIAA Does Well, Our Participants Do Better," TIAA, accessed November 11, 2018, https://www.tiaa.org/public/sharing-profits-with-participants.

12   Lisa A. Runquist, *The ABCs of Nonprofits*, 2nd ed. (Chicago: American Bar Association, 2015), 3–4.

13   Ibid.

14   "Domestic Nonprofit Corporation Forms," Oregon Secretary of State, accessed November 11, 2018, https://sos.oregon.gov/business/Pages/domestic-nonprofit-corporation-forms.aspx.

15   "Form 1023-EZ: Streamlined Application for Recognition of Exemption Under Section 501(c)(3) of the Internal Revenue Code," Internal Revenue Service, accessed November 11, 2018, https://www.irs.gov/forms-pubs/about-form-1023-ez.

16   Bruce Hopkins, *The Law of Tax Exempt Organizations*, 11th ed. (Hoboken, NJ: John Wiley & Sons, 2016), 796–97.

17   "Form 1024: Application For Recognition of Exemption Under Section 501(a)," Internal Revenue Service, accessed November 11, 2018, https://www.irs.gov/pub/irs-pdf/f1024.pdf; "Form 1023: Application for Recognition of Exemption Under Section 501(c)(3) of the Internal Revenue Code," Internal Revenue Service, accessed November 11, 2018, https://www.irs.gov/pub/irs-pdf/f1023.pdf; "Form 1024-A: Application for Recognition of Exemption Under Section 501(c)(4) of the Internal Revenue Code," Internal Revenue Service, accessed November 11, 2018, https://www.irs.gov/pub/irs-pdf/f1024a.pdf.

18   "Form 1023-EZ: Streamlined Application for Recognition of Exemption Under Section 501(c)(3) of the Internal Revenue Code," Internal Revenue Service, accessed November 11, 2018, https://www.irs.gov/forms-pubs/about-form-1023-ez.

2.   WHAT'S THE INTERNAL AFFAIRS DOCTRINE?

1   "Delaware Division of Corporations: About the Division of Corporations," State of Delaware, accessed October 2, 2018, https://corp.delaware.gov/aboutagency/.

2   "Why Did Mark Zuckerberg Incorporate Facebook as a Florida LLC?" Lawtrades.com, accessed October 2, 108, https://www.lawtrades.com/blog/answers/why-did-mark-zuckerberg-incorporate-facebook-as-a-florida-llc-2/.

3   Ibid.

4   Ibid.

5   *The Social Network*, directed by David Fincher (2010; Los Angeles, CA: Columbia Pictures, 2010), DVD; "The Social Network," IMDb, accessed October 2, 2018, https://www.imdb.com/title/tt1285016/quotes?ref_=tt_ql_trv_4.

6   "Facebook's First Big Investor, Peter Thiel, Cashes Out," CNN Business, accessed October 2, 2018, https://money.cnn.com/2012/08/20/technology/facebook-peter-thiel/index.html.

[7] Peter Thiel, *Zero to One: Notes on Startups, or How to Build the Future* (New York: Crown Business, 2014), 80.

[8] "Restated Certificate of Incorporation," United States Securities and Exchange Commission, accessed October 2, 2018, https://www.sec.gov/Archives/edgar/data/1326801/000119312512175673/d287954dex33.htm.

[9] Jeremy Deutsch, "Investor, Beware: Was Your Fund Really Formed in an Investor-Friendly Forum?" *The New York Law Journal*, November 9, 2018, https://www.law.com/newyorklawjournal/2018/11/09/investor-beware-was-your-fund-really-formed-in-an-investor-friendly-forum/?slreturn=20181029082506; Stephen Clinton and Romin Thomson, "How Did Delaware Get So Popular?" *California Business Law Practitioner*, Winter 2013, The Regents of the University of California, http://www.smwb.com/doc/How-Did-Delaware-Get-So-%20Popular.pdf.

[10] *Edgar v. Mite Corp.*, U.S. 457 U.S. 624, 645 (1982), accessed November 28, 2018, https://scholar.google.com/scholar_case?case=2984439589202067076&hl=en&as_sdt=2,5; Norwood P. Beveridge, "The Internal Affairs Doctrine: The Proper Law of a Corporation," *The Business Lawyer* 44, no. 3 (1989): 693–719, http://www.jstor.org/stable/40687015.

[11] Ibid.; David Horowitz and Paul Leaf, "The Internal Affairs Doctrine versus a Conflicting Contractual Choice of Law Provision," The Bureau of National Affairs, November 2, 2012, https://www.kirkland.com/siteFiles/Publications/Bloomberg%20BNA%20(Internal%20Affairs%20Doctrine_%20Leaf,%20Horowitz).pdf.

[12] "Florida Adopts New Limited Liability Company Act," Akerman Law, accessed October 2, 2018, https://www.akerman.com/en/perspectives/florida-adopts-new-limited-liability-company-act.html.

[13] Horowitz and Leaf, "The Internal Affairs Doctrine," https://www.kirkland.com/siteFiles/Publications/Bloomberg%20BNA%20(Internal%20Affairs%20Doctrine_%20Leaf,%20Horowitz).pdf; Clinton and Thomson, "How Did Delaware Get So Popular?"http://www.smwb.com/doc/How-Did-Delaware-Get-So-%20Popular.pdf.

[14] "Form 990: Return of Organization Exempt From Income Tax," American Heart Association, accessed October 2, 2018, https://www.guidestar.org/FinDocuments/2017/135/613/2017-135613797-0ec2c869-9.pdf.

[15] Ibid.

[16] *Edgar v. Mite Corp.*, U.S. 457 U.S. 624, 645 (1982), accessed November 28, 2018, https://scholar.google.com/scholar_case?case=2984439589202067076&hl=en&as_sdt=2,5; Beveridge, "The Internal Affairs Doctrine," 693–719; Horowitz and Leaf, "The Internal Affairs Doctrine," https://www.kirkland.com/siteFiles/Publications/Bloomberg%20BNA%20(Internal%20Affairs%20Doctrine_%20Leaf,%20Horowitz).pdf.

[17] Committee on Nonprofit Organizations, *Model Nonprofit Corporation Act*, 3rd ed. (Chicago: American Bar Association, 2009), 1–3; 17–18.

[18] Ibid.

[19] Deutsch, "Investor, Beware," https://www.law.com/newyorklawjournal/2018/11/09/investor-beware-was-your-fund-really-formed-in-an-investor-friendly-forum/?slreturn=20181029082506; Clinton and Thomson, "How Did Delaware Get So Popular?" http://www.smwb.com/doc/How-Did-Delaware-Get-So-%20Popular.pdf.

[20] "Delaware Division of Corporations: About the Division of Corporations," State of Delaware, accessed October 2, 2018, https://corp.delaware.gov/aboutagency/.

[21] Clinton and Thomson, "How Did Delaware Get so Popular?" http://www.smwb.com/doc/How-Did-Delaware-Get-So-%20Popular.pdf.

[22] "State Laws Governing Nonprofit Corporations," USLegal.com, accessed November 29, 2018, https://nonprofitorganizations.uslegal.com/state-laws-governing-nonprofit-corporations/.

[23] Ibid.; Committee on Nonprofit Organizations, *Model Nonprofit Corporation Act*, 1–3; 17–8.

24   Marion R. Fremont-Smith, *Governing Nonprofit Organizations: Federal and State Law and Regulation* (Cambridge, MA: The Belknap Press of Harvard University Press, 2004), 52–53.

25   "About," The Chan Zuckerberg Initiative, accessed November 29, 2018, https://www.chanzuckerberg.com/about.

26   Ibid.

27   "Initiatives," The Chan Zuckerberg Initiative, accessed November 29, 2018, https://www.chanzuckerberg.com/initiatives.

28   Joel L. Fleishman, *The Foundation: A Great American Secret* (New York: PublicAffairs, 2007), 1–321; Olivier Zunz, *Philanthropy in America: A History* (Princeton, NJ: Princeton University Press, 2012), 1–301.

29   Ibid.

30   "Form 990-PF: Return of Private Foundation," The Bill and Melinda Gates Foundation, accessed November 29, 2018, https://www.guidestar.org/FinDocuments/2016/911/663/2016-911663695-0e7cdc5b-F.pdf.

31   Katherine Schulten, "Mark Zuckerberg Vows to Donate 99% of His Facebook Shares for Charity," *The New York Times*, December 2, 2015, https://www.nytimes.com/2015/12/02/technology/mark-zuckerberg-facebook-charity.html.

32   Peter Reilly, "What Is With This Chan Zuckerberg LLC Thing? Tax Geek Speaks," *Forbes*, December 4, 2015, https://www.forbes.com/sites/peterjreilly/2015/12/04/what-is-with-this-chan-zuckerberg-llc-thing-tax-geeks-speak/#45dea10767b8; Natasha Singer and Mike Isaac, "Mark Zuckerberg's Philanthropy Uses L.L.C. for More Control," *The New York Times*, December 3, 2015, https://www.nytimes.com/2015/12/03/technology/zuckerbergs-philanthropy-uses-llc-for-more-control.html.

33   Ibid.

34   Beveridge, "The Internal Affairs Doctrine," 693–719, http://www.jstor.org/stable/40687015.

35   "Facebook, Inc.: Form 8-K," United States Securities and Exchange Commission, accessed November 29, 2018, https://www.sec.gov/Archives/edgar/data/1326801/000132680115000035/form8kdec2015.htm.

36   Matt Clausen, "Some Restrictions Apply: Donating Restricted Stock," Adler & Colvin, May 14, 2013, https://www.adlercolvin.com/blog/2013/05/14/some-restrictions-apply-donating-restricted-stock/.

37   Singer and Isaac, "Mark Zuckerberg's Philanthropy," https://www.nytimes.com/2015/12/03/technology/zuckerbergs-philanthropy-uses-llc-for-more-control.html.

38   Jeffrey Joyner, "Can an LLC Make Charitable Contributions?" *Small Business Chronicle*, accessed November 29, 2018, https://smallbusiness.chron.com/can-llc-make-charitable-contributions-65814.html.

39   Clinton and Thomson, "How Did Delaware Get so Popular?" http://www.smwb.com/doc/How-Did-Delaware-Get-So-%20Popular.pdf.

40   Fremont-Smith, *Governing Nonprofit Organizations*, 52–53; Committee on Nonprofit Organizations, *Model Nonprofit Corporation Act*, 1–3; 17–18.

3.   WHAT'S A DISSOLUTION PROVISION?

1   Nicholas P. Cafardi and Jaclyn Fabean Cherry, *Understanding Nonprofit and Tax Exempt Organizations* (Newark, NJ: LexisNexis, 2006), 37–38.

2   Lisa Runquist, *The ABCs of Nonprofits* (Chicago: American Bar Association, 2015), 123–24.

3   Colorado Revised Statutes (C.R.S.) § 7-122-102.

4   Cafardi and Fabean Cherry, *Understanding Nonprofit and Tax-Exempt Organizations*, 37–38.

5   Ibid.

⁶ Marion R. Fremont-Smith, *Governing Nonprofit Organizations: Federal and State Law and Regulation* (Cambridge, MA: The Belknap Press of Harvard University Press, 2004), 173–74.

⁷ Ibid.

⁸ "Level 3 Foundation, Inc. Articles of Incorporation," Colorado Secretary of State, accessed November 28, 2018, https://www.sos.state.co.us/biz/ViewImage.do?masterFileId=20141033971&fileId=20141033971.

⁹ "Form 990: Return of Organization Exempt from Income Tax," Level 3 Foundation, accessed November 28, 2018, https://www.guidestar.org/FinDocuments/2016/464/615/2016-464615262-0dc5a220-9.pdf.

¹⁰ "Level 3 Foundation, Inc.," Colorado Secretary of State, https://www.sos.state.co.us/biz/ViewImage.do?masterFileId=20141033971&fileId=20141033971.

4. WHAT ARE BYLAWS?

¹ Marion R. Fremont-Smith, *Governing Nonprofit Organizations: Federal and State Law and Regulation* (Cambridge, MA: The Belknap Press of Harvard University Press, 2004), 158–59.

² Ibid.

³ Lesley Rosenthal, *Good Counsel: Meeting the Legal Needs of Nonprofits* (Hoboken, NJ: John Wiley & Sons, 2012), 23–24.

⁴ Colorado Revised Statutes (C.R.S.) § 7-121-101, et. seq.

⁵ "Form 1023: Application for Recognition of Exemption Under Section 501(c)(3) of the Internal Revenue Code," Internal Revenue Service, accessed November 28, 2018, https://www.irs.gov/pub/irs-pdf/f1023.pdf.

⁶ Rosenthal, *Good Counsel*, 23–24.

⁷ "Form 1023: Application for Recognition of Exemption Under Section 501(c)(3) of the Internal Revenue Code," Internal Revenue Service, accessed November 28, 2018, https://www.irs.gov/pub/irs-pdf/f1023.pdf.

⁸ Rosenthal, *Good Counsel*, 23–24.

⁹ Fremont-Smith, *Governing Nonprofit Organizations*, 158–59.

¹⁰ Ibid.

¹¹ Rosenthal, *Good Counsel*, 23–24.

¹² Fremont-Smith, *Governing Nonprofit Organizations*, 158–59.

¹³ "Global One80, Inc. Articles of Incorporation," Colorado Secretary of State, accessed November 28, 2018, https://www.sos.state.co.us/biz/ViewImage.do?masterFileId=20161813038&fileId=20161813038.

5. WHAT'S AN INDEMNIFICATION PROVISION?

¹ "Nonprofit Bylaw Provision," Hurwit & Associates, accessed October 11, 2018, https://www.hurwitassociates.com/nonprofit-governance-boards-bylaws/sample-bylaw-provision-indemnification.

² "United States Securities and Exchange Commission Form 10-K," Snap, accessed October 11, 2018, https://www.sec.gov/Archives/edgar/data/1564408/000156459018002721/snap-10k_20171231.htm.

³ Ibid.

⁴ Ibid.

⁵ Lesley Rosenthal, *Good Counsel: Meeting the Legal Needs of Nonprofits* (Hoboken, NJ: John Wiley & Sons, 2012), 177–78.

6   Stafford Matthews, "Dentons: Indemnification Clauses," ACC New York, accessed October 12, 2018, https://www.acc.com/chapters/nyc/upload/Indemnification-Clauses-Stafford-Matthews-11-14-13.pdf.

7   Anna Wang, "Indemnity Clauses: Understanding the Basics," Shake LegalShield, May 15, 2014, accessed October 12, 2018, http://www.shakelaw.com/blog/indemnity-clauses-understanding-basics/.

8   Marion R. Fremont-Smith, *Governing Nonprofit Organizations: Federal and State Law and Regulation* (Cambridge, MA: The Belknap Press of Harvard University Press, 2004), 437–38.

9   "D&O Insurance 101: How Much Does a Directors and Officers Lawsuit Cost?", Insureon, accessed October 12, 2018, https://nonprofit.insureon.com/resources/d-and-o/cost.

10   Eileen Morrison, "Enforcing the Duties of Nonprofit Fiduciaries: Advocating for Expanded Standing for Beneficiaries," Boston University School of Law, accessed October 12, 2018, http://www.bu.edu/bulawreview/files/2015/11/MORRISON.pdf; "Who Can Sue a Nonprofit Board?" Nonprofit Risk Management Center, accessed October 12, 2018, https://www.nonprofitrisk.org/resources/articles/who-can-sue-a-nonprofit-board/.

11   Evelyn Brody, "The Legal Framework for Nonprofit Organizations," in *The Nonprofit Sector: A Research Handbook*, 2nd ed. (London: Yale University Press, 2006), 252–53.

12   Pamela Davis, "Directors and Officers Liability Insurance: Why It's Worth the Cost," *Nonprofit Quarterly*, July 13, 2015, https://nonprofitquarterly.org/2015/07/13/nonprofit-insurance-why-its-worth-the-cost/.

13   Fremont-Smith, *Governing Nonprofit Organizations*, 437–38.

14   Andre Juneau, "Nonprofits Especially Need Protection against D&O Liability Risks," *Insurance Journal*, September 17, 2001, https://www.insurancejournal.com/magazines/mag-features/2001/09/17/18503.htm.

15   "Form 990: Return of Organization Exempt from Income Tax," The University of Louisville Foundation, accessed October 19, 2018, https://www.guidestar.org/FinDocuments/2016/237/078/2016-237078461-0e1ddb1f-9.pdf.

16   *The University of Louisville & The University of Louisville Foundation, Inc. v. James Ramsey et al.*, accessed October 19, 2018, https://uoflnews-qmrfqsqodkyjna.netdna-ssl.com/wp-content/uploads/2018/04/Complaint-With-Jury-Trial-Demand-File-Stamped-U-of-L-et-al.-v.-Ramsey-et-al.pdf.

17   Chris Larson, "Update: U of L and its Foundation Sue Ex-President Ramsey, others," *Louisville Business First*, April 25, 2018, https://www.bizjournals.com/louisville/news/2018/04/25/u-of-l-and-its-foundation-will-sue-ex-president.html.

18   "Articles of Amendment to the Articles of Incorporation of University of Louisville Foundation, Inc.," Kentucky Secretary of State, accessed October 19, 2018, http://apps.sos.ky.gov/ImageWebViewer/(S(iqaep1z15d4ric45avj3pd45))/OBDBDisplayImage.aspx?id=7091081.

19   Ibid.

20   Ibid.

21   Larson, "Update: U of L and its Foundation," https://www.bizjournals.com/louisville/news/2018/04/25/u-of-l-and-its-foundation-will-sue-ex-president.html.

6.   WHAT'S A CONFLICT OF INTEREST POLICY?

1   "About Us," The Eli and Edythe Broad Foundation, accessed October 21, 2018, https://broadfoundation.org/about-us/.

2   Ibid.

3   "Form 990-PF: Return of Private Foundation," The Eli and Edythe Broad Foundation, accessed October 21, 2018, https://www.guidestar.org/FinDocuments/2016/954/686/2016-954686318-0ed381aa-F.pdf.

4   "About Us," The Broad Foundation, https://broadfoundation.org/about-us/.

[5]   Ibid.

[6]   "The Broad Art Center at UCLA," The Eli and Edythe Broad Foundation, accessed October 21, 2018, https://broadfoundation.org/grantees/the-broad-art-center-at-ucla/.

[7]   Ibid.

[8]   "Form 990-PF," The Broad Foundation, https://www.guidestar.org/FinDocuments/2016/954/686/2016-954686318-0ed381aa-F.pdf.

[9]   Jonathan Grissom, "Nonprofit Corporations: Board Authority and Fiduciary Duties," San Diego County Bar Association (February 2017), accessed October 21, 2018, https://www.sdcba.org/index.cfm?pg=FTR-Feb-2017-5.

[10]   Lesley Rosenthal, *Good Counsel: Meeting the Legal Needs of Nonprofits* (Hoboken, NJ: John Wiley & Sons, 2012), 36–38.

[11]   Ibid.

[12]   Bruce Hopkins, *The Law of Tax-Exempt Organizations* 11th ed. (Hoboken, NJ: John Wiley & Sons, 2016), 37–372.

[13]   Ibid.

[14]   Rosenthal, *Good Counsel*, 36–38.

[15]   Ibid.

[16]   Ibid.

[17]   Ibid.

[18]   Ibid.

[19]   Ibid.

[20]   "Form 1023: Application for Recognition Under Section 501(c)(3) of the Internal Revenue Code," Internal Revenue Service, accessed October 21, 2018, https://www.irs.gov/pub/irs-pdf/f1023.pdf.

[21]   Ibid.

[22]   Ibid.

[23]   Ibid.

[24]   Ibid.

[25]   Rosenthal, *Good Counsel*, 36–38.

[26]   Ibid.

[27]   Hopkins, *The Law of Tax-Exempt Organizations*, 37–372.

[28]   "Form 1023: Application for Recognition," Internal Revenue Service, https://www.irs.gov/pub/irs-pdf/f1023.pdf.

[29]   Ibid.

7.   HOW DOES A NONPROFIT CORPORATION BECOME A 501(C)(3) ENTITY?

[1]   "How It All Started," Make-A-Wish America, accessed October 21, 2018, http://wish.org/about-us/our-story/how-it-started.

[2]   Ibid.

[3]   Ibid.

[4]   Ibid.

[5]   Ibid.

[6]   Ibid.

[7]   Ibid.

[8]   Ibid.

[9]   Ibid.

[10]   Ibid.

[11]   Ibid.

[12]   Ibid.

[13]   "About Us," Make-A-Wish America, accessed October 22, 2018, http://wish.org/about-us.

14   "Form 1023: Application for Recognition of Exemption Under Section 501(c)(3) of the Internal Revenue Code," Internal Revenue Service, accessed October 22, 2018, https://www.irs.gov/pub/irs-pdf/f1023.pdf.

15   "Form 1023-EZ: Streamlined Application for Recognition of Exemption Under Section 501(c)(3) of the Internal Revenue Code," accessed October 22, 2018, https://www.irs.gov/pub/irs-pdf/f1023ez.pdf.

16   "Form 1023: Application for Recognition," Internal Revenue Service, https://www.irs.gov/pub/irs-pdf/f1023.pdf.

17   Internal Revenue Code (I.R.C.) § Section 501(c)(3).

18   Ibid.

19   "Form 1023: Application for Recognition," Internal Revenue Service, https://www.irs.gov/pub/irs-pdf/f1023.pdf.

20   "The Public Support Test: What a Grant Seeker Should Know," The Brainerd Foundation, accessed October 25, 2018, https://www.brainerd.org/downloads/Public_Support_Test_Memo.pdf.

21   Ibid.

22   Ibid.

23   Ibid.

24   Ibid.

25   Ibid.

26   Ibid.

27   "Form 1023: Application for Recognition," Internal Revenue Service, https://www.irs.gov/pub/irs-pdf/f1023.pdf.

28   Ibid.

29   Ellis Carter, "Accepting Donations Prior to Exemption," CharityLawyerBlog.com, August 12, 2016, http://charitylawyerblog.com/2016/08/12/accepting-donations-prior-to-exemption/.

30   Ibid.

8. WHAT DOES "CHARITABLE" MEAN UNDER SECTION 501(C)(3) OF THE IRS CODE?

1   Internal Revenue Code (I.R.C.) § 501(c)(3).

2   Nicholas P. Cafardi and Jaclyn Fabean Cherry, *Tax Exempt Organizations: Cases and Materials*, 2nd ed. (Newark, NJ: LexisNexis, 2008), 145–47.

3   Bruce Hopkins, *The Law of Tax-Exempt Organizations*, 11th ed. (Hoboken, NJ: John Wiley & Sons, 2016), 67–68.

4   Internal Revenue Code (I.R.C.) § 501(c)(3).

5   "History," Princeton University, accessed October 28, 2018, https://www.visitprinceton.org/princeton-university/history/.

6   "Facts & Figures," Princeton University, accessed October 28, 2018, https://www.princeton.edu/meet-princeton/facts-figures.

7   Ibid.

8   Cafardi and Fabean Cherry, *Tax Exempt Organizations*, 145–47.

9   "Form 1023: Application for Recognition of Exemption Under Section 501(c)(3) of the Internal Revenue Code," accessed October 28, 2018, https://www.irs.gov/pub/irs-pdf/f1023.pdf.

10   Princeton Theological Seminary's homepage, accessed October 28, 2018, https://ptsem.edu/.

11   "Scholarships and Fellowships," Princeton University, accessed October 28, 2018, https://giving.princeton.edu/scholarships-fellowships.

12   Hopkins, *The Law of Tax-Exempt Organizations*, 159–262.

13   Ibid.

14   Ibid.

[15] "Office of Development," Princeton University, accessed October 28, 2018, https://giving.princeton.edu/news-topics/office-development.

[16] Hopkins, *The Law of Tax-Exempt Organizations*, 160–61.

[17] Ibid., 164–65.

[18] Cafardi and Fabean Cherry, *Tax Exempt Organizations*, 30–31.

[19] Ibid.

[20] Hopkins, *The Law of Tax-Exempt Organizations*, 166–67.

[21] Ibid.

[22] "Form 990: Return of Organization Exempt from Income Tax," The New York Public Library, accessed October 28, 2018, https://www.guidestar.org/FinDocuments/2016/131/887/2016-131887440-0e2c5d22-9.pdf.

[23] Ibid.

[24] Ibid.

[25] Ibid.

[26] Ibid.

[27] Hopkins, *The Law of Tax-Exempt Organizations*, 159–262.

[28] Ibid

[29] Ibid.

[30] Hopkins, *The Law of Tax-Exempt Organizations*, 67–68.

9. WHAT'S A 501(C)(3)-PUBLIC CHARITY?

[1] "Form 990: Return of Organization Exempt from Income Tax," Teach for America, accessed October 29, 2018, https://www.guidestar.org/FinDocuments/2017/133/541/2017-133541913-0efba78d-9.pdf.

[2] "History," Teach for America, accessed October 29, 2018, https://www.teachforamerica.org/what-we-do/history.

[3] Ibid.

[4] Ibid.

[5] Ibid.

[6] Ibid.

[7] Ibid.

[8] "Our Approach," Teach for America, accessed October 29, 2018, https://www.teachforamerica.org/what-we-do/approach.

[9] Ibid.

[10] "History," Teach for America, accessed October 29, 2018, https://www.teachforamerica.org/what-we-do/history.

[11] "Teach for All History," Teach for All, accessed October 29, 2018, http://www.teachforallnetwork.com/aboutus_history.html.

[12] Ibid.

[13] "Form 990: Return of Organization," Teach for America, https://www.guidestar.org/FinDocuments/2017/133/541/2017-133541913-0efba78d-9.pdf; "Form 990: Return of Organization Exempt from Income Tax," Teach for All, accessed October 29, 2018, https://www.guidestar.org/FinDocuments/2017/262/122/2017-262122566-0ef67f99-9.pdf.

[14] James J. Fishman and Stephen Schwarz, *Taxation of Nonprofit Organizations: Cases and Materials*, 2nd ed. (New York: Foundation Press, 2006), 98–99.

[15] Bruce Hopkins, *The Law of Tax-Exempt Organizations*, 11th ed. (Hoboken, NJ: John Wiley & Sons, 2016), 82–86.

[16] Ibid., 77–79.

[17] Ibid.

[18] Ibid., 67–69.

[19] Internal Revenue Code (I.R.C.) § 501(c)(3).

[20] Hopkins, *The Law of Tax-Exempt Organizations*, 68–9.

21   Ibid., 68.

22   Ibid., 69–70.

23   Colorado Revised Statutes (C.R.S.) § 7-121-101, et. seq.

24   Internal Revenue Code (I.R.C.) § 501(c)(3).

25   Hopkins, *The Law of Tax-Exempt Organizations*, 69–70.

26   Ibid., 82–86.

27   Ibid.

28   "Operational Test-Internal Revenue Code Section 501(c)(3)," Internal Revenue Code, accessed October 29, 2018, https://www.irs.gov/charities-non-profits/charitable-organizations/operational-test-internal-revenue-code-section-501c3.

29   Hopkins, *The Law of Tax-Exempt Organizations*, 82–86.

30   Fishman and Schwarz, *Taxation of Nonprofit Organizations*, 97–99.

31   Hopkins, *The Law of Tax-Exempt Organizations*, 82–86.

32   Ibid., 357–64.

33   Ibid.

34   Ibid.

35   Ibid.

36   "Exempt Organizations Annual Reporting Requirements–Form 990, Schedules A and B: Public Charity Support Test," Internal Revenue Code, accessed October 29, 2018, https://www.irs.gov/charities-non-profits/exempt-organizations-annual-reporting-requirements-form-990-schedules-a-and-b-public-charity-support-test.

37   Hopkins, *The Law of Tax-Exempt Organizations*, 364–65; Fishman and Schwarz, *Taxation of Nonprofit Organizations*, 544–45.

38   "Form 990: Return of Organization," Teach for America, https://www.guidestar.org/FinDocuments/2017/133/541/2017-133541913-0efba78d-9.pdf; "Form 990: Return of Organization Exempt," Teach for All, https://www.guidestar.org/FinDocuments/2017/262/122/2017-262122566-0ef67f99-9.pdf.

39   Nicholas P. Cafardi and Jaclyn Fabean Cherry, *Understanding Nonprofit and Tax Exempt Organizations* (Newark, NJ: LexisNexis, 2006), 63–66.

40   Internal Revenue Code (I.R.C.) § 501(c)(3).

41   "Form 990: Return of Organization," Teach for All, https://www.guidestar.org/FinDocuments/2017/262/122/2017-262122566-0ef67f99-9.pdf.

42   Internal Revenue Code (I.R.C.) § 501(c)(3).

43   "Form 990: Return of Organization," Teach for America, https://www.guidestar.org/FinDocuments/2017/133/541/2017-133541913-0efba78d-9.pdf.

44   "Form 990: Return of Organization," Teach for All, https://www.guidestar.org/FinDocuments/2017/262/122/2017-262122566-0ef67f99-9.pdf.

45   Cafardi and Fabean Cherry, *Understanding Nonprofit and Tax Exempt Organizations*, 63–6.

46   "Form 990: Return of Organization," Teach for America, https://www.guidestar.org/FinDocuments/2017/133/541/2017-133541913-0efba78d-9.pdf.

47   "Form 990: Return of Organization," Teach for All, https://www.guidestar.org/FinDocuments/2017/262/122/2017-262122566-0ef67f99-9.pdf.

48   Cafardi and Fabean Cherry, *Understanding Nonprofit and Tax Exempt Organizations*, 63–7.

49   "Form 990: Return of Organization," Teach for America, https://www.guidestar.org/FinDocuments/2017/133/541/2017-133541913-0efba78d-9.pdf.

50   "Form 990: Return of Organization," Teach for All, https://www.guidestar.org/FinDocuments/2017/262/122/2017-262122566-0ef67f99-9.pdf.

51   Hopkins, *The Law of Tax-Exempt Organizations*, 24–29.

10. WHAT'S A 501(C)(3)-PRIVATE FOUNDATION?

[1] "Form 990-PF: Return of Private Foundation," Ford Foundation, accessed October 30, 2018, https://www.guidestar.org/FinDocuments/2016/131/684/2016-131684331-0ead99b5-F.pdf.

[2] "About Ford," Ford Foundation, accessed October 30, 2018, https://www.fordfoundation.org/about/about-ford/.

[3] Ibid.; "Financial Snapshot 2016," Ford Foundation, accessed October 30, 2018, https://www.fordfoundation.org/about/library/financial-statements/financial-snapshot-2016/.

[4] "Our Origins," Ford Foundation, accessed October 30, 2018, https://www.fordfoundation.org/about/about-ford/our-origins/.

[5] Ibid.

[6] Ibid.

[7] Internal Revenue Code (I.R.C.) § 501(c)(3).

[8] "Our Origins," Ford Foundation, https://www.fordfoundation.org/about/about-ford/our-origins/.

[9] "Form 990-PF: Return of Private Foundation," The Bill and Melinda Gates Foundation, accessed October 30, 2018, https://www.guidestar.org/FinDocuments/2016/911/663/2016-911663695-0e7cdc5b-F.pdf.

[10] Bruce Hopkins, *The Law of Tax-Exempt Organizations*, 11th ed. (Hoboken, NJ: John Wiley & Sons, 2016), 24–29.

[11] Lesley Rosenthal, *Good Counsel: Meeting the Legal Needs of Nonprofits* (Hoboken, NJ: John Wiley & Sons, 2012), 28–29.

[12] Ibid.

[13] "Form 1023: Application for Recognition of Exemption Under Section 501(c)(3) of the Internal Revenue Code," Internal Revenue Service, accessed October 30, 2018, https://www.irs.gov/pub/irs-pdf/f1023.pdf.

[14] Nicholas P. Cafardi and Jaclyn Fabean Cherry, *Understanding Nonprofit and Tax Exempt Organizations* (Newark, NJ: LexisNexis, 2006), 354–55.

[15] Hopkins, *The Law of Tax-Exempt Organizations*, 344–45.

[16] Ibid.

[17] Ibid., 356–64.

[18] Ibid.

[19] Cafardi and Fabean Cherry, *Understanding Nonprofit and Tax Exempt Organizations*, 354–55.

[20] Hopkins, *The Law of Tax-Exempt Organizations*, 349–50; 82–88.

[21] Ibid., 369–81.

[22] "Form 990-PF: Return of Private Foundation," Daniels Fund, accessed October 30, 2018, https://www.guidestar.org/FinDocuments/2016/841/393/2016-841393308-0dce225e-F.pdf.

[23] "Bill Daniels Biography," Daniels Fund, accessed October 31, 2018, https://www.danielsfund.org/billdaniels/biography.

[24] Ibid.

[25] "Form 990: Return of Organization Exempt from Income Tax," The Cable Center, accessed October 30, 2018, https://www.guidestar.org/FinDocuments/2016/200/315/2016-200315238-0e3dfa4d-9.pdf.

[26] Hopkins, *The Law of Tax-Exempt Organizations*, 372–74.

[27] Ibid.

[28] James J. Fishman and Stephen Schwarz, *Taxation of Nonprofit Organizations: Cases and Materials*, 2nd ed. (New York: Foundation Press, 2006), 608–9.

[29] Hopkins, *The Law of Tax-Exempt Organizations*, 372–74.

[30] Ibid., 370–72.

[31] Ibid.

[32] Ibid.

[33] Cafardi and Fabean Cherry, *Understanding Nonprofit and Tax Exempt Organizations*, 314–15.

[34] Hopkins, *The Law of Tax-Exempt Organizations*, 352–53.

[35] "Daniels Fund Board of Directors," Daniels Fund, accessed November 1, 2018, https://www.danielsfund.org/about-daniels-fund/board-of-directors/board.

[36] Hopkins, *The Law of Tax-Exempt Organizations*, 370–72.

[37] Ibid

[38] Ibid.

[39] Ibid., 374–75.

[40] Ibid.

[41] Ibid.

[42] Ibid., 375–76.

[43] Cafardi and Fabean Cherry, *Understanding Nonprofit and Tax Exempt Organizations*, 321–23.

[44] Ibid.

[45] "Form 990-PF: Return of Private Foundation," Ford Foundation, https://www.guidestar.org/FinDocuments/2016/131/684/2016-131684331-0ead99b5-F.pdf.; "Form 990-PF: Return of Private Foundation," Daniels Fund, https://www.guidestar.org/FinDocuments/2016/841/393/2016-841393308-0dce225e-F.pdf.

[46] "Form 990-PF: Return of Private Foundation," The Bill & Melinda Gates Foundation, https://www.guidestar.org/FinDocuments/2016/911/663/2016-911663695-0e7cdc5b-F.pdf.

11. WHAT'S THE PRIVATE INUREMENT DOCTRINE?

[1] Bruce Hopkins, *The Law of Tax-Exempt Organizations*, 11th ed. (Hoboken, NJ: John Wiley & Sons, 2016), 547–49.

[2] "Neil Gorsuch's Law Firm Years," Big Law Business, accessed November 1, 2018, https://biglawbusiness.com/neil-gorsuchs-law-firm-years/; "About the [Byron] White Center," University of Colorado, accessed November 1, 2018, https://www.colorado.edu/law/research/byron-white-center/about-white-center.

[3] Hopkins, *The Law of Tax-Exempt Organizations*, 372–74.

[4] Internal Revenue Code (I.R.C.) § 501(c)(3) (emphasis added).

[5] Nicholas P. Cafardi and Jaclyn Fabean Cherry, *Understanding Nonprofit and Tax Exempt Organizations* (Newark, NJ: LexisNexis, 2006), 70–71.

[6] Internal Revenue Code (I.R.C.) § 501(c)(6) (emphasis added).

[7] Cafardi and Fabean Cherry, *Understanding Nonprofit and Tax Exempt Organizations*, 70–1.

[8] Marion R. Fremont-Smith, *Governing Nonprofit Organizations: Federal and State Law and Regulation* (Cambridge, MA: The Belknap Press of Harvard University Press, 2004), 248–50.

[9] Cafardi and Fabean Cherry, *Understanding Nonprofit and Tax Exempt Organizations*, 70–71.

[10] Hopkins, *The Law of Tax-Exempt Organizations*, 556–60.

[11] Ibid.

[12] Hopkins, *The Law of Tax-Exempt Organizations*, 556–60; Ibid., 610–13.

[13] Hopkins, *The Law of Tax-Exempt Organizations*, 610–13.

[14] Fremont-Smith, *Governing Nonprofit Organizations*, 258–59.

[15] Cesar Chavez Academy's homepage, accessed November 1, 2018, https://cca.chpa-k12.org/.

[16] Ibid.

[17] Nancy Mitchell, "State: Cesar Chavez 'Squandered Taxpayer Money,'" Chalkbeat, May 5, 2010, https://www.chalkbeat.org/posts/co/2010/05/05/cesar-chavez-audit-deeply-disturbing/.

[18] Ibid.

19 Ibid.
20 Hopkins, *The Law of Tax-Exempt Organizations*, 557–60; Ibid., 613–14.
21 Hopkins, *The Law of Tax-Exempt Organizations*, 613–14.
22 Mitchell, "State: Cesar Chavez," Chalkbeat, https://www.chalkbeat.org/posts/co/2010/05/05/cesar-chavez-audit-deeply-disturbing/.
23 Ibid.
24 Hopkins, *The Law of Tax-Exempt Organizations*, 557–60; Ibid., 613–14.
25 Internal Revenue Code (I.R.C.) § 501(c)(3) (emphasis added).

12.   WHAT'S THE PRIVATE BENEFIT DOCTRINE?

1 Internal Revenue Code (I.R.C.) § 501(c)(7).
2 "About Us," Minnesota Center for Environmental Advocacy, accessed November 2, 2018, http://www.mncenter.org/about-us.html.
3 Internal Revenue Code (I.R.C.) § 501(c)(3).
4 Ibid.
5 Ibid.
6 James J. Fishman and Stephen Schwarz, *Taxation of Nonprofit Organizations: Cases and Materials*, 2nd ed. (New York: Foundation Press, 2006), 99–100.
7 Darryll K. Jones, Steven J. Willis, David A. Brennen, and Beverly I. Moran, *The Tax Law of Charities and Other Exempt Organizations: Cases, Materials, Questions and Answers*, 2nd ed. (St. Paul, MN: Thomson West, 2007), 346–47.
8 Ibid.
9 Ibid.
10 Reg. § 1.501(c)(3)-1(d)(1)(ii).
11 Ibid.
12 Jones, Willis, Brennen, and Moran, *The Tax Law of Charities*, 351–52.
13 Ibid.
14 Ibid.
15 "Private Benefit Doctrine Under IRC 501(c)(3)," Internal Revenue Service, accessed November 2, 2018, https://www.irs.gov/pub/irs-tege/eotopich01.pdf.
16 Ibid.
17 Jones, Willis, Brennen, and Moran, *The Tax Law of Charities*, 350–52.
18 Ibid., 354–59.
19 Ibid.
20 "Private Benefit Doctrine," Internal Revenue Service, https://www.irs.gov/pub/irs-tege/eotopich01.pdf.
21 Ibid.
22 Ibid.
23 Ibid.
24 Internal Revenue Code (I.R.C.) § 501(c)(3).
25 "Private Benefit Doctrine," Internal Revenue Service, https://www.irs.gov/pub/irs-tege/eotopich01.pdf.
26 "Revenue Ruling 75–286," Internal Revenue Service, accessed November 2, 2018, https://www.irs.gov/pub/irs-tege/rr75-286.pdf.

13.   MAY A 501(C)(3) NONPROFIT ENGAGE IN LOBBYING?

1 Internal Revenue Code (I.R.C.) § 501(c)(3).
2 Gary D. Bass, David F. Arons, Kay Guinane, and Matthew F. Carter, *Seen But Not Heard: Strengthening Nonprofit Advocacy* (Washington, DC: The Aspen Institute, 2007), 1–230.

3   "Form 990: Return of Organization Exempt from Income Tax," The Aspen Institute, accessed November 3, 2018, https://www.guidestar.org/FinDocuments/2016/840/399/2016-840399006-0e7bb226-9.pdf.

4   "History," The Aspen Institute, accessed November 3, 2018, https://www.aspeninstitute.org/about/#history.

5   Ibid.

6   Bass, Arons, Guinane, and Carter, *Seen But Not Heard*, 1–230.

7   Ibid., 11.

8   Ibid.

9   Ibid.

10   Nicholas P. Cafardi and Jaclyn Fabean Cherry, *Understanding Nonprofit and Tax Exempt Organizations* (Newark, NJ: LexisNexis 2006), 75–78.

11   Internal Revenue Code (I.R.C.) § 501(c)(3).

12   Cafardi and Fabean Cherry, *Understanding Nonprofit and Tax Exempt Organizations*, 75–78.

13   Ibid., 76–80.

14   Internal Revenue Code (I.R.C.) § 501(c)(3).

15   Cafardi and Fabean Cherry, *Understanding Nonprofit and Tax Exempt Organizations*, 75–78.

16   Ibid.

17   Lesley Rosenthal, *Good Counsel: Meeting the Legal Needs of Nonprofits* (Hoboken, NJ: John Wiley & Sons, 2012), 248–50.

18   Ibid.

19   Bass, Arons, Guinane, and Carter, *Seen But Not Heard*, 191–92.

20   Marion R. Fremont-Smith, *Governing Nonprofit Organizations: Federal and State Law and Regulation* (Cambridge, MA: The Belknap Press of Harvard University Press, 2004), 280–81.

21   Ibid.

22   Ibid.

23   Ibid.

24   "Social Welfare Organizations," Internal Revenue Service, accessed November 3, 2018, https://www.irs.gov/charities-non-profits/other-non-profits/social-welfare-organizations.

25   Ibid.

26   Colorado Common Cause's homepage, accessed November 3, 2018, https://www.commoncause.org/colorado/; "Form 990: Return of Organization Exempt from Income Tax," Common Cause, accessed November 3, 2018, http://www.guidestar.org/FinDocuments/2017/526/078/2017-526078441-0e89721c-9O.pdf; "State Ethics Law Beset by Unintended Consequences," *The Washington Post*, February 19, 2007, accessed November 3, 2018, https://www.washingtontimes.com/news/2007/feb/19/20070219-112748-7289r/.

27   "State Ethics Law," *The Washington Post*, https://www.washingtontimes.com/news/2007/feb/19/20070219-112748-7289r/.

28   "Scholarships" The Boettcher Foundation, accessed November 4, 2018, https://boettcherfoundation.org/colorado-scholarships/.

29   Ibid.

30   "Scholarship Overview," The Daniels Fund, accessed November 4, 2018, https://www.danielsfund.org/scholarships/daniels-scholarship-program/overview.

31   "State Ethics Law," *The Washington Post*, https://www.washingtontimes.com/news/2007/feb/19/20070219-112748-7289r/.

32   "Lobbying," Internal Revenue Service, accessed November 4, 2018, https://www.irs.gov/charities-non-profits/lobbying.

33   Ibid.

34   "State Ethics Law," *The Washington Post*, https://www.washingtontimes.com/news/2007/feb/19/20070219-112748-7289r/.

35   "Judge: Boettcher Can Give Grants Under Amendment 41," The Denver Channel, accessed November 4, 2018, https://www.thedenverchannel.com/lifestyle/education/judge-boettcher-can-give-grants-under-amendment-41.

36   Internal Revenue Code (I.R.C.) § 501(c)(3).

14.   WHAT'S THE JOHNSON AMENDMENT?

1   Philip Bump, "Does More Campaign Money Actually Buy More Votes: An Investigation," The Atlantic, November 11, 2013, https://www.theatlantic.com/politics/archive/2013/11/does-more-campaign-money-actually-buy-more-votes-investigation/355154/.

2   Internal Revenue Code (I.R.C.) § 501(c)(3).

3   Ibid.

4   Nicholas P. Cafardi and Jaclyn Fabean Cherry, Understanding Nonprofit and Tax-Exempt Organizations (Newark, NJ: LexisNexis, 2006), 74–75.

5   Lesley Rosenthal, Good Counsel: Meeting the Legal Needs of Nonprofits (Hoboken, NJ: John Wiley & Sons, 2012), 243.

6   Internal Revenue Code (I.R.C.) § 501(c)(3).

7   Rosenthal, Good Counsel, 243.

8   Marion R. Fremont-Smith, Governing Nonprofit Organizations: Federal and State Law and Regulation (Cambridge, MA: The Belknap Press of Harvard University Press, 2004), 56–57.

9   Ibid.

10   Ibid.

11   Bruce Hopkins, The Law of Tax-Exempt Organizations, 11th ed. (Hoboken, NJ: John Wiley & Sons, 2016), 658.

12   Ibid.

13   Ibid.

14   Ibid.

15   Rosenthal, Good Counsel, 243.

16   Ibid.

17   David Saperstein and Amanda Tyler, "Trump Vowed to Destroy the Johnson Amendment. Thankfully, He Has Failed," The Washington Post, February 7, 2018, https://www.washingtonpost.com/opinions/trump-vowed-to-destroy-the-johnson-amendment-thankfully-he-has-failed/2018/02/07/3cdbce4e-0b67-11e8-95a5-c396801049ef_story.html?utm_term=.eb32880a145c.

18   Ibid.

19   John Wagner and Julie Zauzmer, "Trump Vows to 'Totally Destroy' Restrictions on Churches' Support of Candidates," The Washington Post, February 2, 2017, https://www.washingtonpost.com/politics/trump-vows-to-totally-destroy-restrictions-on-churches-support-of-candidates/2017/02/02/fed9bad2-e981-11e6-bf6f-301b6b443624_story.html?utm_term=.80c87f922e1a.

20   Heather Long, "In Small Win for Democrats, the Final Tax Bill Won't Include a Provision to Allow Churches to Endorse Political Candidates," The Washington Post, December 14, 2017, https://www.washingtonpost.com/news/wonk/wp/2017/12/14/in-small-win-for-democrats-the-final-tax-bill-wont-include-a-provision-to-allow-churches-to-endorse-political-candidates/?utm_term=.9377c4c792ab.

21   Ibid.

22   Ibid.

23   Ibid.

24   Ibid.

25   Cafardi and Fabean Cherry, Understanding Nonprofit and Tax-Exempt Organizations, 275–76.

26   Deborah Stone, Policy Paradox: The Art of Political Decision Making (New York: W. W. Norton & Company, 2002), 1–417.

27 Ibid.
28 Ibid.
29 Long, "In Small Win for Democrats," *The Washington Post*, https://www.washingtonpost.com/news/wonk/wp/2017/12/14/in-small-win-for-democrats-the-final-tax-bill-wont-include-a-provision-to-allow-churches-to-endorse-political-candidates/?utm_term=.9377c4c792ab.
30 Ibid.
31 Ibid.
32 Fremont-Smith, *Governing Nonprofit Organizations*, 56–57.

15. MAY A 501(C)(3) NONPROFIT HAVE A FOR-PROFIT SUBSIDIARY?

1 "Mission, Vision, Values," Foundation Center, accessed November 5, 2018, https://foundationcenter.org/about-us/mission-vision-values; "Foundation Stats," Foundation Center, accessed November 5, 2018, http://data.foundationcenter.org/#/foundations/corporate/nationwide/top:assets/list/2015.
2 Nicholas P. Cafardi and Jaclyn Fabean Cherry, *Understanding Nonprofit and Tax-Exempt Organizations* (Newark, NJ: LexisNexis, 2006), 70–71.
3 Ibid.
4 Colorado Revised Statutes (C.R.S.) § 7-121-101, et. seq.; "Nonprofit Law Basics: Who Owns a Nonprofit?" Cullinane Law Group, accessed November 5, 2018, https://cullinanelaw.com/nonprofit-law-basics-who-owns-a-nonprofit/.
5 "Nonprofit Law Basics," Cullinane Law Group, https://cullinanelaw.com/nonprofit-law-basics-who-owns-a-nonprofit/.
6 Bruce Hopkins, *The Law of Tax-Exempt Organizations*, 11th ed. (Hoboken, NJ: John Wiley & Sons, 2016), 965–66.
7 Ibid.
8 Ibid.
9 Ibid.
10 Cafardi and Fabean Cherry, *Understanding Nonprofit and Tax-Exempt Organizations*, 241–42.
11 Hopkins, *The Law of Tax-Exempt Organizations*, 687–88.
12 Ibid., 965.
13 Ibid., 687–88.
14 Cafardi and Fabean Cherry, *Understanding Nonprofit and Tax-Exempt Organizations*, 253–57.
15 Ibid; "Taxation of Unrelated Business Income (UBIT)," Hurwit & Associates, accessed November 5, 2018, https://www.hurwitassociates.com/taxation-of-unrelated-business-income/taxation-of-unrelated-business-income; Internal Revenue Code (I.R.C.) § 512.
16 Cafardi and Fabean Cherry, *Understanding Nonprofit and Tax-Exempt Organizations*, 330–31.
17 Ibid.
18 "About Us," Share Our Strength, accessed November 5, 2018, https://www.shareourstrength.org/about.
19 "Form 990: Return of Organization Exempt from Income Tax," Share Our Strength, accessed November 5, 2018, https://www.guidestar.org/FinDocuments/2016/521/367/2016-521367538-0dfbbb37-9.pdf.
20 Ibid.
21 Ibid.
22 Ibid.
23 "A Success Story That's Helping Others Succeed," Community Wealth Partners, accessed November 5, 2018, http://communitywealth.com/share-our-strength/.

24   "About Us," Community Wealth Partners, accessed November 5, 2018, http://communitywealth.com/about-us/; "Our Work," Community Wealth Partners, accessed November 5, 2018, http://communitywealth.com/our-work/.

25   "Our Work," Community Wealth Partners, accessed November 5, 2018, http://communitywealth.com/our-work/.

26   Ibid.

27   "About Us," Share Our Strength, https://www.shareourstrength.org/about.

28   "Share Our Strength, Inc. and Subsidiary Consolidated Financial Statements and Supplemental Information for the Year Ended December 31, 2012 and Report Thereon," Share Our Strength, accessed November 5, 2018, https://www.nokidhungry.org/sites/default/files/2017-12/2012-audit.pdf.

29   "Form 990: Return of Organization," Share Our Strength, https://www.guidestar.org/FinDocuments/2016/521/367/2016-521367538-0dfbbb37-9.pdf

30   "Share Our Strength, Inc.," Share Our Strength, https://www.nokidhungry.org/sites/default/files/2017-12/2012-audit.pdf.

31   J. Gregory Dees, Jed Emerson, and Peter Economy, *Enterprising Nonprofits: A Toolkit for Social Entrepreneurs* (New York: John Wiley & Sons, 2001), 1–321.

16.   WHAT ARE THE IRS FORM 1024 AND FORM 1024-A?

1   Malcolm Gladwell, *The Tipping Point* (New York: Little, Brown and Company, 2000), 30–88.

2   Ibid.

3   Ibid.; Wayne Baker, *Achieving Success through Social Capital: Tapping the Hidden Resources in Your Personal and Business Networks* (New York: John Wiley & Sons, 2000), 1–231.

4   Francis Fukuyama, "Social Capital, Civil Society and Development," *Third World Quarterly* vol. 22, no. 1 (February 2001), 7–20.

5   "About," Quarterly Forum, accessed November 5, 2018, https://www.quarterlyforum.org/about/.

6   "About Form 1024: Application for Recognition of Exemption under Section 501(a)," Internal Revenue Code, accessed November 5, 2018, https://www.irs.gov/forms-pubs/about-form-1024.

7   "About Form 1024," Internal Revenue Service, https://www.irs.gov/forms-pubs/about-form-1024-a.

8   "Summary: QF Group, Inc.", Colorado Secretary of State, accessed November 5, 2018, https://www.sos.state.co.us/biz/BusinessEntityCriteriaExt.do.

9   "About Form 1024," Internal Revenue Code, https://www.irs.gov/forms-pubs/about-form-1024.

10   Ibid.

11   Ibid.

12   Ibid.

13   Bruce Hopkins, *The Law of Tax-Exempt Organizations*, 11th ed. (Hoboken, NJ: John Wiley & Sons, 2016), 821–22.

14   Ibid.

15   Ibid.

16   Ibid., 46–47.

17   Ibid.

18   "Trevor Potter Helps Stephen Colbert Form 'Anonymous Shell Corporation' to Avoid Disclosure," Campaign Legal Center, accessed November 5, 2018, https://campaignlegal.org/update/trevor-potter-helps-stephen-colbert-form-anonymous-shell-corporation-avoid-disclosure.

19   Ibid.

20   Ibid.

21   Ibid.

22   Trevor Potter, "How Stephen Colbert Schooled Americans in Campaign Finance," *Time*, December 16, 2014, http://time.com/3600116/stephen-colbert-report-finale-super-pac/.

23   "Trevor Potter Helps Stephen Colbert," https://campaignlegal.org/update/trevor-potter-helps-stephen-colbert-form-anonymous-shell-corporation-avoid-disclosure.

24   "The Colbert Report—Super PAC Segments (Comedy Central)," The Peabody Awards, accessed November 5, 2018, http://peabodyawards.com/award-profile/the-colbert-report-super-pac-segments.

25   52 U.S.C. § 30101(17)

26   Dave Levinthal and Sarah Kleiner, "Supreme Court Lets Stand a Decision Requiring 'Dark Money' Disclosure," *The Atlantic*, https://www.theatlantic.com/politics/archive/2018/09/supreme-court-lets-stand-a-decision-requiring-dark-money-disclosure/570670/; " 'Dark Money' Gets a Little Light: CREW v. FEC and Its Implications for the 2018 Midterms," K&L Gates, accessed December 14, 2018, https://www.lexology.com/library/detail.aspx?g=e1f82545-1680-49b7-8e58-2ee1522a2933.

27   " 'Dark Money' Gets a Little Light," K&L Gates, https://www.lexology.com/library/detail.aspx?g=e1f82545-1680-49b7-8e58-2ee1522a2933.

28   Ibid.

29   Ibid.

30   Ibid.

31   "The Colbert Report," The Peabody Awards, http://peabodyawards.com/award-profile/the-colbert-report-super-pac-segments.

17.   WHAT'S A 501(C)(2)?

1   Bruce Hopkins, *The Law of Tax-Exempt Organizations*, 11th ed. (Hoboken, NJ: John Wiley & Sons, 2016), 493–98; "Single Parent Title Holding Corporations," Internal Revenue Service, accessed November 6, 2018, https://www.irs.gov/irm/part7/irm_07-025-002.

2   James J. Fishman and Stephen Schwarz, *Taxation of Nonprofit Organizations: Cases and Materials*, 2nd ed. (New York: Foundation Press, 2006), 809–10.

3   Ibid.

4   Internal Revenue Code (I.R.C.) § 501(c)(4).

5   "Title-Holding Corporations," Internal Revenue Service, accessed November 6, 2018, https://www.irs.gov/pub/irs-tege/eotopicc86.pdf.

6   Hopkins, *The Law of Tax-Exempt Organizations*, 493–98.

7   Fishman and Schwarz, *Taxation of Nonprofit Organizations*, 809–10; Hopkins, *The Law of Tax-Exempt Organizations*, 493–98; "Single Parent Title Holding Corporations," Internal Revenue Service, https://www.irs.gov/irm/part7/irm_07-025-002.

8   Pennsylvania Consolidated Statutes (Pa. Cons. Stat.) § 5101; Pennsylvania Consolidated Statutes (Pa. Cons. Stat.) § 5306.

9   "Single Parent Title Holding Corporations," Internal Revenue Service, https://www.irs.gov/irm/part7/irm_07-025-002.

10   Ibid.

11   Ibid.

12   Ibid.

13   Ibid.

14   Hopkins, *The Law of Tax-Exempt Organizations*, 493–98.

15   Ibid.

16   Nicholas P. Cafardi and Jaclyn Fabean Cherry, *Understanding Nonprofit and Tax Exempt Organizations* (Newark, NJ: LexisNexis, 2006), 206.

17   "Single Parent Title Holding Corporations," Internal Revenue Service, https://www.irs.gov/irm/part7/irm_07-025-002.

18. WHAT'S A 501(C)(4)?

[1] "History," AARP, accessed November 6, 2018, https://www.aarp.org/about-aarp/company/info-2016/history.html.

[2] Ibid.

[3] "About AARP," AARP, accessed November 6, 2018, https://www.aarp.org/about-aarp/.

[4] "Mission and Vision," AARP, accessed November 6, 2018, https://states.aarp.org/aarps-mission-and-vision/.

[5] "Benefits and Discounts," AARP, accessed November 6, 2018, https://www.aarp.org/benefits-discounts/.

[6] "Mission and Vision," AARP, https://states.aarp.org/aarps-mission-and-vision/; "Social Welfare Organizations," Internal Revenue Services, accessed November 6, 2018, https://www.irs.gov/charities-non-profits/other-non-profits/social-welfare-organizations.

[7] Internal Revenue Code (I.R.C.) § 501(c)(4).

[8] Ibid.

[9] Bruce Hopkins, *The Law of Tax Exempt Organizations*, 11th ed. (Hoboken, NJ: John Wiley & Sons, 2016), 391–99.

[10] Ibid., 386.

[11] Ibid., 385–99.

[12] James Fishman and Stephen Schwarz, *Taxation of Nonprofit Organizations: Cases and Materials*, 2nd ed. (New York: Foundation Press, 2006), 313; Nicholas P. Cafardi and Jaclyn Fabean Cherry, *Understanding Nonprofit and Tax Exempt Organizations* (Newark, NJ: LexisNexis, 2006), 191–94.

[13] Hopkins, *The Law of Tax Exempt Organizations*, 386.

[14] Cafardi and Fabean Cherry, *Understanding Nonprofit and Tax Exempt Organizations*, 194–95.

[15] Internal Revenue Code (I.R.C.) § 501(c)(3); Internal Revenue Code (I.R.C.) § 501(c)(4).

[16] Hopkins, *The Law of Tax Exempt Organizations*, 397.

[17] Internal Revenue Code (I.R.C.) § 501(c)(4); Hopkins, *The Law of Tax Exempt Organizations*, 385–99.

[18] "Consolidated Financial Statements Together with Report of Independent Certified Public Accountants AARP December 31, 2017 and 2016," AARP, accessed November 6, 2018, https://www.aarp.org/content/dam/aarp/about_aarp/about_us/2018/aarp-2017-audited-financial-statement.pdf.

[19] "Form 990: Return of Organization Exempt from Income Tax," AARP, accessed November 7, 2018, https://www.guidestar.org/FinDocuments/2016/951/985/2016-951985500-0e895bd4-9O.pdf.

[20] Cafardi and Fabean Cherry, *Understanding Nonprofit and Tax Exempt Organizations*, 194–95.

[21] "Form 990: Return of Organization," AARP, https://www.guidestar.org/FinDocuments/2016/951/985/2016-951985500-0e895bd4-9O.pdf.

[22] Ibid.

[23] Liz Kennedy and Sean McElwee, "Do Corporations and Unions Face the Same Rules for Political Spending?" Demos, July 23, 2014, https://www.demos.org/publication/do-corporations-unions-face-same-rules-political-spending.

[24] Hopkins, *The Law of Tax Exempt Organizations*, 397.

[25] Ibid.

[26] Laura Davison and Bill Allison, "Many Political Tax-Exempts No Longer Required to Report Donors," Bloomberg, July 16, 2018, https://www.bloomberg.com/news/articles/2018-07-17/many-political-tax-exempts-no-longer-required-to-report-donors.

[27] Ibid.

[28] Michelle Ye Hee Lee and Jeff Stein, "'Dark Money' Groups Don't Need to Disclose Donors to IRS, Treasury Says," *The Washington Post*, July 17, 2018, https://www.washingtonpost.com/politics/dark-money-groups-dont-need-to-disclose-donors-to-irs-treasury-says/2018/07/17/38f5d8aa-89d0-11e8-a345-a1bf7847b375_story.html.

29   Ibid.
30   Internal Revenue Code (I.R.C.) § 501(c)(4).
31   Cafardi and Fabean Cherry, *Understanding Nonprofit and Tax Exempt Organizations*, 194–95.
32   Internal Revenue Code (I.R.C.) § 501(c)(3); Internal Revenue Code (I.R.C.) § 501(c)(4).

19.   WHAT'S A 501(C)(6)?

1   "Best Places to Live," *Money*, accessed November 7, 2018, https://money.cnn.com/magazines/moneymag/best-places/2013/snapshots/PL0846355.html.
2   Ibid.
3   Louisville Chamber of Commerce's homepage, accessed November 7, 2018, https://louisvillechamber.com/#!event-list.
4   "Become a Member of the Chamber and Enjoy All the Benefits," Louisville Chamber of Commerce, accessed November 7, 2018, https://louisvillechamber.com/become-a-member/.
5   Internal Revenue Code (I.R.C.) § 501(c)(6); Bruce Hopkins, *The Law of Tax Exempt Organizations*, 11th ed. (Hoboken, NJ: John Wiley & Sons, 2016), 46–7.
6   Nicholas P. Cafardi and Jaclyn Fabean Cherry, *Understanding Nonprofit and Tax Exempt Organizations* (Newark, NJ: LexisNexis, 2006), 212–17.
7   Ibid.
8   Internal Revenue Code (I.R.C.) § 501(c)(6).
9   "Form 990: Return of Organization Exempt from Income Tax," Louisville Chamber of Commerce, accessed November 7, 2018, https://www.guidestar.org/FinDocuments/2016/840/892/2016-840892240-0ebb39bf-9O.pdf.
10   Ibid.
11   Sean Gregory, "Why the NFL Suddenly Wants to Pay Taxes," *Time*, April 28, 2015, http://time.com/3839164/nfl-tax-exempt-status/.
12   Kate Rogers, "Tax-Exempt? The NFL's Nonprofit Status by the Numbers," CNBC, September 12, 2014, https://www.cnbc.com/2014/09/12/tax-exempt-the-nfls-nonprofit-status-by-the-numbers.html; Kara Beer, 'Tis the Season," *Philanthropy Daily*, September 15, 2014, https://www.philanthropydaily.com/tis-the-season-2/.
13   Internal Revenue Code (I.R.C.) § 501(c)(6).
14   Sean Gregory, "Why the NFL Suddenly Wants to Pay Taxes," *Time*, http://time.com/3839164/nfl-tax-exempt-status/.
15   Ibid.
16   Ibid.
17   "Form 990: Return of Organization Exempt from Income Tax," National Football League, accessed November 7, 2018, https://www.guidestar.org/FinDocuments/2015/131/922/2015-131922622-0ca543a0-9O.pdf.
18   Joe Pinsker, "Why the NFL Decided to Start Paying Taxes," *The Atlantic*, April 28, 2015, https://www.theatlantic.com/business/archive/2015/04/why-the-nfl-decided-to-start-paying-taxes/391742/.
19   "Form 990: Return of Organization Exempt from Income Tax," American Dental Association, accessed November 7, 2018, https://www.guidestar.org/FinDocuments/2016/360/724/2016-360724690-0e68e8d2-9O.pdf.
20   Ibid.
21   Ibid.
22   "Andreas Antonopoulos Leaves Bitcoin Foundation Over 'Complete Lack of Transparency,'" CCN, accessed November 7, 2018, https://www.ccn.com/andreas-antonopoulos-leaves-bitcoin-foundation-complete-lack-transparency/; "Form 990: Return of Organization Exempt from Income Tax," Bitcoin Foundation, accessed November 7, 2018, https://www.guidestar.org/FinDocuments/2016/461/671/2016-461671796-0dcca0c9-9O.pdf.

23   Cafardi and Fabean Cherry, *Understanding Nonprofit and Tax Exempt Organizations* (Newark, NJ: LexisNexis, 2006), 212–17.
24   "Form 990: Return of Organization Exempt from Income Tax," American Dental Association, https://www.guidestar.org/FinDocuments/2016/360/724/2016-360724690-0e68e8d2-9O.pdf.

20.   WHAT'S A 501(C)(7)?

1   "Financial Information," The Ability Experience, accessed November 9, 2018, https://abilityexperience.org/about/financial-information/.
2   "About-Ability Experience," The Ability Experience, accessed November 9, 2018, https://abilityexperience.org/about/.
3   "Form 990: Return of Organization Exempt from Income Tax," Pi Kappa Phi Fraternity, accessed November 9, 2018, https://www.guidestar.org/FinDocuments/2017/570/340/2017-570340150-0ebed563-9O.pdf.
4   "Social Clubs," Internal Revenue Service, accessed November 9, 2018, https://www.irs.gov/other-non-profits/social-clubs; Bruce Hopkins, *The Law of Tax Exempt Organizations*, 11th ed. (Hoboken, NJ: John Wiley & Sons, 2016), 25.
5   "Social Clubs," Internal Revenue Service, https://www.irs.gov/other-non-profits/social-clubs.
6   Nicholas P. Cafardi and Jaclyn Fabean Cherry, *Understanding Nonprofit and Tax Exempt Organizations* (Newark, NJ: LexisNexis, 2006), 217.
7   Hopkins, *The Law of Tax Exempt Organizations*, 429.
8   Cafardi and Fabean Cherry, *Understanding Nonprofit and Tax Exempt Organizations*, 217.
9   Ibid.; Internal Revenue Code (I.R.C.) § 501(c)(7).
10   Cafardi and Fabean Cherry, *Understanding Nonprofit and Tax Exempt Organizations*, 218.
11   Ibid., 217.
12   Ibid., 218
13   Ibid., 218.
14   Hopkins, *The Law of Tax Exempt Organizations*, 433–35.
15   Ibid.
16   Ibid.
17   Ibid.
18   "Form 990: Return of Organization Exempt from Income Tax," The Augusta Country Club, accessed November 9, 2018, https://www.guidestar.org/FinDocuments/2016/580/148/2016-580148720-0e6a0ac4-9O.pdf.
19   Ibid.
20   Ibid.
21   Ibid.
22   Internal Revenue Code (I.R.C.) § 501(c)(7).
23   Ibid.
24   Michael Buteau and Janet Paskin, "118 Rich and Powerful People Who Are Members of Augusta National," Bloomberg, April 10, 2015, https://www.bloomberg.com/graphics/2015-augusta-national-golf-club-members/.
25   Ibid.

21. WHAT ARE THE IRS FORM 990 AND FORM 990-PF?

[1] "Financials," World Wildlife Fund, accessed November 10, 2018, https://www.worldwildlife.org/about/financials.

[2] World Wildlife Fund's homepage, accessed November 10, 2018, https://www.worldwildlife.org/.

[3] Ibid.

[4] "About Us," World Wildlife Fund, accessed November 10, 2018, https://www.worldwildlife.org/about.

[5] "World Wildlife Fund, Inc. and Subsidiaries Consolidated Financial Statements and Independent Auditor's Report Years Ended June 30, 2017 and 2016," World Wildlife Fund, accessed November 10, 2018, http://assets.worldwildlife.org/financial_reports/33/reports/original/WWF_-_Institutional_Audit_Report_FY17.pdf?1519855210&_ga=2.148947125.246739612.1543378750-2067346590.1541872146.

[6] Ibid.

[7] Ibid.

[8] "Form 990 Resources and Tools," Internal Revenue Service, accessed November 10, 2018, https://www.irs.gov/charities-non-profits/form-990-resources-and-tools; Lisa A. Runquist, *The ABCs of Nonprofits*, 2nd ed. (Chicago: American Bar Association, 2015), 73–75.

[9] Bruce Hopkins, *The Law of Tax-Exempt Organizations*, 11th ed. (Hoboken, NJ: John Wiley & Sons, 2016), 145–46.

[10] "About Form 990-PF, Return of Private Foundation," Internal Revenue Service, accessed November 10, 2018 https://www.irs.gov/forms-pubs/about-form-990-pf.

[11] "Annual Electronic Filing Requirements for Small Exempt Organizations-Form 990-N (e-Postcard)," Internal Revenue Service, accessed November 10, 2018, https://www.irs.gov/charities-non-profits/annual-electronic-filing-requirement-for-small-exempt-organizations-form-990-n-e-postcard.

[12] Ibid.

[13] Ibid

[14] Runquist, *The ABCs of Nonprofits*, 73–75.

[15] "Annual Electronic Filing Requirements," Internal Revenue Service, https://www.irs.gov/charities-non-profits/annual-electronic-filing-requirement-for-small-exempt-organizations-form-990-n-e-postcard.

[16] Runquist, *The ABCs of Nonprofits*, 73–75.

[17] "Form 990-EZ: Short Form Return of Organization Exempt from Income Tax," Internal Revenue Service, accessed November 10, 2018, https://www.irs.gov/pub/irs-pdf/f990ez.pdf.

[18] Hopkins, *The Law of Tax-Exempt Organizations*, 882–83.

[19] Ibid.

[20] "Form 990: Return of Organization Exempt from Income Tax," Internal Revenue Service, accessed November 10, 2018, https://www.irs.gov/pub/irs-pdf/f990.pdf.

[21] Hopkins, *The Law of Tax-Exempt Organizations*, 893–97.

[22] Ibid.

[23] Ibid., 884–85; Runquist, *The ABCs of Nonprofits*, 73–75.

[24] "Nonprofit Law Basics: Do Nonprofits File Tax Returns? What Is a 990?" Cullinane Law Group, accessed November 10, 2018, https://cullinanelaw.com/nonprofit-law-basics-does-our-nonprofit-have-to-file-tax-returns-or-an-annual-reporting-return-with-the-irs/.

[25] Ibid., Hopkins, *The Law of Tax-Exempt Organizations*, 889–90.

[26] Ibid., 890–91.

[27] "Form 990: Return of Organization Exempt from Income Tax," World Wildlife Fund, accessed November 10, 2018, http://assets.worldwildlife.org/financial_reports/32/reports/original/Public_inspection_990_WORLD_WILDLIFE_FUND_INC.pdf?1519855180&_ga=2.210512278.246739612.1543378750-2067346590.1541872146.

28 Ibid.
29 Ibid.
30 Ibid.
31 Ibid.
32 Ibid.
33 Ibid.
34 Ibid.
35 Ibid.
36 Ibid.
37 Michael Conover, "Excise Tax 'Bite' on Nonprofit Compensation," *BDO*, July 2, 2018, https://www.bdo.com/blogs/nonprofit-standard/july-2018/excise-tax-bite-on-nonprofit-compensation.
38 "Form 990: Return of Organization," World Wildlife Fund, http://assets.worldwildlife.org/financial_reports/32/reports/original/Public_inspection_990_WORLD_WILDLIFE_FUND_INC.pdf?1519855180&_ga=2.210512278.246739612.1543378750-2067346590.1541872146.
39 Ibid.
40 Ibid.
41 Ibid.
42 "Form 990: Return of Organization," Internal Revenue Service, https://www.irs.gov/pub/irs-pdf/f990.pdf

22.   WHO ARE INDEPENDENT CONTRACTORS?

1 Thomas McLaughlin, *Streetsmart Financial Basics for Nonprofit Managers*, 3rd ed. (Hoboken, NJ: John Wiley & Sons, 2009), 165–66.
2 Ibid.
3 "Independent Contractor (Self-Employed) or Employee?" Internal Revenue Service, accessed November 13, 2018, https://www.irs.gov/businesses/small-businesses-self-employed/independent-contractor-self-employed-or-employee; Lesley Rosenthal, *Good Counsel: Meeting the Legal Needs of Nonprofits* (Hoboken, NJ: John Wiley & Sons, 2012), 175–77.
4 McLaughlin, *Streetsmart Financial Basics*, 165–66.
5 Rosenthal, *Good Counsel*, 175–77.
6 Ibid.
7 "Independent Contractor Defined," Internal Revenue Service, accessed November 13, 2018, https://www.irs.gov/businesses/small-businesses-self-employed/independent-contractor-defined.
8 Ibid.
9 Ibid.
10 McLaughlin, *Streetsmart Financial Basics*, 165–66.
11 Ibid.
12 "Topic No. 762-Independent Contractor vs. Employee," Internal Revenue Service, accessed November 27, 2018, https://www.irs.gov/taxtopics/tc762.
13 Colorado Revised Statutes (C.R.S.) § 8-40-202; "Independent Contractors," Colorado Department of Labor and Employment, accessed November 13, 2018, https://www.colorado.gov/pacific/cdle/independent-contractors.
14 "Who Is an Employee? Determining Independent Contractor Status," United States Department of Labor, accessed November 13, 2018, https://www.dol.gov/oasam/programs/history/herman/reports/futurework/conference/staffing/9.1_contractors.htm; Michael Marr, "Independent Contractor or Employee: Do You Pass the 'Economic Realities' Test?" LexisNexis, August 12, 2015, https://www.lexisnexis.com/legalnewsroom/labor-employment/b/labor-employment-top-blogs/posts/

independent-contractor-or-employee-do-you-pass-the-economic-realities-test;   Rosenthal, *Good Counsel*, 175–77.

15   Rosenthal, *Good Counsel*, 175–77.

23. WHAT ARE LOW-PROFIT LIMITED LIABILITY COMPANIES (L3CS) AND PROGRAM-RELATED INVESTMENTS (PRIS)?

1   "Jeff Cherry: Executive Director," Conscious Venture Lab, accessed November 11, 2018, http://www.consciousventurelab.com/our-mission/jeff-cherry/.

2   "Our Mission," Conscious Venture Lab, accessed November 11, 2018, http://www.consciousventurelab.com/our-mission/.

3   Ibid.

4   Ibid.

5   "Portfolio Companies," Conscious Venture Lab, accessed November 12, 2018, http://www.consciousventurelab.com/portfolio-companies/.

6   "Our Mission," Conscious Venture Lab, http://www.consciousventurelab.com/our-mission/.

7   Conscious Venture Lab's homepage, accessed November 11, 2018, http://www.consciousventurelab.com/.

8   Marion R. Fremont-Smith, *Governing Nonprofit Organizations: Federal and State Law and Regulation* (Cambridge, MA: The Belknap Press of Harvard University Press, 2004), 272–73.

9   Ibid.

10   Bruce Hopkins, *The Law of Tax Exempt Organizations*, 11th ed. (Hoboken, NJ: John Wiley & Sons, 2016), 373–74.

11   Ibid., 130.

12   Hana Muslic, "The Jargon-Free Guide to Low Profit Limited Companies (L3C)," Nonprofit Hub, June 1, 2017, https://nonprofithub.org/starting-a-nonprofit/jargon-free-guide-l3c/.

13   Hopkins, *The Law of Tax Exempt Organizations*, 375.

14   Ibid.

15   Ibid., 376.

16   Ibid.

17   Ibid.

18   Ibid.

19   Ibid.

20   Ibid.

21   Ibid.

22   Ibid., 376.

23   Flexible Capital Fund's homepage, accessed November 11, 2018, http://flexiblecapitalfund.com/.

24   Ibid.

25   "Flex Fund Background," Flexible Capital Fund, accessed November 11, 2018, http://flexiblecapitalfund.com/who-we-are/.

26   Ibid.

27   Hopkins, *The Law of Tax Exempt Organizations*, 375.

28   Ibid., 376.

24. WHAT ARE BENEFIT CORPORATIONS?

1   Yvon Chouinard, *Let My People Go Surfing: The Education of a Reluctant Businessman* (New York: Penguin Books, 2005).

2   Ibid., 168.

3   Ibid., 170–71.

4 Ibid., 171.

5 Ibid., 196.

6 Ibid., 200.

7 "Certified B Corporation," Patagonia, accessed November 12, 2018, https://www.patagonia.com/b-lab.html.

8 Rona Fried, "Patagonia Among California's First Benefit Corporations," SustainableBusiness.com, January 4, 2012, https://www.sustainablebusiness.com/patagonia-among-california39s-first-benefit-corporations-49961/.

9 Bart King, "Patagonia Is First to Register for 'Benefit Corporation' Status in California," SustainableBrands.com, January 4, 2012, https://www.sustainablebrands.com/news_and_views/articles/patagonia-first-register-%E2%80%98benefit-corporation%E2%80%99-status-california

10 Erik J. Estrada and Alan H. Frosh, "An Overview of Benefit Corporations: A Proposed Solution to the Social Entrepreneur's Dilemma," DLR Online: The Online Supplement to the Denver Law Review, March 22, 2012, http://www.denverlawreview.org/dlr-onlinearticle/2012/3/22/an-overview-of-benefit-corporations-a-proposed-solution-to-t.html.

11 Internal Revenue Code (I.R.C.) § 501(c)(3).

12 Estrada and Frosh, "An Overview of Benefit Corporations," DLR Online, http://www.denverlawreview.org/dlr-onlinearticle/2012/3/22/an-overview-of-benefit-corporations-a-proposed-solution-to-t.html.

13 Ibid.

14 Bruce Hopkins, *The Law of Tax-Exempt Organizations*, 11th ed. (Hoboken, NJ: John Wiley & Sons, 2016), 131.

15 Estrada and Frosh, "An Overview of Benefit Corporations," DLR Online, http://www.denverlawreview.org/dlr-onlinearticle/2012/3/22/an-overview-of-benefit-corporations-a-proposed-solution-to-t.html.

16 Ibid.

17 "Certified B Corporation," BCorporation.net, accessed November 12, 2018, https://bcorporation.net/.

18 "Patagonia Works: Annual Benefit Corporation Report," Patagonia, accessed November 12, 2018, https://www.patagonia.com/static/on/demandware.static/-/Library-Sites-PatagoniaShared/default/dw824fac0f/PDF-US/2017-BCORP-pages_022218.pdf.

19 Ibid.

20 Ibid

21 Ibid

22 Ibid

23 Ibid

24 Ibid

25 Ibid

26 Hopkins, *The Law of Tax-Exempt Organizations*, 131.

27 "Certified B Corporation," BCorporation.net, https://bcorporation.net/.

25. WHAT ARE ARTICLES OF INCORPORATION?

1 Marissa Peretz, "Want to Engage Millennials? Try Corporate Social Responsibility," *Forbes*, September 27, 2017, https://www.forbes.com/sites/marissaperetz/2017/09/27/want-to-engage-millennials-try-corporate-social-responsibility/#5ab464f56e4e.

2 Ibid.

3 "Community Giving," Wells Fargo, accessed November 13, 2018, https://www.wellsfargo.com/about/corporate-responsibility/community-giving/; Max Miceli, "Google Tops Reputation Rankings for Corporate Responsibility," U.S. News & World Report, accessed November 13, 2018, https://www.usnews.com/news/articles/2015/09/17/google-tops-reputation-rankings-for-corporate-responsibility; "Salesforce Foundation," Salesforce, accessed November 13, 2018, https://www.salesforce.org/about-us/salesforce-foundation/.

[4] Daniel H. Pink, *Drive: The Surprising Truth About What Motivates Us* (New York: Riverhead Books, 2009), 1–270.

[5] "Certified B Corporation," BCorporation.net, accessed November 13, 2018, https://bcorporation.net/.

[6] "Articles of Incorporation: Level 3 Foundation, Inc.," Colorado Secretary of State, accessed November 27, 2018, https://www.sos.state.co.us/biz/ViewImage.do?masterFileId=20141033971&fileId=20141033971.

[7] Lisa A. Runquist, *The ABCs of Nonprofits*, 2nd ed. (Chicago: American Bar Association, 2015) 12–13.

[8] "Nonprofit Services," Oregon Secretary of State, accessed November 13, 2018, https://sos.oregon.gov/business/Pages/nonprofit.aspx.

[9] "A Manager's Guide to the Colorado Revised Nonprofit Corporation Act & Other Statutes," Orten, Cavanagh & Holmes: Attorneys At Law, accessed November 13, 2018, https://www.ochhoalaw.com/a-manager-s-guide-to-the-colorado-revised-nonprofit-corporation-act-other-statutes.

[10] Ibid.

[11] Ibid.

[12] Ibid.

[13] "Form 1023: Application for Recognition of Exemption Under Section 501(c)(3) of the Internal Revenue Code," Internal Revenue Service, accessed November 13, 2018, https://www.irs.gov/pub/irs-pdf/f1023.pdf.

[14] Runquist, *The ABCs of Nonprofits*, 14–16.

[15] Lesley Rosenthal, *Good Counsel: Meeting the Legal Needs of Nonprofits* (Hoboken, NJ: John Wiley & Sons, 2012), 24.

[16] Runquist, *The ABCs of Nonprofits*, 14–16.

[17] Colorado Revised Statutes (C.R.S.) § 7-121-101, et. seq.

[18] Bruce Hopkins, *The Law of Tax-Exempt Organizations*, 11th ed. (Hoboken, NJ: John Wiley & Sons, 2016), 68–71.

[19] Ibid.

[20] Ibid.

[21] Ibid.

26. WHY IS A BOARD OF DIRECTORS LEGALLY RESPONSIBLE FOR A NONPROFIT'S FINANCES?

[1] Lesley Rosenthal, *Good Counsel: Meeting the Legal Needs of Nonprofits* (Hoboken, NJ: John Wiley & Sons, 2012), 8–9.

[2] Marion R. Fremont-Smith, *Governing Nonprofit Organizations: Federal and State Law and Regulation* (Cambridge, MA: The Belknap Press of Harvard University Press, 2004), 201–5.

[3] Ibid., 226–27.

[4] Rosenthal, *Good Counsel*, 20–21.

[5] Ibid., 8–9.

[6] Ibid.

[7] Ibid.

[8] Daniel L. Kurtz, *Board Liability: A Guide for Nonprofit Directors* (Mt. Kisco, NY: Moyer Bell, 1989), 84–85.

[9] "Financial Information," El Pomar Foundation, accessed November 27, 2018, https://www.elpomar.org/About-Us/financials/.

[10] "University of Colorado Foundation," University of Colorado, accessed November 27, 2018, https://giving.cu.edu/about-us/university-colorado-foundation.

[11] Rosenthal, *Good Counsel*, 8–9.

27. WHAT ARE A NONPROFIT'S TWO BOTTOM LINES?

[1] Thomas McLaughlin, *Streetsmart Financial Basics for Nonprofit Managers*, 3rd ed. (Hoboken, NJ: John Wiley & Sons, 2009), 19–22.

[2] Simon Sinek, *Start with Why: How Great Leaders Inspire Everyone to Take Action* (New York: Penguin Group, 2009), 1–228.

[3] "Mission Statement," Imagine Charter School, accessed November 14, 2018, https://www.imaginefirestone.org/apps/pages/index.jsp?uREC_ID=824538&type=d&pREC_ID=1205852.

[4] Steven Ott, *Understanding Nonprofit Organizations: Governance, Leadership, and Management* (Boulder, CO: Westview Press, 2001), 127–30.

[5] Ibid.

[6] "Mission Statement," Imagine Charter School, https://www.imaginefirestone.org/apps/pages/index.jsp?uREC_ID=824538&type=d&pREC_ID=1205852.

[7] McLaughlin, *Streetsmart Financial Basics*, 19–22.

[8] Clara Miller, "Linking Money and Mission: An Introduction to Nonprofit Capitalization," Nonprofit Finance Fund, January 1, 2001, https://nff.org/report/linking-mission-and-money-introduction-nonprofit-capitalization.

[9] McLaughlin, *Streetsmart Financial Basics*, 19–22.

[10] Ibid., 24.

[11] Ibid., 21.

[12] Ibid.

[13] "Mission & Values," Vail Health Center, accessed November 14, 2018, https://www.vailhealth.org/about/mission-values.

[14] Ibid.

[15] Ibid.

[16] Ibid.

[17] "Form 990: Return of Organization Exempt from Income Tax," Vail Health Center, accessed November 14, 2018, https://www.guidestar.org/FinDocuments/2016/840/563/2016-840563230-0e7444d1-9.pdf.

[18] Ibid.

[19] "History," Vail Health Center, accessed November 14, 2018, https://www.vailhealth.org/about/history.

[20] McLaughlin, *Streetsmart Financial Basics*, 19–22.

28. WHAT'S A BALANCE SHEET?

[1] "About John D. and Catherine T. MacArthur," The MacArthur Foundation, accessed November 15, 2018, https://www.macfound.org/about/our-history/about-the-macarthurs/.

[2] "Our History," The MacArthur Foundation, accessed November 15, 2018, https://www.macfound.org/about/our-history/.

[3] Ibid.

[4] Ibid.

[5] Ibid.

[6] "Big Bets: Striving Toward Transformative Change in Areas of Profound Concern," The MacArthur Foundation, accessed November 15, 2018, https://www.macfound.org/pages/about-our-big-bets/.

[7] "MacArthur Fellows," The MacArthur Foundation, accessed November 15, 2018, https://www.macfound.org/programs/fellows/; "MacArthur Fellows Frequently Asked Questions," The MacArthur Foundation, accessed November 15, 2018, https://www.macfound.org/fellows-faq/.

[8] "MacArthur Fellows Frequently Asked Questions," The MacArthur Foundation, accessed November 15, 2018, https://www.macfound.org/fellows-faq/.

9   "100&Change," The MacArthur Foundation, accessed November 15, 2018, https://www.macfound.org/programs/100change/strategy/.

10   Steven A. Finkler, *Finance andAccounting for Nonfinancial Managers* (Paramus, NJ: Prentice Hall, 1996), 19.

11   Ibid.

12   Ibid., 17.

13   Ibid., 6.

14   Ibid., 214; Thomas McLaughlin, *Streetsmart Financial Basics for Nonprofit Managers*, 3rd ed. (Hoboken, NJ: John Wiley & Sons, 2009), 42–43.

15   McLaughlin, *Streetsmart Financial Basics*, 42–45.

16   Ibid., 45–47.

17   Ibid., 47.

18   Ibid., 47–48.

19   Finkler, *Finance andAccountingfor Nonfinancial Managers*, 16–17.

20   Ibid.

21   "John D. and Catherine T. MacArthur Foundation Consolidated Financial Statements December 31, 2017 and 2016," The MacArthur Foundation, accessed November 15, 2018, https://www.macfound.org/media/files/FINAL_2017_MacArthur_Foundation_audit_report.pdf.

22   Ibid.

23   Ibid.

24   Ibid.

25   Ibid.

26   Ibid.

27   McLaughlin, *Streetsmart Financial Basics*, 93.

28   "John D. and Catherine T. MacArthur Foundation Consolidated Financial Statements," The MacArthur Foundation, accessed November 15, 2018, https://www.macfound.org/media/files/FINAL_2017_MacArthur_Foundation_audit_report.pdf.

29   "Our History," The MacArthur Foundation, https://www.macfound.org/about/our-history/.

29.   WHAT'S AN INCOME STATEMENT?

1   Thomas McLaughlin, *Streetsmart Financial Basics for Nonprofit Managers*, 3rd ed. (Hoboken, NJ: John Wiley & Sons, 2009), 37–120; Edward McMillan, *Not-for-Profit Accounting, Tax, and Reporting Requirements*, 4th ed. (Hoboken, NJ: John Wiley & Sons, 2010), 1–179.

2   Tracy D. Connors and Christopher T. Callaghan, *Financial Management for Nonprofit Organizations* (New York: AMACOM Book Division, 1982), 237.

3   Ibid.

4   Clara Miller, "Hidden in Plain Sight: Understanding Nonprofit Capital Structure," Nonprofit Finance Fund, March 1, 2003, https://nff.org/commentary/hidden-plain-sight-understanding-nonprofit-capital-structure.

5   McMillan, *Not-for-Profit Accounting*, 191.

6   Steven A. Finkler, *Finance and Accounting for Nonfinancial Managers* (Paramus, NJ: Prentice Hall, 1996), 22–23.

7   Ibid.

8   Laurence Scot, *The Simplified Guide to Not-For-Profit Accounting, Formation, and Reporting* (Hoboken, NJ: John Wiley & Sons, 2010), 139–54.

9   Ibid., 143.

10   McLaughlin, *Streetsmart Financial Basics*, 64.

11   Ibid., 30

12   Scot, *The Simplified Guide*, 110–11.

13   Ibid., 109–11.

[14] Finkler, *Finance and Accountingfor Nonfinancial Managers*, 22–23.

[15] Ibid.

[16] "Audited Financial Statements National Council of Nonprofits December 31, 2017," National Council of Nonprofits, accessed November 17, 2018, https://www.councilofnonprofits.org/sites/default/files/documents/final-audited-financial-statements-fy2017.PDF.

[17] Ibid.

[18] "Form 990: Return of Organization Exempt from Income Tax," National Council of Nonprofits, accessed November 17, 2018, https://www.councilofnonprofits.org/sites/default/files/documents/final-national-council-of-nonprofits-fy2017-form990.pdf.

[19] "About Us," National Council of Nonprofits, accessed November 17, 2018, https://www.councilofnonprofits.org/about-us.

[20] "Audited Financial Statements," National Council of Nonprofits, https://www.councilofnonprofits.org/sites/default/files/documents/final-audited-financial-statements-fy2017.PDF.

[21] Ibid.

[22] Ibid.

[23] Ibid.

[24] Ibid.

[25] Ibid.

[26] Ibid.

[27] Ibid.

30. HOW'S THE BALANCE SHEET LINKED TO THE INCOME STATEMENT?

[1] Nicholas P. Cafardi and Jaclyn Fabean Cherry, *Understanding Nonprofit and Tax Exempt Organizations* (Newark, NJ: LexisNexis, 2006), 318–19.

[2] Internal Revenue Code (I.R.C.) § 4942.

[3] Ibid.; Cafardi and Fabean Cherry, *Understanding Nonprofitand Tax Exempt Organizations*, 318–19.

[4] Steven A. Finkler, *Finance and Accounting for Nonfinancial Managers* (Paramus, NJ: Prentice Hall, 1996), 20–21.

[5] Ibid., 19–20.

[6] Thomas McLaughlin, *Streetsmart Financial Basics for Nonprofit Managers* (Hoboken, NJ: John Wiley & Sons, 2009), 41–42.

[7] Finkler, *Finance and Accounting for Nonfinancial Managers*, 19–20.

[8] McLaughlin, *Streetsmart Financial Basics*, 41–42; Finkler, *Finance and Accounting for Nonfinancial Managers*, 19–20.

[9] Peter Konrad and Alys Novak, *Financial Management for Nonprofits: Keys to Success*, 3rd ed. (Littleton, CO: Discover Communications, 2004) 44–49.

[10] Finkler, *Finance and Accounting for Nonfinancial Managers*, 22–23.

[11] Guidestar's homepage, accessed December 1, 2018, https://www.guidestar.org/Home.aspx.

[12] "Who We Are," Clinica Tepeyac, accessed November 17, 2018, http://clinicatepeyac.org/who-we-are/financials.html.

[13] "Form 990: Return of Organization Exempt from Income Tax," La Clinica Tepeyac, accessed November 17, 2018, https://www.guidestar.org/FinDocuments/2015/841/285/2015-841285505-0cee2f22-9.pdf.

[14] Ibid.

[15] Ibid.

[16] Ibid.

[17] "Accounting: Income Statements," Inc., accessed November 17, 2018, https://www.inc.com/encyclopedia/income-statements.html.

31. WHAT'S THE STATEMENT OF CASH FLOWS?

[1] "Annual Report," Boys and Girls Clubs of America, accessed November 17, 2018, https://www.bgca.org/about-us/annual-report; "Form 990: Return of Organization Exempt from Income Tax," Boys and Girls Clubs of America, accessed November 17, 2018, https://www.bgca.org/about-us/annual-report.

[2] "Our Mission and Story," Boys and Girls Clubs of America, accessed November 17, 2018, https://www.bgca.org/about-us/our-mission-story.

[3] Ibid.

[4] Ibid.

[5] Ibid.

[6] Ibid.

[7] Ibid.

[8] "Annual Report," Boys and Girls Clubs of America, accessed November 17, 2018, https://www.bgca.org/about-us/annual-report

[9] Ibid.

[10] Ibid.; Laurence Scot, *The Simplified Guide to Not-for-Profit Accounting, Formation, and Reporting* (Hoboken, NJ: John Wiley & Sons, 2010) 76–81.

[11] Scot, *The Simplified Guide*, 76–81.

[12] Ibid.; Steven Finkler, *Finance and Accounting for Nonfinancial Managers* (Paramus, NJ: Prentice Hall, 1996), 24–25.

[13] Ibid

[14] Ibid.

[15] Peter Konrad and Alys Novak, *Financial Management for Nonprofits: Keys to Success*, 3rd ed. (Littleton, CO: Discover Communications, 2004), 48.

[16] Scot, *The Simplified Guide*, 76–81.

[17] Ibid.

[18] "Annual Report," Boys and Girls Clubs of America, https://www.bgca.org/about-us/annual-report; "Boys and Girls Clubs of America and Subsidiaries Consolidated Financial Statements December 31, 2016 and 2015 (With Independent Auditor's Report Thereon)," Boys and Girls Clubs of America, accessed November 17, 2018, https://www.bgca.org/about-us/annual-report.

[19] Ibid.

[20] Ibid.

[21] Ibid.

[22] Ibid.

[23] Ibid.

[24] Ibid.

[25] Ibid.

[26] Ibid.

[27] Ibid.

[28] Ibid.

[29] Ibid

32. HOW'S THE BALANCE SHEET LINKED TO THE STATEMENT OF CASH FLOWS?

[1] Steven Finkler, *Finance and Accounting for Nonfinancial Managers* (Paramus, NJ: Prentice Hall, 1996), 6.

[2] Thomas McLaughlin, *Streetsmart Financial Basics for Nonprofit Managers*, 3rd ed. (Hoboken, NJ: John Wiley & Sons, 2009), 42.

[3] Ibid., 45.

[4] Ibid., 46.

[5]   Matthew R. Rice, Robert A. DiMeo, and Matthew P. Porter, *Nonprofit Asset Management: Effective Investment Strategies and Oversight* (Hoboken, NJ: John Wiley & Sons, 2012), 8–9.

[6]   Ibid.

[7]   "David Packard: American Engineer," Encyclopedia Britannica, accessed November 18, 2018, https://www.britannica.com/biography/David-Packard.

[8]   "About Our History," The David and Lucile Packard Foundation, accessed November 18, 2018, https://www.packard.org/about-the-foundation/our-history/.

[9]   Ibid.

[10]   Ibid.

[11]   Ibid.

[12]   Ibid.   ·

[13]   "The David and Lucile Packard Foundation Consolidated and Individual Financial Statements December 31, 2016," The David and Lucile Packard Foundation, accessed November 18, 2018, https://www.packard.org/about-the-foundation/how-we-operate/investments-finance/financial-statements/.

[14]   Ibid.

[15]   Ibid.

[16]   Ibid.

[17]   Ibid.

33.   WHAT'S THE STATEMENT OF FUNCTIONAL EXPENSES?

[1]   Thomas Stanley and William Danko, *The Millionaire Next Door: The Surprising Secrets of America's Wealthy* (Lanham, MD: Taylor Trade Publishing, 1996), 1–246.

[2]   Ibid.

[3]   Ibid.

[4]   "Our History," St. Jude Children's Research Hospital, accessed November 18, 2018, https://www.stjude.org/about-st-jude/history.html?sc_icid=us-mm-history.

[5]   "Jennifer Aniston, Sofia Vergara, Michael Strahan, Jimmy Kimmel, Luis Fonsi join Marlo Thomas for 13th Annual St. Jude Thanks and Giving® Campaign," St. Jude Children's Research Hospital, accessed November 18, 2018, https://www.stjude.org/media-resources/news-releases/2016-fundraising-news/st-jude-thanks-and-giving-celebrity-partners.html.

[6]   "Form 990: Return of Organization Exempt from Income Tax," St. Jude Children's Research Hospital, accessed November 18, 2018, https://www.stjude.org/content/dam/en_US/shared/www/about-st-jude/financial-information/990-form-alsac-fy17.pdf.

[7]   "Timeline: From Dream to Reality," St. Jude Children's Research Hospital, accessed November 18, 2018, https://www.stjude.org/about-st-jude/history/timeline.html.

[8]   "Our Mission Statement," St. Jude Children's Research Hospital, accessed November 18, 2018, https://www.stjude.org/about-st-jude.html?sc_icid=us-mm-missionstatement#mission.

[9]   "Jennifer Aniston, Sofia Vergara, Michael Strahan," St. Jude Children's Research Hospital, https://www.stjude.org/media-resources/news-releases/2016-fundraising-news/st-jude-thanks-and-giving-celebrity-partners.html.

[10]   "Financial Reports," St. Jude Children's Research Hospital, accessed November 18, 2018, https://www.stjude.org/about-st-jude/financials.html.

[11]   Ibid.

[12]   Peter Konrad and Alys Novak, *Financial Management for Nonprofits: Keys to Success*, 3rd ed. (Littleton, CO: Discovery Communications, 2004), 47.

[13]   Ibid.

[14]   Ibid.

[15]   Ibid.

[16]   Ibid.

[17]   Ibid.

[18]   Ibid.

[19]   Edward McMillan, *Not-for-Profit Accounting Tax and Reporting Requirements*, 4th ed. (Hoboken, NJ: John Wiley & Sons, 2010), 22.

[20]   "Financial Reports," St. Jude Children's Research Hospital, https://www.stjude.org/about-st-jude/financials.html.

[21]   "St. Jude Children's Research Hospital, Inc. Combined Financial Statements as of and for the Years Ended June 30, 2017 and 2016, and Independent Auditors' Report," St. Jude Children's Research Hospital, accessed November 18, 2018, https://www.stjude.org/content/dam/en_US/shared/www/about-st-jude/financial-information/fy17-combined-audited-financial-statements.pdf.

[22]   Ibid.

[23]   Ibid.

[24]   Ibid.

[25]   Ibid.

[26]   Ibid.

[27]   Ibid.

34. HOW'S THE INCOME STATEMENT LINKED TO THE STATEMENT OF FUNCTIONAL EXPENSES?

[1]   Stephanie Strom, "Charities Now Seek Bankruptcy Protection," *New York Times*, February 19, 2009, https://www.nytimes.com/2009/02/20/us/20bankrupt.html.

[2]   Ibid.

[3]   Ibid.

[4]   Ibid.

[5]   Ibid.

[6]   Lesley Rosenthal, *Good Counsel: Meeting the Legal Needs of Nonprofits* (Hoboken, NJ: John Wiley & Sons, 2012), 7–9.

[7]   Strom, "Charities Now Seek Bankruptcy Protection," New York Times, https://www.nytimes.com/2009/02/20/us/20bankrupt.html.

[8]   Edward McMillan, *Not-for-Profit Accounting, Tax and Reporting Requirements*, 4th ed. (Hoboken, NJ: John Wiley & Sons, 2010), 22.

[9]   Ibid.

[10]   "Form 990: Return of Organization Exempt from Income Tax," Independent Sector, accessed November 18, 2018, https://independentsector.org/wp-content/uploads/2016/08/2015-form990.pdf.

[11]   "2016 IRS Form 990," Independent Sector, accessed November 18, 2018, https://independentsector.org/resource/2016-form-990/.

[12]   Ibid.

[13]   Ibid.

[14]   Ibid.

[15]   Ibid.

[16]   "2015 IRS Form 990," Independent Sector, accessed November 18, 2018, https://independentsector.org/resource/2015-form-990/.

[17]   Ibid.

[18]   Ibid.

[19]   "2016 IRS Form 990," Independent Sector, https://independentsector.org/resource/2016-form-990/; "About," Independent Sector, accessed November 18, 2018, https://independentsector.org/about/.

35. WHAT ARE UNRESTRICTED, TEMPORARILY RESTRICTED, AND PERMANENTLY RESTRICTED FUNDS?

[1] "Big Brothers Big Sisters of Metropolitan Chicago Financial Statements June 30, 2018," Big Brothers Big Sisters of Metropolitan Chicago, accessed November 19, 2018, https://bbbschgo.org/wp-content/uploads/2018/10/FY18-BBBSMC-Audited-Financial-Statements.pdf; "Form 990: Return of Organization Exempt from Income Tax," Big Brothers Big Sisters of Metropolitan Chicago, accessed November 19, 2018, https://bbbschgo.org/wp-content/uploads/2018/10/FY18-Tax-Return-Form-990.pdf.

[2] "Form 990: Return of Organization," Big Brothers Big Sisters of Metropolitan Chicago, https://bbbschgo.org/wp-content/uploads/2018/10/FY18-Tax-Return-Form-990.pdf.

[3] "About Us," Big Brothers Big Sisters of Metropolitan Chicago, accessed November 19, 2018, https://bbbschgo.org/about/.

[4] "Programs," Big Brothers Big Sisters of Metropolitan Chicago, accessed November 19, 2018, https://bbbschgo.org/programs/.

[5] "About Us," Big Brothers Big Sisters of Metropolitan Chicago, https://bbbschgo.org/about/.

[6] "Big Brothers Big Sisters of Metropolitan Chicago Financial Statements June 30, 2018," Big Brothers Big Sisters of Metropolitan Chicago, https://bbbschgo.org/wp-content/uploads/2018/10/FY18-BBBSMC-Audited-Financial-Statements.pdf

[7] Ibid.

[8] Ibid.

[9] Edward McMillan, Not-for-Profit Accounting, Tax and Reporting Requirements, 4th ed. (Hoboken, NJ: John Wiley & Sons, 2010), 163–64.

[10] Thomas McLaughlin, *Streetsmart Financial Basics for Nonprofit Managers*, 3rd ed. (Hoboken, NJ: John Wiley & Sons, 2009), 92–93.

[11] Ibid.

[12] Ibid.

[13] Ibid.

[14] McMillan, *Not-for-Profit Accounting*, 219.

[15] Ibid.

[16] Ibid., 164.

[17] McLaughlin, *Streetsmart Financial Basics*, 92–93.

[18] Ibid.

[19] Ibid.

[20] Ibid.

[21] "Big Brothers Big Sisters of Metropolitan Chicago Financial Statements June 30, 2018," Big Brothers Big Sisters of Metropolitan Chicago, https://bbbschgo.org/wp-content/uploads/2018/10/FY18-BBBSMC-Audited-Financial-Statements.pdf.

[22] Ibid.

[23] Ibid.

[24] Ibid.

[25] Ibid.

[26] Ibid.

[27] Ibid.

[28] Ibid.

[29] Ibid.

[30] Ibid.

[31] Ibid.

[32] Lesley Rosenthal, *Good Counsel: Meeting the Legal Needs of Nonprofits* (Hoboken, NJ: John Wiley & Sons, 2012), 116–17.

36.   WHAT ARE THE CURRENT RATIO AND WORKING CAPITAL?

[1]   Dean Baker, "The Housing Bubble and the Great Recession: Ten Years Later," Center for Economic and Policy Research, September 2018, http://cepr.net/images/stories/reports/housing-bubble-2018-09.pdf.

[2]   Ibid.

[3]   Steven Finkler, *Finance and Accounting for Nonfinancial Managers* (Paramus, NJ: Prentice Hall, 1996), 20.

[4]   Thomas McLaughlin, *Streetsmart Financial Basics for Nonprofit Managers*, 3rd ed. (Hoboken, NJ: John Wiley & Sons, 2009), 75–76.

[5]   Ibid.

[6]   Ibid.

[7]   Ibid., 42.

[8]   Ibid., 45–46.

[9]   Ibid.

[10]   Peter Konrad and Alys Novak, *Financial Management for Nonprofits: Keys to Success*, 3rd ed. (Littleton, CO: Discovery Communications, 2004), 113.

[11]   Ibid.

[12]   Ibid.

[13]   "Annual Reports and 990 Forms," Habitat for Humanity International, accessed November 19, 2018, https://www.habitat.org/about/annual-reports-990s.

[14]   "Frequently Asked Questions," Habitat for Humanity International, accessed November 19, 2018, https://www.habitat.org/about/faq#what.

[15]   Ibid.

[16]   Habitat for Humanity of Utah County's homepage, accessed November 19, 2018, https://www.habitatuc.org/.

[17]   "Form 990: Return of Organization Exempt from Income Tax," Habitat for Humanity of Utah County, accessed November 19, 2018, https://www.habitatuc.org/pdfs/H4H-PublicDisclosure2016-990and990T-TaxFiling.pdf.

[18]   "Habitat for Humanity Restore," Habitat for Humanity of Utah County, accessed November 19, 2018, https://www.habitatuc.org/restore.htm.

[19]   "Habitat for Humanity of Utah County Financial Statements June 30, 2017," Habitat for Humanity of Utah County, accessed November 19, 2018, https://www.habitatuc.org/pdfs/audit-HabitatForHumanity2017-06FinalFinancialStatements132782.pdf.

[20]   Ibid.

37.   WHAT ARE THE DEBT RATIO, EQUITY RATIO, AND THE DEBT-TO-EQUITY RATIO?

[1]   Clara Miller, "Hidden in Plain Sight: Understanding Capital Structure," *Nonprofit Quarterly*, March 21, 2003, https://nonprofitquarterly.org/2003/03/21/hidden-in-plain-sight-understanding-capital-structure/.

[2]   Ibid.

[3]   Ron Mattocks, *Zone of Insolvency: How Nonprofits Avoid Hidden Liabilities and Build Financial Strength* (Hoboken, NJ: John Wiley & Sons, 2008), 100.

[4]   Ibid.

[5]   Ibid.

[6]   Ibid.

[7]   Ibid.

[8]   Steven Finkler, *Finance and Accounting for Nonfinancial Managers* (Paramus, NJ: Prentice Hall, 1996), 19.

[9]   Konrad and Novak, *Financial Management for Nonprofits*, 113.

[10]   Ibid.

[11] Ibid.

[12] "Delivering Clear Impact: Financial Statements and Report of Independent Certified Public Accountants and Single Audit Reports: YMCA of the USA April 2018," YMCA of the USA, accessed November 20, 2018, https://s3.amazonaws.com/ymca-ynet-prod/files/organizational-profile/2017-audited-financial-statements.pdf.

[13] Ibid.

[14] Ibid.

[15] Ibid.

[16] Clara Miller, "Hidden in Plain Sight," *Nonprofit Quarterly*, https://nonprofitquarterly.org/2003/03/21/hidden-in-plain-sight-understanding-capital-structure/.

38.   WHAT'S SO IMPORTANT ABOUT THE "NOTES" SECTION IN AUDITED FINANCIAL STATEMENTS?

[1] Peter Konrad and Alys Novak, *Financial Management for Nonprofits: Keys to Success*, 3rd ed. (Littleton, CO: Discovery Communications, 2004), 112.

[2] Laurence Scot, *The Simplified Guide to Not-for-Profit Accounting, Formation, and Reporting* (Hoboken, NJ: John Wiley & Sons, 2010), 85–86.

[3] Ibid.

[4] Ibid.

[5] Konrad and Novak, *Financial Management for Nonprofits*, 112; Scot, *The Simplified Guide*, 85–86.

[6] Konrad and Novak, *Financial Management for Nonprofits*, 112.

[7] Ibid.

[8] Konrad and Novak, *Financial Management for Nonprofits*, 112; Scot, *The Simplified Guide*, 85–86.

[9] William P. Barrett, "The Largest U.S. Charities for 2016," *Forbes*, December 14, 2016, https://www.forbes.com/sites/williampbarrett/2016/12/14/the-largest-u-s-charities-for-2016/#7c10face4abb; "IRS Information Returns: Form 990," Alzheimer's Association, accessed November 21, 2018, https://www.alz.org/about/finances/irs-information-returns-form-990.

[10] "About," Alzheimer's Association, accessed November 21, 2018, https://www.alz.org/about.

[11] "Consolidated Financial Statements and Report of Independent Certified Public Accountants: Alzheimer's Association June 30, 2017," Alzheimer's Association, accessed November 21, 2018, https://www.alz.org/media/Documents/audited-financial-statements-fy2017.pdf.

[12] Ibid.

[13] Ibid.

[14] Ibid.

[15] Ibid.

[16] Ibid.

[17] Ibid.

[18] Ibid.

[19] Ibid.

[20] Ibid.

[21] Ibid.

39.   WHAT'S TIME VALUE OF MONEY?

[1] Geraldine Fabrikant, "Harvard's Endowment Grew 10% Last Year, but Some Rivals Did Better," *The New York Times*, September 28, 2018, https://www.nytimes.com/2018/09/28/business/harvard-endowment-gains.html.

[2] Ibid.

3   Steven Finkler, *Finance and Accounting for Nonfinancial Managers* (Paramus, NJ: Prentice Hall, 1996), 156–61.

4   Ibid.

5   "What Is the Time Value of Money?" Corporate Finance Institute, accessed November 21, 2018, https://corporatefinanceinstitute.com/resources/knowledge/valuation/time-value-of-money/.

6   "Form 990: Return of Organization Exempt from Income Tax," Capital Area Food Bank, accessed November 21, 2018, https://1qf95e43hn5t3dvchxhlkupz-wpengine.netdna-ssl.com/wp-content/uploads/2018/01/CAFB-2017-06-Tax-Form-990-Public-Disclosure-Copy-signed.pdf.

7   Ibid.

8   Ibid.

9   "About Us," Capital Area Food Bank, accessed November 21, 2018, https://www.capitalareafoodbank.org/about-cafb/.

10   "Form 990: Return of Organization Exempt from Income Tax," Capital Area Food Bank, https://1qf95e43hn5t3dvchxhlkupz-wpengine.netdna-ssl.com/wp-content/uploads/2018/01/CAFB-2017-06-Tax-Form-990-Public-Disclosure-Copy-signed.pdf.

11   "Capital Area Food Bank and Capital Area Food Bank Foundation Consolidated Financial Statements and Supplemental Information: For the Fiscal Year Ended June 30, 2018," Capital Area Food Bank, accessed November 21, 2018, https://1qf95e43hn5t3dvchxhlkupz-wpengine.netdna-ssl.com/wp-content/uploads/2018/10/cafb_201806_audit_final_fs__ug.pdf.

12   Ibid.

13   Finkler, *Finance and Accounting for Nonfinancial Managers*, 156–61.

14   "What Is the Time Value of Money?" Corporate Finance Institute, https://corporatefinanceinstitute.com/resources/knowledge/valuation/time-value-of-money/.

40.   WHAT'S THE DIFFERENCE BETWEEN AN AUDIT, A REVIEW, AND A COMPILATION?

1   "Form 990: Return of Organization Exempt from Income Tax," Internal Revenue Service, accessed November 21, 2018, https://www.irs.gov/pub/irs-pdf/f990.pdf; "Form 990-PF: Return of Private Foundation," Internal Revenue Service, accessed November 21, 2018, https://www.irs.gov/pub/irs-pdf/f990pf.pdf.

2   "Does Your Nonprofit Need to Have an Independent Audit?" National Council of Nonprofits, accessed November 21, 2018, https://www.councilofnonprofits.org/nonprofit-audit-guide/need-independent-audit.

3   Tracy D. Connors and Christopher T. Callaghan, *Financial Management for Nonprofit Organizations* (New York: AMACOM Book Division, 1982), 209–20.

4   Ibid.

5   Ibid.

6   Ibid.

7   Ibid.

8   Ibid.; Thomas McLaughlin, *Streetsmart Financial Basics for Nonprofit Managers*, 3rd ed. (Hoboken, NJ: John Wiley & Sons, 2009), 113–14.

9   Ibid.

10   Connors and Callaghan, *Financial Management for Nonprofit Organizations*, 209–20; McLaughlin, *Streetsmart Financial Basics*, 113–14.

11   Ibid.

12   "Does Your Nonprofit Need to Have an Independent Audit?" National Council of Nonprofits, https://www.councilofnonprofits.org/nonprofit-audit-guide/need-independent-audit.

13   Ibid.

14   McLaughlin, *Streetsmart Financial Basics*, 113–14.

¹⁵ Connors and Callaghan, *Financial Management for Nonprofit Organizations*, 209–20.

¹⁶ Ibid.

¹⁷ "Does Your Nonprofit Need to Have an Independent Audit?" National Council of Nonprofits, https://www.councilofnonprofits.org/nonprofit-audit-guide/need-independent-audit.

¹⁸ Ibid.

41. WHAT'S THE DIFFERENCE BETWEEN CASH-BASIS AND ACCRUAL-BASIS ACCOUNTING?

¹ "Reforming the Pass-Through Deduction," Tax Foundation, accessed November 22, 2018, https://taxfoundation.org/reforming-pass-through-deduction-199a/; John Wagner, "Trump Signs Sweeping Tax Bill into Law," *The Washington Post*, December 22, 2017, https://www.washingtonpost.com/news/post-politics/wp/2017/12/22/trump-signs-sweeping-tax-bill-into-law/?noredirect=on&utm_term=.a65997ded2c4.

² Internal Revenue Code (I.R.C.) § 199A.

³ Kelly Phillips Erb, "What Tax Reform Means for Small Businesses and Pass-Through Entities," *Forbes*, December 22, 2017, https://www.forbes.com/sites/kellyphillipserb/2017/12/22/what-tax-reform-means-for-small-businesses-pass-through-entities/#760c213b6de3.

⁴ Davis Graham and Stubbs LLP's homepage, accessed November 22, 2018, https://www.dgslaw.com/.

⁵ Phillips Erb, "What Tax Reform Means," *Forbes*, https://www.forbes.com/sites/kellyphillipserb/2017/12/22/what-tax-reform-means-for-small-businesses-pass-through-entities/#760c213b6de3.

⁶ "Reforming the Pass-Through Deduction," Tax Foundation, accessed November 22, 2018, https://taxfoundation.org/reforming-pass-through-deduction-199a/.

⁷ Daniel Wiessner, "U.S. Judge Says Uber Drivers Are Not Company's Employees," Reuters, April 12, 2018, https://www.reuters.com/article/us-uber-lawsuit/u-s-judge-says-uber-drivers-are-not-companys-employees-idUSKBN1HJ31I; Paayal Zaveri and Deirdre Bosa, "The New Tax Law Creates a Huge Boon for Uber and Lyft Drivers," CNBC, February 5, 2018, https://www.cnbc.com/2018/02/05/uber-lyft-drivers-and-other-contractors-get-2018-tax-law-benefit.html.

⁸ "Tax Cuts and Jobs Act, Provision 11011 Section 199A-Qualified Business Income Deduction FAQs," Internal Revenue Service, accessed November 22, 2018, https://www.irs.gov/newsroom/tax-cuts-and-jobs-act-provision-11011-section-199a-qualified-business-income-deduction-faqs.

⁹ Phillips Erb, "What Tax Reform Means," *Forbes*, https://www.forbes.com/sites/kellyphillipserb/2017/12/22/what-tax-reform-means-for-small-businesses-pass-through-entities/#760c213b6de3.

¹⁰ Edward McMillan, *Not-for-Profit Accounting, Tax, and Reporting Requirements*, 4th ed. (Hoboken, NJ: John Wiley & Sons, 2010), 177.

¹¹ Ibid.

¹² Ibid.

¹³ "Form 990-PF: Return of Private Foundation," Boettcher Foundation, accessed November 22, 2018, https://www.guidestar.org/FinDocuments/2016/840/404/2016-840404274-0de2e214-F.pdf.

¹⁴ McMillan, *Not-for-Profit Accounting*, 177.

¹⁵ Tracy D. Connors and Christopher T. Callaghan, *Financial Management for Nonprofit Organizations* (New York: AMACOM Book Division, 1982), 76–78.

¹⁶ Ibid.

¹⁷ Laurence Scot, *The Simplified Guide to Not-for-Profit Accounting, Formation, and Reporting* (Hoboken, NJ: John Wiley & Sons, 2010), 59–60.

18   Thomas McLaughlin, *Streetsmart Financial Basics for Nonprofit Managers*, 3rd ed. (Hoboken, NJ: John Wiley & Sons, 2009), 71.

19   "Form 990: Return of Organization Exempt from Income Tax," Medecins Sans Frontieres USA, (d/b/a Doctors Without Borders USA, Inc.), accessed November 22, 2018, https://doctorswithoutborders.org/sites/default/files/2018-08/2018-07-dwb_990.pdf.

20   Ibid.

21   "Form 990: Return of Organization Exempt from Income Tax," Medecins Sans Frontieres USA, (d/b/a Doctors Without Borders USA, Inc.), https://www.doctorswithoutborders.org/sites/default/files/2018-06/dwb_990_pd_0.pdf.

22   McMillan, *Not-for-Profit Accounting*, 177.

23   Ibid.

24   "Form 990: Return of Organization Exempt From Income Tax," Medecins Sans Frontieres USA, (d/b/a Doctors Without Borders USA, Inc.), https://doctorswithoutborders.org/sites/default/files/2018-08/2018-07-dwb_990.pdf.

25   Connors and Callaghan, *Financial Management for Nonprofit Organizations*, 76–78.

26   Ibid.

42.   WHAT DOES IT MEAN TO CAPITALIZE AN ASSET AND THEN DEPRECIATE THAT ASSET?

1   "Mayo Clinic: Ranked #1 in the Nation," Mayo Clinic, accessed November 23, 2018, https://www.mayoclinic.org/about-mayo-clinic/quality/top-ranked.

2   "Mayo Clinic: Consolidated Financial Report December 31, 2017," Mayo Clinic, accessed November 23, 2018, https://cdn.prod-carehubs.net/n1/802899ec472ea3d8/uploads/2018/03/Mayo-Clinic-2017-Consolidated-Financials-Word_FINAL-SECURED_v3-SHORT-FORM.pdf.

3   Ibid.

4   Ibid.

5   Ibid.

6   Ibid.

7   Ibid.

8   Edward McMillan, *Not-for-Profit Accounting, Tax, and Reporting Requirements*, 4th ed. (Hoboken, NJ: John Wiley & Sons, 2010), 246.

9   Thomas McLaughlin, *Streetsmart Financial Basics for Nonprofit Managers*, 3rd ed. (Hoboken, NJ: John Wiley & Sons, 2009), 146–47.

10   Peter Konrad and Alys Novak, *Financial Management for Nonprofits: Keys to Success*, 3rd ed. (Littleton, CO: Discovery Communications, 2004), 61–62.

11   Ibid.

12   Ibid.

13   Ibid.

14   Ibid.

15   Ibid.

16   "About Publication 946, How to Depreciate Property," Internal Revenue Service, accessed November 23, 2018, https://www.irs.gov/forms-pubs/about-publication-946.

17   "Publication 946 (2017), How to Depreciate Property," Internal Revenue Service, https://www.irs.gov/publications/p946.

18   Konrad and Novak, *Financial Management for Nonprofits*, 61–62.

19   Ibid.

20   Ibid.

21   "What We Do: Keeping Families Close," Ronald McDonald House Charities, accessed November 23, 2018, https://rmhc-denver.org/what-we-do/.

22   Ibid.

23   Konrad and Novak, *Financial Management for Nonprofits*, 61–62.

[24]   "Form 990: Return of Organization Exempt from Income Tax," Ronald McDonald House Charities of Denver, accessed November 23, 2018, https://www.guidestar.org/FinDocuments/2017/840/728/2017-840728926-0f5c0d6d-9.pdf.

[25]   Ibid.

[26]   "IRS Issues New Regulations Requiring a Written Capitalization Policy to be in Place by January 1 to Qualify for Special Tax Treatment," Batts, Morrison, Wales, & Lee, accessed November 23, 2018, https://www.nonprofitcpa.com/irs-issues-new-regulations-requiring-written-capitalization-policy-place-january-1st-qualify-special-tax-treatment/; "Fixed Asset or Expense?" Nonprofit Accounting Academy, accessed November 23, 2018, https://www.nonprofitaccountingacademy.com/fixed-asset-expense/.

[27]   "Fixed Asset or Expense?" Nonprofit Accounting Academy, https://www.nonprofitaccountingacademy.com/fixed-asset-expense/.

[28]   Konrad and Novak, *Financial Management for Nonprofits*, 61–62.

43.   WHAT'S THE DIFFERENCE BETWEEN FIXED COSTS AND VARIABLE COSTS?

[1]   William Foster and Jeffrey L. Bradach, "Should Nonprofits Seek Profits?" *Harvard Business Review*, February (2005), https://hbr.org/2005/02/should-nonprofits-seek-profits.

[2]   "Case Study: Appreciating Depreciation-Thinking Strategically about Fixed Assets-Boston Center for the Arts," Nonprofit Finance Fund, accessed November 23, 2018, https://www.nonprofitfinancefund.org/sites/default/files/paragraphs/file/download/BCACaseStudy.pdf.

[3]   "Mission," Boston Center for the Arts, accessed November 23, 2018, http://www.bcaonline.org/aboutthebca/mission.html.

[4]   "Case Study: Appreciating Depreciation," Nonprofit Finance Fund, https://www.nonprofitfinancefund.org/sites/default/files/paragraphs/file/download/BCACaseStudy.pdf.

[5]   Ibid.

[6]   Ibid.

[7]   Ibid.

[8]   Ibid.

[9]   Ibid.

[10]   Thomas McLaughlin, *Streetsmart Financial Basics for Nonprofit Managers*, 3rd ed. (Hoboken, NJ: John Wiley & Sons, 2009), 108–09; Peter Konrad and Alys Novak, *Financial Management for Nonprofits: Keys to Success*, 3rd ed. (Littleton, CO: Discovery Communications, 2004), 97–98.

[11]   Konrad and Novak, *Financial Management for Nonprofits*, 97–98.

[12]   Ibid.

[13]   Ibid.

[14]   Ibid.

[15]   McLaughlin, *Streetsmart Financial Basics*, 107–8.

[16]   Konrad and Novak, *Financial Management for Nonprofits*, 97–98.

[17]   McLaughlin, *Streetsmart Financial Basics*, 107–8.

[18]   "Case Study: Appreciating Depreciation," Nonprofit Finance Fund, https://www.nonprofitfinancefund.org/sites/default/files/paragraphs/file/download/BCACaseStudy.pdf.

44.   WHAT'S ZERO-BASED BUDGETING?

[1]   "Peter F. Drucker," Drucker School of Management, Claremont Graduate University, accessed November 24, 2018, https://www.cgu.edu/school/drucker-school-of-management/peter-f-drucker/.

[2]   Murray Dropkin, Jim Halpin, and Bill La Touche, *The Budget-Building Book for Nonprofits: A Step-By-Step Guide for Managers and Boards*, 2nd ed. (San Francisco: Jossey-Bass, 2007), 30–32.

3   Ibid.
4   Ibid.
5   Ibid.
6   Ibid.
7   Ibid.
8   Ibid.
9   Ibid.
10   Ibid.
11   Ibid.

45.   WHAT'S UNRELATED BUSINESS TAXABLE INCOME (UBTI)?

1   "Form 990: Return of Organization Exempt from Income Tax," Goodwill Industries International, accessed November 24, 2018, http://www.goodwill.org/wp-content/uploads/2018/04/2017-Goodwill-Industries-Internation-Form-990.pdf.

2   "About Us," Goodwill Industries International, accessed November 24, 2018, http://www.goodwill.org/about-us/.

3   Ibid.

4   Ibid.

5   Ibid.

6   Ibid.

7   Ibid.

8   Ibid.

9   Internal Revenue Code (I.R.C.) § 512.

10   Lesley Rosenthal, *Good Counsel: Meeting the Legal Needs of Nonprofits* (Hoboken, NJ: John Wiley & Sons, 2012), 147–49.

11   Ibid.

12   "All about Cookies," Girl Scouts, accessed November 24, 2018, https://www.girlscouts.org/en/cookies/all-about-cookies.html.

13   Ibid.

14   "Unrelated Business Income Tax Exceptions and Exclusions," Internal Revenue Service, accessed November 24, 2018, https://www.irs.gov/charities-non-profits/charitable-organizations/unrelated-business-income-tax-exceptions-and-exclusions.

15   Reg. § 1.513-1.

16   Ibid.

17   Ibid.

18   "Request for Comments Regarding the Calculation of Unrelated Business Taxable Income under § 512(a)(6) for Exempt Organizations with More than One Unrelated Trade or Business; Interim and Transition Rules for Aggregating Certain Income in the Nature of Investments; and the Treatment of Global Intangible Low-Taxed Income Inclusions for Purposes of the Unrelated Business Income Tax," Internal Revenue Service, accessed November 24, 2018, https://www.irs.gov/pub/irs-drop/n-18–67.pdf.

19   Ibid.

20   "Employer's Tax Guide to Fringe Benefits," Internal Revenue Service, accessed November 24, 2018, https://www.irs.gov/pub/irs-pdf/p15b.pdf; "Request for Comments Regarding the Calculation of Unrelated Business Taxable Income," Internal Revenue Service, https://www.irs.gov/pub/irs-drop/n-18–67.pdf.

21   "Priv. Ltr. Rul. 201423030," Internal Revenue Service, accessed November 24, 2018, https://www.irs.gov/pub/irs-wd/201423030.pdf.

22   Ibid.

23   Ibid.

24 Ibid.
25 Ibid.
26 Ibid.
27 Ibid.
28 Ibid.
29 Ibid.
30 Ibid.
31 Ibid.
32 Ibid.

46. WHAT ARE INTERNAL CONTROLS?

1 "TEDx Program," TED, accessed November 24, 2018, https://www.ted.com/about/programs-initiatives/tedx-program.

2 "TEDx Events," TED, accessed November 24, 2018, https://www.ted.com/tedx/events.

3 "Our Organization," TED, accessed November 24, 2018, https://www.ted.com/about/our-organization; "About Us," TEDxMileHigh, accessed November 24, 2018, https://www.tedxmilehigh.com/about/

4 "About Us," TEDxMileHigh, https://www.tedxmilehigh.com/about/

5 "Announcing the Full Lineup for TEDxMileHigh: Uncommon," TEDxMileHigh, accessed November 24, 2018, https://www.tedxmilehigh.com/full-lineup-uncommon/.

6 Ibid.

7 Ibid.

8 "Articles of Incorporation," ActionMileHigh, accessed November 24, 2018, https://www.sos.state.co.us/biz/BusinessEntityDetail.do?quitButtonDestination=BusinessEntityResults&nameTyp=ENT&masterFileId=20101686510&entityId2=20101686510&fileId=20101686510&srchTyp=ENTITY.

9 "SEC Implements Internal Control Provisions of Sarbanes-Oxley Act; Adopts Investment Company R&D Safe Harbor," United States Securities and Exchange Commission, accessed November 24, 2018, https://www.sec.gov/news/press/2003–66.htm.

10 Peter Konrad and Alys Novak, *Financial Management for Nonprofits: Keys to Success*, 3rd ed. (Littleton, CO: Discovery Communications, 2004), 86–89.

11 Ibid.

12 Thomas McLaughlin, *Streetsmart Financial Basics for Nonprofit Managers*, 3rd ed. (Hoboken, NJ: John Wiley & Sons, 2009), 219–37.

13 Ibid.

14 Konrad and Novak, *Financial Management for Nonprofit*), 86–89.

15 Ibid.

16 McLaughlin, *Streetsmart Financial Basics*, 219–37.

17 Ibid., 235–36.

18 Ibid.

19 Ibid.

20 "Form 990: Return of Organization Exempt from Income Tax," TEDx Portland, accessed November 24, 2018, https://www.guidestar.org/FinDocuments/2016/274/884/2016-274884880-0e9f72d4-9.pdf.

21 Ibid.

22 TEDxPortland's homepage, accessed November 24, 2018, http://www.tedxportland.com/.

23 Konrad and Novak, *Financial Management for Nonprofits*, 86–89.

24 McLaughlin, *Streetsmart Financial Basics*, 219–37.

47. WHAT'S A CAPITAL CAMPAIGN?

1   "About Us," The Butterfly Pavilion, accessed November 25, 2018, https://butterflies.org/about-us/.

2   Ibid.

3   Ibid.

4   "Form 990: Return of Organization Exempt from Income Tax," Rocky Mountain Butterfly Consortium (d/b/a, Butterfly Pavilion), accessed November 25, 2018, https://butterflies.org/app/uploads/2018/09/Form990_2016.pdf.

5   "The Boettcher Times: A Colorado Legacy," The Boettcher Foundation, accessed November 25, 2018, https://boettcherfoundation.org/download-file/?file_id=/wp-content/uploads/2015/06/The-Boettcher-Times-A-Colorado-Legacy.pdf.

6   Ibid.

7   "Form 990: Return of Organization Exempt From Income Tax," Rocky Mountain Butterfly Consortium (d/b/a, Butterfly Pavilion), https://butterflies.org/app/uploads/2018/09/Form990_2016.pdf.

8   "Executive Summary: Facility Expansion and Renovation: Planning for Capital Campaign Projects and Campaigns," The Gates Family Foundation, accessed November 25, 2018, https://www.gatesfamilyfoundation.org/sites/default/files/docs/Planning%20Tools%20Summary.pdf.

9   Ibid.

10   Ibid.

11   Ibid.

12   Ibid.

13   Ibid.

14   "The Campaign for BU Law," Boston University, accessed November 25, 2018, https://www.bu.edu/law/alumni/campaign/ priorities/.

15   "Campaign for BU Law Priorities," Boston University, https://www.bu.edu/law/alumni/campaign/priorities/.

16   "Sumner Redstone Gives $18 Million to School of Law," Boston University, accessed November 25, 2018, http://www.bu.edu/today/2012/sumner-redstone-gives-18-million-to-school-of-law/.

17   "Message from Law School Campaign Chair," Boston University, accessed November 25, 2018, https://www.bu.edu/law/alumni/campaign/message-from-chair/.

18   Ibid.

19   "Executive Summary: Facility Expansion and Renovation," The Gates Family Foundation, https://www.gatesfamilyfoundation.org/sites/default/files/docs/Planning%20Tools%20Summary.pdf.

20   Ilona Bray, *Effective Fundraising for Nonprofits: Real-World Strategies That Work* (Berkeley, CA: Nolo, 2008), 1–460; K. Scott Sheldon, *Successful Corporate Fundraising: Effective Strategies for Today's Nonprofits* (New York: John Wiley & Sons, 2000), 41–42.

48. WHAT ARE A DONOR-ADVISED FUND, CHARITABLE REMAINDER TRUST, AND CHARITABLE LEAD TRUST?

1   "Donor-Advised Fund Timeline," Council on Foundations, accessed November 25, 2018, https://www.cof.org/sites/default/files/documents/files/DAF-timeline.pdf.

2   "Donor-Advised Funds," Internal Revenue Service, https://www.irs.gov/charities-non-profits/charitable-organizations/donor-advised-funds.

3   Joel L. Fleishman, *The Foundation: A Great American Secret* (New York: PublicAffairs, 2007), 269.

4   Ibid.

5   Harvey J. Platt, *Your Living Trust and Estate Plan: How to Maximize Your Family's Assets and Protect Your Loved Ones*, 3rd. ed. (New York: Allworth Press, 2002), 45.

6   Ibid., 46.

7   Ibid., 45.

8   Ibid., 132.

9   Ibid.; Internal Revenue Code (I.R.C.) § 664, accessed November 25, 2018, https://www.law.cornell.edu/uscode/text/26/664.

10   Internal Revenue Code (I.R.C.) § 664, https://www.law.cornell.edu/uscode/text/26/664.

11   Platt, *Your Living Trust and Estate Plan*, 131–37.

12   Ibid.

13   Ibid., 134.

14   Ibid.

15   Ibid.

16   Ibid.

17   Ibid., 134–36.

18   "Donor-Advised Funds," Children's Hospital Colorado Foundation, accessed November 25, 2018, https://childrenscoloradofoundation.giftplans.org/index.php?cID=241.

19   "More Ways to Give Stock," Children's Hospital Colorado Foundation, accessed November 25, 2018, http://www.childrenscoloradofoundation.org/ways-to-give/other-ways-to-give.html.

Bibliography

■ ■ ■

"100&Change," The MacArthur Foundation, accessed November 15, 2018, https://www.macfound.org/programs/100change/strategy/.

"2015 IRS Form 990," Independent Sector, accessed November 18, 2018, https://independentsector.org/resource/2015-form-990/.

"2016 IRS Form 990," Independent Sector, accessed November 18, 2018, https://independentsector.org/resource/2016-form-990/.

AARP, accessed November 6, 2018, https://www.aarp.org/about-aarp/.

The Ability Experience, accessed November 9, 2018, https://abilityexperience.org/about/.

"Accounting: Income Statements," Inc., accessed November 17, 2018, https://www.inc.com/encyclopedia/income-statements.html.

"All About Cookies," Girl Scouts, accessed November 24, 2018, https://www.girlscouts.org/en/cookies/all-about-cookies.html.

Alzheimer's Association, accessed November 21, 2018, https://www.alz.org/about.

"Andreas Antonopoulos Leaves Bitcoin Foundation Over 'Complete Lack of Transparency,'" CCN, accessed November 7, 2018, https://www.ccn.com/andreas-antonopoulos-leaves-bitcoin-foundation-complete-lack-transparency/.

"Announcing the Full Lineup for TEDxMileHigh: Uncommon," TEDxMileHigh, accessed November 24, 2018, https://www.tedxmilehigh.com/full-lineup-uncommon/.

"Annual Electronic Filing Requirements for Small Exempt Organizations—Form 990-N (e-Postcard)," Internal Revenue Service, accessed November 10, 2018, https://www.irs.gov/charities-non-profits/annual-electronic-filing-requirement-for-small-exempt-organizations-form-990-n-e-postcard.

"Annual Report," Boys and Girls Clubs of America, accessed November 17, 2018, https://www.bgca.org/about-us/annual-report.

"Annual Reports and 990 Forms," Habitat for Humanity International, accessed November 19, 2018, https://www.habitat.org/about/annual-reports-990s.

Arnsberger, Paul, Melissa Ludlum, Margaret Riley, and Mark Stanton, "A History of the Tax-Exempt Sector: An SOI Perspective," Internal Revenue Service, accessed November 11, 2018, https://www.irs.gov/pub/irs-soi/tehistory.pdf.

"Articles of Amendment to the Articles of Incorporation of University of Louisville Foundation, Inc.," Kentucky Secretary of State, accessed October 19, 2018, http://apps.sos.ky.gov/ImageWebViewer/(S(iqaep1z15d4ric45avj3pd45))/OBDBDisplayImage.aspx?id=7091081.

"Articles of Incorporation," ActionMileHigh, accessed November 24, 2018, https://www.sos.state.co.us/biz/BusinessEntityDetail.do?quitButtonDestination=BusinessEntityResults&nameTyp=ENT&masterFileId=20101686510&entityId2=20101686510&fileId=20101686510&srchTyp=ENTITY.

"Articles of Incorporation: Level 3 Foundation, Inc.," Colorado Secretary of State, accessed November 27, 2018, https://www.sos.state.co.us/biz/ViewImage.do?masterFileId=201410 33971&fileId=2014103397.

"Audited Financial Statements National Council of Nonprofits December 31, 2017," National Council of Nonprofits, accessed November 17, 2018, https://www.councilofnonprofits. org/sites/default/files/documents/final-audited-financial-statements-fy2017.PDF.

Baker, Dean, "The Housing Bubble and the Great Recession: Ten Years Later," Center for Economic and Policy Research, September 2018, http://cepr.net/images/stories/reports/ housing-bubble-2018-09.pdf.

Baker, Wayne, *Achieving Success Through Social Capital: Tapping the Hidden Resources in Your Personal and Business Networks* (New York: John Wiley & Sons, 2000).

Barrett, William P., "The Largest U.S. Charities for 2016," *Forbes*, December 14, 2016, https://www.forbes.com/sites/williampbarrett/2016/12/14/the-largest-u-s-charities-for-2016/#7c10face4abb.

Bass, Gary D., David F. Arons, Kay Guinane, and Matthew F. Carter, *Seen but not Heard: Strengthening Nonprofit Advocacy* (Washington, DC: The Aspen Institute, 2007).

"Become a Member of the Chamber and Enjoy All the Benefits," Louisville Chamber of Commerce, accessed November 7, 2018, https://louisvillechamber.com/become-a-member/.

Beer, Kara, 'Tis the Season," *Philanthropy Daily*, September 15, 2014, https://www. philanthropydaily.com/tis-the-season-2/.

"Benefits and Discounts," AARP, accessed November 6, 2018, https://www.aarp.org/ benefits-discounts/.

"Best Places to Live," *Money*, accessed November 7, 2018, https://money.cnn.com/magazines/ moneymag/best-places/2013/snapshots/PL0846355.html.

Beveridge, Norwood P. "The Internal Affairs Doctrine: The Proper Law of a Corporation," *The Business Lawyer* 44, no. 3 (1989): 693–719, http://www.jstor.org/stable/40687015.

"Big Bets: Striving Toward Transformative Change in Areas of Profound Concern," The MacArthur Foundation, accessed November 15, 2018, https://www.macfound.org/pages/ about-our-big-bets/.

Big Brothers Big Sisters of Metropolitan Chicago, accessed November 19, 2018, https:// bbbschgo.org/about/.

"Big Brothers Big Sisters of Metropolitan Chicago Financial Statements June 30, 2018," Big Brothers Big Sisters of Metropolitan Chicago, accessed November 19, 2018, https://bbbschgo.org/wp-content/uploads/2018/10/FY18-BBBSMC-Audited-Financial-Statements.pdf.

"Bill Daniels Biography," Daniels Fund, accessed October 31, 2018, https://www.danielsfund. org/billdaniels/biography.

"The Boettcher Times: A Colorado Legacy," The Boettcher Foundation, accessed November 25, 2018, https://boettcherfoundation.org/download-file/?file_id=/wp-content/uploads/2015/ 06/The-Boettcher-Times-A-Colorado-Legacy.pdf.

"Boys & Girls Clubs of America and Subsidiaries Consolidated Financial Statements December 31, 2016 and 2015 (With Independent Auditor's Report Thereon)," Boys and Girls Clubs of America, accessed November 17, 2018, https://www.bgca.org/about-us/annual-report.

Bray, Ilona, *Effective Fundraising for Nonprofits: Real-World Strategies That Work* (Berkeley, CA: Nolo, 2008).

"The Broad Art Center at UCLA," The Eli and Edythe Broad Foundation, accessed October 21, 2018, https://broadfoundation.org/grantees/the-broad-art-center-at-ucla/.

Brody, Evelyn, "The Legal Framework for Nonprofit Organizations," *The Nonprofit Sector: A Research Handbook*, 2nd ed. (London: Yale University Press, 2006).

Bryce, Herrington J., *Players in the Public Policy Process: Nonprofits as Social Capital and Agents* (New York: Palgrave Macmillan 2005), 1–283.

Bump, Philip, "Does More Campaign Money Actually Buy More Votes: An Investigation," *The Atlantic*, November 11, 2013, https://www.theatlantic.com/politics/archive/2013/11/does-more-campaign-money-actually-buy-more-votes-investigation/355154/.

Buteau, Michael, and Janet Paskin, "118 Rich and Powerful People Who Are Members of Augusta National," *Bloomberg*, April 10, 2015, https://www.bloomberg.com/graphics/2015-augusta-national-golf-club-members/.

Butterfly Pavilion, accessed November 25, 2018, https://butterflies.org/about-us/.

Cafardi, Nicholas P., and Jaclyn Fabean Cherry, *Tax Exempt Organizations: Cases and Materials*, 2nd ed. (Newark, NJ: LexisNexis, 2008).

"The Campaign for BU Law," Boston University, accessed November 25, 2018, https://www.bu.edu/law/alumni/campaign/.

"Campaign for BU Law Priorities," Boston University, accessed November 25, 2018, https://www.bu.edu/law/alumni/campaign/priorities/.

Capital Area Food Bank, accessed November 21, 2018, https://www.capitalareafoodbank.org/about-cafb/.

"Capital Area Food Bank and Capital Area Food Bank Foundation Consolidated Financial Statements and Supplemental Information: For the Fiscal Year Ended June 30, 2018," Capital Area Food Bank, accessed November 21, 2018, https://1qf95e43hn5t3dvchxhlkupz-wpengine.netdna-ssl.com/wp-content/uploads/2018/10/cafb_201806_audit_final_fs__ug.pdf.

Carter, Ellis, "Accepting Donations Prior to Exemption," *CharityLawyerBlog.com*, August 12, 2016, http://charitylawyerblog.com/2016/08/12/accepting-donations-prior-to-exemption/.

"Case Study: Appreciating Depreciation—Thinking Strategically About Fixed Assets—Boston Center for the Arts," Nonprofit Finance Fund, accessed November 23, 2018, https://www.nonprofitfinancefund.org/sites/default/files/paragraphs/file/download/BCACaseStudy.pdf.

"Certified B Corporation," BCorporation.net, accessed November 12, 2018, https://bcorporation.net/.

"Certified B Corporation," Patagonia, accessed November 12, 2018, https://www.patagonia.com/b-lab.html.

Chan Zuckerberg Initiative, accessed November 29, 2018, https://www.chanzuckerberg.com/about.

Chernow, Ron, *Alexander Hamilton* (New York: The Penguin Press, 2004), 36–40.

Chouinard, Yvon, *Let My People Go Surfing: The Education of a Reluctant Businessman* (New York: Penguin Books, 2005).

Clausen, Matt, "Some Restrictions Apply: Donating Restricted Stock," *Adler & Colvin*, May 14, 2013, https://www.adlercolvin.com/blog/2013/05/14/some-restrictions-apply-donating-restricted-stock/.

Clinton, Stephen, and Romin Thomson, "How Did Delaware Get so Popular?" *California Business Law Practitioner*, Winter 2013, The Regents of the University of California, http://www.smwb.com/doc/How-Did-Delaware-Get-So-%20Popular.pdf.

"The Colbert Report—Super PAC Segments (Comedy Central)," The Peabody Awards, accessed November 5, 2018, http://peabodyawards.com/award-profile/the-colbert-report-super-pac-segments.

Colorado Common Cause's homepage, accessed November 3, 2018, https://www.common-cause.org/colorado/.

Committee on Nonprofit Organizations, *Model Nonprofit Corporation Act*, 3rd ed. (Chicago: American Bar Association, 2009).

"Community Giving," Wells Fargo, accessed November 13, 2018, https://www.wellsfargo.com/about/corporate-responsibility/community-giving/.

Community Wealth Partners, accessed November 5, 2018, http://communitywealth.com/about-us/.

Connors, Tracy D., and Christopher T. Callaghan, *Financial Management for Nonprofit Organizations* (New York: AMACOM Book Division, 1982).

Conover, Michael, "Excise Tax 'Bite' on Nonprofit Compensation," *BDO*, July 2, 2018, https://www.bdo.com/blogs/nonprofit-standard/july-2018/excise-tax-bite-on-nonprofit-compensation.

Conscious Venture Lab's homepage, accessed November 11, 2018, http://www.conscious-venturelab.com/.

"Consolidated Financial Statements and Report of Independent Certified Public Accountants: Alzheimer's Association June 30, 2017," Alzheimer's Association, accessed November 21, 2018, https://www.alz.org/media/Documents/audited-financial-statements-fy2017.pdf.

"Consolidated Financial Statements Together with Report of Independent Certified Public Accountants AARP December 31, 2017 and 2016," AARP, accessed November 6, 2018, https://www.aarp.org/content/dam/aarp/about_aarp/about_us/2018/aarp-2017-audited-financial-statement.pdf.

"D&O Insurance 101: How Much Does a Directors and Officers Lawsuit Cost?" Insureon, accessed October 12, 2018, https://nonprofit.insureon.com/resources/d-and-o/cost.

"Daniels Fund Board of Directors," Daniels Fund, accessed November 1, 2018, https://www.danielsfund.org/about-daniels-fund/board-of-directors/board.

"'Dark Money' Gets a Little Light: CREW v. FEC and Its Implications for the 2018 Midterms," K&L Gates, accessed December 14, 2018, https://www.lexology.com/library/detail.aspx?g=e1f82545-1680-49b7-8e58-2ee1522a2933.

The David and Lucile Packard Foundation, accessed November 18, 2018, https://www.packard.org/about-the-foundation/our-history/.

"The David and Lucile Packard Foundation Consolidated and Individual Financial Statements December 31, 2016," The David and Lucile Packard Foundation, accessed November 18, 2018, https://www.packard.org/about-the-foundation/how-we-operate/investments-finance/financial-statements/.

"David Packard: American Engineer," Encyclopedia Britannica, accessed November 18, 2018, https://www.britannica.com/biography/David-Packard.

Davis, Pamela, "Directors and Officers Liability Insurance: Why It's Worth the Cost," *Nonprofit Quarterly*, July 13, 2015, https://nonprofitquarterly.org/2015/07/13/nonprofit-insurance-why-its-worth-the-cost/.

Davis Graham & Stubbs LLP's homepage, accessed November 22, 2018, https://www.dgslaw.com/.

Davison, Laura, and Bill Allison, "Many Political Tax-Exempts No Longer Required to Report Donors," *Bloomberg*, July 16, 2018, https://www.bloomberg.com/news/articles/2018-07-17/many-political-tax-exempts-no-longer-required-to-report-donors.

Dees, J. Gregory, Jed Emerson, and Peter Economy, *Enterprising Nonprofits: A Toolkit for Social Entrepreneurs* (New York: John Wiley & Sons, 2001).

"Delaware Division of Corporations: About the Division of Corporations," State of Delaware, accessed October 2, 2018, https://corp.delaware.gov/aboutagency/.

"Delivering Clear Impact: Financial Statements and Report of Independent Certified Public Accountants and Single Audit Reports: YMCA of the USA April 2018," YMCA of the USA, accessed November 20, 2018, https://s3.amazonaws.com/ymca-ynet-prod/files/organizational-profile/2017-audited-financial-statements.pdf.

Deutsch, Jeremy, "Investor, Beware: Was Your Fund Really Formed in an Investor-Friendly Forum?", *The New York Law Journal*, November 9, 2018, https://www.law.com/newyorklawjournal/2018/11/09/investor-beware-was-your-fund-really-formed-in-an-investor-friendly-forum/?slreturn=20181029082506.

"Does Your Nonprofit Need to Have an Independent Audit?", National Council of Nonprofits, accessed November 21, 2018, https://www.councilofnonprofits.org/nonprofit-audit-guide/need-independent-audit.

"Domestic Nonprofit Corporation Forms," Oregon Secretary of State, accessed November 11, 2018, https://sos.oregon.gov/business/Pages/domestic-nonprofit-corporation-forms.aspx.

"Donor-Advised Funds," Children's Hospital Colorado Foundation, accessed November 25, 2018, https://childrenscoloradofoundation.giftplans.org/index.php?cID=241.

"Donor Advised Funds," Internal Revenue Service, accessed November 25, 2018, https://www.irs.gov/charities-non-profits/charitable-organizations/donor-advised-funds.

"Donor Advised Fund Timeline," Council on Foundations, accessed November 25, 2018, https://www.cof.org/sites/default/files/documents/files/DAF-timeline.pdf.

Dropkin, Murray, Jim Halpin, and Bill La Touche, *The Budget-Building Book for Nonprofits: A Step-by-Step Guide for Managers and Boards*, 2nd ed. (San Francisco, CA: Jossey-Bass, 2007).

Drucker, Peter F.," Drucker School of Management, Claremont Graduate University, accessed November 24, 2018, https://www.cgu.edu/school/drucker-school-of-management/peter-f-drucker/.

Edgar v. Mite Corp., U.S. 457 U.S. 624, 645 (1982), accessed November 28, 2018, https://scholar.google.com/scholar_case?case=2984439589202067076&hl=en&as_sdt=2,5.

The Eli and Edythe Broad Foundation, accessed October 21, 2018, https://broadfoundation.org/about-us/.

"Employer's Tax Guide to Fringe Benefits," Internal Revenue Service, accessed November 24, 2018, https://www.irs.gov/pub/irs-pdf/p15b.pdf.

Erb, Kelly Phillips, "What Tax Reform Means For Small Businesses & Pass-Through Entities," *Forbes*, December 22, 2017, https://www.forbes.com/sites/kellyphillipserb/2017/12/22/what-tax-reform-means-for-small-businesses-pass-through-entities/#760c213b6de3.

Estrada, Erik J., and Alan H. Frosh, "An Overview of Benefit Corporations: A Proposed Solution to the Social Entrepreneur's Dilemma," *DLR Online: The Online Supplement to the Denver Law Review*, March 22, 2012, http://www.denverlawreview.org/dlr-onlinearticle/2012/3/22/an-overview-of-benefit-corporations-a-proposed-solution-to-t.html.

Estrada, Erik J., "At the Governor's Table: The Case for the Nonprofit Cabinet Member," *DLR Online: The Online Supplement to the Denver Law Review*, February 22, 2017, http://www.denverlawreview.org/dlr-onlinearticle/2017/2/22/at-the-governors-table-the-case-for-the-nonprofit-cabinet-me.html#_ftn3.

"Executive Summary: Facility Expansion & Renovation: Planning for Capital Campaign Projects & Campaigns," The Gates Family Foundation, accessed November 25, 2018, https://www.gatesfamilyfoundation.org/sites/default/files/docs/Planning%20Tools%20Summary.pdf.

"Exempt Organizations Annual Reporting Requirements-Form 990, Schedules A and B: Public Charity Support Test," Internal Revenue Code, accessed October 29, 2018, https://www.irs.gov/charities-non-profits/exempt-organizations-annual-reporting-requirements-form-990-schedules-a-and-b-public-charity-support-test.

Fabrikant, Geraldine, "Harvard's Endowment Grew 10% Last Year, but Some Rivals Did Better," *New York Times*, September 28, 2018, https://www.nytimes.com/2018/09/28/business/harvard-endowment-gains.html.

"Facebook, Inc.: Form 8-K," United States Securities and Exchange Commission, accessed November 29, 2018, https://www.sec.gov/Archives/edgar/data/1326801/000132680115000035/form8kdec2015.htm.

"Facebook's First Big Investor, Peter Thiel, Cashes Out," CNN Business, accessed October 2, 2018, https://money.cnn.com/2012/08/20/technology/facebook-peter-thiel/index.html.

"Facts & Figures," Princeton University, accessed October 28, 2018, https://www.princeton.edu/meet-princeton/facts-figures.

"Financial Information," El Pomar Foundation, accessed November 27, 2018, https://www.elpomar.org/About-Us/financials/.

"Financial Information," The Ability Experience, accessed November 9, 2018, https://abilityexperience.org/about/financial-information/.

"Financial Reports," St. Jude Children's Research Hospital, accessed November 18, 2018, https://www.stjude.org/about-st-jude/financials.html.

"Financials," World Wildlife Fund, accessed November 10, 2018, https://www.worldwildlife.org/about/financials.

"Financial Snapshot 2016," Ford Foundation, accessed October 30, 2018, https://www.fordfoundation.org/about/library/financial-statements/financial-snapshot-2016/.

Finkler, Steven A., *Finance and Accounting for Nonfinancial Managers* (Paramus, NJ: Prentice Hall, 1996).

Fishman, James, and Stephen Schwarz, *Taxation of Nonprofit Organizations: Cases and Materials*, 2nd ed. (New York: Foundation Press, 2006).

"Fixed Asset or Expense," Nonprofit Accounting Academy, accessed December 1, 2018, https://www.nonprofitaccountingacademy.com/fixed-asset-expense/.

"Fixed Asset or Expense?", Nonprofit Accounting Academy, accessed November 23, 2018, https://www.nonprofitaccountingacademy.com/fixed-asset-expense/.

Fleishman, Joel L., *The Foundation: A Great American Secret* (New York: Public Affairs, 2007), 1–321.

"Flex Fund Background," Flexible Capital Fund, accessed November 11, 2018, http://flexiblecapitalfund.com/who-we-are/.

Flexible Capital Fund's homepage, accessed November 11, 2018, http://flexiblecapitalfund.com/.

"Florida Adopts New Limited Liability Company Act," Akerman Law, accessed October 2, 2018, https://www.akerman.com/en/perspectives/florida-adopts-new-limited-liability-company-act.html.

Ford Foundation, accessed October 30, 2018, https://www.fordfoundation.org/about/about-ford/.

"Form 1023: Application for Recognition of Exemption Under Section 501(c)(3) of the Internal Revenue Code," accessed October 28, 2018, https://www.irs.gov/pub/irs-pdf/f1023.pdf.

"Form 1023-EZ: Streamlined Application for Recognition of Exemption Under Section 501(c)(3) of the Internal Revenue Code," accessed October 22, 2018, https://www.irs.gov/pub/irs-pdf/f1023ez.pdf.

"Form 1024: Application for Recognition of Exemption Under Section 501(a)," Internal Revenue Code, accessed November 5, 2018, https://www.irs.gov/forms-pubs/about-form-1024.

"Form 1024: Application for Recognition of Exemption Under Section 501(a)," Internal Revenue Service, accessed November 11, 2018, https://www.irs.gov/pub/irs-pdf/f1024.pdf.

"Form 1024-A: Application for Recognition of Exemption Under Section 501(c)(4) of the Internal Revenue Code," Internal Revenue Service, accessed November 11, 2018, https://www.irs.gov/pub/irs-pdf/f1024a.pdf.

"Form 1024-A: Application for Recognition of Exemption Under Section 501(c)(4) of the Internal Revenue Code," Internal Revenue Service, accessed November 5, 2018, https://www.irs.gov/forms-pubs/about-form-1024-a.

"Form 990: Return of Organization Exempt from Income Tax," AARP, accessed November 7, 2018, https://www.guidestar.org/FinDocuments/2016/951/985/2016-951985500-0e895bd4-9O.pdf.

"Form 990: Return of Organization Exempt from Income Tax," American Dental Association, accessed November 7, 2018, https://www.guidestar.org/FinDocuments/2016/360/724/2016-360724690-0e68e8d2-9O.pdf.

"Form 990: Return of Organization Exempt from Income Tax," American Heart Association, accessed October 2, 2018, https://www.guidestar.org/FinDocuments/2017/135/613/2017-135613797-0ec2c869-9.pdf.

"Form 990: Return of Organization Exempt from Income Tax," The Aspen Institute, accessed November 3, 2018, https://www.guidestar.org/FinDocuments/2016/840/399/2016-8403-99006-0e7bb226-9.pdf.

"Form 990: Return of Organization Exempt from Income Tax," The Augusta Country Club, accessed November 9, 2018, https://www.guidestar.org/FinDocuments/2016/580/148/2016-580148720-0e6a0ac4-9O.pdf.

"Form 990: Return of Organization Exempt from Income Tax," Big Brothers Big Sisters of Metropolitan Chicago, accessed November 19, 2018, https://bbbschgo.org/wp-content/uploads/2018/10/FY18-Tax-Return-Form-990.pdf.

"Form 990: Return of Organization Exempt from Income Tax," Bitcoin Foundation, accessed November 7, 2018, https://www.guidestar.org/FinDocuments/2016/461/671/2016-4616-71796-0dcca0c9-9O.pdf.

"Form 990: Return of Organization Exempt from Income Tax," Boys and Girls Clubs of America, accessed November 17, 2018, https://www.bgca.org/about-us/annual-report.

"Form 990: Return of Organization Exempt from Income Tax," The Cable Center, accessed October 30, 2018, https://www.guidestar.org/FinDocuments/2016/200/315/2016-2003-15238-0e3dfa4d-9.pdf.

"Form 990: Return of Organization Exempt from Income Tax," Capital Area Food Bank, accessed November 21, 2018, https://1qf95e43hn5t3dvchxhlkupz-wpengine.netdna-ssl.com/wp-content/uploads/2018/01/CAFB-2017-06-Tax-Form-990-Public-Disclosure-Copy-signed.pdf.

"Form 990: Return of Organization Exempt from Income Tax," Common Cause, accessed November 3, 2018, http://www.guidestar.org/FinDocuments/2017/526/078/2017-52607-8441-0e89721c-9O.pdf.

"Form 990: Return of Organization Exempt from Income Tax," Goodwill Industries International, accessed November 24, 2018, http://www.goodwill.org/wp-content/uploads/2018/04/2017-Goodwill-Industries-Internation-Form-990.pdf.

"Form 990: Return of Organization Exempt from Income Tax," Habitat for Humanity of Utah County, accessed November 19, 2018, https://www.habitatuc.org/pdfs/H4H-PublicDisclosure2016-990and990T-TaxFiling.pdf.

"Form 990: Return of Organization Exempt from Income Tax," Independent Sector, accessed November 18, 2018, https://independentsector.org/wp-content/uploads/2016/08/2015-form990.pdf.

"Form 990: Return of Organization Exempt from Income Tax," Internal Revenue Service, accessed November 10, 2018, https://www.irs.gov/pub/irs-pdf/f990.pdf.

"Form 990: Return of Organization Exempt from Income Tax," La Clinica Tepeyac, accessed November 17, 2018, https://www.guidestar.org/FinDocuments/2015/841/285/2015-841285505-0cee2f22-9.pdf.

"Form 990: Return of Organization Exempt from Income Tax," Level 3 Foundation, accessed November 28, 2018, https://www.guidestar.org/FinDocuments/2016/464/615/2016-464615262-0dc5a220-9.pdf.

"Form 990: Return of Organization Exempt from Income Tax," Louisville Chamber of Commerce, accessed November 7, 2018, https://www.guidestar.org/FinDocuments/2016/840/892/2016-840892240-0ebb39bf-9O.pdf.

"Form 990: Return of Organization Exempt from Income Tax," Medecins Sans Frontieres USA, (d/b/a Doctors Without Borders USA), accessed November 22, 2018, https://doctorswithoutborders.org/sites/default/files/2018-08/2018-07-dwb_990.pdf.

"Form 990: Return of Organization Exempt from Income Tax," National Council of Nonprofits, accessed November 17, 2018, https://www.councilofnonprofits.org/sites/default/files/documents/final-national-council-of-nonprofits-fy2017-form990.pdf.

"Form 990: Return of Organization Exempt from Income Tax," National Football League, accessed November 7, 2018, https://www.guidestar.org/FinDocuments/2015/131/922/2015-131922622-0ca543a0-9O.pdf.

"Form 990: Return of Organization Exempt from Income Tax," The New York Public Library, accessed October 28, 2018, https://www.guidestar.org/FinDocuments/2016/131/887/2016-131887440-0e2c5d22-9.pdf.

"Form 990: Return of Organization Exempt from Income Tax," Pi Kappa Phi Fraternity, accessed November 9, 2018, https://www.guidestar.org/FinDocuments/2017/570/340/2017-570340150-0ebed563-9O.pdf.

"Form 990: Return of Organization Exempt from Income Tax," Rocky Mountain Butterfly Consortium (d/b/a, Butterfly Pavilion), accessed November 25, 2018, https://butterflies.org/app/uploads/2018/09/Form990_2016.pdf.

"Form 990: Return of Organization Exempt from Income Tax," Ronald McDonald House Charities of Denver, accessed November 23, 2018, https://www.guidestar.org/FinDocuments/2017/840/728/2017-840728926-0f5c0d6d-9.pdf.

"Form 990: Return of Organization Exempt from Income Tax," Share Our Strength, accessed November 5, 2018, https://www.guidestar.org/FinDocuments/2016/521/367/2016-52136-7538-0dfbbb37-9.pdf.

"Form 990: Return of Organization Exempt from Income Tax," St. Jude Children's Research Hospital, accessed November 18, 2018, https://www.stjude.org/content/dam/en_US/shared/www/about-st-jude/financial-information/990-form-alsac-fy17.pdf.

"Form 990: Return of Organization Exempt from Income Tax," Teach for All, accessed October 29, 2018, https://www.guidestar.org/FinDocuments/2017/262/122/2017-26212-2566-0ef67f99-9.pdf.

"Form 990: Return of Organization Exempt from Income Tax," Teach for America, accessed October 29, 2018, https://www.guidestar.org/FinDocuments/2017/133/541/2017-13354-1913-0efba78d-9.pdf.

"Form 990: Return of Organization Exempt from Income Tax," TEDx Portland, accessed November 24, 2018, https://www.guidestar.org/FinDocuments/2016/274/884/2016-2748-84880-0e9f72d4-9.pdf.

"Form 990: Return of Organization Exempt from Income Tax," The University of Louisville Foundation, accessed October 19, 2018, https://www.guidestar.org/FinDocuments/2016/237/078/2016-237078461-0e1ddb1f-9.pdf.

"Form 990: Return of Organization Exempt from Income Tax," Vail Health Center, accessed November 14, 2018, https://www.guidestar.org/FinDocuments/2016/840/563/2016-840563230-0e7444d1-9.pdf.

"Form 990: Return of Organization Exempt from Income Tax," World Wildlife Fund, accessed November 10, 2018, http://assets.worldwildlife.org/financial_reports/32/reports/original/Public_inspection_990_WORLD_WILDLIFE_FUND_INC.pdf?1519855180&_ga=2.210512278.246739612.1543378750-2067346590.1541872146.

"Form 990-EZ: Short Form Return of Organization Exempt from Income Tax," Internal Revenue Service, accessed November 10, 2018, https://www.irs.gov/pub/irs-pdf/f990ez.pdf.

"Form 990-PF: Return of Private Foundation," The Bill and Melinda Gates Foundation, accessed November 29, 2018, https://www.guidestar.org/FinDocuments/2016/911/663/2016-911663695-0e7cdc5b-F.pdf.

"Form 990-PF: Return of Private Foundation," Boettcher Foundation, accessed November 22, 2018, https://www.guidestar.org/FinDocuments/2016/840/404/2016-840404274-0de-2e214-F.pdf.

"Form 990-PF: Return of Private Foundation," Daniels Fund, accessed October 30, 2018, https://www.guidestar.org/FinDocuments/2016/841/393/2016-841393308-0dce225e-F.pdf.

"Form 990-PF: Return of Private Foundation," The Eli and Edythe Broad Foundation, accessed October 21, 2018, https://www.guidestar.org/FinDocuments/2016/954/686/2016-954686318-0ed381aa-F.pdf.

"Form 990-PF: Return of Private Foundation," Ford Foundation, accessed October 30, 2018, https://www.guidestar.org/FinDocuments/2016/131/684/2016-131684331-0ead99b5-F.pdf.

"Form 990-PF: Return of Private Foundation," Internal Revenue Service, accessed November 10, 2018, https://www.irs.gov/forms-pubs/about-form-990-pf.

"Form 990-PF: Return of Private Foundation," Internal Revenue Service, accessed November 21, 2018, https://www.irs.gov/pub/irs-pdf/f990pf.pdf.

"Form 990 Resources and Tools," Internal Revenue Service, accessed November 10, 2018, https://www.irs.gov/charities-non-profits/form-990-resources-and-tools.

Foster, William, and Jeffrey L. Bradach, "Should Nonprofits Seek Profits?", *Harvard Business Review*, February (2005), https://hbr.org/2005/02/should-nonprofits-seek-profits.

"Foundation Stats," Foundation Center, accessed November 5, 2018, http://data.foundationcenter.org/#/foundations/corporate/nationwide/top:assets/list/2015.

Fremont-Smith, Marion R., *Governing Nonprofit Organizations: Federal and State Law and Regulation* (Cambridge, MA: The Belknap Press of Harvard University Press, 2004).

"Frequently Asked Questions," Habitat for Humanity International, accessed November 19, 2018, https://www.habitat.org/about/faq#what.

Fried, Rona, "Patagonia Among California's First Benefit Corporations," *Sustainable-Business.com*, January 4, 2012, https://www.sustainablebusiness.com/patagonia-among-california39s-first-benefit-corporations-49961/.

Fukuyama, Francis, "Social Capital, Civil Society and Development," *Third World Quarterly* 22, no. 1 (February 2001).

Gladwell, Malcolm, *The Tipping Point* (New York: Little, Brown and Company, 2000).

Global One80, "Articles of Incorporation," Colorado Secretary of State, accessed November 28, 2018, https://www.sos.state.co.us/biz/ViewImage.do?masterFileId=20161813038&fileId=2016181303.

Goodwill Industries International, accessed November 24, 2018, http://www.goodwill.org/about-us/.

Gregory, Sean, "Why the NFL Suddenly Wants to Pay Taxes," *Time*, April 28, 2015, http://time.com/3839164/nfl-tax-exempt-status/.

Grissom, Jonathan, "Nonprofit Corporations: Board Authority and Fiduciary Duties," San Diego County Bar Association (February 2017), accessed October 21, 2018, https://www.sdcba.org/index.cfm?pg=FTR-Feb-2017-5.

"Habitat for Humanity of Utah County Financial Statements June 30, 2017," Habitat for Humanity of Utah County, accessed November 19, 2018, https://www.habitatuc.org/pdfs/audit-HabitatForHumanity2017-06FinalFinancialStatements132782.pdf.

Habitat for Humanity of Utah County's homepage, accessed November 19, 2018, https://www.habitatuc.org/.

"Habitat for Humanity Restore," Habitat for Humanity of Utah County, accessed November 19, 2018, https://www.habitatuc.org/restore.htm.

"History," AARP, accessed November 6, 2018, https://www.aarp.org/about-aarp/company/info-2016/history.html.

"History," The Aspen Institute, accessed November 3, 2018, https://www.aspeninstitute.org/about/#history.

"History," Princeton University, accessed October 28, 2018, https://www.visitprinceton.org/princeton-university/history/.

"History," Teach for America, accessed October 29, 2018, https://www.teachforamerica.org/what-we-do/history.

"History," Vail Health Center, accessed November 14, 2018, https://www.vailhealth.org/about/history

Hopkins, Bruce, *The Law of Tax-Exempt Organizations*, 11th ed. (Hoboken, NJ: John Wiley & Sons, 2016).

Horowitz, David, and Paul Leaf, "The Internal Affairs Doctrine versus a Conflicting Contractual Choice of Law Provision," *The Bureau of National Affairs*, November 2, 2012, https://www.kirkland.com/siteFiles/Publications/Bloomberg%20BNA%20(Internal%20 Affairs%20Doctrine_%20Leaf,%20Horowitz).pdf.

"How It All Started," Make-A-Wish America, accessed October 21, 2018, http://wish.org/ about-us/our-story/how-it-started.

"Independent Contractor (Self-Employed) or Employee?" Internal Revenue Service, accessed November 13, 2018, https://www.irs.gov/businesses/small-businesses-self-employed/ independent-contractor-self-employed-or-employee.

"Independent Contractor Defined," Internal Revenue Service, accessed November 13, 2018, https://www.irs.gov/businesses/small-businesses-self-employed/independent-contractor-define.

"Independent Contractors," Colorado Department of Labor and Employment, accessed November 13, 2018, https://www.colorado.gov/pacific/cdle/independent-contractors.

Independent Sector, accessed November 18, 2018, https://independentsector.org/about/.

"Initiatives," Chan Zuckerberg Initiative, accessed November 29, 2018 https://www.chanz-uckerberg.com/initiatives.

"IRS Information Returns: Form 990," Alzheimer's Association, accessed November 21, 2018, https://www.alz.org/about/finances/irs-information-returns-form-990.

"IRS Issues New Regulations Requiring a Written Capitalization Policy to be in Place by January 1 to Qualify for Special Tax Treatment," Batts Morrison Wales & Lee, accessed November 23, 2018, https://www.nonprofitcpa.com/irs-issues-new-regulations-requiring-written-capitalization-policy-place-january-1st-qualify-special-tax-treatment/.

"Jeff Cherry: Executive Director," Conscious Venture Lab, accessed November 11, 2018, http://www.consciousventurelab.com/our-mission/jeff-cherry/.

"Jennifer Aniston, Sofia Vergara, Michael Strahan, Jimmy Kimmel, Luis Fonsi Join Marlo Thomas for 13th Annual St. Jude Thanks and Giving® Campaign," St. Jude Children's Research Hospital, accessed November 18, 2018, https://www.stjude.org/ media-resources/news-releases/2016-fundraising-news/st-jude-thanks-and-giving-celebrity-partners.html.

"John D. and Catherine T. MacArthur Foundation Consolidated Financial Statements December 31, 2017 and 2016," The MacArthur Foundation, accessed November 15, 2018, https://www.macfound.org/media/files/FINAL_2017_MacArthur_Foundation_audit_report.pdf.

Jones, Darryll K., Steven J. Willis, David A. Brennen, and Beverly I. Moran, *The Tax Law of Charities and Other Exempt Organizations: Cases, Materials, Questions and Answers*, 2nd ed. (St. Paul, MN: Thomson West, 2007).

Joyner, Jeffrey, "Can an LLC Make Charitable Contributions?" Small Business Chronicle, accessed November 29, 2018, https://smallbusiness.chron.com/can-llc-make-charitable-contributions-65814.html.

"Judge: Boettcher Can Give Grants Under Amendment 41," The Denver Channel, accessed November 4, 2018, https://www.thedenverchannel.com/lifestyle/education/ judge-boettcher-can-give-grants-under-amendment-41.

Juneau, Andre, "Nonprofits Especially Need Protection against D&O Liability Risks," *Insurance Journal*, September 17, 2001, https://www.insurancejournal.com/magazines/ mag-features/2001/09/17/18503.htm.

Kennedy, Liz, and Sean McElwee, "Do Corporations & Unions Face the Same Rules for Political Spending?", *Demos*, July 23, 2014, https://www.demos.org/publication/ do-corporations-unions-face-same-rules-political-spending.

King, Bart, "Patagonia Is First to Register for 'Benefit Corporation' Status in California," *SustainableBrands.com*, January 4, 2012, https://www.sustainablebrands.com/news_and_ views/articles/patagonia-first-register-%E2%80%98benefit-corporation%E2%80%99-status-california.

Konrad, Peter, and Alys Novak, *Financial Management for Nonprofits: Keys to Success*, 3rd ed. (Littleton, CO: Discover Communications, 2004).

Kurtz, Daniel L., *Board Liability: A Guide for Nonprofit Directors* (Mt. Kisco, NY: Moyer Bell, 1989).

Larson, Chris, "Update: U of L and its Foundation Sue Ex-President Ramsey, Others," *Louisville Business First*, April 25, 2018, https://www.bizjournals.com/louisville/news/2018/04/25/u-of-l-and-its-foundation-will-sue-ex-president.html.

"Level 3 Foundation, Inc. Articles of Incorporation," Colorado Secretary of State, accessed November 28, 2018, https://www.sos.state.co.us/biz/ViewImage.do?masterFileId=201410 33971&fileId=2014103397.

Levinthal, Dave, and Sarah Kleiner, "Supreme Court Lets Stand a Decision Requiring 'Dark Money' Disclosure," *The Atlantic*, September 18, 2018, https://www.theatlantic.com/politics/archive/2018/09/supreme-court-lets-stand-a-decision-requiring-dark-money-disclosure/570670/.

"Lobbying," Internal Revenue Service, accessed November 4, 2018, https://www.irs.gov/charities-non-profits/lobbying.

Long, Heather, "In Small Win for Democrats, the Final Tax Bill Won't Include a Provision to Allow Churches to Endorse Political Candidates," *The Washington Post*, December 14, 2017, https://www.washingtonpost.com/news/wonk/wp/2017/12/14/in-small-win-for-democrats-the-final-tax-bill-wont-include-a-provision-to-allow-churches-to-endorse-political-candidates/?utm_term=.9377c4c792ab.

Louisville Chamber of Commerce's homepage, accessed November 7, 2018, https://louisvillechamber.com/#!event-list.

"MacArthur Fellows," The MacArthur Foundation, accessed November 15, 2018, https://www.macfound.org/programs/fellows/.

"MacArthur Fellows Frequently Asked Questions," The MacArthur Foundation, accessed November 15, 2018, https://www.macfound.org/fellows-faq/.

MacArthur Foundation, accessed November 15, 2018, https://www.macfound.org/about/our-history/about-the-macarthurs/.

Make-A-Wish America, accessed October 22, 2018, http://wish.org/about-us.

"A Manager's Guide to the Colorado Revised Nonprofit Corporation Act & Other Statues," Orten Cavanagh & Holmes: Attorneys at Law, accessed November 13, 2018, https://www.ochhoalaw.com/a-manager-s-guide-to-the-colorado-revised-nonprofit-corporation-act-other-statutes.

Marr, Michael, "Independent Contractor or Employee: Do You Pass the 'Economic Realities' Test?" LexisNexis, August 12, 2015, https://www.lexisnexis.com/legalnewsroom/labor-employment/b/labor-employment-top-blogs/posts/independent-contractor-or-employee-do-you-pass-the-economic-realities-test.

Matthews, Stafford, "Dentons: Indemnification Clauses," ACC New York, accessed October 12, 2018, https://www.acc.com/chapters/nyc/upload/Indemnification-Clauses-Stafford-Matthews-11-14-13.pdf.

Mattocks, Ron, *Zone of Insolvency: How Nonprofits Avoid Hidden Liabilities and Build Financial Strength* (Hoboken, NJ: John Wiley & Sons, 2008).

"Mayo Clinic: Consolidated Financial Report December 31, 2017," Mayo Clinic, accessed November 23, 2018, https://cdn.prod-carehubs.net/n1/802899ec472ea3d8/uploads/2018/03/Mayo-Clinic-2017-Consolidated-Financials-Word_FINAL-SECURED_v3-SHORT-FORM.pdf.

"Mayo Clinic: Ranked #1 in the Nation," Mayo Clinic, accessed November 23, 2018, https://www.mayoclinic.org/about-mayo-clinic/quality/top-ranked.

McLaughlin, Thomas, *Streetsmart Financial Basics for Nonprofit Managers*, 3rd ed. (Hoboken, NJ: John Wiley & Sons, 2009).

McMillan, Edward, *Not-for-Profit Accounting, Tax, and Reporting Requirements*, 4th ed. (Hoboken, NJ: John Wiley & Sons, 2010).

"Message From Law School Campaign Chair," Boston University, accessed November 25, 2018, https://www.bu.edu/law/alumni/campaign/message-from-chair/.

Miceli, Max, "Google Tops Reputation Rankings for Corporate Responsibility," *U.S. News & World Report*, accessed November 13, 2018, https://www.usnews.com/news/articles/2015/09/17/google-tops-reputation-rankings-for-corporate-responsibility.

Miller, Clara, "Hidden in Plain Sight: Understanding Capital Structure," *Nonprofit Quarterly*, March 21, 2003, https://nonprofitquarterly.org/2003/03/21/hidden-in-plain-sight-understanding-capital-structure/.

Miller, Clara, "Linking Money and Mission: An Introduction to Nonprofit Capitalization," *Nonprofit Finance Fund*, January 1, 2001, https://nff.org/report/linking-mission-and-money-introduction-nonprofit-capitalization.

Minnesota Center for Environmental Advocacy, accessed November 2, 2018, http://www.mncenter.org/about-us.html.

"Mission," Boston Center for the Arts, accessed November 23, 2018, http://www.bcaonline.org/aboutthebca/mission.html.

"Mission, Vision, Values," Foundation Center, accessed November 5, 2018, https://foundationcenter.org/about-us/mission-vision-values.

"Mission & Values," Vail Health Center, accessed November 14, 2018, https://www.vailhealth.org/about/mission-values.

"Mission and Vision," AARP, accessed November 6, 2018, https://states.aarp.org/aarps-mission-and-vision/.

"Mission Statement," Imagine Charter School, accessed November 14, 2018, https://www.imaginefirestone.org/apps/pages/index.jsp?uREC_ID=824538&type=d&pREC_ID=1205852.

Mitchell, Nancy, "State: Cesar Chavez 'Squandered Taxpayer Money,'" *Chalkbeat*, May 5, 2010, https://www.chalkbeat.org/posts/co/2010/05/05/cesar-chavez-audit-deeply-disturbing/.

"More Ways to Give Stock," Children's Hospital Colorado Foundation, accessed November 25, 2018, http://www.childrenscoloradofoundation.org/ways-to-give/other-ways-to-give.html.

Morgenson, Gretchen, "The Finger-Pointing at the Finance Firm TIAA," *The New York Times*, October 21, 2017, https://www.nytimes.com/2017/10/21/business/the-finger-pointing-at-the-finance-firm-tiaa.html.

Morrison, Eileen, "Enforcing the Duties of Nonprofit Fiduciaries: Advocating for Expanded Standing for Beneficiaries," Boston University School of Law, accessed October 12, 2018, http://www.bu.edu/bulawreview/files/2015/11/MORRISON.pdf.

Muslic, Hana, "The Jargon-Free Guide to Low Profit Limited Companies (L3C)," *Nonprofit Hub*, June 1, 2017, https://nonprofithub.org/starting-a-nonprofit/jargon-free-guide-l3c/.

National Council of Nonprofits, accessed November 17, 2018, https://www.councilofnonprofits.org/about-us.

"Neil Gorsuch's Law Firm Years," Big Law Business, accessed November 1, 2018, https://biglawbusiness.com/neil-gorsuchs-law-firm-years/.

"Nonprofit Bylaw Provision," Hurwit & Associates, accessed October 11, 2018, https://www.hurwitassociates.com/nonprofit-governance-boards-bylaws/sample-bylaw-provision-indemnification.

"Nonprofit Law Basics: Do Nonprofits File Tax Returns? What Is a 990?" Cullinane Law Group, accessed November 10, 2018, https://cullinanelaw.com/nonprofit-law-basics-does-our-nonprofit-have-to-file-tax-returns-or-an-annual-reporting-return-with-the-irs/.

"Nonprofit Law Basics: Who Owns a Nonprofit?" Cullinane Law Group, accessed November 5, 2018, https://cullinanelaw.com/nonprofit-law-basics-who-owns-a-nonprofit/.

"Nonprofit Services," Oregon Secretary of State, accessed November 13, 2018, https://sos.oregon.gov/business/Pages/nonprofit.aspx.

"Office of Development," Princeton University, accessed October 28, 2018, https://giving.princeton.edu/news-topics/office-development.

"Operational Test-Internal Revenue Code Section 501(c)(3)," Internal Revenue Code, accessed October 29, 2018, https://www.irs.gov/charities-non-profits/charitable-organizations/operational-test-internal-revenue-code-section-501c3.

Ott, Steven, *Understanding Nonprofit Organizations: Governance, Leadership, and Management* (Boulder, CO: Westview Press, 2001).

"Our Approach," Teach for America, accessed October 29, 2018, https://www.teachforamerica.org/what-we-do/approach.

"Our History," The MacArthur Foundation, accessed November 15, 2018, https://www.macfound.org/about/our-history/.

"Our History," St. Jude Children's Research Hospital, accessed November 18, 2018, https://www.stjude.org/about-st-jude/history.html?sc_icid=us-mm-history.

"Our Mission," Conscious Venture Lab, accessed November 11, 2018, http://www.consciousventurelab.com/our-mission/.

"Our Mission & Story," Boys and Girls Clubs of America, accessed November 17, 2018, https://www.bgca.org/about-us/our-mission-story.

"Our Mission Statement," St. Jude Children's Research Hospital, accessed November 18, 2018, https://www.stjude.org/about-st-jude.html?sc_icid=us-mm-missionstatement#mission.

"Our Organization," TED, accessed November 24, 2018, https://www.ted.com/about/our-organization.

"Our Origins," Ford Foundation, accessed October 30, 2018, https://www.fordfoundation.org/about/about-ford/our-origins/.

"Our Work," Community Wealth Partners, accessed November 5, 2018, http://communitywealth.com/our-work/.

"Patagonia Works: Annual Benefit Corporation Report," Patagonia, accessed November 12, 2018, https://www.patagonia.com/static/on/demandware.static/-/Library-Sites-PatagoniaShared/default/dw824fac0f/PDF-US/2017-BCORP-pages_022218.pdf.

Peretz, Marissa, "Want to Engage Millennials? Try Corporate Social Responsibility," *Forbes*, September 27, 2017, https://www.forbes.com/sites/marissaperetz/2017/09/27/want-to-engage-millennials-try-corporate-social-responsibility/#5ab464f56e4e.

Pink, Daniel H., *Drive: The Surprising Truth about What Motivates Us* (New York: Riverhead Books, 2009).

Pinsker, Joe, "Why the NFL Decided to Start Paying Taxes," *The Atlantic*, April 28, 2015, https://www.theatlantic.com/business/archive/2015/04/why-the-nfl-decided-to-start-paying-taxes/391742/.

Platt, Harvey J., *Your Living Trust and Estate Plan: How to Maximize Your Family's Assets and Protect Your Loved Ones*, 3rd ed.(New York: Allworth Press, 2002).

"Portfolio Companies," Conscious Venture Lab, accessed November 12, 2018, http://www.consciousventurelab.com/portfolio-companies/.

Potter, Trevor, "How Stephen Colbert Schooled Americans in Campaign Finance," *Time*, December 16, 2014, http://time.com/3600116/stephen-colbert-report-finale-super-pac/.

Princeton Theological Seminary's homepage, accessed October 28, 2018, https://ptsem.edu/.

"Priv. Ltr. Rul. 201423030," Internal Revenue Service, accessed November 24, 2018, https://www.irs.gov/pub/irs-wd/201423030.pdf.

"Private Benefit Doctrine Under IRC 501(c)(3)," Internal Revenue Service, accessed November 2, 2018, https://www.irs.gov/pub/irs-tege/eotopich01.pdf.

"Programs," Big Brothers Big Sisters of Metropolitan Chicago, accessed November 19, 2018, https://bbbschgo.org/programs/.

"Publication 946, How to Depreciate Property," Internal Revenue Service, accessed November 23, 2018, https://www.irs.gov/forms-pubs/about-publication-946.

"Publication 946 (2017), How to Depreciate Property," Internal Revenue Service, https://www.irs.gov/publications/p946.

"The Public Support Test: What a Grant Seeker Should Know," The Brainerd Foundation, accessed October 25, 2018, Fhttps://www.brainerd.org/downloads/Public_Support_Test_Memo.pdf.

Putnam, Robert, *Bowling Alone: The Collapse and Revival of American Community* (New York: Simon & Schuster, 2000), 15–414.

Quarterly Forum, accessed November 5, 2018, https://www.quarterlyforum.org/about/.

"Reforming the Pass-Through Deduction," Tax Foundation, accessed November 22, 2018, https://taxfoundation.org/reforming-pass-through-deduction-199a/.

Reilly, Peter, "What Is with This Chan Zuckerberg LLC Thing? Tax Geek Speaks," *Forbes*, December 4, 2015, https://www.forbes.com/sites/peterjreilly/2015/12/04/what-is-with-this-chan-zuckerberg-llc-thing-tax-geeks-speak/#45dea10767b8.

"Request for Comments Regarding the Calculation of Unrelated Business Taxable Income under § 512(a)(6) for Exempt Organizations with More than One Unrelated Trade or Business; Interim and Transition Rules for Aggregating Certain Income in the Nature of Investments; and the Treatment of Global Intangible Low-Taxed Income Inclusions for Purposes of the Unrelated Business Income Tax," Internal Revenue Service, accessed November 24, 2018, https://www.irs.gov/pub/irs-drop/n-18–67.pdf.

"Restated Certificate of Incorporation," United States Securities and Exchange Commission, accessed October 2, 2018, https://www.sec.gov/Archives/edgar/data/1326801/000119312512175673/d287954dex33.htm.

"Revenue Ruling 75–286," Internal Revenue Service, accessed November 2, 2018, https://www.irs.gov/pub/irs-tege/rr75-286.pdf.

Rice, Matthew R., Robert A. DiMeo, and Matthew P. Porter, *Nonprofit Asset Management: Effective Investment Strategies and Oversight* (Hoboken, NJ: John Wiley & Sons, 2012).

Rogers, Kate, "Tax-Exempt? The NFL's Nonprofit Status by the Numbers," *CNBC*, September 12, 2014, https://www.cnbc.com/2014/09/12/tax-exempt-the-nfls-nonprofit-status-by-the-numbers.html.

Rosenthal, Lesley, *Good Counsel: Meeting the Legal Needs of Nonprofits* (Hoboken, NJ: John Wiley & Sons, 2012).

Runquist, Lisa A., *The ABCs of Nonprofits*, 2nd ed. (Chicago: American Bar Association, 2015).

"Salesforce Foundation," Salesforce, accessed November 13, 2018, https://www.salesforce.org/about-us/salesforce-foundation/.

Saperstein, David, and Amanda Tyler, "Trump Vowed to Destroy the Johnson Amendment. Thankfully, He Has Failed," *The Washington Post*, February 7, 2018, https://www.washingtonpost.com/opinions/trump-vowed-to-destroy-the-johnson-amendment-thankfully-he-has-failed/2018/02/07/3cdbce4e-0b67-11e8-95a5-c396801049ef_story.html?utm_term=.eb32880a145c.

Schloss, Irving S., and Deborah V. Abildsoe, *Understanding TIAA-CREF: How to Plan for a Secure and Comfortable Retirement* (New York: Oxford University Press, 2000).

Scholarship Overview," The Daniels Fund, accessed November 4, 2018, https://www.danielsfund.org/scholarships/daniels-scholarship-program/overview.

"Scholarships and Fellowships," Princeton University, accessed October 28, 2018, https://giving.princeton.edu/scholarships-fellowships.

"Scholarships," The Boettcher Foundation, accessed November 4, 2018, https://boettcher-foundation.org/colorado-scholarships/.

Schulten, Katherine, "Mark Zuckerberg Vows to Donate 99% of His Facebook Shares for Charity," *The New York Times*, December 2, 2015, https://www.nytimes.com/2015/12/02/technology/mark-zuckerberg-facebook-charity.html.

Scot, Laurence, *The Simplified Guide to Not-for-Profit Accounting, Formation and Reporting* (Hoboken, NJ: John Wiley & Sons, 2010).

"SEC Implements Internal Control Provisions of Sarbanes-Oxley Act; Adopts Investment Company R&D Safe Harbor," United States Securities and Exchange Commission, accessed November 24, 2018, https://www.sec.gov/news/press/2003–66.htm.

Share Our Strength, accessed November 5, 2018, https://www.shareourstrength.org/about.

"Share Our Strength, Inc. and Subsidiary Consolidated Financial Statements and Supplemental Information for the Year Ended December 31, 2012 and Report Thereon," Share Our Strength, accessed November 5, 2018, https://www.nokidhungry.org/sites/default/files/2017-12/2012-audit.pdf.

Sheldon, K. Scott, *Successful Corporate Fundraising: Effective Strategies for Today's Nonprofits* (New York: John Wiley & Sons, 2000).

Sinek, Simon, *Start with Why: How Great Leaders Inspire Everyone to Take Action* (New York: Penguin Group, 2009).

Sinek, Simon, "How Great Leaders Inspire Action," TEDx, accessed December 1, 2018, https://www.youtube.com/watch?v=qp0HIF3SfI4&t=41s.

Singer, Natasha, and Mike Isaac, "Mark Zuckerberg's Philanthropy Uses L.L.C. for More Control," *The New York Times*, December 3, 2015, https://www.nytimes.com/2015/12/03/technology/zuckerbergs-philanthropy-uses-llc-for-more-control.html.

"Single Parent Title Holding Corporations," Internal Revenue Service, accessed November 6, 2018, https://www.irs.gov/irm/part7/irm_07-025-002.

"Social Clubs," Internal Revenue Service, accessed November 9, 2018, https://www.irs.gov/other-non-profits/social-clubs.

The Social Network, directed by David Fincher (2010; Los Angeles, CA: Columbia Pictures, 2010), DVD.

"The Social Network," IMBd, accessed October 2, 2018, https://www.imdb.com/title/tt1285016/quotes?ref_=tt_ql_trv_4.

"Social Welfare Organizations," Internal Revenue Service, accessed November 3, 2018, https://www.irs.gov/charities-non-profits/other-non-profits/social-welfare-organizations.

"Social Welfare Organizations," Internal Revenue Services, accessed November 6, 2018, https://www.irs.gov/charities-non-profits/other-non-profits/social-welfare-organizations.

"St. Jude Children's Research Hospital, Inc. Combined Financial Statements as of and for the Years Ended June 30, 2017 and 2016, and Independent Auditors' Report," St. Jude Children's Research Hospital, accessed November 18, 2018, https://www.stjude.org/content/dam/en_US/shared/www/about-st-jude/financial-information/fy17-combined-audited-financial-statements.pdf.

Stanley, Thomas, and William Danko, *The Millionaire Next Door: The Surprising Secrets of America's Wealthy* (Lanham, MD: Taylor Trade Publishing, 1996).

"State Ethics Law Beset by Unintended Consequences," *The Washington Post*, February 19, 2007, accessed November 3, 2018, https://www.washingtontimes.com/news/2007/feb/19/20070219-112748-7289r/.

"State Laws Governing Nonprofit Corporations," USLegal.com, accessed November 29, 2018, https://nonprofitorganizations.uslegal.com/state-laws-governing-nonprofit-corporations/.

Sterbenz, Christina, "Nelson Mandela Never Said One of His Most Famous 'Quotes'," Business Insider, October 11, 2013, https://www.businessinsider.com/nelson-mandelas-deepest-fear-misquotation-2013-10.

Stone, Deborah, *Policy Paradox: The Art of Political Decision Making* (New York: W.W. Norton & Company, 2002).

Strom, Stephanie, "Charities Now Seek Bankruptcy Protection," *The New York Times*, February 19, 2009, https://www.nytimes.com/2009/02/20/us/20bankrupt.html.

"A Success Story That's Helping Others Succeed," Community Wealth Partners, accessed November 5, 2018, http://communitywealth.com/share-our-strength/.

"Summary: QF Group, Inc.", Colorado Secretary of State, accessed November 5, 2018, https://www.sos.state.co.us/biz/BusinessEntityCriteriaExt.do.

"Sumner Redstone Gives $18 Million to School of Law," Boston University, accessed November 25, 2018, http://www.bu.edu/today/2012/sumner-redstone-gives-18-million-to-school-of-law/.

"Taxation of Unrelated Business Income (UBIT)," Hurwit & Associates, accessed November 5, 2018, https://www.hurwitassociates.com/taxation-of-unrelated-business-income/taxation-of-unrelated-business-income.

"Tax Cuts and Jobs Act, Provision 11011 Section 199A-Qualified Business Income Deduction FAQs," Internal Revenue Service, accessed November 22, 2018, https://www.irs.gov/newsroom/tax-cuts-and-jobs-act-provision-11011-section-199a-qualified-business-income-deduction-faqs.

"Teachers Insurance and Annuity Association," Encyclopedia.com, accessed November 11, 2018, https://www.encyclopedia.com/books/politics-and-business-magazines/teachers-insurance-and-annuity-association.

"Teach for All History," Teach for All, accessed October 29, 2018, http://www.teachforallnetwork.com/aboutus_history.html.

"TEDx Events," TED, accessed November 24, 2018, https://www.ted.com/tedx/events.

TEDxMileHigh, accessed November 24, 2018, https://www.tedxmilehigh.com/about/.

TEDxPortland's homepage, accessed November 24, 2018, http://www.tedxportland.com/.

TEDx Program," TED, accessed November 24, 2018, https://www.ted.com/about/programs-initiatives/tedx-program.

Thiel, Peter, *Zero to One: Notes on Startups, or How to Build the Future* (New York: Crown Business, 2014).

"This Is the True Joy in Life," Habits for Well Being, accessed December 3, 2018, https://www.habitsforwellbeing.com/this-is-the-true-joy-in-life/.

"Timeline: From Dream to Reality," St. Jude Children's Research Hospital, accessed November 18, 2018, https://www.stjude.org/about-st-jude/history/timeline.html.

"Title-Holding Corporations," Internal Revenue Service, accessed November 6, 2018, https://www.irs.gov/pub/irs-tege/eotopicc86.pdf.

Tocqueville, Alexis de, *Democracy in America*, 1st ed., trans. Henry Reeve, Esq. (New York: Adlard and Saunders, 1838), 595.

"Topic No. 762 - Independent Contractor vs. Employee," Internal Revenue Service, accessed November 27, 2018, https://www.irs.gov/taxtopics/tc762.

"Trevor Potter Helps Stephen Colbert Form 'Anonymous Shell Corporation' to Avoid Disclosure," Campaign Legal Center, accessed November 5, 2018, https://campaignlegal.org/update/trevor-potter-helps-stephen-colbert-form-anonymous-shell-corporation-avoid-disclosure.

"United States Securities and Exchange Commission Form 10-K," Snap, accessed October 11, 2018, https://www.sec.gov/Archives/edgar/data/1564408/000156459018002721/snap-10k_20171231.htm.

University of Colorado, accessed November 1, 2018, https://www.colorado.edu/law/research/byron-white-center/about-white-center.

"University of Colorado Foundation," University of Colorado, accessed November 27, 2018, https://giving.cu.edu/about-us/university-colorado-foundation.

The University of Louisville & The University of Louisville Foundation, Inc. v. James Ramsey et al., accessed October 19, 2018, https://uoflnews-qmrfqsqodkyjna.netdna-ssl.com/wp-content/uploads/2018/04/Complaint-With-Jury-Trial-Demand-File-Stamped-U-of-L-et-al.-v.-Ramsey-et-al.pdf.

"Unrelated Business Income Tax Exceptions and Exclusions," Internal Revenue Service, accessed November 24, 2018, https://www.irs.gov/charities-non-profits/charitable-organizations/unrelated-business-income-tax-exceptions-and-exclusions.

"U of L and its Foundation Sue Ex-President Ramsey, others," *Louisville Business First*, April 25, 2018, https://www.bizjournals.com/louisville/news/2018/04/25/u-of-l-and-its-foundation-will-sue-ex-president.html.

Wagner, John, "Trump Signs Sweeping Tax Bill into Law," *The Washington Post*, December 22, 2017, https://www.washingtonpost.com/news/post-politics/wp/2017/12/22/trump-signs-sweeping-tax-bill-into-law/?noredirect=on&utm_term=.a65997ded2c4.

Wagner, John, and Julie Zauzmer, "Trump Vows to 'Totally Destroy' Restrictions on Churches' Support of Candidates," *The Washington Post*, February 2, 2017, https://www.washingtonpost.com/politics/trump-vows-to-totally-destroy-restrictions-on-churches-support-of-candidates/2017/02/02/fed9bad2-e981-11e6-bf6f-301b6b443624_story.html?utm_term=.80c87f922e1a.

Wang, Anna, "Indemnity Clauses: Understanding the Basics," Shake LegalShield, May 15, 2014, accessed October 12, 2018, http://www.shakelaw.com/blog/indemnity-clauses-understanding-basics/.

"What Is the Time Value of Money?" Corporate Finance Institute, accessed November 21, 2018, https://corporatefinanceinstitute.com/resources/knowledge/valuation/time-value-of-money/.

"What We Do: Keeping Families Close," Ronald McDonald House Charities, accessed November 23, 2018, https://rmhc-denver.org/what-we-do/.

"When TIAA Does Well, Our Participants Do Better," TIAA, accessed November 11, 2018, https://www.tiaa.org/public/sharing-profits-with-participants.

"Who Can Sue a Nonprofit Board?" Nonprofit Risk Management Center, accessed October 12, 2018, https://www.nonprofitrisk.org/resources/articles/who-can-sue-a-nonprofit-board/.

"Who Is an Employee? Determining Independent Contractor Status," United States Department of Labor, accessed November 13, 2018, https://www.dol.gov/oasam/programs/history/herman/reports/futurework/conference/staffing/9.1_contractors.htm.

"Who We Are," Clinica Tepeyac, accessed November 17, 2018, http://clinicatepeyac.org/who-we-are/financials.html.

"Who We Are," TIAA, accessed November 11, 2018, https://www.tiaa.org/public/why-tiaa/who-we-are.

"Why Did Mark Zuckerberg Incorporate Facebook as a Florida LLC?" Lawtrades.com, accessed October 2, 108, https://www.lawtrades.com/blog/answers/why-did-mark-zuckerberg-incorporate-facebook-as-a-florida-llc-2/.

Wiessner, Daniel, "U.S. Judge Says Uber Drivers Are Not Company's Employees," Reuters, April 12, 2018, https://www.reuters.com/article/us-uber-lawsuit/u-s-judge-says-uber-drivers-are-not-companys-employees-idUSKBN1HJ31I.

World Wildlife Fund, accessed November 10, 2018, https://www.worldwildlife.org/about.

"World Wildlife Fund, Inc. and Subsidiaries Consolidated Financial Statements and Independent Auditor's Report Years Ended June 30, 2017 and 2016," World Wildlife Fund, accessed November 10, 2018, http://assets.worldwildlife.org/financial_reports/33/reports/original/WWF_-_Institutional_Audit_Report_FY17.pdf?1519855210&_ga=2.148947125.246739612.1543378750-2067346590.1541872146.

World Wildlife Fund's homepage, accessed November 10, 2018, https://www.worldwildlife.org/.

Ye Hee Lee, Michelle, and Jeff Stein, "'Dark Money' Groups Don't Need to Disclose Donors to IRS, Treasury Says," *The Washington Post*, July 17, 2018, https://www.washingtonpost.com/politics/dark-money-groups-dont-need-to-disclose-donors-to-irs-treasury-says/2018/07/17/38f5d8aa-89d0-11e8-a345-a1bf7847b375_story.html.

Zaveri, Paayal, and Deirdre Bosa, "The New Tax Law Creates a Huge Boon for Uber and Lyft Drivers," CNBC, February 5, 2018, https://www.cnbc.com/2018/02/05/uber-lyft-drivers-and-other-contractors-get-2018-tax-law-benefit.html.

Zunz, Olivier, *Philanthropy in America: A History* (Princeton, NJ: Princeton University Press, 2012).

Index

■ ■ ■